Moscow Nights

The Shakespeare Riots:
Revenge, Drama, and Death in
Nineteenth-Century America

The Last Crusade: The Epic Voyages
of Vasco da Gama

The Travels by Marco Polo
(editor, translator)

MOSCOW NIGHTS

NIGHTS

*The Van Cliburn Story—How One Man
and His Piano Transformed the Cold War*

NIGEL CLIFF

HARPER

An Imprint of HarperCollinsPublishers

HarperCollins books may be purchased for educational, business,
or sales promotional use. For information, please email the Special
Markets Department at SPsales@harpercollins.com.

FIRST EDITION

Designed by Fritz Metsch

Library of Congress Cataloging-in-Publication Data
has been applied for.

ISBN 978-0-06-233316-2

16 17 18 19 20   RRD   10 9 8 7 6 5 4 3 2 1

For my son, Orlando

Contents

THIRD MOVEMENT:
Pianoforte

Moscow Nights

Introduction

ON MAY 28, 1958, ticker tape snowed from the sky above Broadway, darkening an already gray New York City day and flurrying around rapturous, flag-waving crowds. High school bands marched, Fire Department colors trooped, and at the center of it all was a young American perched on the back of an open-top Continental, grinning in disbelief and crossing his hands over his heart. He was as tall, thin, and blond as Charles Lindbergh, but he was not a record-setting aviator. Nor was he an Olympic athlete or a world statesman or a victor in war. The cause of the commotion was a twenty-three-year-old classical pianist from a small town in Texas who had recently taken part in a music competition.

"What's goin' on here?" a stalled taxi driver yelled to a cop. "A parade? Fer the *piano player?*"

The cabbie had a point. No musician had ever been honored like this. No American pianist had been front-page news, let alone a household name. But the confetti was whirling, the batons were twirling, and on a damp morning a hundred thousand New Yorkers were cheering and climbing on cars and screaming and dashing up for a kiss. In the summer of 1958, Van Cliburn was not only the most famous musician in America. He was just about the most famous *person* in America—and barring the president, quite possibly the most famous American in the world.

Things got stranger. At a time when the United States and the Soviet Union were bitter enemies in a perilous Cold War, the Russians had gone mad for him before Americans had. Two months earlier he had arrived in Moscow, a gangly, wide-eyed kid on his first overseas trip, to try his luck in the First International Tchaikovsky Competition. Such was the desperate state of world affairs that even musical talent counted as ammunition in the battle of beliefs, and everyone understood that the Soviets had cranked open the gates only to prove that their virtuosos were the best. Yet for once in the tightly plotted Cold War, the authors had to tear up the script, for the real story of the Tchaikovsky Competition was beyond the imagination of the most ingenious propagandist. The moment the young American with the shock of flaxen curls sat before the piano, a powerful new weapon exploded across the Soviet Union. That weapon was love: one man's love for music, which ignited an impassioned love affair between him and an entire nation.

It came at a critical time. Five months earlier the Soviet Union had sensationally beaten the United States into space. Even now, shiny metal *sputniks* were whizzing above American roofs, which suddenly seemed puny shields against a newly menacing sky. In this hallucinatory and panicked age, Van Cliburn gained the trappings of a rock star: sold-out stadiums, platinum albums, screaming groupies, and vindictive rivals. The implausible extent of his fame was captured when the Elvis Presley Fan Club of Chicago switched allegiance and changed its name to the Van Cliburn Fan Club. He brought millions of people to classical music, yet more than a pianist, he was a talisman: a locus of hopes that through his music he could heal a troubled world.

He hoped so, too, but the moment of youthful glory that made him also trapped him. An innocent required to play a global role, a gregarious charmer obsessed with privacy, a model of piety with a rebellious streak, a driven man who could be hopelessly dysfunctional, a patriot who loved Communist Russia, a man-child who was old when young and young when old, a lover of aristocracy proud of his humble Texas roots, a modest man who was not above embellishing his own legend—Van was both what he seemed and not what he seemed. As the Cold War lurched from one crisis to another, he played on, returning emotionally to Moscow, courted by presidents and Politburo members, watched by the FBI and KGB, and closely guarding a secret that could have destroyed him overnight. In those days when clashing ideologies counted no cost in human lives too high, he stood impotently by while several of his fellow competitors met with tragic fates. While superpower relations plumbed new depths, he disappeared to become America's most famous recluse, his one-man musical peace mission seemingly a busted flush. Yet, just when all looked lost, the legend of Van Cliburn would rise again to answer the call of history.

Based on numerous interviews and newly revealed evidence from Russian and American archives, this book tells the full story of Van Cliburn and the Tchaikovsky Competition for the first time. That story is inextricably linked to the Cold War, which turned a music competition into an event of global significance, and its main players, especially Nikita Khrushchev and the U.S. presidents he tangled with: Eisenhower, Kennedy, Johnson, and Nixon. It also takes us through the remarkable careers of the piano concertos by Tchaikovsky and Rachmaninoff, written at the height of Romanticism, that supplied the unlikely sound track to three decades of global conflict.

If Van's tale resonates particularly strongly today, that may be because events overtook the writing of this book. A window on a recent but seemingly vanished world now opens onto terrain that looks all too familiar. While we contemplate talk of a new Cold War, it can be illuminating to recall that Russia and America have had a love-hate relationship for a long while. Both nations became world powers at the same time, as multiethnic states with one foot in Europe with its old-world refinement and the other in their vast rude hinterlands. Both were ideologically extreme nations with utopian identities: America the shining city on a hill; Russia the third Rome and the chalice of true faith, be it Orthodox or Communist. Yet whereas America promoted happiness through freedom, Russia sought stability through autocracy. And while America's exemplary heroes were businessmen and industrialists, Russia's were artists who peered into the human soul with an unmatched intensity.

The conflict between these young-old nations defined the second half of the twentieth century not only because of their military might but also because of the stark choice thrown up by their distinctly different views of human nature. Yet deep down there was common ground, waiting to be rediscovered. It was unexpected that it happened through music, but in a way it was a return to form. In the late nineteenth and early twentieth centuries there was no place that loved Russian music more than America—not even Russia itself.

Prelude in Two Parts

BY 1874, Peter Ilyich Tchaikovsky had been professor of theory and harmony at the Moscow Conservatory for each of the eight long years since it opened its doors. The grand title belied a desultory salary (fifty rubles a month), and the thirty-four-year-old musician supplemented his income by working as a roving critic. Both jobs took him away from composing, which had yet to earn him more than lukewarm praise. To Russians his music was too Western, to Europeans too unmannered; one Viennese critic contemptuously likened it to "the brutish, grim jollity of a Russian church festival" where "we see nothing but common, ravaged faces, hear rough oaths, and smell cheap liquor." So when Tchaikovsky decided to write his first piano concerto that year, he set out to meld Western and Russian musical practices into a new style that would win universal approval and finally let him quit his tiresome post. In bold strokes he conceived a big, virtuosic work brimming with catchy folk themes: a melody he heard performed by blind beggars at a market and others taken from Russian and Ukrainian folk songs and a French chansonette, "Il faut s'amuser, danser et rire." By late December the concerto was sketched out, and he inscribed a dedication to Nikolai Rubinstein, the founder and director of the conservatory and a fine pianist in his own right. Tchaikovsky hoped Rubinstein would agree to give the premiere, and on Christmas Eve, before heading out to a party, Rubinstein asked the reticent composer to play the concerto through.

Dusk was settling as the two men met in the deserted school and chose a classroom. Outside, the snow muffled the bells pealing the Royal Hours and the chatter of girls waiting to tell their marriage fortunes. All was peaceful as Tchaikovsky took his place at the piano and Rubinstein settled down to listen.

The composer played the tumultuous first movement. Rubinstein did not move or say a word. Fearing the worst, Tchaikovsky toiled through the entire concerto. Again there was silence.

"Well?" he ventured.

Rubinstein began quietly, continued intemperately, and finally, Tchaikovsky thought, let fly like "Zeus hurling thunderbolts." The concerto was utterly worthless, absolutely unplayable, bad, trivial, and vulgar. Some passages were so trite and clumsy that nothing could be done with them; others were plagiarism, pure and simple. The director sprang to the piano and dashed off crude parodies of Tchaikovsky's choicest phrases: "Here for instance, this"—making a monstrous jangle—"now what's all that? And this? How can any-one . . ." he trailed away, leaving a thick vapor of disdain and disap-pointment in the air.

Tchaikovsky was notoriously touchy about his music, and felt vio-lated. "An impartial bystander would necessarily have believed that I was a stupid, ignorant, conceited note-scratcher, who was so impudent as to show his scribble to a celebrated man," he would write his pa-troness Nadezhda von Meck three years later, still bitterly aggrieved. He stormed out and headed upstairs to his studio. Rubinstein followed and pulled him into another empty room. The whole piece was im-possible, Rubenstein repeated, and would have to be completely over-hauled, but if Tchaikovsky reworked it according to his instructions, and did so in good time, he would consent to play it at his concert.

"I shall not alter a single note," the indignant composer retorted. "I shall publish the work exactly as it is!" In the event, he made one change: he scratched out the dedication to Rubinstein and wrote in the name of the pianist Hans von Bülow, whose acquaintance he had just made. Bülow was a giant of the German music scene who had married musical royalty in the tall, angular form of Franz Liszt's daughter Cosima before losing her to Richard Wagner, two of whose greatest operas, *Tristan und Isolde* and *Die Meistersinger von Nürnberg*, Bülow had conducted at their premieres. As soon as Bülow received the score, he wrote an effusive letter of praise to a delighted and relieved Tchaikovsky.

Bülow was about to embark on an American tour, and he premiered the concerto in Boston on October 25, 1875. Only four first violins could be rounded up in time, and the rest of the orchestra was patchy at best. An American composer reported the result: "They had not rehearsed much and the trombones got in wrong in the 'tutti' in the middle of the first movement, whereupon Bülow sang out in a perfectly audible voice, 'The brass may go to hell.'" One Boston Brahmin declared in a review that the concerto was hardly destined to become classical, but it was a sensation with the public, even more so when it was repeated in less straitlaced New York a month later. Bülow featured it in 139 of his 172 American concerts. Anton Rubinstein, the fiery, raven-haired, fat-fingered virtuoso who founded the St. Petersburg Conservatory and the Romantic Russian school of piano playing, took it up. Even his paler, steelier brother, Nikolai, eventually relented and played it many times. Tchaikovsky made a peace offering by dedicating his Second Piano Concerto to Nikolai, but the pianist died before he could perform it. Instead, in 1881, it, too, premiered in the United States, with the English-born pianist Madeline Schiller and the Philharmonic Society of New York.

Tchaikovsky was fascinated that his work had been more warmly welcomed in the United States than in his own country. In 1891, now world-famous and long liberated from his teaching duties, he eagerly accepted an invitation to open the newly built Carnegie Hall. "It turns out that I am ten times better known in America than in Europe," he wrote his nephew from New York:

At first when they told me that, I thought that it was an exaggerated compliment, but now I see that it is the truth. Works of mine that are still unknown in Moscow are performed here several times a season, and whole reviews and commentaries are written on them (e.g., *Hamlet*). I am far more of a big shot here than in Russia. Is it not curious!!!

The visitor was impressed by the vastness of the city, the hospitality of his hosts, and the comfort of his hotel room, with its gas and electric light, private bathroom and lavatory, and apparatus for speaking to reception. Yet his thoughts turned constantly to home, and he decided that at fifty he was too old to experience travel as anything other than a mild form of punishment. Well-wishers and autograph hunters mobbed him everywhere he went, giving him no quarter, and when he conducted his own works in the new hall, including the now-canonical Piano Concerto no. 1, the bright lights on Fifty-Seventh Street flared on a line of carriages that crawled for a quarter of a mile queuing to drop off eager concertgoers. After a brief tour he left, never to come back, and two years later he was dead.

The First Piano Concerto went on to become the calling card of many a visiting virtuoso; in the following decades, both Sergei Rachmaninoff and Vladimir Horowitz made sensational American debuts with the work. But it would take a young pianist from Texas to make it the most famous piece of classical music in the world. Tchaikovsky would have been less surprised than most.

. . . AND ANOTHER ABOUT RACHMANINOFF

IN 1941 a twenty-seven-year-old Soviet spy named Alexander Feklisov set out from his Manhattan office and headed downtown on an urgent mission. Among his regular duties, Feklisov was the handler of Julius Rosenberg, later to be executed alongside his wife, Ethel, for nuclear espionage, but for now all normal activity was on hold. Earlier that year Adolf Hitler had launched the most massive and perhaps most brutal invasion in history against the Soviet Union, and the spy's delicate assignment was to press New York's leading Russian émigrés to contribute to the defense of the motherland they had fled.

Feklisov made for the Russian bathhouse on the corner of Second Street and Second Avenue. As he opened the doors, the smooth, sweet sound of a well-trained choir flowed out. In the big reception hall, middle-aged men with sheets knotted round their waists were sitting on couches singing Russian and Ukrainian songs, perfectly in tune and unison. One very tall old man with his back turned to the newcomer was strumming along quietly on a guitar.

After undressing, Feklisov went to get a beer and asked the barman what was going on. "Don't you know them?" the man asked in surprise. "This is the world-famous choir of the Don Cossacks, with its leader Sergei Zharov." He pointed to Zharov, a short man seated next to the tall guitarist. As the spy's glance moved onto the guitar player's long gray face, he recognized him as Sergei Rachmaninoff.

"They often come here," the barman added, "and sing whenever they feel up to it. Sometimes Rachmaninoff comes along, and then they sing under his direction."

The Cossacks chanted the low first notes of "Vecherniy Zvon," a beloved folk song that evoked an evening chorus of Russian church bells. Suddenly the languid composer was transformed. He drew himself up; broke in several times with instructons about pauses, tempo, and volume; then got up, put his guitar aside, and started conducting. Now the portly choir sang each word distinctly and precisely, in rapturous voices trembling with nostalgia:

> *Evening bells*
> *Evening bells*
> *How many thoughts*
> *They arouse!*
> *O youthful days*
> *Where I was born and bred*

Where I first loved
Where father's house stands

And now how I,
On forever parting,
Have heard the bells
For my last time.

The spy sat transfixed, transported despite himself to an old Russia that no longer existed and that he had barely known. At the end, Rachmaninoff and the choir got dressed, knocked back a shot of vodka, and drifted out into the chilly New York night. Feklisov never met the great musician again, but soon afterward an unknown man arrived at his office in the East Sixty-First Street consulate and handed over a large chunk of Rachmaninoff's concert fees, along with assurances of his love and devotion to his homeland.

The Russian Revolution had been a gift to American music lovers. Fleeing the Bolsheviks on an open sled with his wife, his two daughters, and a bag of notebooks and scores, in 1918 Rachmaninoff had retaken New York—where nine years earlier he had premiered his most famous piano concerto, the Third—outdazzling even the American debut of his brilliant compatriot Sergei Prokofiev, who had arrived earlier that year, though perhaps not the white-hot piano virtuoso Vladimir Horowitz, who defected in 1925 with American dollar bills and British pound notes stuffed into his shoes. Rachmaninoff made a great deal of money in America, but even after transforming his New York home into the scene of all-Russian soirees, complete with Russian guests, servants, and rituals, he was painfully homesick and scrupulously avoided agents of the despised Soviet regime. Feklisov grew so curious about the fabled musician that he bought a ticket to see him at Carnegie Hall out of his own pocket.

The first wave of Russian refugees already dominated American music when a second influx arrived. In 1939 the composer Igor Stravinsky steamed away from war-torn Europe and settled in sunny

West Hollywood, where he joined an unlikely Los Angeles diaspora that included the choreographer George Balanchine (born Giorgi Balanchivadze in St. Petersburg), the Lithuanian violinist Jascha Heifetz, and the sensational pianist Arthur Rubinstein, born in a region of Poland then ruled by the Russian Empire. Horowitz moved in, as did Rachmaninoff, who bought a house in Beverly Hills not far from the self-consciously diminutive Stravinsky, who called his fellow Russian composer a "six-and-a-half-foot scowl."

The year after Feklisov's visit to the baths, the capitalist United States and the Communist Soviet Union became unlikely allies in World War II. Music was an effective way of strengthening the ties of war, less blatant and perhaps more effective than Hollywood movies that whitewashed Stalin's scandalous show trials or featured Soviet collective farms filled with Ukrainian peasants (millions of whom, in real life, had been wiped out by famine) dancing merrily in pressed white shirts with flowers twined in their tresses. The greatest musical bond was forged when the microfilmed score of Dmitri Shostakovich's *Leningrad Symphony* (written during the hellish 872-day siege of the former St. Petersburg in which a million perished) was flown to the West and performed in London and New York before its premiere in Leningrad. In New York the symphony was the subject of a pitched battle between conductors, and in six months it was performed sixty-two times across America.

Never, not even in Tchaikovsky's time, had Russian music been more admired, honored, or glorified; never had it been more *American*.

FIRST MOVEMENT

Sognando

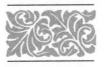

· I ·

The Prodigy

RILDIA BEE O'Bryan Cliburn's proudest day was the day her son was born. She was thirty-seven and had been married to Harvey Lavan Cliburn for eleven childless years. He was two years younger, a native of Mississippi whom she had met at an evening prayer meeting soon after breaking an engagement to a dentist. When she went to him one day in 1933 and said, "Sug, I think we're going to have a little baby," it seemed a miracle to them both. The following July 12 he came to her bedside at Tri-State Sanitarium in Shreveport, Louisiana—room 322, the number part of their personal liturgy—and smiled. "Babe," he said in his laconic drawl, "we have a little boy, and this is our family." The smiles dimmed when they differed over what to name the child—he wanted his son to have his name; she was not minded to raise a Junior—before harmony was restored with a compromise. The birth certificate duly recorded the debut of "Harvey Lavan (Van) Cliburn," but Rildia Bee made sure the child was never called anything but Van.

Her second-proudest day was the day she met Sergei Rachmaninoff. It was two years earlier, and she was on a committee of musically minded ladies who had invited the Russian to Shreveport. The Cliburns had moved to the city after her father, William Carey O'Bryan, who was mayor of McGregor, Texas, as well as a judge, state legislator, and newspaperman, convinced his son-in-law to make a career in oil. At the time, Harvey was a railroad station agent, but since his dream of being a doctor had been dashed in the Great War, and one thing was as good as another, he gamely signed up as a roving crude oil purchasing agent. Rildia Bee's dream was to be a concert pianist, and she had indeed been on the brink of a career when her parents pulled her back from the unseemly business of performing in public. Since her mother, Sirrildia, had been a semiprofessional actress—the only kind in those parts—that seemed a little unfair, but perhaps it was not, because Sirrildia refashioned herself into that primmest of creatures, a local historian, and the family was trying to put its stage days behind it. Rildia Bee dutifully demoted herself to teaching piano, which was why she was on the Shreveport concert committee and came to tend personally to Rachmaninoff.

Backstage at the big new Art Deco Municipal Auditorium, she had little to do except hand the famous Russian a glass of orange juice or water, and she never got to tell him that, pianistically speaking, they were almost family. When she was a student at the Cincinnati conservatory, Rildia Bee had one day attended a recital by the famed pianist Arthur Friedheim, who despite his Germanic name was born to an aristocratic family in St. Petersburg when it was the Imperial Russian capital. Mesmerized, she followed him to New York, where she became one of his best students at the Institute of Musical Art, a forerunner to the Juilliard School. Friedheim had studied with the fiery Anton Rubinstein, the founder of the St. Petersburg Conservatory, before he balked at Rubinstein's chaotic teaching style and defected to the superstar Hungarian Franz Liszt, becoming Liszt's foremost pupil and, later, his secretary. Rachmaninoff counted Rubinstein as his greatest pianistic inspiration, and in his playing markedly resembled Friedheim, who had died less than a month earlier, leaving Rachmaninoff the greatest living exponent of the school of pianism that Rildia Bee adored. Perhaps it was just as well she never knew how depressing he found the experience of performing in Shreveport. "Business is lamentable," he wrote a friend the next day:

We play in an empty but huge hall, which is very painful. To-day the local paper writes about the absence of the public! Fur-thermore, a few people dropped in to apologize because "there were so few of us." The day before yesterday there was a foot-ball game here, with 15 thousand spectators. Well, wasn't I right to say over and over that our day is interested only in muscles? Within five or ten years, concerts will no longer be given.

To rub it in, the Shreveport paper reviewed his concert as if it had been a football game, under the headline RACHMANINOFF WINS BY LARGE MARGIN IN MONDAY NIGHT GAME! The lugubrious pianist went away from Shreveport and never returned. Yet Rildia Bee told the story of her backstage brush with greatness whenever she could, and as soon as her son was old enough to understand, she told it to him at bedtime. He lapped it up because not only was she hopeless at nurs-ery rhymes, but by then he was already playing the piano.

The story of how that happened went like this. A music room opened off the modest parlor of their little white frame house on Stevenson Street, and as a baby, Van sat in the corner listening to Mother's lessons. Sometimes he crawled over and touched the keys gently, one by one, testing them. When he was a plump three-year-old, a local kid named Sammy Talbot came at his usual time and played Crawford's "Arpeggio Waltz," an intermediate piece that in-volved hand crossing. Sammy had been working on it for a while and was getting quite good. Rildia Bee dismissed him at the end and had ducked out to do some chores when the notes came rippling back. "Tell Sammy to go home, his mother's gonna be worried about him!" she called out to Van, but the music carried on. She looked in the par-lor, and there was Van sitting on the piano bench, picking the piece out perfectly.

"You! Do you want to learn how to play the piano?" she asked.

"Yes, Mother," he said with a child's fearless certainty.

"Well," she said briskly, "you're not going to play by ear. You're going to know what you're doing." So she entered him in her composition book for regular lessons and began teaching him the grand staff. Harvey knocked together a blackboard, with one side lined and the other blank, and Rildia Bee chalked in the arcana of music, the secret language that Van was to become an adept in:

adagio,
allegro,
allegretto,
rubato.

He took to it like other children take to their toys. Occasionally he messed about with his tricycle and truck and tried to avoid taking lessons or practicing—an hour a day at first, in three periods. Usually, though, as soon as Rildia Bee clapped her hands three times or started playing, he came running. When they were seated side by side, or he on her lap, there was no wasting time. "Now, when we're taking a lesson, I want you to think of me as your teacher, not your mommy," she told him from the start. At four he was lifted onto a stool at a local women's college to make his debut, and at five, after hearing Rachmaninoff play on the radio, he informed his parents over dinner that he was going to be a concert pianist. Harvey frowned. "Well, son, we'll see about that," he said. Rildia Bee had planted the notion in the boy's head, he murmured. An affable but reticent man with a crop of tight dark curls severely barbered at the back and sides, Harvey nursed his own hope that Van would become a medical missionary.

Yet Rildia Bee, whose warm manner and spirited laugh masked a steely resolve, had poured her forbidden dreams into her only child, and she was always going to get her way. By then, not even Christmas kept Van from the piano, except for one unseasonably chilly (for Louisiana) Christmas Day in 1939. That day, he unwrapped his present, a picture book of world history, and contentedly leafed through it until he stopped at a spread showing the Moscow Kremlin. A riot of colorful onion domes belonging to St. Basil's Cathedral jostled over the old fortress's long red walls like the candy-striped turbans of a deputation of Eastern kings. He looked up, wide-eyed, his soul swelling with childlike surprise.

"Mommy, Daddy, take me there," he pleaded. "Take me there, *please.*" Perhaps the architecture chimed in his young mind with the stories of Rachmaninoff and the other Russians whose music he had already begun to love.

"Maybe someday, sonny," they said, smiling. It was impossible of course, even if intercontinental travel had been within their means. Soviet Russia was a closed and alien world of secret police and show trials, murderous purges and forced labor camps masterminded by its all-powerful strongman, Joseph Stalin. Besides, there was a war on in Europe. Four months earlier Stalin and Adolf Hitler had signed a notorious nonaggression pact and had promptly invaded Poland from opposite ends.

*   *   *

THE FAMILY Buick left the municipal bustle of Shreveport and headed west along the I-20, crossing the state line outside sleepy Waskom, Texas. Back when Rildia Bee was about to go into labor, she had proposed to Harvey that they take the half-hour drive so her baby could be born a Texan, and she had been only half-joking. The Lone Star State ran deep in her family, beginning with Grandfather Solomon, a circuit rider, hellfire evangelist, and math teacher who was a founder of Baylor University and the First Baptist Church of Waco and pastor to Sam Houston, who had virtually hauled the republic into the United States. Now, at last, Harvey's employer had relocated them back where she belonged.

From Waskom the road led behind the pine curtain that cast its green shade across East Texas. In this subtropical land of shadows, so unlike the fabled Texas of cattle and cacti, ten-gallon hats and jinglin' spurs to the west, there was space and peace, with little to hear for miles but rustling boughs.

Half an hour farther on, the unmistakable spindly towers of Kilgore came into view. The little city had been a railroad way station until 1930, when a "poor boy" drilling test mounted by a seventy-year-old charlatan named Columbus Marion "Dad" Joiner unexpectedly gushed forth a roaring geyser of crude. Thus Joiner, who had staged the lackadaisical operation to extract funds from widows to whom he professed undying love and from Depression-struck farmers desperate for a lucky strike, discovered the East Texas Oilfield, the biggest in the contiguous United States and at the time in the world. When it emerged that he had peddled the rights several times over, "Dad" was finessed into selling up to H. L. Hunt, who played a much meaner hand of poker, and Joiner died virtually penniless. Kilgore, meanwhile, sprouted oil derricks the way regular towns raised telegraph poles and traffic lights: at their densest, there were more than a thousand downtown, including forty-four on a single block, many in backyards, with their legs hard up against those of their neighbors. Tents, shanties, and ramshackle honkytonks heaving with prospectors, roustabouts, gamblers, and whores spilled along Main Street. Texas Rangers and the National Guard followed in pursuit of "hot" oil smugglers and oil pirates, among them some of East Texas's leading citizens, who drilled long slanting holes to draw off their neighbors' crude.

The wooden skeletons still commanded the sky when the Cliburns arrived in 1940, topped at Christmas with illuminated stars in reds, greens, and blues like a forest of deconstructed firs. Yet, by then, the boomtown jamboree had moved on to leave a pleasant if scattered town of ten thousand. Big oil had bought up most of the leases, and among the operators was Magnolia Petroleum Company, an affiliate of Socony-Vacuum Oil of New York. Harvey was their purchasing agent for East Central Texas, Arkansas, Louisiana, Mississippi, and Alabama, a title that was bigger than his annual salary, which was around ten thousand dollars. Soft-spoken and sensitive, he was never cut out to be a player in the high-stakes oil business. While H. L. Hunt, an old family friend, became the richest man in the world, the Cliburns moved their modest belongings into a tiny one-story white house with a cedar shake roof eight blocks from downtown on South Martin Street. The cozy living room was just big enough for Rildia Bee's baby grands—a Steinway and a Bechstein placed six to nine so she could look her students in the eyes—together with a nine-by-twelve red floral rug, a few chairs, and an old windup Victrola.

At the back of the small plot was a hedge with a strategic gap that led directly to Kilgore Heights Elementary School. This was important because Van could squeeze out after morning practice wearing his little tweed suit, hair combed back and face scrubbed pink, but more important because, during recess, his classmates could squeeze *in* for piano lessons. On his first day of school, Miss Gray, his first-grade teacher, stopped by his desk during a spelling lesson and stared at his hands. "Van, you have such long hands, you ought to play the piano," she said. He smiled, and a few days later, when they were trying to find him a role in the class play, the maudlin *Tom Thumb Wedding*, he offered to take over the accompaniment. Oleta Gray literally jumped out of her seat when Van launched into the Bridal Chorus from *Lohengrin*.

A minute after the last bell, he was back home at the piano, and he was at the keys again after dinner—except on church nights, which were as often as four times a week. Music and religion were the twin themes of his young life. Harvey was the Sunday school superintendent, Rildia Bee played the organ, and they all sang in the choir. With rehearsing, attending church dinners and prayer meetings, memorizing the King James Bible, praying for foreign missionaries, and shaming lapsed parishioners, First Baptist took up a good deal of what childhood the piano left. In return, it taught Van generosity, humility, and pluck: the last not least during Sword Drill, when children stood at attention, drew their Bibles, and on the word *Charge!* thumbed furiously through to find the day's book, chapter, and verse.

Added to those qualities was service, which was a constant refrain at home as well as at church. While Van was still tiny, Harvey had him seat his mother at mealtimes and open the door for her. In his first year at elementary school, he set him to studying table etiquette and serving dinner. When Van was ready, they invited two couples over and had him serve them. "If you do not know how to serve, you are not worthy to be served" was their mantra, and it became his. Playing was serving, too, Rildia Bee taught, and she took every chance to have Van perform in public. He played at ladies' teas and the Rotary. He played in the chapel of rest at Rader Funeral Home, a few blocks over, before he could read the hymn titles. He played at the Southwestern Bible and Evangelical Conference, the Baptist Sunday School Convention, and the Texas Music Teachers Association State Convention. At the National Piano Playing Auditions in Fort Worth, he rattled off fifteen pieces and was graded "superior" fifteen times. He wowed the Musical Arts Society of Muskogee, Oklahoma, and audiences in Nacogdoches, Texas, and Clinton and Brookhaven, Mississippi. Excuses did not wash. Shortly before a concert in Kilgore, when he was still six, he ran into a tree and knocked out a front tooth, adding another gap to the two already there. "I can't play without any teeth," he wheedled. "Just don't smile," Rildia Bee replied. "The rest will be done by your hands— and God." She had a way of pretending to let him decide whether to accept an invitation while giving him no choice whatsoever. "Well, you know you are free," she would say. "If you say no, oh! you can do anything you want, but if you say yes"—in a singsong staccato now— "there—will—be—restrictions, and you will have freedom only after you do this much now in the morning and that much after dinner, and then if you want to go to the movies, wonderful . . ."

Little by little a performer was created: poised in public, outwardly older than his years, a showman who, like many only children, desperately wanted to please everyone he knew, which in a small town meant everyone. Only he was aware how acutely he suffered from nerves before every concert, beginning when he was four. Yet, even then, he knew it wasn't stage fright: it was a heart-wrenching feeling of responsibility to the beautiful music to which he had to do justice, to the audience he had to serve.

*   *   *

WHEN VAN was ten, Harvey reached a decision. "Well, all right then, young fella," he said, "if that's the way it's gonna be, we'll just git with it. There's not gonna be any halfway best around here. If you're gonna be a concert pianist you're gonna be the best there is." He built a music room on the garage so Van could practice whenever he liked. Now he was at the piano three hours a day, four if schoolwork allowed, and eventually as much as five. Sometimes he rebelled, but Rildia Bee was not above moral blackmail. On one day that he cried off practice, Harvey badly wanted to see a movie. "It hurts me *terribly*," Rildia Bee told Van, "but we have to show we have strength. No we are *not* going, no matter what he says." Van went to the piano, abjectly telling himself what a bad boy he was, and conquered a passage that had troubled him. "Thank you, Mother, thank you, Daddy," he said afterward. "I know you were only trying to help me." Rildia Bee left the room, but not before he saw her tear up. If he was really naughty, the ultimate sanction was to ban the NBC Blue Network Saturday broadcast from the Met. He had adored opera since he was four and had sat motionless through a dress rehearsal and three performances of *Carmen*. He wanted to be a bass baritone, playing the glamorous toreador Escamillo or the tyrannous police chief Scarpia or the tormented czar Boris Godunov, but when his voice broke at puberty, he was left with an indifferent baritone at best.

Operas were for special occasions, but concerts were part of the plan. Sometimes he felt as if he were growing up on Highway 80, where the forests gave way to sparser trees and open plains, rushing up to Dallas or anywhere a big-name performer was playing, pulling over to stanch one of his nosebleeds with the kit they always had at hand, sleeping on the backseat during the drive home. The hum of tires on tarmac relaxed him, and on the cusp of his teens, he announced that he wanted to be a taxi driver. Mother was not amused, which was perhaps the point.

He was never a regular kid, and he knew it. When he entered Kilgore Junior High he was already growing like a beanstalk in a wet spring, and basketball coach Q. L. Bradford made a beeline for him. Rildia Bee graciously steered the coach away: she appreciated his interest, she said, but it was impossible; her son's fingers were insured for a million dollars and were made for playing the piano, not shooting or dribbling a ball. The school band director had a friendlier reception when he dropped by: Van got himself a uniform, learned how to play the clarinet, and marched up and down tootling away, safely on the sidelines, when the Bulldogs played football. But when he moved to high school, Rildia Bee quickly buttonholed his physical education instructor, Bob Waters, who spoke to the principal, C. L. Newsome, who excused Van from classes. One day, when he was playing ball in the street with some friends, he jammed his finger, and she restricted that kind of play, too. He was not bothered enough about sports to care, but when he won the leading role of Mr. Belvedere, an elderly babysitter with a mysterious past, in the class play *Sitting Pretty*, he was desperate to take it and forlorn when Rildia Bee decreed that the rehearsals would encroach too much on his practice time. As a small protest, he became president of the Thespian Club and the Spanish Club, and a member of the Student Council.

His school friends liked his quick laugh and antsy friendliness and wicked impressions, but he had precious little time to hang out with them. He had a desperate crush on a pretty young Latin teacher named Winifred Hamilton and moped with another boy who shared it, but the few girls he managed to date were all Rildia Bee's students. In his heart, though, he sensed that Mother knew best. She taught him to work hard enough to make it look easy when he played in public. She trained him to make a percussion instrument sing like a lyric instrument. She told him not to play faster than he could appreciate the music, that playing more slowly with greater rhythmic precision sounded faster than letting the notes tumble over one another. Music was a serious business, she lectured: "It stimulates both sides of the brain and enlivens the soul." That dictum and her others were wired into his brain: "Sing it before you play it." "You must find a singing sound." "Listen for the eye of the sound." "The first instrument was the human voice." Once, she took Van to audition for the famous Spanish pianist and Metro-Goldwyn-Mayer star José Iturbi. "You already have the best teacher," Iturbi told him. "You see, Mother?" Van said impatiently, and refused to hear of studying under anyone else.

It was always Mother, and Daddy of course, who was away a lot—"Sonny Boy," he'd say as he left in search of fairly priced crude, "now, you take care of your mother"—but who knew his son better than many fathers in an emotionally glacial age. If a friend had dared warn about the risks of raising a prodigy—for there were plenty of examples of infant marvels who startled grown-ups with their dazzling finger work only to lead lives misshapen by their devouring talent—Van would have understood least of all. He loved the company of adults, their attention and their stories of past times. By age eight, he had read his first book about English antique silver (in which his aunt was an expert) and learned all the markings by heart. He was born old, he said while still young. The past was the most beautiful place to be, and music was his time machine.

*   *   *

AS WORLD War II ended, Van's yearning to visit Russia faded like an old photograph, leaving only a nostalgic dream. But he had Russia's music at his fingertips, and that was nearly as good. Rildia Bee enjoyed reminding him that he was getting the teaching of the great masters, Franz Liszt and Anton Rubinstein, thirdhand; she had had it secondhand, she brightly added. Deep in East Texas she kept the Romantic flame burning pure and true, untainted by modern influences, and passed the torch on to her son. He had the demonstrative nature, the physical equipment, and a natural nobility of expression that perfectly suited the grandly expressive Russian style.

Van's first big chance to show it off came when he was twelve and Tchaikovsky's Piano Concerto no. 1 appeared on the list of pieces eligible for the annual Texas State Music Contest sponsored by Texas Gulf Sulphur Company. He memorized it in twenty-one days, Rildia Bee crossing each day off on the blackboard, and won the two-hundred-dollar prize. Then he played it with the Houston Symphony Orchestra, a plump pink boy with wavy ginger hair in a tweed suit and wide-collared shirt grinning behind the piano and sounding as if he'd been born a hundred years before. At the end, the orchestra as well as the audience jumped to its feet. It was as if the fresh-faced kid had mysteriously channeled the soul of Tchaikovsky, the most Russian composer of them all.

Perhaps it was just as well that Van was unable to visit Tchaikovsky's homeland, because it bore little similiarity to the country of his dreams. Barely two years after the end of the war, a Cold War was setting in between the Soviet Union and its former allies. Behind the Kremlin walls that so appealed to Van's childish imagination, Joseph Stalin was driving his scientists to replicate the atomic bombs that America had exploded above Hiroshima and Nagasaki. As the dictator sought security by toying with the fates of neighboring nations, an Iron Curtain fell across Europe, and the shadow of totalitarianism and police government settled on its eastern half. In the Soviet Union, too, the relative freedoms of war retreated before a new campaign of fear. Once more, black secret police vans mockingly painted with advertisements for scarce meat and scarcer Soviet champagne roamed the streets, and routine torture, forced confessions, sham trials, mass deportations, summary executions, and arranged accidents began all over again.

To scour away the effects of exposure to the West during the wartime alliance, Stalin launched a campaign to expunge foreign influence from Soviet society—especially that of America, which was denounced from loudspeakers strung along streets as "the warmonger and imperialist oppressor." The arts were not immune, and of all Soviet arts, classical music was first.

High art had survived the Russian Revolution thanks to the leading role of the intelligentsia, who had simply declared the arts socialized. Lenin had envisioned concert halls packed with workers absorbing the improving strains of the classics. Stalin, a fanatical consumer of culture who attended Tchaikovsky's *Swan Lake* thirty times, saw music as a useful tool of ideology. In 1936 the dictator had lured Sergei Prokofiev back to Russia after nearly two decades' exile in America and Europe. Now he turned on him and Dmitri Shostakovich, Prokofiev's rival for the title of greatest Soviet composer. In February 1948 the Central Committee of the Communist Party issued a resolution that attacked both men, together with other leading composers, for exhibiting bourgeois tendencies. In Soviet speak, a lexicon in which words acquired the opposite of their usual meaning, *bourgeois* signified avant-garde styles of Western origin. Allied to it was *formalism*, connoting a work of uninhibited creativity. Such "degenerate music" was rejected as difficult and therefore useless for developing proletarian culture; in its place was prescribed *socialist realism*, which was not intended to portray life as it actually was but rather as it would be in the ideal workers' paradise. In practice, this amounted to bad imitations of Tchaikovsky's stodgier successors, seasoned with hummable melodies and rousing heroic themes, but since composers were paid and given privileges by the state, so long as they obeyed party precepts their livelihood needed have no correlation with their talent. That much was clear when speakers at the ensuing First All-Union Congress of Soviet Composers dismissed Comrade Prokofiev's music as "grunting and scraping," ridiculed Comrade Shostakovich's oeuvre as a "muddled, nerve-wracking" hubbub exhibiting a neurotic and repulsive pathology, and labeled both men "enemies of Russian music." In Stalinist Russia, this was an attack on not just their careers but potentially their lives. Prokofiev found many of his works banned and the rest suppressed for fear of official displeasure; heavily in debt, he secluded himself to conserve his energy for composing. His estranged Spanish wife, Lina, was arrested on a charge of espionage and hauled off to the Lubyanka, the yellow neoclassical prison at the core of the Soviet police state. After nine months of torture she was sentenced to twenty years in the Gulag, the notorious chain of forced labor camps scattered across Soviet territory, on the basis of an extracted confession that was, anyway, a bureaucratic formality: in those days, there was a specific category for spouses and children of the condemned, "Traitor of Motherland Family Member."

As for Shostakovich, he had been here before, in 1936, when he was

denounced and ostracized so severely that for months his life hung
in the balance. He embraced the new attacks with abject humility.
"Once again," he wrote in an open letter, "I moved in the direction
of formalism and have begun to speak a language the people do not
understand . . . I know that the Party is right. I am deeply grateful for
the criticism." Even so, his music was boycotted, his family's privileges were rescinded, and he was fired from his job at the conservatory, where composers scrambled to accuse one another of formalism
in hopes of deflecting the charge from their own work. Reserved and
testy, alternately apologetic and irritable, Shostakovich busied himself with synchronizing the clocks in his apartment, cleaning obses-
sively, and checking the performance of the postal service by mailing
himself cards.

In a system where one man's word was law, fortunes could change
with dizzying speed, and in 1949 Stalin decided he needed Shostakovich as a delegate to the Cultural and Scientific Congress for World
Peace being held in New York that March. The meeting was among
the most daring and successful creations of the Cominform (short
for Communist Information Bureau), which Stalin had set up two
years earlier as a lavishly funded vehicle for coordinating international political warfare. As the Congress filled the Art Deco halls of
the Waldorf-Astoria, American liberals, including composers Leonard Bernstein and Aaron Copland, spoke in favor of peaceful cooperation, while other liberals mounted a picket outside, one brandishing a
placard reading "Shostakovich! Jump thru the window!" in reference
to a recent defection from the Soviet consulate.

Shostakovich was the celebrity witness to the glories of Soviet
culture, but the luxury accommodation was no recompense for the
humiliation he suffered. At the official press conference, he stood up,
his face a "bag of ticks and grimaces," his eyes downcast behind thick
wire-rimmed glasses, and read from a prepared statement, accusing
Western "hatemongers" of "preparing world opinion for the transi-
tion from cold war to outright war." In the audience was the Russian-
born composer Nicolas Nabokov, who, like his first cousin Vladimir,

had fled the revolution and taken U.S. citizenship. Nabokov watched Shostakovich read in a shaky voice before breaking off a short way through, leaving a "suave radio baritone" to finish his speech, and decided to expose the sham. Jumping to his feet, Nabokov loudly asked if the composer supported the recent Soviet vilification of his great compatriot Igor Stravinsky. Shostakovich worshipped Stravinsky as a composer, if not always as a man, but he was forced to parrot the official line. To Nabokov, this was proof enough that Shostakovich was "not a free man, but an obedient tool of his government."

Later that year, in his oratorio *The Song of the Forests*, Shostakovich extolled Stalin as the "great gardener," and rehabilitated himself a second time. Nabokov, meanwhile, became secretary-general of the Paris-based Congress for Cultural Freedom, a CIA client organization that covertly funded moderate left-wing European intellectuals as an antidote to far-left-wing European intellectuals who claimed that culture and communism were better bedfellows than culture and liberal democracy. Music featured heavily among its many projects, including a festival staged in Paris called Masterpieces of the Twentieth Century, which was designed to pick up the baton of modernism the Soviets had dropped. Heading the program was *The Rite of Spring*, with its composer, Stravinsky, whom Nabokov had sought out in Los Angeles, prominently in attendance.

Music was no longer a bond between East and West; on the contrary, both sides manipulated it to point up their differences. The cultural chasm widened as the Soviets exploded their first nuclear device in August 1949, as China fell to Mao Zedong's Communists weeks later, and as U.S. forces went back into action in Korea the following summer. America fell prey to a hysterical Red Scare, fanned by Senator Joe McCarthy, which sought to expose Communists and fellow travelers in every area of public life, including classical music. In this toxic atmosphere, anything Russian was beyond the pale. One producer at the Voice of America, the nation's external broadcaster, asked the music library for a recording of a popular piece called "Song of India" and found that the Red baiters had banned it. "It's by

Rimsky-Korsakov," the librarian explained, "and we're not supposed to use anything by Russians."

For the crew-cut American pianists who came of age in the 1950s, the steely tones and coiled rhythms of modern music were all the rage. Germanic composers were also firmly back in favor: Bach, Mozart, Beethoven, and Schubert were the undisputed masters. As for Russian music and the whole Romantic repertoire, with its cult of the inspired virtuoso (including the Hungarian Liszt and the Polish Chopin), it was suddenly as out of fashion as powdered wigs and pistols at dawn. To a mop-haired seventeen-year-old who arrived in New York in the fall of 1951, this came as an awful shock.

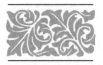

· *2* ·

Room 412

A TALL pile of loud clothes was flapping along the hallway of the Juilliard School toward the elevator where the legendary Rosina Lhévinne was standing. Barely inhabiting the colorful threads was a rawboned creature with enormous waving hands, a snub nose, and a frizz of gingery blond curls that bounced nearly up to the ceiling. The kid was six foot four, maybe six foot seven with the hair. Rosina, who stood five foot two, craned her neck to find a spotty, boyish face beaming down at her with intent.

"Honey," Van Cliburn announced, "ah've come to study with y'all."

Joe, the school's Irish elevator operator, might well have spluttered, for this was not the way to address New York's most revered piano teacher. At seventy-one, the Russian-born Madame Lhévinne was loved and feared in equal measure. One observer suggested she combined the autocracy of Catherine the Great with the coarseness of a droshky driver. If you could get through your pieces in room 412 at Juilliard, it was said, you could play anywhere in the world.

Rosina scanned the speaker's face. She had not seen him before, but the voice was familiar: a honey-and-mesquite drawl that was at once grave and impish. He had telephoned her the other day from the Buckingham Hotel, where he was staying with his mother. During three summers, the pair had traveled up from Texas and enrolled Van in school in order to find the right teacher, and Rildia Bee had then written the school with their final choice: Rosina Lhévinne. Now they had received the school registration card only to find Van had been assigned to another teacher's class. They felt hurt, bewildered, and betrayed.

Rosina explained that her classes, which were always oversubscribed, were unfortunately full. She had not heard Van play at the auditions, and he would have to make do with one of her assistants. "Perhaps," she had offered over the telephone, "I can take you next year."

"But I must study with you, Mrs. Lhévinne," the voice had come back, its unrushed tones curling round every word. "Even if you can give me only ten minutes a week, I'll consider myself your pupil. However"—and here the voice lingered with a warning edge—"if you definitely can't take me and I go to another teacher, I'll stay with that teacher until I graduate. What I want you to know about me, Mrs. Lhévinne, is that I'm very loyal."

"Shhh," Rildia Bee had whispered from the other room of the little suite. As usual, Harvey had stayed back home in Texas.

"No, Mother," Van had said firmly when he put the phone down. "She's a very nice lady, but I want her to know—when I begin, I stay and I end."

As luck would have it, Rosina already had two students from Texas. Jeaneane Dowis, a pretty, preppy, quick-witted brunette from Grapevine, was eighteen but had been at Juilliard for two years already. Her friend James Mathis, from Dallas, also eighteen, had just joined the Lhévinne class. Together they put in a word for Van: at the very least, they said, Madame should hear him play.

* * *

JUILLIARD OCCUPIED a sandwich of limestone buildings at West 122nd Street, between Claremont Avenue and Broadway, in the Morningside Heights neighborhood of Upper Manhattan. One slice was the handsome Edwardian mansion of the old Institute of Musical Arts; the other, in streamlined Art Deco by the Empire State Building architects, was added when the institute merged with the school founded, after much skullduggery, with the fortune of textile merchant Augustus D. Juilliard. Six hundred artistic souls crammed into a tangle of pastel green corridors and stairways and halls, each confidently expecting a dazzling solo career and almost all destined to be brutally disappointed. Pianists, numbering two hundred or so, were the dominant tribe; there were also violinists, cellists, wind and brass players, percussionists, singers, composers, conductors, and, this year, dancers, whom the musicians noticed chiefly on account of their odor. Like monks in a cell, the musical novices shut themselves in rehearsal studios for ten hours a day, banding together to keep rivals away and scaring off freshmen with tall tales of razor blades planted between piano keys. Social life was intense but strained. United by a cultish devotion to the school and their art, students were jealously divided by the pressure to outplay one another to obtain a hearing. Some crumpled under the competition; others basked in a glow of conscious exclusivity, buoyed with the pleasant sensation of filling their space well.

As for the faculty, they were the students a few decades on. Teachers' reputations depended on their attracting talented pupils, and they competed shamelessly for the best. Once they had them, they hated seeing them play for colleagues or talk to members of another class. Hierarchy was engraved in brass on the doors of their studios, recording how long they had survived. Rosina Lhévinne's nameplate bore the year 1924, when she and her husband, Josef, joined the faculty. Both had graduated with gold medals from the Moscow Conservatory in the 1890s, but after being trapped in Germany by the First World War and losing their savings in the Russian Revolution, they had sailed for America, where Josef made a sensational debut at Carnegie Hall and they taught in tandem, she bearing the brunt of the work while he was away performing and philandering. When Josef passed away in 1944, a year after his classmate and friend Sergei Rachmaninoff, Rosina became America's foremost link to the golden age of Russian Romanticism. At seventy-one, she was Juilliard's undisputed star teacher.

More perhaps than any other young American, Van revered that tradition, with its virtuosos who painted stories from the keyboard with a religious passion. To his mind, Romantic Russian music was so exquisitely, painfully beautiful that he knew it could only be the breath of God. Aside from Rildia Bee, he could not imagine studying with anyone else but Rosina, which was why he was here in the famous fourth-floor studio with its double walls and cork floor, ready to play his way into her hard-won affections.

Rosina sat in her high-backed green-upholstered chair as Van raised his huge, bony hands. They were as big as Josef's, she noticed, big enough to play a twelfth and stretch thirteen notes, middle C to A, with long, tapered fingers that could get between the keys. But what were they doing? His left hand was drumming the opening fanfare of Liszt's Twelfth Hungarian Rhapsody, a storm-racked chandelier of crashing chords that serious pianists were supposed to spurn. A deep, ominous tremolando, the same fanfare with the right hand, and another tremulous roll. Then the lightest chords, tripping off the fingers of his right hand while his left played the wistful melody. Both hands away, flying along the keyboard like a ballerina's feet barely brushing the floor. A moment of tranquillity, his head back now, eyes closed, forehead creased at the exquisite beauty of the thing, his soul swelling with every note. Long before then, Rosina had her answer. The unusual boy was not only playing with startling control and power, but he was also constructing something uncommonly noble, sensitive, and heartfelt. More than that, he had a big, sweeping approach that she had not seen in years: a grand style that uncannily echoed the dashing virtuosos of her youth.

His playing thrilled a deep Russian chord in her. She found space in her class.

*   *   *

DURING THE Great Depression many of Morningside Heights' apartment buildings degenerated into single-room-occupancy hotels of such squalor that they scared off even students. Neighboring Columbia University had recently begun a program of crash gentrification by buying up whole blocks and returning them to family housing, and 15 Claremont Avenue, a handsome ten-story structure three blocks from Juilliard, was one of the beneficiaries. The five-room apartment leased by Mr. and Mrs. Allen Spicer was generously sized, the room for rent had its own bath, and best of all, there was an ornate Chickering grand in the living room.

Bristle-haired Allen Spicer worked in the traffic department of the New York Telephone Company. His chubby, white-haired wife, Hazel, was secretary to the principal of a Bronx high school. They needed the extra income, but Mrs. Spicer was reluctant to take responsibility for a roomer as young as Van. Rildia Bee charmingly waved away her doubts and asked if her son might be allowed to practice on the piano for an hour or two a day. Mrs. Spicer reluctantly agreed, so long as she didn't have to listen to scales. Van moved in, and Rildia Bee left her only child for the first time.

He loved his parents deeply, but in many ways the move was a relief. His Texas adolescence, he once admitted, had been a living hell: "You can't love music enough to want to play it without other kids thinking you're queer or something." In his early teens he shot up to his full height, his shoe size nearly matching his years, and his hair kinked into an uncontrollable frizz. When unisex salons were widely regarded as abominations and the epithet *longhair*, signifying an artist or intellectual, was akin to *sissy*, he had been easy pickings for school jocks. As well as retreating still further into music, he had unburdened his awkwardness into old-fashioned poems: one, published in the *National Anthology of High School Poetry* in 1950, was bleakly titled "The Void." Though he was no genius at academic work—his IQ was measured at a high but unspectacular 119—he had sweated through summer sessions in the dusty brick groves of Kilgore College to graduate high school at sixteen, twelfth in a class of 103, with the highest ratings for personality, attitude, attendance, associates, chance of success, and character, though only a "satisfactory" for leadership, and ready to get out of town as fast as he could.

Like any teenager away from home the first time, he cut loose some strings. His room was a pigsty. Every day, Rildia Bee sent him the *Kilgore News Herald*, and the unread copies piled up with the other clutter until it threatened to block the door. Occasionally he stayed up all night and tackled a batch. "My room looks wonderful and I'll never let it get untidy again," he'd vow to Hazel Spicer in the morning, but it always did. He was terrible at writing home; after weeks of silence he telephoned, reversing the charges. Against his parents' strict precepts, he tried smoking and drinking: "Just a little rum," he said when he joined the Spicers in their late-afternoon rum and Coke. The biggest relief after years as a special case was Juilliard's unabashed elitism. In a place where violinists strode down the hall throwing off double-stops and triple-stops, he no longer stood out for devotion to his craft.

Yet he still stood out. It was hard not to when his blond pompadour bobbed above the heads of everyone else and his contagious laugh echoed down the hall. He was perpetually putting his paddle-like arms round anyone who came within their ambit, which disarmed most but annoyed some. A young voice student named Leontyne Price was shocked when he, a Lhévinne student, spoke to her in the cafeteria, a major arena for student showboating, where the tribes normally kept their own counsel. Then there was his Texas-ness, which he wore more strongly than the Dallas contingent, despite years of speech and drama lessons with a neighbor, Mrs. Leo Satterwhite Allen, whose son had studied with Rildia Bee. The typical Juilliard student was the son of Eastern European Jewish intellectuals raised in a wood polish world of museums and Chekhov plays and studied language. Van went round with his brightly patterned shirts and his wide, floppy collars, his southern accent and down-home humor and artless affection for everyone. "Boy, isn't it wonderful," he'd say, shaking his head in wonder, when he liked something. Students who considered themselves intellectuals talked down to him, but what they found most outlandish was his taste in music: Tchaikovsky, Rachmaninoff, Liszt—his heroes were so cringingly unfashionable that it was hard to take him seriously as an artist. That pained him,

more on account of his beloved music than his ego, which his up-
bringing and gentleness kept modestly bound.

Since he was dismissed as a hayseed he began playing the enfant
terrible, banging out jazz and pop tunes, thumping the keyboard as
if he had boxing gloves on, and fooling his classmates into thinking
he coasted on his admittedly spectacular musical instincts. To the
Spicers' consternation, he started coming home in the early hours and
leaving notes for Hazel: "Hello, darling! I'm home! Whee! Wake me
up so I can talk to you in the morning. Love, Van." They soon solved
the mystery of his late nights. When the night caretaker at Juilliard
threw Rosina's gang out of the practice studios, Van walked with them
as far as the 110th Street subway station, but instead of joining them
for a beer, he took the downtown 1 train, with its screeching brakes
and wicker seats, to Fifty-Seventh Street and disappeared down the
service stairs at the back of a tall stone building. Squeezing past the
trash cans, he tugged on a heavy sliding door and entered a window-
less basement lit by factory-style fluorescent lights and crisscrossed
by pipes. There, parked against drably painted walls, were his nightly
dates: a bank of several dozen nine-foot concert grands. This was the
basement of Steinway Hall, where pianists on the roster of Steinway
Artists could choose an instrument for their next performance from
a storied fleet that included Rachmaninoff's favorite, number CD-18.
At night, after the white-coated technicians had finished their tuning
and buffing, the black beauties were available for practice. Some students used the basement as a musical club, where friends gathered
to dispense gossip and criticism. Van took the last time slot, when
he could be alone and concentrate while the world was asleep. In the
morning he was perpetually late for his nine o'clock class. This drove
Rosina crazy and irritated his classmates, who thought he was dopey
and pitched in to buy him a Big Ben alarm clock. He started picking
up chocolates or flowers on the way to school and presenting them to
Rosina with his excuses, which made him even later.

To his peers' equal bemusement, three times a week he rode the
subway to Fifty-Seventh Street to attend Calvary Baptist Church.

In true New York style, the church was interrupted by its own sky-scraper, with a Gothic portal supporting a dozen floors of apart-ments and a tower perched up high. Inside, a proscenium arch and gallery gave it the look of a Broadway theater, but the fellowship was warm, hands were raised high, and here in Mammon the living God felt present in daily life. Van's fellow Texan Jeaneane Dowis was as suspicious as any of Van's worn-on-the-sleeve faith, but he kept ask-ing her out for dinner, and a free meal was not to be sniffed at. She and Jimmy Mathis, Rosina's other Texan pianist, became Van's best friends. Jimmy had short dark hair; a sensitive, clammy face; and a penchant for making a hysterical drama out of anything. "*Well,* far be it from *me* to say," he'd begin in the tones of a bossy schoolmarm, before delivering an outrageous zinger. The threesome ate together at Aki Dining Room on West 119th Street, where a full dinner could be had for ninety-nine cents, gabbing all the time about the superior virtues of Texas. When they were apart, Van was on the phone with them by the hour. Mr. Spicer had a free telephone that went with his job, but he consulted his conscience, decided it was wrong to put Van's calls on it, and installed a separate line. His conscience thanked him when Van racked up staggeringly high bills.

Many evenings, Van bought a twenty-five-cent student ticket for Carnegie Hall from Joseph Patelson Music House on Fifty-Sixth Street, a little place with bins full of out-of-print sheet music that was universally known as the half-price shop; or he and his two friends queued for seventy-five-cent standing places at the Metropolitan Op-era, down on Broadway. One night at the Met, a wealthy lady beck-oned him to take her spare seat down front, and from then on he bought standing but sat in an orchestra seat. Occasionally he went to the jazz clubs on Fifty-Second Street, or the Village Vanguard down-town, where Ella Fitzgerald might be singing or Art Tatum and Os-car Peterson playing piano. Some said the improvised spontaneity of jazz inflected American classical music, but Van didn't take it very seriously and liked cocktail piano and World War II songs just as well.

There was music everywhere in New York in 1951. There was everything in New York, though many neighborhoods retained a quirky small-town feel. The city was rushing with the energies unleashed after the war. The West Side piers were busy with ships and freight, the billboard lights of Times Square glowed bright, and the colleges were full of men and women on the GI program. For a young man with a few dollars chasing his dream, it was an exciting time to be alive.

* * *

IT WAS the brightest of times and the darkest of times. Cities across America were shooting skyward, but toward what future? With the map of Eurasia now overwhelmingly colored red, President Truman made it America's overriding priority to resist at all costs what one official termed "the Kremlin's ultimate intentions to enslave mankind." Secret plans were drawn up for a fourfold increase in defense spending, a burgeoning of the atomic stockpile, and a possible Third World War, which experts predicted was most likely to start, and end, in 1957. In New York, schoolchildren were issued dog tags so their bodies could be identified in case of a nuclear blast, and families upstate were warned to expect a flood of refugees. "Every effort will be made to place people of similar interests with you," officials assured them, as if Armageddon would resemble summer camp. Allegorizing how the world had got in this fix, movie theaters were showing *The Day the Earth Stood Still*, in which a well-meaning alien pleads for world harmony and an end to the weapons race only to meet with suspicion and violence from officials and citizens alike.

Since the human consciousness protects itself by refusing to countenance its own demise, many searched for a silver lining to the atomic cloud. In bookstores, a thin volume entitled *How to Survive an Atomic Bomb* was a best seller; its recommendations include practicing lying on the floor, ideally with no one watching; and wearing loose-fitting clothing and a hat to minimize burns. Reciting jingles or the multiplication table might help control fear during a nuclear attack, the book advises, but, in any case, life should be back to normal within a month or two. In an even more Pollyannaish vein, an engineer drew up plans for giant subterranean elevators that would lower

New York City's skyscrapers in an atomic emergency; he calculated that the Empire State Building could be dropped as far as the eighty-sixth floor in fifty-eight seconds, "leaving only the tower unprotected to avoid expense of added cellar depth." Others saw in atomic energy not the flash of extinction but a dazzling future of cheap power, mass leisure, and a cultural and intellectual renaissance. Families would live in houses heated and cooled by walls of radioactive uranium and lit by panels glowing with the "fluorescence which occurs around U-235." They would brush their teeth with atomic toothpaste, eat crops grown with radioactive fertilizer and meat from giant mutant cattle, and drive atomic cars that ran for a year on "a pellet of atomic energy the size of a vitamin pill." One expert proposed melting the polar ice cap by bombing the Arctic, gifting "the entire world a moister, warmer climate" and opening vast areas for development; others suggested leveling the Rocky Mountains with atom bombs to increase rainfall across the Great Plains and using the weapons "generally to tidy up the awkward parts of the world." This was a brave new era limited only by man's imagination—and by reality, which soon set in. "If an atomic-powered taxi hit an atomic-powered streetcar at Forty-second and Lex," explained the editor of *Astounding Science Fiction*, a publication not renowned for dryness, "it would completely destroy the whole Grand Central area." Melting the ice cap, *Science Digest* pointed out, would be not only calamitous, but also ruinously expensive. Domestic applications of atomic power sources, noted *Scientific American*, were limited by the inconvenient fact that they weighed a minimum of twenty tons, excluding the cooling system and radiation shield.

Faced with such impossible calculations, most people did the only sensible thing: they tuned out, hoped for the best, and got on with their lives.

*   *   *

INSIDE ROOM 412 it was evilly hot. Rosina was a famous hypochondriac and sat wrapped in shawls, winter and summer, against imaginary drafts. "Open the window a little less!" she croaked if someone dared nudge it. When her full complement of fifteen or twenty students crammed into the studio, they begged her to step outside while they aired it.

Behind the two pianos hung a small portrait of Josef Lhévinne and a bigger one of Anton Rubinstein. In 1889, the year she met Josef, when she (then Rosina Bessie) was nine and he (then Josef Levin) was fourteen and had shown up at her door as a substitute piano teacher, Rubinstein selected Josef to play Beethoven's *Emperor Concerto* under his baton and, at the end, publicly embraced him, declaring him his successor. The rest of their story was legend. Rosina followed Josef into the conservatory, and a week after her graduation they married. Friends gave the marriage a year at most, but when Rosina overheard a remark that she was the better pianist of the two, she immediately stopped playing and devoted herself to Josef's career. It was in search of opportunities for him that they moved to western Europe and Frenchified their name from Levin to Lhévinne.

In class, Rosina presided from her green chair, which was known as "the throne," her short, wavy hair augmented with a steel-gray wig that sometimes lost its moorings. Behind the little-old-lady act lay a complex character. She was both a cuddly matriarch who shamelessly matchmade lonely first-year students and a master manipulator who kept control by withholding praise and playing classmates against one another. She told earthy jokes and pealed with laughter, but also suffered bouts of depression that left her coldly inscrutable, "with hooded eyes like a dour toad." Her advice changed with her mood, but if a student dared complain, she waved it off: "Certainly, you know, that was Monday and today is Friday," she'd purr in her thick Russian accent. She had a famously tortured relationship with the English language. When a journalist asked how she prepared for a concert, she replied, "After a little practice and a simple lunch I go to my room to rest and finger my passages."

On the subject of Romantic music, she was oracular. She taught the old Russian style, gently regularized to suit American tastes, which to Van was second nature. Since bravura pieces were easy for him, she started him with Mozart's Sonata in E-flat Major and Bach's Partita in E Minor. "Very talented, quick, not *very* accurate," she noted on a page headed "Cliburn, Harvey" in one of the little ring binders she used in class. They moved on to Chopin, Liszt, and Beethoven; and then Hindemith, Schumann, and Prokofiev. Like all the best students, Van had arrived a fully formed musician, and her interventions were modest, but he responded so strongly and felt the music so deeply that she began to look forward to their Friday 11:00 a.m. sessions with great joy. One day she suggested a different approach to a Chopin piece, and he got up and paced the room. "It's too beautiful," he said. "I can't stand it. I can't stand it."

The semesters went by, each seeming longer than it was because of the work packed in, the beginnings and endings marked by the increasingly raucous parties Jimmy Mathis threw at the fifteen-room apartment at West Seventy-Second Street and Riverside Drive that he shared with some other students. Van was always in the middle of the crush, playing the piano with a bevy of women singing along, chain-smoking now between pieces. It was hard not to like the gangly, goofy kid, even when he began to rack up prizes. In April 1952 it was the G. B. Dealey Memorial Award, named after a publisher of the *Dallas Morning News*, which earned him three hundred dollars, a performance with the Dallas Symphony Orchestra, and a solo recital. June of that year brought the Kosciuszko Foundation Chopin Award and a thousand dollars, a handy sum that paid off some of his mounting debts, as did a six-hundred-dollar Juilliard grant the following spring. Money was still short, and when he filled in the school's Placement Bureau form, he offered himself for tuition at five dollars an hour and recitals at three hundred dollars "or less," though he drew the line at playing hotels, nightclubs, or resorts. On the back page, Rosina added her endorsement:

> Harvey Levan [*sic*] ("Van") Cliburn possesses a most outstanding talent. He is a born virtuoso with dash and sweep which carry away the listener. In addition, he has the unusual

combination of virtuosity with a rare, innate sensitivity for music . . .

Mr. Cliburn has excellent stage presence and, to my mind, if he continues to work as sincerely as he does now he will be one of the most promising young pianists of the day.

Suddenly it was the end of the year. Late as usual, Van rushed back to the Spicers' with one classmate to help him pack and another to stand outside holding a cab that would take him to the airport. He threw his things helter-skelter into a suitcase and jumped on it until it closed. Then he ran out with the bulging bag in one hand, a briefcase stuffed with music in the other, and his spare pair of shoes sticking out of his coat pockets.

*   *   *

ROSINA'S CLASS was convinced it ran Juilliard, or at least the piano department, but within it, sudden fierce rivalries bubbled up and soured the air. In Van's second year, an ambitious seventeen-year-old with a crew cut named Daniel Pollack joined as a full scholarship student: "Excellent talent," Rosina had noted at his entrance examination. Pollack was six months younger than Van, was nearly as tall at six foot two, and the year before arriving had won an appearance with his hometown orchestra, the Los Angeles Philharmonic. He was bent on proving himself, and since both his parents had been born in Russia, he had a stronger claim on its heritage than Van. With their different characters, it was apparent to the class that the two did not warm to each other.

The new school year also brought the annual competition to perform as soloist with the Juilliard Symphony Orchestra. To Van and Rosina's glee, the prize piece was announced as Tchaikovsky's Piano Concerto no. 1, and they worked on it together for several weeks. Rosina was an unassailable authority where the Tchaikovsky was concerned. If a student dared argue when she told him to pedal during a passage that was marked "staccato" and was always played staccato, she would sweetly say, "But Tchaikovsky told Mr. Lhévinne to pedal there." After the class heats, Jeaneane Dowis, who had been banned from competing after winning two years in a row, ventured an opinion that Van's playing bordered on cheap thrills, which made Rosina so angry that she refused to speak to her for five days. Van went forward to the semifinals. "Well, we don't really need to have any finals," a jury member said at the end. "Van won the competition."

That January, he played the concerto in the Juilliard Concert Hall. The gangly Texan sat tall in the saddle. His fidgety geniality stilled into steady resolve. His huge hands hovered like hawks' wings and dropped fearlessly, flying with abandon. His interpretation was built on a grand scale and burnished to a lustrous glow. There was an eighteen-year-old's overexuberance about his tempo changes and dynamics, and he missed a few notes, but Rosina, listening in the audience, was transported. It was Anton Rubinstein's bravura and beauty she was hearing: the dramatic Russian spirit, virile and volcanic, a little brash and crazy, tempered by Liszt's long, lyrically elegant line, with a dash of American steadiness that stayed the thrillingly supple phrasing.

At the end of his second year, she graded him "Excellent." She had always admired him, and now she had come to love him, for his plucky joie de vivre, his childlike wonder, and his desperate naïveté. Still, there were many in the Juilliard hothouse who were convinced Van would never reach the top. The boy was a lovable mess—one day, he fell asleep and nearly missed his own showcase—but more to the point, he was a lovable *Texan* mess.

With Europe rebuilding after the war and the Iron Curtain impassable, unprecedented opportunities were opening up for American musicians. Yet almost to a man—women in the field were still a rarity—the rising stars were New York Jews of Russian and Eastern European heritage. There was no mystery to this. Back in Imperial Russia most Jews had been restricted to a region known as the Pale of Settlement, where they were heavily taxed, banned from sensitive jobs, forced to enroll their sons in military service, and devastated by pogroms. Under these hardships, many had emigrated and some had converted to Russian Orthodoxy, including the grandfather of Anton and Nikolai Rubinstein. When the Rubinstein brothers founded the St. Petersburg and Moscow conservatories, they established diplomas that permitted Jews to live beyond the Pale, and music became an escape route for poor Russian and Eastern European Jews much as athletics would be for African Americans. Their descendants were the inheritors of that tradition, the people whom audiences expected and trusted to interpret European music. It was true that the foremost American pianist of the early twentieth century was born Lucy Hickenlooper in San Antonio, Texas. But she changed her name to Olga Samaroff, and when she married the conductor Leopold Stokowski, she bolted his name on for double protection. The idea of a blond Southern Baptist called Van becoming a star virtuoso was downright peculiar. He was too domestic.

*　　*　　*

IF VAN hid his hunger for success from his peers, to the Spicers he appeared tremendously, determinedly ambitious. When he was home at night they had to prise him away from the Chickering before the neighbors complained. If they had friends round, he insisted on playing for them. For a time he practiced while sitting on the floor, to strengthen his wrists. One day he came in wringing his hands after a long session: "I never want to see a piano again," he cried, but fifteen minutes later he was hard at work, caught up in the music, singing and humming as he played, stopping to murmur, "Isn't that beautiful?"

The Spicers' only child, a daughter, had died five years before, and Van became like a son to them. They worried that he had few interests outside music. The Spicers were hot Yankee fans, but he loathed sports. His room gave no clues to a special girl: there were only three pictures in it, of Mother, Daddy, and Rosina Lhévinne. He was obsessed with Barbara Stanwyck movies; otherwise, his main nonmusical interest seemed to be people, whose company he unaffectedly adored. Allen Spicer, an Old Princetonian, was especially perturbed that Van never opened a book or newspaper. The boy paid little attention when the United States detonated the first hydrogen bomb on an atoll in the Pacific Ocean, or when Dwight D. Eisenhower won the 1952 presidential election by a landslide, in part by attacking the Truman administration for not doing enough to combat the creeping Communist threat.

"Van," said Allen, "if you don't read the headlines, you won't even know if there's a war on."

Van grinned. He lived in a world of eternal verities, where time was an illusion. If, in the spring of 1953, he heard about the convulsions shaking the tormented empire his beloved Russia had become, he could scarcely have imagined that they would soon give him the chance to silence his musical skeptics.

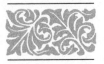

· *3* ·

The Successor

AT DUSK on March 1, 1953, Dacha no. 1 was eerily quiet. Not a curtain had twitched since the early hours when the four dinner guests staggered out after the usual boozy bacchanalia, collapsed in the backs of their limousines, and sped back to Moscow. For the first time anyone could remember, the master of the house told the guards to turn in for the night, and they slept soundly until ten. Normally he woke between then and midday, but the morning had gone and then the afternoon, and now they were beginning to get scared, scared at what might have happened and even more scared that they might have to disobey his orders not to disturb him.

At around 6:00 p.m., a light came on in the small dining room. The guards breathed a little and waited, at full alert, but 10:00 p.m. came, and still there was no call.

"Go on, you go, it's your responsibility," junior guard Pavel Lozgachev said to the head guard, Starostin.

"I'm afraid," he murmured.

"Fine, be afraid, but I'm not about to play the hero," Lozgachev retorted. Just then a package arrived from the Central Committee, and delivering the mail was Lozgachev's duty.

"All right, then," he said. "Wish me luck, boys."

The thickset sentry stomped down the long corridor that joined the lodge to the main house. They always made a noise to warn the

Boss they were coming, while pulling themselves into the attitude he liked: erect, not too soldierly.

The door to the small dining room was open, revealing wood-paneled walls newly covered with blown-up magazine photos of young children: a boy on skis, toddlers picnicking under a cherry tree. Lozgachev stepped in, and suddenly his legs abandoned him. The Boss was lying on the carpet in his vest and pajama bottoms, an acrid stain spreading round him. He grunted and weakly raised his hand.

Somehow the guard moved across the room. "Comrade Stalin, what's wrong?" he asked. "Should I call a doctor?"

This was a dangerous proposition. Since November, Stalin had arrested hundreds of medics, including his personal physician, on suspicion of plotting to murder him and other top leaders. Many were Jewish; Stalin had convinced himself that Jews, with their links to America, were incurable enemies of the state. "Beat them until they confess!" he ordered his torturers. "Beat, beat and beat again. Put them in chains, grind them into powder!" The propagandists announced the results: "It has been established that all these killer-doctors, monsters in human form . . . were hired agents of foreign intelligence services." With *Pravda* declaring that America and Britain were "feverishly preparing for a new world war," public trials of the medical fifth column were due to open in four days' time.

"Dz . . . Dz . . . ," Stalin mumbled incoherently. Next to him were a copy of *Pravda* and his pocket watch, which had stopped at half past six. His eyelids closed, and he gently snored. Lozgachev shakily picked up the intercom phone. "Come to the house quick," he said, sweat beading on his forehead. Starostin arrived in seconds, followed by two other guards. They stopped short.

"Let's put him on the sofa," Lozgachev said. They heaved the stout body onto the pink upholstered divan, and Starostin went off to phone Ignatiev, the head of the secret police. Ignatiev panicked and told him to phone Lavrenty Beria, the powerful security supremo.

The other guards moved Stalin from the pink divan to the sofa in the large dining room, where the air was fresher. He shivered, and they rolled down his sleeves and covered him with a blanket.

Beria was unavailable, but Starostin reached Georgy Malenkov, Stalin's latest favorite and heir apparent. Malenkov tried to phone Beria as well but called back after half an hour to say he couldn't find him. Another half hour went by, and Beria himself called. "Don't say anything to anyone about Comrade Stalin's illness," he instructed them.

Meanwhile, Malenkov got hold of Nikolai Bulganin, the suave deputy premier, and Nikita Khrushchev, the voluble, roly-poly party head in Moscow. These three and Beria had been Stalin's dinner companions the previous night. For years the dictator had presided over his empire from his table, plying his increasingly bloated cronies with strong liquor and relishing their loss of control almost as much as he enjoyed hearing them inform on one another to gain favor. After the meal, the mustachioed host would play the gramophone and watch the others cut a rug; one night he made Khrushchev squat down and perform a spinning, kicking Cossack dance called the *gopak*, which even the performer likened to a cow hoofing on ice. "When Stalin says dance, a wise man dances," Khrushchev ruefully remarked, summing up the operation of the entire Soviet government. When the torment ended, at around 5:00 a.m., they would totter out, relieved to have survived: "One never knows if one's going home or to prison," Bulganin once confided to Khrushchev. One by one, their comrades had disappeared, until the four were the last men standing.

"Look, the security boys have phoned from Stalin's place," Malenkov told Khrushchev. "They are very worried, something's happened to Stalin. We've got to go there." Khrushchev should go ahead, he added, and he and the others would follow. Khrushchev was surprised: when he had left, Stalin had been pretty drunk, but in fine fettle, jabbing his rotund protégé in the belly and warbling "Mikita," in a takeoff of Khrushchev's Ukrainian accent.

At 3:00 a.m. a car approached through the birches, golden pines, and camouflaged antiaircraft guns and drove up to the gates in the double perimeter fence. Malenkov and Beria got out. They made an odd pair: Malenkov, the finicky former keeper of the party records, resembling a portly baker, with his bloated torso and slicked hair; Beria, the brilliant KGB butcher and notorious pervert, equally rotund but the very picture of a shifty cartoon detective, with his turned-up collar and black trilby jammed on his head, over a pince-nez with thick lenses that made his eyes pop out.

"What's up with the Boss?" Malenkov asked one of the guards. His boots squeaked, and as he went inside he took them off and tucked them under his arm.

Lozgachev was still with Stalin, who was snoring.

"What are you panicking for?" Beria asked, swearing at him. "The Boss is sound asleep. Let's go, Malenkov!" The guard explained what had happened, but Beria told him not to bother them or disturb Comrade Stalin. The two men left.

Alone with Stalin, Lozgachev began to imagine the dire consequences if the *vozhd* died on his watch. He woke up the chief guard and persuaded him to call the inner circle again.

Sometime after 7:00 a.m., Khrushchev finally showed up.

"How's the Boss?" he asked.

"He's very poorly," Lozgachev replied. "There's something wrong."

"The doctors are on their way," Khrushchev reassured him.

The room filled up as the party bosses arrived, several openly weeping. Stalin's eyes briefly opened, gleaming with their usual tiger intensity, and seemed to flicker with recognition. "Comrade Stalin," his old comrade Kliment Voroshilov spoke up, "we, all your true friends and colleagues, are here. How are you feeling, dear friend?" But the moment of lucidity had gone.

By half past nine the doctors finally arrived. None of them had treated Stalin before, and their hands shook as they examined him. A dentist dropped the dictator's false teeth. The others fumbled at his shirt, and Lozgachev tore it off. To the guard's intense relief, the doctors diagnosed a cerebral hemorrhage: a massive stroke.

Ignatiev, the executor of the doctors' plot, who had been head of the secret police for less than two years, hovered outside, too scared to enter. "Come in, don't be shy," Lozgachev said, waving him in. When Stalin had let fly at him a few months earlier, Ignatiev had a heart attack.

Stalin's daughter, Svetlana, arrived direct from her French class and was met by Khrushchev and Bulganin, who hugged her, weeping. Later her brother Vasily showed up, drunk as usual. After the previous year's May Day parade, when Vasily authorized a flyby in bad weather conditions and crashed two Tu-4 bombers, Stalin fired him as Moscow Air Force commander. Not knowing the reason for the summons, Vasily had brought his maps, in case he had to account for himself. After a minute, he lurched off to the guards' lodge and screamed that his father had been murdered, then weaved out to his car and went home.

More doctors arrived and consulted. They applied leeches behind Stalin's ears and a cold compress to his head, injected him with camphor, administered magnesium sulfate enemas, took a urine sample, and left instructions to feed him sweet tea or soup from a spoon. Later, a coffin-like iron lung was wheeled in, accompanied by wide-eyed young specialists. Occasionally Stalin let out a groan.

Bulganin stayed with the patient while the other three leaders drove to the Kremlin for a conference in the Boss's office. Present in the room were the ten members of the old Politburo, which Stalin had replaced the previous year with a much larger Presidium. Beria, Malenkov, and Khrushchev were there, together with old Voroshilov and Khrushchev's mentor "Iron Lazar" Kaganovich, a former shoemaker turned manager of heavy industry and mass terror. Also in attendance were former foreign minister Vyacheslav Molotov, a cold-blooded hard-liner whom Lenin had nicknamed "Iron Butt," and former foreign trade minister Anastas Mikoyan, an emphatic Armenian with dark, glittering eyes and flashing, clenched teeth. Both were Kremlin stalwarts whom Stalin had recently fired and publicly denounced. Within hours of his stroke, the old order had restored itself to power.

The doctors presented their reports, and the horse trading began.

As the day wore on, it continued in whispers by the deathbed and back in the Kremlin that night.

For one moment on the morning of the fourth, Stalin seemed to regain consciousness. He gestured to a magazine clipping, a picture of a little girl feeding a lamb from a horn, and pointed to himself. "He sort of smiled," Khrushchev thought. Iron Butt Molotov saw a flash of the old self-deprecating wit. Beria, who had begun venting his pent-up hatred of Stalin, rushed over, dropped to his knees, and kissed Stalin's hand. Then, when the Boss sank again, Beria shot him a look of scorn and disgust. Svetlana caught it and thought Beria a monster. Once, Beria had dandled her on his knee; now she saw his flabby, sickly face "twisted by ambition, cruelty, cunning and a lust for power . . . He was a magnificent modern specimen of the artful courtier, the embodiment of Oriental perfidy, flattery and hypocrisy who had succeeded in confounding even my father."

Later in the day, the patient worsened again. That night, three of the "poisoner-doctors" were summoned from their cells in the Lubyanka. "Which specialist would you recommend for one of our most important people who has just had a stroke?" their torturers asked them. The doctors suggested several experts who were in prison and dismissed most of those at Stalin's side as incompetents, which put their interlocutors in a delicate position.

The following morning, Stalin paled, shook, and vomited blood. His breath came slow and shallow. Beria rushed back to the Boss's office, opened his safe, and searched for documents that might incriminate him and his cronies. As he expected, many of the files contained denunciations and evidence against him, Khrushchev, Malenkov, and others, including interrogation papers already filled out with answers. Systematically he began to destroy them.

Shortly before 10:00 p.m., Stalin's features twisted, and he began choking to death. One last time, he opened his eyes and with an awful look raised his left hand, pointing upward, perhaps trying to shake his finger or claw for air. Svetlana thought he was bringing a curse down on them all. Then he was gone.

A brawny medic began rhythmically pumping the dictator's chest. "Listen, please stop that!" Khrushchev spoke up from by the door. "The man is dead. What do you want? To bring him back to life?"

The leaders lined up in pairs to kiss the body. Most, even those whose lives had been on the line under Stalin, were crying. Beria, who went first, was glowing.

Silence fell. Then Beria barged out, shouting to the chief guard with immodest urgency, "Khrustalev, the car!"

"He's off to take power," Mikoyan said to Khrushchev. A great dealmaker like many of his fellow Armenians, Mikoyan was famous among the leaders for his glistening shrewdness.

The others lingered for a moment. Then, in a frenzy, they rushed all at once for the door.

*   *   *

TWO DAYS later, just after the 1:00 a.m. news, radio receivers tuned to Moscow emitted a strange spluttering sound followed by a flat drone. Somber orchestral music struck up and played in place of the usual hourly bulletins and the early-morning exercise class and political lecture. Suddenly it stopped, and after a delay bells pealed out. Another silence was broken by the soaring strains of the Soviet national anthem, which during the Second World War Stalin had substituted for "The Internationale."

Finally, a familiar voice came on, the same voice that had brought news of wartime victories, thick with emotion. The heart of Joseph Vissarionovich, the collaborator and follower of the genius of Lenin's work, the wise leader and teacher of the Communist Party and the Soviet people, had stopped beating. However heavy the blow, the nation was steely in its unity under the beloved fraternal family led by the party, the correctness of whose policies had been proven time and again. It would rise to new successes and crush foreign aggressors. After the usual pieties about peace, the voice concluded with a variation on the old line on the death of kings, with the Communist Party in place of the eternal crown.

It was an unnatural family that rewarded children if they orphaned themselves by accusing their parents of thought crimes, and an unnatural father who beamed down from the icy walls of labor camp orphanages, cradling a little girl whose parents had died in the Terror above the slogan "Thank you, Comrade Stalin, for a happy childhood." Yet many, perhaps most, Soviets believed that the millions arrested under Stalin had been guilty of something. They believed it because they loved and worshipped Stalin as much as they feared him. For three decades they had woken up with his name on their lips, and their children had gone to school singing songs in his praise. His statue towered over squares and strode before public buildings. His bust was in every airport, train station, bus station, and schoolroom; his portrait in every room of every museum and draped stories high on buildings during celebrations. Workers went to their factory or collective farm proud that it bore his name, and went home to streets, towns, and cities renamed in his honor. Greatest of all was Stalingrad, which had bled and nearly died for him during the worst of all wars but had never surrendered. He had led them to victory, and even when it unaccountably yielded more terror, many of his victims had extolled him as they died. Now he was gone, and millions wept for the Guiding Light of Communism, the Genius Leader of Progressive Mankind, the man they had called God.

It was hard to imagine such a man dying of natural causes, and rumors spread that his deputies and doctors had done away with him: perhaps because of his rumored plan to deport Moscow's Jews and start another Terror, or perhaps because powerful figures had begun to worry that Stalin's belief in the inevitability of war with the West would become a self-fulfilling prophecy. Of course there were less principled possibilities, too. Age and absolute power had recently made Stalin more dangerous than ever: sterile inside and morbidly suspicious, jittery and unpredictable. "I'm finished," he once told Khrushchev and Mikoyan in a moment of candor. "I don't even trust myself." So long as he was alive, even the most powerful potentates were all, as Khrushchev said, temporary people. Both Mikoyan and Molotov, whose wife Stalin had sent to the Gulag, stood accused of spying and were an inch from the noose. Even Beria was waiting for the deathblow. Perhaps they had been afraid to call in the doctors sooner, lest the Boss accuse them of plotting murder. Perhaps they had delayed calling them to hasten the end. Or, just possibly, someone had been brave enough to slip a slow-acting poison into Stalin's light Georgian wine.

The theories multiplied, but already there was a more pressing question on everyone's lips. "Our father is dead," they said. "What will we do now?"

* * *

SVIATOSLAV RICHTER, the Soviet Union's greatest pianist, was on tour in Georgia when he received a telegram requiring his immediate return to Moscow. Owing to atrocious weather, the usual flights were full, and the thirty-seven-year-old Richter, who was impervious to fear but hated flying anyway, shared a plane with hundreds of wreaths sent as a tribute to the Georgian-born dictator. Soon after takeoff, the storm worsened and the funereal plane was forced to land at Sukhumi, on the Black Sea, where Richter spent an uncomfortable night before flying on to Moscow in the morning.

In the capital the newspapers were heavily edged in black, and the radio was broadcasting back-to-back requiems. The Metro and shops were shut, and the brightly colored trams bore green wreaths. The streets were filled with hundreds of thousands of mourners, many sobbing or holding Stalin's portrait aloft like a holy icon, heading for the House of Unions, near the Kremlin. As more poured in, those at the front were crushed against the security trucks ringing the building. "Save me!" they screamed as they were trampled underfoot. As many as two thousand died: the last victims of the twisted genius who had turned the Bolshevik system of government by fear into a personal cult of death.

Like the rest of the city center, the House of Unions was decked with black-bordered red flags at half-mast. In the building's former incarnation as the Nobles' Club, the gold-and-white Columned Hall, with its two-tiered chandeliers, had been the focal point of Moscow's wintertime marriage market. Here Lenin had lain in state, and during the show trials, Stalin had puffed on his pipe behind a screen while his rivals accused themselves of incredible crimes. Now he was laid out amid clumps of palm trees and banks of flowers, a Plexiglas dome displaying his embalmed face like an iced cake under a glass cloche. A full symphony orchestra, a quartet, and the celebrated violinist David Oistrakh were already in position. Richter took his place at an upright piano positioned directly beneath the coffin. When he stepped on the pedals, they clonked uselessly to the floor. There was a pile of scores nearby, and he asked an orchestra member to help him wedge them underneath. As they bent down, plainclothes agents started running along the gallery. "They think I'm planting a bomb," he realized, and pedals or no pedals, he sat down to plunk out the slow movement from Bach's D Minor Concerto.

For two days the musicians played nonstop in an icy draft as policemen propelled the crowds through at such a rate that it felt as if the hall were a continuation of the street. Richter glanced sideways and idly wondered if the people had come to check that Stalin was really dead. For his part, he was supremely indifferent. During the war, his German father was arrested on the usual trumped-up charges of spying and was executed by firing squad, in a garbage dump, along with twenty-three others, but Richter mostly blamed his mother, who refused to leave town because her lover had moved in with them and who afterward ran off with him, never to be heard from since. Otherwise, he treated the regime as a nuisance to be ignored whenever possible.

Outside, on Pushkinskaya, thousands were still shuffling along. It was nearly midnight, and Stalin's corpse was due to be removed. Malenkov, the favorite, turned up looking scared stiff. "Ha ha! There's someone who's afraid he'll be killed," thought the pianist. The orchestra had come to the end of Tchaikovsky's Symphony no. 6, the great withdrawing hymn written days before the composer's death, and it started again from the beginning. At the worst moment, a military band outside began honking Chopin's "Funeral March," and to Richter's disgust, the symphony fell apart.

The pallbearers heaved the coffin, with its solitary marshal's hat, onto their shoulders, and as the cortege moved out, Richter was finally able to leave the hall. "Our new leaders!" the street loudspeakers boomed as he went home to take a shower. The pianist was key to the Soviet belief that its system bred excellence, a state-sponsored demonstration of the superior life under socialism and the greater glories ahead. Yet Richter was an unreliable idol. In the thick of Stalin's purges, he had refused to attend the Moscow Conservatory's obligatory weekly classes in Marxism-Leninism and the history of the Communist Party, and had twice been expelled, though both times he was readmitted at the insistence of his teacher, Heinrich Neuhaus. He could never remember his own telephone number or apartment number, and he intermittently plunged from manic periods into black depressions. During one long bout, he took a plastic lobster everywhere, letting go only the instant he went onstage.

The procession wove past the U.S. embassy on Mokhovaya Street, turned into Red Square, and halted. Four short, flabby figures trudged up the steps to the tribune of the granite mausoleum where Stalin had reviewed his troops and received his people's adulation. To seasoned Kremlinologists, the order of the eulogists was a sure sign of where power now lay. Malenkov, somber and swaddled in fur, had replaced Stalin as the most powerful man in the Soviet Union. As well as being named chairman of the Council of Ministers, or premier, he topped the list of members of the Presidium of the Central Committee, the real policy-making body, and of the Secretariat of the Central Committee, the bureaucracy that administered party business. Beria, in his bulky overcoat and trilby, was minister for internal affairs, back in direct charge of the security services. Molotov, the arch Stalinist with his gray coat, gray hair, and gray mustache, visibly distraught over Stalin's death (though his wife was still in Stalin's prison), had been reinstated as foreign minister. Khrushchev, at fifty-eight, looking like an overgrown Boy Scout with jug ears poking out beneath a flowerpot-shaped hat, was restricted to introducing the others. Like them, he retained his membership in the Presidium, and like Malenkov, he was also a member of the Secretariat. Yet he had been replaced as head of the Moscow party without being given new responsibilities, and few paid him much heed.

After the speeches, the embalmed body was installed in Lenin's mausoleum, alongside the founder of the Soviet state, who had let it be known (too late, too privately) that his protégé was unfit for power.

*   *   *

AS THE final masterpiece in the long Stalinist performance came to an end, another notable funeral was taking place in Moscow. Sergei Prokofiev had died on March 5, less than an hour before his former patron and tormentor.

Prokofiev's body was laid out in an open casket in the dank cellars of the Union of Soviet Composers, the scene of his earlier denunciation. There were no flowers left in the city, but his neighbors provided a few potted plants. On March 7 the mourners who carried his coffin to Novodevichy Cemetery—among them his old rival and fellow sufferer Dmitri Shostakovich—struggled against the tide of humanity surging to pay its last respects to Stalin. Politics had stifled art, but art made a subtle protest. Richter had heard of the great composer's death on his way to Moscow, and it was later whispered that he and the other musicians in the Columned Hall had actually been playing for Prokofiev.

If so, perhaps they were celebrating the music more than the man. Prokofiev's spurned wife, Lina, first suspected he had died when she heard his music on a radio at her labor camp in the far north; it had not been broadcast for years. Since her arrest, she had had no contact with the husband she had accompanied to Russia, but eventually a letter arrived from her son describing his last moments. "And what a cruel—tragic—coincidence," the young man wrote—but the censor's black pen had struck out the rest.

*   *   *

THE SOVIET Union was one of the world's two nuclear superpowers. It was the earth's largest state by area and the imperial overlord of Eastern Europe. It was the bellwether of international communism and the patron of Mao's China. It had the world's second-largest industrial capacity and a literate, educated workforce. Its organs of state functioned as one body, and its people were passive, acquiescent, and proud of their nation's breakneck industrialization, free health care and schooling, and great victory in the war. With their fortitude and the Kremlin's goading, the reconstruction of devastated cities and industries was almost complete. For all its many faults (a climate of fear, the dead hand of bureaucracy, widespread poverty, limited incentives to work, the denial of individual rights in the name of equality, the inversion of rational thought by state diktat, the ease with which a dictator could delegitimize the machinery of state), the Soviet Union was at the height of its power.

Yet the men who inherited that power were on unfamiliar ground. For as long as they could remember, their purpose in life had been to compete for Stalin's approval. It was never going to be easy to work together.

Malenkov's reign lasted barely a week. Khrushchev and Beria ganged up to remove him from the Secretariat, and a revised list was issued, with Khrushchev's name at the top. The sinister Beria was now the kingpin, and with astonishing facility he began to undo his life's work. Within days, he banned the torture he had so enthusiastically meted out, restored freedom of movement to millions he had driven into exile, proposed some autonomy for the non-Russian nations he had worked to destroy, freed more than a million from the Gulag camps he controlled, moved to pressure the Chinese and North Koreans into ending the Korean War, and even proposed allowing Germany to reunify as a capitalist country in return for compensation and guarantees of neutrality. During the May Day parades, he stood next to Molotov on the viewing balcony of the Lenin-Stalin mausoleum and whispered in his ear, "I did him in! I saved you all!" Iron Butt, his beloved wife now restored to him by Beria, took it that Beria was claiming credit for Stalin's death.

Brutal, clever, and utterly unprincipled, Beria stood revealed as a careerist who had never believed in communism and who dreamed of being a world statesman. But he was moving too far, too fast for the rest of the leadership, who anyway despised him for humiliating them at Stalin's dinners with schoolboy pranks (slipping a ripe tomato onto Molotov's chair or into Mikoyan's trouser pocket, or writing "PRICK" on a sheet of paper and pinning it to Khrushchev's back) and even more for his well-known predilection for cruising the streets in his burly black ZiL in search of underage girls. Of more material concern were the several divisions of troops that he had brought in to police Stalin's funeral and kept in Moscow, fueling rumors that he was secretly preparing for a coup.

Khrushchev sensed an opportunity. Like most of the leadership, he was a fanatical believer in Marxism-Leninism. The barely educated son of poor peasants, before discovering politics he had eked out a living as a miner, herd boy, railwayman, brick factory laborer, and metal fitter. "We wiped our noses on our sleeves and kept our trousers up with a piece of string" was his typically picturesque summary of his childhood. In the first years after the revolution, he later recalled, he and his comrades had no idea how to use a toilet and squatted on the seat, putting numerous bathrooms beyond use. Stalin had once chortled that Khrushchev was incapable of grasping statistics but had to be humored because he was the only real proletarian among the leadership. Now, with one eye on his political advantage and another on the mortal danger he was convinced Beria posed to the party, Khrushchev made his move.

"Beria is getting his knives ready for us," he said to Malenkov.

"Well, what can we do?" pondered the accommodating premier, who was himself against nuclear weapons and for talks with the West. "I see, but what steps can we take?"

Khrushchev suggested a scheme, and to his surprise Malenkov

agreed to go along with it. Operating in secrecy, they won over a majority of the leadership, crucially including Marshal Georgy Zhukov, the hero of the Second World War, who was now deputy defense minister. An ambitious peasant like Khrushchev, Zhukov had been sidelined by Stalin and hated Beria for his murderous inroads on the army command.

Three months after Stalin's death, the plotters called a meeting of the Presidium at which Beria was the only item on the agenda. Beria protested in astonishment, but Malenkov laid out the charges. When he finished, he invited others to add their concerns, and Khrushchev launched into a foul-mouthed diatribe. "What's going on, Nikita?" asked the startled Beria. After Stalin's dinners, Beria had often taken Khrushchev home paralytically drunk and tucked him in his bed, which he had invariably wet. "Why are you searching for fleas in my trousers?"

After two and a half hours, Malenkov pressed a concealed button that rang a buzzer outside. Zhukov burst in with ten officers and seized Beria. Apparently unprompted, a bodyguard blurted out that Beria had raped his twelve-year-old stepdaughter. In a typically Stalinist touch, the former security supremo was charged with being an agent of Anglo-American imperialism. When, in December 1953, a secret court convicted him of treason, terrorism, and counterrevolutionary conspiracy, he "flung himself about the courtroom weeping and begging for mercy." Stripped to his underpants, his hands in irons, he was hung mewling from a hook on the wall. A general shoved a cloth in his mouth, wrapped a bandage round his eyes, and fired point-blank into his forehead. Several officers followed suit. Libraries and schools across the Soviet Union closed so that staff could rip Beria's face out of their books. His long entry in the *Great Soviet Encyclopedia* was pasted over with one about the Bering Sea.

On street corners, newly emboldened Russians got drunk and beat up the local militiaman. In the Gulag camps, riots broke out among political prisoners, who had largely been excluded from the amnesty. But the hopes of change stirring in Soviet breasts were not to be realized yet. Ukrainian women in national dress linked arms and were crushed by tanks. Automatic weapons mowed down camp strikers.

That September, Khrushchev had been named first secretary of the Central Committee of the Communist Party, the single most powerful position in the Soviet Union. Now, with Beria dead, only Malenkov and Molotov stood in the way of his assuming total control. Spherical, loudmouthed, and jovial, he had always had the advantage of being underestimated. The U.S. ambassador dismissed him as boozy and "not especially bright." The British ambassador, the resplendently named Sir William Goodenough Hayter, described him as "rumbustious, impetuous, loquacious, free-wheeling, and alarmingly ignorant of foreign affairs." He was incapable of following complex reasoning, Hayter added, and the far more educated, intelligent, and agreeable Malenkov had to explain things to Khrushchev in "words of one syllable." The celebrated Russian writer Boris Pasternak was unimpressed by both men and said so more bluntly: "For so long we were ruled over by a madman and a murderer, and now by a fool and a pig."

To the West, the fool and the pig were not necessarily an improvement. That August, the Soviets had exploded their first hydrogen bomb—and unlike the American prototype tested earlier, it was ready for immediate use. Stalin had been a known if feared quantity, but there was no telling what these thermonuclear-armed nonentities might try.

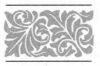

· *4* ·

Van Cliburn Days

NOT TWO years had passed since Van fastened a small orchid on the gown of a pretty blonde named Rosemary Butts and escorted her to the junior-senior prom at Kilgore College. Now fifteen hundred East Texans were waiting for him in the same hall, which was less known for piano recitals than for the ice-white smiles and mountain-high legs of the Rangerettes, the world's first precision drill team. By mayoral proclamation, April 9, 1953, was Van Cliburn Day in Kilgore.

Yet the young hero was nowhere to be seen. As far as he was concerned, the Rangerettes' motto, "Beauty Knows No Pain," applied equally well to concert pianists, who were expected to play exquisitely whatever their state of mind. His usual solution was to arrive at the last minute, or well after, and then pray, walk onstage, and play.

After half an hour the crowd began to squirm. Rumors spread that Van was still at home, talking long-distance to a girl in New York. Tempers were starting to fray when he finally traipsed out, sat down at the piano, and dashed off a florid rendition of "The Star-Spangled Banner." The audience clambered to its feet, stirred by the unexpected pageantry, and with lumps in their throats cheered loudly before the concert began. When it did, they tipped to the edge of their seats, feeling each note as if they were the strings the hammer had hit. The nervous energy that shook Van's frame, electrifying audiences as if each person were receiving his vital spark, was his burden and his blessing.

During intermission the president of Kilgore Music Club, a Mrs. Raymond Whittlesey, presented Van with a check for six hundred dollars, to further his musical education. He had already brought credit to the oil patch communities of East Texas and Louisiana, she said, and they were mighty proud of him. He was overwhelmed, he replied, and would remember the help of the people he knew if he ever did anything really big. The delay had only added to the excitement, and the concert ended with a roar that would have pleased any college grid star. Later in the year he was back for two "East Texas Days," proclaimed in his honor by the mayor of Shreveport, which was not inclined to let Kilgore reap all the glory. Both communities had made heavy demands on their talented youngster's time, but in return they had taught him a lesson unavailable to his worldlier peers: that when he performed, it was not just for the cognoscenti who wanted to hear his take on a familiar piece, but also for the doctor, lawyer, merchant, or fire chief who could not play the piano himself. To play to serve, to value all: experience like that was hard to buy.

That year, Van summered at Chautauqua, in western New York State, the original location of a nineteenth-century adult education movement that spawned camps nationwide. He stayed in the lakeside summerhouse of Mrs. Stephen I. Munger of Dallas and played with the festival orchestra under the baton of Walter Hendl, music director of the Dallas Symphony Orchestra. The numerous Texans in the audience, reported the *Chautauquan*, "seemed barely able to keep from drawing their 'shootin' irons,' and 'whoopies' trembled on their lips." Texans were famously supportive of their own, but Van's unusual ability to embrace and grip an audience was attracting wider attention. Juilliard's bald, urbane dean, Mark Schubart, a former *New York Times* music editor, was sure Van was something special the moment he heard him. "After all," he pointed out when asked, "not all people who talk like Texans are dumb." Schubart phoned Bill Judd at Columbia Artists Management, Inc., the mega-agency that dominated concert promoting, which everyone called CAMI. "I've never done this before," Schubart told him, "but there's a pianist here named Van Cliburn that you ought to hear."

"I've been hearing *about* him," Judd replied, and asked if he could listen discreetly. When Van played Mozart and Prokofiev one afternoon in the Juilliard auditorium, Judd was sitting in the back. He later declared that Van was the only artist he was completely certain about from the first. The way Van looked did no harm, either; with a little metropolitan gloss, the strikingly tall, baby-faced Texan was beginning to cut quite a figure.

Judd was a four-martini-lunch man who started mixing again at dinnertime and "worked from home" in the mornings. Yet he had an impeccable pedigree—his father was manager of the Boston Symphony—and was an important vice president in the most glamorous division of CAMI, called Judson, O'Neill, and Judd. It was highly unusual to offer a student a contract, but when Judd made his play, Van politely thanked him and promised to think it over. He was in pressing need of some fees—in January 1954 he dropped by the Juilliard Placement Bureau to remind them that he would still like some students—but he had his hopes set elsewhere. A few months earlier he had gone to the Capitol Theatre, a four-thousand-seat movie palace near Times Square, to see a feature called *Tonight We Sing*. The film was a schmaltzy take on the rags-to-riches life and career of Sol Hurok, a legendary Russian-born impresario who represented many of the world's top artists, and Van was swept away. Another of his childhood dreams had been to appear in lights under the famed rubric "S. Hurok Presents," and while he made overtures to Hurok, he dragged his feet with Judd. The surprised manager pursued his nineteen-year-old quarry for more than a year, with improved contracts, dinner invitations, and concert tickets, which Van accepted with great grace without coming near to signing.

"How good, really, do you think Van is?" Allen Spicer asked Judd over a libation one evening, when the manager had swung by to press his suit. "Tell it to me so that a businessman can understand it."

"Well, let me put it this way," Judd replied. "First, he is one whale of a piano player. And second, he's better than even *he* knows."

Judd's faith was about to be put to the test.

*   *   *

THE LEVENTRITT Competition had no formal rules, application forms, cash prizes, or repertoire beyond requiring a concerto by Mozart, Beethoven, or Brahms. It took place only in years when its prime movers, the conductor George Szell and the pianist Rudolf Serkin, heard there was talent at large. Yet it was the toughest contest for young instrumentalists in America. To carry off the title—there were no runners-up—a pianist had to be ready to play a solo engagement with the New York Philharmonic and sustain a concert career. That set the bar so high that for four years an annual crop of thirty or forty entrants had not produced a single winner.

The competition was shepherded by Rosalie Leventritt, a petite southern belle with smiling violet-blue eyes and an impish humor whose spacious apartment at 850 Park Avenue was the unofficial headquarters of New York's classical musicians. Entrants had to submit evidence of professional experience, and bright, jolly Naomi Graffman, who two years earlier had married the last winner, the brilliant young pianist Gary Graffman, went through forty-eight packages with Mrs. Leventritt's daughter, who was also called Rosalie but who had sensibly married early and become a Berner. Most consisted of a few sheets of typed paper, but Harvey Cliburn had put together a scrapbook as thick as a phone directory with a picture of Van aged six on the cover. Newspaper clippings and more photos spilled from its pages. There were numerous articles about the G. B. Dealey Award, which neither Naomi nor Rosalie had heard of, and full details on some twenty-four concerts in unlikely places such as Muskogee, Oklahoma; Clinton, Mississippi; Hot Springs, Arkansas; and Paris, Texas. The two women ran their own sweepstakes based on the submissions, and between fits of giggles, Naomi burst out, "He's going to win!"

Van prepared thirteen pieces, including three concertos, and practiced hard; to reach peak form, he played a benefit for a Shreveport college, another for a Riverdale retirement home, and a concert at Calvary Baptist. The opening sessions were held in Steinway Hall, in front of a lineup of American musical aristocracy. Dominant in every way was the six-foot-four, barrel-chested Arthur Judson, a founder of CBS, president of CAMI, and manager of the New York Philharmonic, who ascribed his ruddy cheeks to permanent rage at dealing with artists. Alongside Szell and Serkin were conductors Dimitri Mitropoulos and Leonard Bernstein and pianists Nadia Reisenberg, Leopold Mannes, and Eugene Istomin. The chairman was Abram Chasins, the stuffy but gifted music director of WQXR, the *New York Times* radio station.

Van strolled in with his wild hair, and Naomi Graffman was enchanted. He was so tall, and so thin that he looked even taller. "And not even Jewish!" she marveled. "How odd to see a *cowboy* play the piano." But all visions of bucking broncos vanished the instant he began to play. Afterward her husband got a call from Serkin.

"You must come to the finals," he gushed. "There's this marvelous, incredible talent! His Liszt, Chopin, Schumann—beautiful."

"Did he play Mozart?" asked Graffman, a bespectacled classicist who dismissed Tchaikovsky and Rachmaninoff as razzle-dazzle Russians.

"Nah, that wasn't good at all," said Serkin, "but he's such a great talent."

Van called his friends from Calvary Baptist: "You won't forget to pray for me, will you? It buoys me up when I know you're praying."

The finals were held at the Town Hall on West Forty-Third Street. In past years the deliberations had grown so heated that judges physically attacked one another: Serkin, who stood six foot three, once grabbed the four-foot-seven Polish pianist Mieczyslaw Horszowski when the latter was sixty years into his century-long life and gave him a good shaking. Whether from fear of a recurrence of discord or simply so they could listen with detachment, the jurors were placed several seats apart and required to communicate in writing.

Van played the Tchaikovsky concerto, his technique dazzling, his expression reverent, his sound liquid and songlike. In the last movement, the roller coaster hurtled triumphantly home. "He really loves music, loves to play it, and loves the way *he* plays it," noted Bernstein. "It's so honest and refreshing." Before excusing him, the judges asked Van if he would play the Brahms B-flat Concerto, which he had also listed.

"May I explain," Van replied quietly but firmly, "that I have been ill much of this past week. I feel it would be an injustice not only to myself but, far more important, to this great work and to the patience and integrity of this jury if I attempted to play the Brahms. Would you permit me to play something else?"

He played Liszt's Twelfth Hungarian Rhapsody, the old showpiece he had used to get into Rosina's class, as audaciously and nobly as ever. Jaws dropped, and the judges emitted yelps of pleasure. At the end, Van sat waiting for instructions. "Would y'all mahnd if Ah went and got a glass of WAWtuh?" he asked after a minute, or so Gary Graffman heard. While he stepped out, the jury scribbled furiously on their index cards. Naomi saw Arthur Judson drop his on the floor and, at the end, she picked it up. "Not this year," his note read in his spidery writing: "Perhaps another time." The other judges differed. As it happened, Van's leading opponent was a newcomer to Rosina's class, the intense, intellectual John Browning, whose elegantly reserved style appealed to Jeaneane Dowis but not to Jimmy Mathis, which finally broke up the Texas threesome, especially after Dowis and Browning started going steady. Browning played perfectly— almost too perfectly; against Van's big, heartfelt sound, he came across as slick and somewhat bloodless.

Van went home to the Spicers' and hovered by the telephone until it rang. "Congrats!" Bill Judd shouted. "Arthur Judson just got back to the office and said that the verdict was unanimous." Even the obdurate Judson had bent before the prevailing wind.

"Hazel, Hazel, I've won, I've won!" Van cried, running into the living room and squeezing his landlady in a bear hug, and then jumping until she feared for the integrity of her floor. "Isn't it wonderful? Go get dressed up and we'll go out for dinner!"

"Oh no, Van, go call up a girl," she demurred.

"You go get ready," he said, ignoring her: "I've got to call up Rosina right away." He started dialing his teacher's number and then stopped. "No. It's no good," he said. "I'm going up there to tell her myself." He grabbed his overcoat with its missing buttons and dashed out, calling to Hazel to wait for him.

The doorbell rang and rang at 185 Claremont Avenue, a few doors down from Juilliard. Eventually Rosina answered, and Van barged into the tiny apartment, nearly knocking her over. "Honey, I got it! Honey, I won!" he shouted, twirling her round. When they both calmed down they called Kilgore to tell Van's parents.

Afterward, Van slumped on the sofa, his head in his hands. "Oh, what a responsibility," he groaned. "What a dreadful responsibility!" Silently he contemplated a future in which he would always be judged against this success.

"I'd better be going," he said, jumping up.

On the way back, he took a detour to visit Calvary organist Clifford Tucker in the hospital and cheer him up with the news. It was late by the time he got home, but he dragged Hazel to Asti, in the Village, a hangout for musicians who played when they liked and paid for their food when they could. He had already endeared himself to flamboyant owner Adolfo Mariani, and the waiter refused to give him the check. "He's such a *good* boy," thought Mrs. Spicer as she dotingly watched him take over the piano.

The following month, on April 30, Van played Bach, Mozart, Brahms, Chopin, Debussy, and Ravel for his Juilliard diploma recital. Rosina graded him "excellent" again. Teacher and student were now extravagantly in love. Van had gone from addressing her in letters as "Dear Mrs. Lhévinne" to simply "Darling." "My best love to you, darling," he signed off, or more grandiloquently, "I won't even try to tell you how very deeply I appreciate, admire, respect, and, of course, forever love you, for I will only let Time supply the moment's all too inadequate phrases." In May he graduated, and in her little ring binder, where she drafted reports, Rosina noted, "Most promising student I have had."

It was morning when the class gathered on the steps of the old Claremont Avenue building for their commencement photograph, and Van was missing. Jimmy Mathis boldly told the photographer and school officials they would be pretty sorry not to have him in the picture and marched off to the Spicers' to wake him up. He then ran back with Van and the two jumped into the edge of the frame. The camera clicked, half an hour late.

*   *   *

THAT NOVEMBER, on the same date that Rachmaninoff had played in Shreveport in 1932, a coincidence that superstitiously thrilled him, twenty-year-old Van Cliburn stepped in front of the lights at Carnegie Hall. Dimitri Mitropoulos was on the podium, with the forces of the New York Philharmonic ranged in front of him. Unusually for a Sunday afternoon, the cavernous hall was crowded; this was partly explained by the presence of what the Graffmans conjectured must have been planeloads of Texans. The couple surveyed the parterre and decided it looked like the Alamo. In pride of place were Rildia Bee and Harvey, who Naomi thought was a "farmery-looking person."

The long, tall Texan ambled out, bowed modestly, sat unfussily, focused his energies into his hands, and plunged them into the opening chords of the Tchaikovsky. If some of the regular concertgoers expected showiness, what they got was a young man with a brilliant sound who was determined to communicate his beloved music to the best of his considerable ability. The end of the first movement brought an unconventional chorus of cheers and bravos—from the orchestra as well as the audience. After the third movement, they jumped to their feet and called him back seven times, and when the commotion died down, half the hall jostled backstage to the green room. The Graffmans took Rosalie Leventritt with them and chortled at the sight of hundreds of tall, red-faced Texans "ho-ho-hoing" as they clomped up the long staircase. Van was smiling and shaking hands and gazing gently into the eyes of every well-wisher, especially the youngest. He spotted the small, delicate Rosalie struggling up the stairs. "Honey, see all these people?" he cried. "Well, they all comin' to yo' party!" When she got to the top, he picked her up off her feet and twirled her round as she screamed with laughter. The two were getting on famously: he trusted her because of her southern accent, and she was utterly charmed by him, even though her tastes ran to the more intimate works of Brahms, Schubert, and Schumann.

Later that afternoon, a few hundred hungry Texans piled into the celadon-green sitting room of Leventritt's Park Avenue apartment. Rosalie begged her regulars to go easy on the food; the epicurean Gary Graffman nobly denied himself a second helping of the famous tomato aspic bursting with juicy jumbo shrimp. Van had sent a dozen long-stemmed roses, and someone had stuck them in an eleventh-century Song dynasty vase. It started leaking over the piano, first a trickle, then a flood. Rosalie was beginning to crack up when Van breezed in, sat at the piano, fixed his soft eyes on his patroness, and played the Schumann-Liszt "Widmung." "Du meine Seele, du mein Herz," he sang along, swaying into the music: "You are my soul, you are my heart."

The next morning, the reviews of Van's Carnegie Hall performance were good but not effusive. One exception was Louis Biancolli of the *New York World-Telegram and Sun*: "This is one of the most genuine and refreshing keyboard talents to come out of the West—or anywhere else—in a long time," he wrote. "Van Cliburn is obviously going places, except that he plays as if he had already been there."

*   *   *

AFTER DRAWING a blank from Sol Hurok, Van finally signed with CAMI, and in January 1955 its Midwest representative Schuyler Chapin, who was married to Betty Steinway of the piano-manufacturing clan, wangled him a rare appearance on NBC's *Tonight*, starring Steve Allen. "Longhair" music was usually considered the kiss of death for a talk show, and Van didn't even have a name, but he played Ravel's Toccata and a Chopin étude, and caused a minor sensation. Viewers sent in letters and telegrams and jammed the switchboard. The Baltimore and Ohio Railroad employees' club called for a booking. Across the Midwest, Chapin was asked about "that extraordinary guy with the hair we saw on TV." Suddenly the concerts mounted up: that season, Van played twenty orchestral dates and ten recitals, the latter running through Bach, Beethoven, Brahms, Chopin, Debussy, Liszt, Medtner, Mozart, Prokofiev, Rachmaninoff, Ravel, Scarlatti, Schumann, and Stravinsky. When the Cleveland Summer Orchestra asked him to play Rachmaninoff's Piano Concerto no. 2 in C Minor, he learned it in two weeks. Audiences reacted so intensely that Van stood overwhelmed amid thundering applause, shaking hands over and over with the conductor and concertmaster, begging the orchestra to share the bows. Critics raved about the young musical Adonis with the flashing fingers and the unquenchable fire, likening his impact to that of Franz Liszt bursting on the Paris music world, also age twenty. "Tear out this name, write it somewhere, get to know it: Van Cliburn," urged a Denver paper, declaring him "the most important young pianist of his generation."

This was sensational, though frequent mentions of cowboys and rodeos made it plain that the fascination stemmed in part from finding such talent in such an unusual person from such an unusual place. Meanwhile, Van's impact on the *Tonight* show had been great enough that its host, Steve Allen, wanted him back. He was featured again that April, but this time he followed a slapstick act, played an obscure piece by Medtner followed by a long, reflective work by Chopin, and died. Novelty in the American entertainment world had a nasty habit of wearing off fast.

*   *   *

THE SAME month that Van was competing for the Leventritt, the United States detonated its first viable thermonuclear weapon at Bikini Atoll in the Marshall Islands. By using nuclear fission, the mechanism of the atom bomb, to set off a secondary fusion reaction, scientists exponentially increased its destructive power. At fifteen megatons (the equivalent of 750 Hiroshima bombs) the "Castle Bravo" test produced a yield that was twice what was expected. Strong winds blew the radioactive fallout far across the Pacific Ocean, killing a Japanese tuna fisherman ninety miles away and contaminating the catch. If a single thermonuclear blast could have global ecological consequences, the world darkly brooded, what would be the effect of many? Experts provided the answer: just a hundred H-bombs could "create on the whole globe conditions impossible for life."

Nine months later, tuna was still being condemned by the ton; the following year, radioactive rain fell on Chicago. Soon deadly strontium 90 began to turn up in the milk supply, prompting fears of a generation prone to bone cancer and leukemia. A study found fifty-times-higher-than-normal levels of the same radioactive isotope, a product of nuclear fission, in hundreds of thousands of milk teeth. The postwar generation was rushing ahead without the basic comfort of assuming its children would survive. Doomsters argued about whether this unprecedented loss of faith in the future would lead to riotous living, mercenary individualism, or glassy-eyed nihilism. The only certainty was that it would be traumatic.

Radiation, the invisible killer, buried the atomic boom in a thick concrete coffin and boosted activists of every stripe into the saddles of their hobbyhorses, with the prophets of domestic bliss leading the charge. It was not really a paradox that a world facing unfathomable threats decided that security began at home. To social conservatives, American families in their picket fence fortresses were moral crusaders who preserved the nation's fiber in the face of enemy assaults. In an about-face from the permissive 1920s and the Depression-hit '30s, the postwar generation was settling down earlier, having bigger families, and divorcing less. Boosters recommended twenty-one as the best age to tie the knot; twenty-three was past it. Since marriage and the production of lots of well-mannered children were patriotic duties, expressions of responsible citizenship, it followed that other lifestyles gave succor to America's enemies, which meant Reds. When sexologist Alfred Kinsey reported that premarital sex, homosexuality, and adultery were widespread, he was accused of giving succor to international communism.

Homosexuality caused the greatest stink. Officially classed as a psychiatric disorder, during the Cold War it was treated as a contagious social disease that threatened the nation's security and sapped the virility that had tamed a continent. In 1950 the U.S. Senate had set the tone with a report entitled "Employment of Homosexuals and Other Sex Perverts in Government," which equated gay men in consenting relationships with violent pedophiles. "Those who engage in overt acts of perversion," the authors declared, "lack the emotional stability of normal persons . . . One homosexual can pollute a government office." As thousands lost their jobs, gay hunts became as ferocious as Red hunts; in the minds of prosecutors, who forced those who confessed to being "perverts" to name their "accomplices," the two were barely distinguishable. Plainclothes FBI agents fanned through the nation's parks and movie houses, bars and restaurants, to entrap the lonely and unwary, arresting a thousand a year in Washington alone. Eisenhower's cynical "Silent Generation" either condoned the persecutions or raised a Bogartian eyebrow. Taught as children that the Russians were allies and the Japanese and Germans were enemies, only to be told the opposite when they were barely in their teens, most kept their noses clean and walked on by. The pressure to conform was irresistible.

In the spring of 1955, Van ran into a tall, lissome Texan brunette named Donna Sanders at a concert. They had met a year and half earlier, on registration day at Juilliard, when Donna, an aspiring singer who had won an episode of the *Arthur Godfrey Talent Scouts* variety show on CBS, had enrolled on a scholarship fresh out of high school. She briefly became part of Van's set before quitting after a few months to take up a role alongside a young Shirley MacLaine in the chorus of *Me and Juliet*, a Rodgers and Hammerstein musical that was opening on Broadway.

This time Van asked Donna out. Their dates were patchy because he was often away touring and because, as she soon realized, the piano came first for him. By now he had moved out of the Spicers' and was living temporarily in a little eleventh-floor apartment at the Buckingham Hotel. When he was practicing for a concert, Donna reported, "he'd shove the telephone under his bed and muffle it, and for days he'd be absolutely incommunicado." There were other oddities. He was so obsessed with protecting his hands that he never wore a ring, for fear it would cut him, and he was scared of cooking, in case he burned his fingers. Strangest of all: "Van gets terribly depressed every time he has a birthday. He explained to me that it was terribly difficult to grow out of being a child prodigy."

Occasionally the two went to the theater or the Met. Once, they drove with friends to Palisades Park, a popular amusement park on a bluff above the Hudson in New Jersey, overlooking Manhattan. Van was pressured into riding the Cyclone roller coaster and got off green-faced, swearing it was the last time. Sometimes they went together to Calvary Baptist, where Van had become a much-loved character, famous for ragging the old gospel hymns during choir rehearsals, rolling his eyes and flying up and down the organ keyboard with terrible tremolos and horribly lush chords until the minister walked in, at which point Van turned demure as a nun. As they were both observant Southern Baptists, he and Donna never got beyond light petting, and there was never a formal understanding. When Van went home to Texas for the summer, and Donna went to perform in *Arabian Nights* at the Jones Beach Marine Theater on Long Island, he called it off without quite saying so, and by the time he came back to New York, she was engaged to a fellow cast member.

After the breakup Donna's roommate, a pert, green-eyed, twenty-year-old blond soprano named Jean Heafner, took it upon herself to console Van. They talked constantly on the phone, sighing over his problems for an hour and a half at a stretch. Jean, who was keen on Van herself, was romantically convinced that he and Donna loved each other and "were as engaged as two people could be without a ring" but were fated to be kept apart by a third party. "He's married to his music," she explained. "What can you do with a guy who's spent his life pounding black on white?" If Van ever cut loose a little, she added, he did a fine job of covering it up.

Jean was at Juilliard for graduate study, and one day she was gossiping when a girl said to her, "Isn't that rough on Donna? You know, Van's queer." Jean refused to believe it. From what she had seen he was strictly the all-American boy. Yet the more she thought about it, the more she became convinced that Rildia Bee was responsible for the end of the affair. Domineering or overprotective mothers were also targets during the Cold War, accused of a social crime called Momism; psychologists asserted as scientific fact that such mothers prevented their sons from forming normal relationships with women and turned them into effeminates, which of course put them on the path to communism.

Vladimir Horowitz famously quipped that there were three types of pianists: Jewish pianists, gay pianists, and bad pianists. There were also gay Jewish pianists, such as Horowitz, who, during a separation from the legendary conductor Arturo Toscanini's daughter, Wanda, was snapped with a bevy of half-naked men at George Cukor's notorious Hollywood parties. In fact, in the 1950s, that fearful-smug decade that percolated with the overpowering smell of the middle class, the music world was a very close-knit, very gay enclave. Juilliard, whose dean, Mark Schubart, was gay, was no exception. Jimmy Mathis was as out as they came. John Browning was out to his clique; Jeaneane Dowis was not the only girl to be used as a beard. Some of the girls were gay, too, though they were even more discreet than the men, who gossiped among themselves but seldom if ever with outsiders. Van, who loved women passionately and platonically, was never particularly closeted with friends he trusted. Yet with his family and the outside world it was a different matter. It was not just the danger; he was a southern gentleman who would never have dreamed of exposing his sexuality and discomfiting others. Better by far to keep it unspoken. Whatever the psychological fallout, it was a burden many shared.

*   *   *

IN 1955 *The Juilliard Review* listed the salaries of musicians fortunate enough to have full-time jobs. It was sobering reading. A few hundred lucky souls working in the movies made $8,677 a year on average; a few thousand playing in traveling dance bands made around $6,000. From there it was a long way down to the 2,671 people working in the symphony, who took home $1,980 annually. Only opera and ballet paid worse: average salaries there hovered around $1,000, and though top artists made far more, that meant most made much less.

By that measure, Van was doing fine. He was the first American pianist for whom CAMI asked $1,000 per performance from the get-go, and in his first full year out, he earned about $19,000 gross. Commission, travel, and publicity expenses reduced that to $150 a week, but with his parents' help he signed a lease on three rooms at the Osborne Apartment House, a large brownstone rental house at 205 West Fifty-Seventh Street, on New York's Music Row. The grotto-like lobby was a Gilded Age dream of the Renaissance that transported visitors to the time, six years after it was completed, in 1885, when residents could step across the road to watch Tchaikovsky open Carnegie Hall. Yet the mosaics and murals were dulled and dusty, rust ran from the faucets, and the building had become a haunt of actors, writers, artists, and musicians, who appreciated its location and the thirty-inch walls that muffled noise.

Apartment 9B was not one of the grand suites with richly carved fireplaces and fourteen-foot ceilings that faced the street. During the Depression many apartments had been divided up, with the former sleeping quarters at the back chopped off and turned into studios. Here the ceilings were eight feet high, and the windows faced the backs of buildings on Fifty-Eighth Street, which suited Van: the gloom helped him sleep in. He had the telephone company install a long cord so he could talk from bed to bathroom, and he set about decorating: dove gray for the living room walls and bright Chinese red for the tiny kitchenette, which resembled the inside of a lacquered box. The cupboards were perpetually empty; there were only enough glasses for two or three to drink simultaneously. A sofa bed for his parents took up one wall of the living room; a loaned seven-foot Steinway muffled with a quilt occupied the rest. After moving in, he began frequenting museums and antique shops for inspiration, and snapped up bargains at auctions: murky oils for a dollar apiece and old mirrors, which he propped against the fireplace to mask the painted brick.

It was a cozy life. He ate in smart restaurants, thanks to friends who liked his company, or dined alone at Carnegie Hall Tavern, where the waiters advised him to order the pot roast sandwich and ladled an entrée-size portion on two slices of rye. Underneath the Osborne was a florist's shop, where he spent his lunch money on bouquets for CAMI's secretaries, who worked out of the Steinway Building, a block over, next door to Calvary Baptist. Bill Judd had an office in the Osborne itself, and every morning at ten Naomi Graffman, who had left the Leventritt Foundation to work for Judd, telephoned Mrs. Hughes on the Osborne's switchboard:

"Would you call Van for me, please?"

Buzz—buzz—buzz—buzz.

"Rise and shine!"

"U-u-u-h."

She'd call back at ten-minute intervals until he surfaced, around eleven, and at 12:45 the door to the left of her typewriter desk opened and his curly head poked in. "Honey, ah'm hungry," he said. They'd go downstairs to Beefburger Hall and lunch on thirty-five-cent hamburgers or, if Naomi was feeling flush, forty-five-cent cheeseburgers. To Naomi, who was older than Van by five years, Van was a sweet, galumphing schoolboy with big eyes for everything and his nose pressed against the window. He always seemed impossibly cheery— except once, when his parents failed to let him know where they were for forty-eight hours and he went berserk, calling every place he could think of until finally he tracked them down.

*   *   *

WITH SOL Hurok unresponsive and the Soviet Union impenetrable, Van's Russian dreams had become a faraway fantasy. Then, in October 1955, three months after he grimaced through his twenty-first birthday, the first gust of change blew from Moscow to New York. It came in the burly form of Emil Gilels, a golden-toned virtuoso who was usually accounted the Soviet Union's second-best pianist after Sviatoslav Richter, which by any measure put him among the greatest in the world. As the first Soviet musician to visit the United States since the war, he was big news, and passersby stared as his wave of red-blond hair bobbed along Fifty-Seventh Street. Naomi Graffman went a whole stage further and tailed him as he bought a stuffed Snoopy at Rappaport's Toy Bazaar, ordered blintzes at the Carnegie Deli, and stocked up on jockey shorts at M. H. Lamston, the celebrities' five-and-dime. Afterward he walked into Steinway Hall, chose a concert grand to be shipped to Moscow, and peeled off hundred-dollar bills from his pocket. Naomi drew the line at following him to a meeting with Rosina Lhévinne or another with the left-leaning Marilyn Monroe, whom Gilels cordially invited to Moscow.

Gilels made his debut at Carnegie Hall with the Philadelphia Orchestra and Eugene Ormandy, Rachmaninoff's favorite conductor. As he played the inevitable Piano Concerto no. 1 by Tchaikovsky, the audience's mood transformed from uneasy to ecstatic. With the help of a Juilliard classmate who was doing some ushering, Van managed to snag one of the seats crammed onto the stage for a later performance. He had a direct view of the keyboard as Gilels played Stravinsky's piano arrangement of *Petrushka*, his 1911 burlesque score for the Ballets Russes. By coincidence, Van was studying the music and had left it sitting open on his piano; afterward he went home and, certain he could never play it so well, put it away for good.

Within weeks the Soviet violinist David Oistrakh followed, and astonished Americans with his virtuosic intensity. Culture mavens began to fret aloud that America was leaving the field to the Soviets, and they found an unlikely ally in President Eisenhower. Covert operations such as floating excerpts from Scripture across the Iron Curtain on balloons or air-dropping T. S. Eliot's fiendishly difficult *Four Quartets* on Russia were having limited success, and Ike was beginning to suspect that a direct appeal to the emotions might better counteract Soviet propaganda that caricatured America as a nation of jive-dancing, gum-chewing rubes and goons. The old soldier even went so far as to urge his hawkish secretary of state, John Foster Dulles, to include "the singing of a beautiful hymn" within his definition of psychological warfare, and Congress authorized an emergency presidential fund to support "Cold War cultural exchange." It then voted to slash the budget in half on the basis that "soft power" was hooey dreamed up by namby-pamby liberals, but in 1956 it reversed course and made Ike's fund a permanent body.

The Cold War had achieved what no amount of advocacy ever did: it had persuaded the U.S. government publicly to support the arts. The International Exchange Program expanded fast, supporting twelve orchestras in its first three years and, over five years, more than one hundred performers and groups who visited more than ninety countries. The State Department was in overall charge, but unlike the CIA, whose pipe-smoking Ivy Leaguers clandestinely funneled huge sums into atonal music and abstract art, it left the choice of performers mostly to panels of practicing artists, in an attempt to promote diversity. That policy backfired when the artists turned out to be more conservative than the government. The Music Panel, which met every two or three weeks in New York, repeatedly spurned foreign-born musicians and had to be lectured that America benefited from being seen as culturally diverse. It was so prejudiced against jazz that a separate jazz panel had to be spun off. It rejected Leonard Bernstein's hit musical *West Side Story* on the grounds that "showing the gang warfare in New York will not help our cultural relations." Frustrated officials could have been forgiven for envying the Soviet system, which regarded artists as the property of the state and systematically selected, trained, and sent abroad its best. Still, in its messy way, the American effort notched up successes. African American performers were particularly admired abroad, an important consideration in light of *Brown v. Board of Education* and Soviet denunciations of America's Jim Crow laws and decaying inner cities.

At first the Soviet Bloc was excluded from the exchanges. "We are not planning to send performers behind the iron curtain because they have controlled audiences who can hiss the players off the boards," a State Department official informed an early Music Panel meeting, though the real reason may have been a lack of confidence in American artists. Juilliard's president, Bill Schuman, a vocal member of the group, vigorously protested but was warned that he was exceeding his remit by straying into policy.

The issue was still being hotly debated when Nikita Khrushchev delivered the most explosive speech in the history of the Soviet Union.

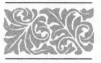

· 5 ·

The Secret Speech

THE TWENTIETH Congress of the Communist Party of the Soviet Union was officially over. For ten days, fifteen hundred comrades from fifty-six countries had applauded through speech after speech endorsing the ideology and policies of the new regime. They had gone back to their hotels and were preparing to carry the torch home when the Soviet contingent was hastily summoned back. The session was not on the timetable, and the foreign delegates were not invited. There was no notice of what was to be discussed, and no preparation for what was about to happen. Shortly after midnight on February 25, 1956, Nikita Sergeyevich Khrushchev got to his feet and buried Stalin a second time.

Gesticulating wildly, Khrushchev revealed that a dreadful perversion had infected Marxism-Leninism. A cult of personality had elevated a criminal to the status of a god. Stalin, he said, had twisted the government into a vehicle of repression and a machine of lies. He had imprisoned, tortured, and murdered innocent people and deported entire nations on a paranoid whim. Having killed four-fifths of the army command before World War II, Stalin, like a boy with his toys, had planned military operations using a globe. Dashing from accusation to denunciation, Khrushchev suddenly paused and spoke intimately. "Stalin was a very distrustful man, sickly suspicious," he recalled. "We know this from our work with him. He could look at a man and say: 'Why are your eyes so shifty today?' or 'Why are you turning so much today and avoiding looking at me directly in the eyes?'" Possessing unlimited power, Khrushchev added, the *vozhd* had "indulged in great willfulness and choked a person morally and physically."

The speech was not elegant or even very coherent, but its simplicity made it devastating. Like the miner he had once been, Khrushchev shone his lamp into the cells and tunnels of Stalinist Russia and ruggedly set the charges that would dynamite them into the earth. The shock was so great that several delegates collapsed and had to be carried out. The rest sat in stunned silence. Of course there was no denying the scale of the purges that had happened on Stalin's watch. They had touched them all. Of 1,966 delegates to the Seventeenth Party Congress in 1934, 1,108 had been declared enemies of the people and 848 had been executed. Of 139 full and candidate members of the Central Committee, 98 had been accused of treason. Still, to blame Stalin himself? They had not come to hear this savage demolition of everything they had worked and fought for. They had never expected to hear it. Marxism-Leninism was a secular religion that demanded blind faith, and Stalin had been its presiding deity. How could the great leader have been a deluded murderer?

Only one group looked on with burning vindication. To put a human face on moral outrage, Khrushchev had invited along a hundred former party members who had recently been released from the Gulag camps. They were a tiny fraction of the victims he was talking about, survivors of the convulsions in the body politic that had consumed perhaps twenty million lives and stunted many more in less than a quarter century, and they were there to bear witness.

After four hours, Khrushchev sat down. The customary storm of applause never came. The audience filed out quietly, their world upside down.

* * *

THEY WERE coming back in droves, those nonpeople with no value to whose victimhood Khrushchev's speech referred, stripped of humanity in the bare struggle to survive. They walked along haltingly, "with horrifyingly empty eyes," unable to cross the street without orders, trying to readjust to life, if they were lucky, with the families from whom they'd been torn. Some compulsively recounted their sufferings and those of their dead comrades, driven to document the unspeakable even as it drove them mad. Others had forgotten their family members' names, or even their own. Sleepless from fear and plagued by envy, they struggled to rediscover love and feeling itself. Their accusers crossed the road to avoid them or looked straight through them; a few gentler souls were consumed by delayed guilt. The novelist Alexander Fadeyev, who as secretary of the Writers' Union had authorized writers' arrest warrants, lurched drunkenly at his victims, trying to befriend them. One day he sobered up, wrote a note to the Central Committee—"I thought I was guarding a temple, and it turned out to be a latrine"—and shot himself.

Stalin had worked the mincer, but many had provided the meat. Khrushchev later admitted that he himself was up to his elbows in blood. "Everyone who rejoices in the successes achieved in our country, the victories of our party led by the great Stalin, will find only one word suitable for the mercenary, fascist dogs," he had screamed to 200,000 people gathered in Red Square during the 1936 show trials: "That word is execution!" The following year, as the Moscow Party boss, he handily exceeded his quota of 30,000 enemies of the people to be arrested and 5,000 executed, boasting to Stalin that he had rounded up 41,305, of whom 8,500 deserved to die. As party leader of Ukraine, he had sped up the arrests there until there were scarcely any politicians, officials, or army commanders left to run the country.

It had been an act of fear to keep silent, an act of fanaticism or callous self-advancement to lend support. Yet Khrushchev's speech was an act of courage—he was haunted by guilt, and his humanity had risen to demand it. The risk was huge, but it was also more calculated than it seemed. By blaming everything on Stalin, he deflected guilt both from himself and the Communist Party, which after a painful reckoning could once again become the conduit for the people's enthusiasm and energy. Khrushchev was never very clear about Marxist-Leninist theory—to his mind, it boiled down to giving everyone goulash—but he believed with all his heart that it would bring unprecedented happiness. The glorious Soviet system, the most progressive and democratic developed by mankind, the perpetual engine of history—in his account, it and the party itself were also Stalin's victims, not the facilitators, encouragers, perpetrators, and justifiers of judicially approved genocide.

The Stalinists were aghast, but with peasant cunning, Khrushchev had weakened them. The previous year, he had accused Malenkov of ganging up with Beria, demoted him to minister of electric power stations, and replaced him in the chair of the Presidium. He had attacked Iron Butt Molotov for conducting a bellicose foreign policy, and though the old revolutionary clung to his job, he was greatly diminished. So far so good, but Stalin's ghost was hard to exorcise, and threats lay all around. Khrushchev would need all his native wit and guile to attempt the monumental task he had set for himself: that of building communism without terror.

*   *   *

BECAUSE OF its restricted audience, Khrushchev's denunciation became known as the Secret Speech, but he never intended it to be anything of the sort. The following night, it was read to the foreign delegates, very slowly, so they could take notes. The Polish leader Boleslaw Bierut had a heart attack and died. Transcripts crisscrossed the Soviet Union, to be read aloud to millions of party members. Some outdid Khrushchev in decrying the former regime, some saw no point in raking through old muck, and others angrily defended Stalin. In Georgia, his birthplace, four days of riots broke out.

The speech leaked out of the Soviet Union via Israeli intelligence, and on June 5 it was published in the *New York Times*. Over the years the trickle of Gulag survivors who made it to the West had tried to raise awareness of Stalin's atrocities, but without the images that seared the Nazi concentration camps into humanity's conscience, it was easy to dismiss their talk as hysteria. Most people had no stomach for another monstrous crime of civilization, especially one perpetrated by a wartime ally against the Nazi evil. Meanwhile, to Communists and fellow travelers, it was inconceivable that a society built on equality and fraternity could be guilty of crimes whose enormity approached that of Hitler's. Now the Soviet leader himself had confirmed the worst, and as many of Stalin's apologists recoiled, a distinct strand of Eurocommunism was born.

During the Congress, Khrushchev had also ditched Marxist-Leninist orthodoxy about the inevitability of war. Socialism would triumph, he confidently predicted, because it was a superior system; meanwhile, the USSR must live with the West, as it was either that or "the most destructive war in history." In America, policy makers reacted warily. Most foresaw a split in the Soviet leadership and thought it would suit America's interests. CIA chief Allen Dulles, the dour John Foster's playboy brother, thought Khrushchev was drunk and warned that his emotional nature made him "the most dangerous person to lead the Soviet Union since the October Revolution." In the end they decided to do nothing and see what happened. Still, to put out feelers, the State Department sent the Boston Symphony Orchestra to Russia that September.

The effect was sensational. "The usually decorous elite of the Soviet capital went wild," the New York Times reported, adding that the word in the hall was that the Americans were better than any Soviet orchestra, even at playing the Soviet national anthem. "'Culture' is no longer a sissy word," declared C. D. Jackson, a leading presidential adviser on psychological warfare. But the glow was short-lived. When Sol Hurok tried to bring over the Moiseyev Dance Company, with its spectacular routines based on Soviet folk dances, negotiations foundered on the U.S. requirement that foreign visitors be fingerprinted; Khrushchev angrily retorted that Soviet citizens would never submit to an indignity "reserved for criminals." Then, within weeks of the Boston orchestra's triumph, student demonstrations in Hungary snowballed into a national revolution against Soviet domination. At first the Red Army stood fast as the regime fell, but when the new government announced its withdrawal from the Warsaw Pact, the

Soviet Bloc security system formed the previous year as a counter-weight to NATO, Khrushchev reluctantly ordered in the tanks. His hope that nations would choose communism of their own free will diminished with every shell, and as thousands died and hundreds of thousands scrambled to escape, all cultural exchange was called off.

Eisenhower, who presented a sunny, homey face to the world but spent sleepless nights staring anxiously at the ceiling, was never going to risk war by intervening in Eastern Europe. Besides, his criticism of the Soviet invasion was blunted by the infuriating coincidence that the Israelis, French, and British had chosen exactly the same moment to launch a surprise invasion of Egypt to seize the recently nation-alized Suez Canal—without consulting the Americans. Ike angrily brooded that the Soviets "might be ready to undertake any wild ad-venture. They are as scared and furious as Hitler was in his last days." His fears seemed justified when Khrushchev threatened to deploy troops to the Middle East and fire nuclear-tipped rockets at Egypt's attackers. The threat was widely held responsible for the humiliating cease-fire that Britain announced the following day, and Egypt's pres-ident, Gamal Abdel Nasser, publicly praised the Soviet Union as his country's savior and special friend. In private he was well aware that concerted U.S. diplomatic and financial pressure had saved him, but the Soviet Union's prestige rose across the Middle East and the Third World, while America's sank along with that of its irksome allies.

For Khrushchev, luck had transformed a disaster into a triumph. He had not had the slightest intention of firing rockets at anyone, but the mere threat seemed to have magically stopped a major Western offensive in its tracks. Greatly emboldened, he bet his career and his country's future on building a monster rocket that could hit New York and Washington before America's bombers were even scram-bled. The beast was already under development at a top-secret mis-sile research center north of Moscow. Ten stories high, with a flared skirt of four huge booster rockets, the R-7 was designed to reach the East Coast of the United States in less than half an hour.

His motives were both tactical and practical. The Soviet bomber fleet and its nuclear arsenal lagged far behind America's, and Khrushchev had his sights set on slashing the military budget, not adding punishingly expensive new programs. He needed the savings to pay for two grand projects that he was convinced would prove the Soviet system's ability to deliver. The first was a mass building program of prefabricated suburban apartment blocks that would rescue Soviet citizens from Stalinist communal apartments, with their padlocked cupboards in shared kitchens and their rows of toilet seats hung on hooks in shared bathrooms. The second was a visionary scheme to turn eighty million acres of Central Asian steppe into workable farmland that required the relocation of three hundred thousand farmworkers and fifty thousand tractors.

The fact that the hideously complex rocket technology was not yet proven did not dissuade him from his plan, and neither did the staggering cost of building multiple launch pads. Rockets, he pointed out to Kremlin skeptics, "are not cucumbers; they cannot be eaten, and only so many are necessary to repel aggression." Since the Suez ploy had been so successful, he decided the existence of the missiles was anyway not so important as the *belief* that they existed. Buoyed up with impatience and excitement, in speech after speech he began to threaten the West with nuclear annihilation. The speeches were all the more spine-chilling for being delivered in the reckless tone of a playground bully. The Soviet Union, he blustered, was turning out missiles "like sausages." The missiles were so far ahead of America's that they could wipe out cities like swatting gnats. Asking visiting American politicians where they were from, he would circle their hometown on a map—to remind him, he affably explained to them, to spare it when the rockets flew. The fib was so successful that the West began diverting astonishing sums to compete with the nonexistent Soviet rockets, which was satisfying in a way but also meant that if the truth were ever discovered, the whole game would be up.

*   *   *

PURSUING HIS grinning megalomaniac act, the Kremlin showman also began to uncouple a few links in the Iron Curtain. Boasting that the Soviet Union not only was unafraid of comparison with the rest of the world but also positively welcomed it, he announced that in the summer of 1957 the capital would open its gates and host the Sixth World Festival of Youth and Students.

For unreconstructed Old Bolsheviks it was all too much. A plot that had been brewing since the Secret Speech now came to a head. Malenkov was the leader: humiliated by his power station billet, he was newly threatened by Khrushchev's attempts to decentralize industrial management. Molotov joined him; after stoically arguing against peaceful coexistence, he had been removed as foreign minister by Khrushchev, who made him the (iron) butt of many jokes. After some persuasion, Khrushchev's old mentor "Iron Lazar" Kaganovich came on board, too: the unrepentant Stalinist had been disoriented by the recent changes. The suave Bulganin, Khrushchev's close ally, who had taken over from Malenkov as premier, wavered but eventually fell in with the plotters.

The showdown took place at a Presidium meeting held late on June 18, 1957, a date chosen because many Khrushchev loyalists were absent from Moscow then. Malenkov immediately disputed Khrushchev's right to preside and moved that Bulganin assume the chair. Most of those present were taken by surprise, but unease at Khrushchev's behavior was widespread, and the vote carried. Malenkov bitterly accused Khrushchev of undermining collective leadership by making up policy on the hoof and demanded that he resign. In the heated debate that followed, the plotters labeled Khrushchev's agricultural policies (including his authorization of limited private production) a "rightist deviation" and his foreign policy "Trotskyist and opportunist." His tomfoolery was summed up by his mania for planting corn, a crop that was unsuited to many Soviet regions. It was time to hit the brakes on de-Stalinization, before the entire system flew apart.

Over Khrushchev's strenuous objections the plotters moved to vote on dismissing him as first secretary. The motion carried seven to four, but to their surprise, the flinty-eyed rustic refused to budge, declaring the action illegal on the grounds that some Presidium members had not been notified of the meeting. He insisted on putting the matter to a vote by the full Central Committee, but his opponents refused, knowing full well that Khrushchev had packed it with his own people. Bulganin had stationed guards around the building, but a Khrushchev ally got word out to some Central Committee members who were in Moscow. Eighteen or twenty arrived, forced their way past the guards, and delivered a petition demanding a Central Committee plenum.

Uproar broke out in the Presidium chamber, and some of the missing members returned to find their colleagues deadlocked. Khrushchev's supporters, meanwhile, summoned Central Committee members from the provinces and foreign embassies; Georgy Zhukov, now minister of defense, flew many in on military planes. Three hundred nine made it to Moscow in time; at least a third owed their positions to Khrushchev. The plenum opened four days after the first showdown and turned into an eight-day-long attack on the plotters. Speakers vied to accuse them of factionalism and complicity in Stalin's purges, reviling them as murderers, criminals, and sadists whose hands dripped with innocent blood. "Only you are completely pure, Comrade Khrushchev!" Malenkov bitterly retorted. "Didn't you sign death warrants in Ukraine?" Kaganovich asked rhetorically. "All of us together aren't worth Stalin's shit!" Khrushchev screamed. "You are young! We will correct your brains!" barked the increasingly senile Voroshilov, the ceremonial head of state, jumping up and waving his arms. Yet by the end he, too, had denounced the plotters, as had Bulganin. When Zhukov appeared and added his voice, Malenkov and Kaganovich confessed their guilt; only Molotov doggedly held out. Dubbed the Anti-Party Group, they were removed from their jobs and expelled from the Presidium and the Central Committee.

Khrushchev had lately made a habit of turning up with his friend and ally Mikoyan, now deputy premier, to the National Day parties thrown by foreign embassies. When the next one came round, he made a beeline for the gaggle of Western correspondents, to boast that his opponents were alive and being found employment for which they were qualified. Show trials belonged to the past, but their jobs had been chosen with a sense of humor. Molotov, Stalin's globetrotting foreign minister, was dispatched as ambassador to landlocked Outer Mongolia. Malenkov, an electrical engineer, became manager of a hydroelectric plant in eastern Kazakhstan; though life there was limited, Stalin's intended successor was later said to be happier away from the pressures of the Kremlin. Kaganovich, the master builder of Moscow's glorious Metro, was sent to run a cement plant east of the Urals. Voroshilov and Bulganin were reprimanded but stayed in their posts. Khrushchev rewarded Zhukov by making him a full member of the Presidium, but he was scared of the war hero's popularity and power. Four months later he sent him on a tour of the Balkans and sacked him for "Bonapartism" while he was away.

Now, beyond doubt, Khrushchev was first among equals. It was still not enough.

*　　*　　*

ON JULY 28, a month after the ructious plenum, the World Festival of Youth and Students took over Moscow. Its political bias was evident from the list of previous host cities (Prague, Budapest, East Berlin, Bucharest, and Warsaw), and its joint organizers, the World Federation of Democratic Youth and the International Union of Students, were known in the West as Kremlin fronts. Still, thirty-four thousand young people from one hundred thirty countries arrived in the broiling Soviet capital for two weeks of music and sport, among them sixteen hundred Britons and one hundred sixty Americans who consisted of rebels traveling against State Department advice and a roughly equal number of CIA plants. Three million Muscovites came out to welcome them as they paraded on trucks to Lenin Stadium for the opening ceremony. As the Americans waved the Stars and Stripes, the crowds strained past the police lines, bombarding the visitors with souvenir pins and candy and shouting the festival slogan *Mir i druzhba!*—"Peace and friendship!" The locals were supposed to meet foreigners in groups, under KGB or police supervision; one young Soviet journalist whose father had just returned from the Gulag panicked as a truckload of Italians laughingly pulled her aboard. Yet the operation spun out of control, and Moscow's youth was soon reveling in unprecedented and virtually unfettered contact with Westerners. The Soviets asked for news about émigrés such as Stravinsky, and the visitors asked why Moscow was so poor and shabby even though it had just been given an expensive face-lift. In the sunny evenings, they clustered on the broad pavements of Gorky Street, the main drag known to Americophiles as "Brodvay," and engaged in passionate discussion. Many Muscovites repeated the old line that the United States was in the grip of monopoly capitalists who were gearing up to achieve world domination in a terrible new battle. They could not understand why the West was so antagonistic toward them. "Why should anyone want to oppose the Soviet Union?" an interpreter asked an American journalist; the Communist Party was so clearly correct on all international questions that it was hard to imagine another viewpoint.

To the authorities this novel exchange of opinions was alarming, not least because they had a major problem with disaffected youth. In Stalin's last years, the USSR had experienced a sharp rise in juvenile delinquency, ranging from mass slacking to violent and sometimes lethal assaults in schools. At first it was blamed on a long-standing Tarzan cult, which inspired otherwise normal Soviet youngsters to swing yodeling from trees and through upper-story windows while sporting shaggy haircuts and dressing "like parrots"; then on Western-style fashionistas, who wore zoot suits, bell-bottoms, and risqué ties and who spoke only English (or, in the case of two educated hooligans who created a disturbance in the Hotel Moskva, English and Latin). The party youth organization Komsomol had recently declared war on the hipsters, who were known in Russian as *stilyagi*, together with "aristocrats and other loafers and hooligans," going so far as to suggest they should be sent to labor camps. Yet during the festival the *stilyagi* were far from alone in gaping at the visitors' blue jeans, which became smoking hot items on the black market, or obsessing over American cosmetics, gadgets, cars, and cigarettes. Nor were all the youngsters who flocked to jazz bands out to cause trouble, despite the common saying "Today you're playing jazz and tomorrow you're going to sell out your motherland." Millions listened to Willis Conover's nightly jazz program on the Voice of America, mocking budget-busting efforts to jam it, and the outlawed music was so popular that when the first American exchange students arrived at Moscow University, they "told wild tales of Russian youth lusting to trade dormitory sex for jazz and pop recordings." After a concert by a British jazz group at the festival, one young Russian sneaked backstage past the KGB guards and recited like a mantra the names of American jazz legends; in return he got his first professional lesson on the saxophone, which Stalin had banned as an enemy instrument, and for the duration of their stay he posed as the sixth member of the quintet. Naturally, Western music did not win the festival song contest: that honor went to a sentimental ditty called "Moscow Nights." To the surprise of its authors, who had originally written it as "Leningrad Nights" and who thought it was a bit of nonsense, it also won the overall first prize and was on everyone's lips.

As events reached a climax, the streets filled with Muscovites and foreigners dancing the jitterbug and holding hands in front of banners of Lenin. Brief, torrid affairs broke out between Russian girls and foreign men, especially black men. The dark fields and woods near the visitors' hotels on the edge of the city filled with furiously copulating couples. Trucks equipped with searchlights and manned by surly Komsomol marshals in identical rough boiler suits revved up to catch them in the act and arrest the women, but in regimented Moscow, a city of hierarchies and lonely people, the lure of exotic foreigners was too strong, and the festival was followed nine months later by what was awkwardly called the "inter-baby boom."

Ignoring the U.S. government's dire warnings, forty-one Americans boarded a train, as a brass band played and a thousand Muscovites held out flowers, and set off on a three-week, all-expenses-paid tour of Communist China. That handy bit of propaganda could not disguise the fact that the festival was an unmitigated disaster for Khrushchev. Young people coupling in the undergrowth were not what he had meant by peaceful coexistence. Worse, many Soviet youths appeared drawn to the West by disaffection as much as by positive attraction. Their apathy toward Communist ideals and their cynicism about the achievements of socialism were profoundly shocking to men and women schooled in the revolutionary class struggle.

*   *   *

KHRUSHCHEV WAS determined not to put up the shutters, but he could ill afford to court ridicule again. Luckily the Ministry of Culture had a suggestion that was both reassuringly decorous and virtually guaranteed to impress Soviet genius on citizens and foreigners alike. The idea, which probably originated with the Union of Soviet Composers, was to hold a high-profile music competition in Moscow.

With musicians such as Emil Gilels wowing the West, classical music had become prime evidence in the Soviets' triumphalist case that their political system was the perfected culmination of everything that had gone before. Khrushchev was no aesthete—he complained of seeing *Swan Lake* so often that the mere prospect made him feel sick—but nor had it crossed his mind to cut arts spending. The Soviet republics supported 503 permanent year-round theater companies, 314 middle schools of the arts, 48 higher schools, and 43 advanced conservatories and theatrical and art institutes, while the Ministry of Culture had direct charge of 900,000 arts workers. Many were employed in the famously tough system of music training that funneled children as young as seven to specialist music schools, where the best were prepared for eight years' further study at a conservatory. These incubators of excellence were famous for producing fast, brilliant pianists, who were considered unbeatable. Violinists were equally strong, and the two instruments were natural choices for the upcoming contest. The shackles of socialist realism had finally fallen from Soviet composers after the Secret Speech, and many Russian and Soviet masterpieces were chosen for the program—including some that were seldom if ever heard abroad, which, intentionally or not, made life harder for foreign participants.

The proposal was taken to the Central Committee, which was persuaded not so much by the cultural benefits as by the propaganda prospects both at home and abroad, and raised no objections. As for the competition's namesake, in a country that was still deeply wedded to its heritage, it could only be Tchaikovsky, whose name now adorned the Moscow Conservatory where the composer had so unhappily taught.

The first international competition to be held on Soviet soil was always going to be newsworthy. The catalyst that would make it potentially explosive was about to take off from a top-secret site thirteen hundred miles southeast of Moscow.

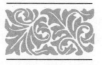

· 6 ·

The Red Moon

AT 10:27 p.m. Moscow time on October 4, 1957, the desert of Kazakhstan was cold, silent, and dark.

At 10:28 there was a loud hiss and a dull roar, as if tectonic plates were shifting deep underfoot. A fiery glow flickered across the flat scrub and dunes, unmasking a hundred-foot-high monster held by four restraining arms. Flames spilled out of a pit in the sand, and smoke plumed into the air. There was a bright flash, and the roar grew deeper and more deafening than a thousand bass drums. The glow dipped and then intensified to a dazzling white as incandescent gases jetted up in columns. The roar and the drumming mixed with a hellish crackling that seemed to come from the center of an incinerating forest, and a blinding point of light rose above the ground. From the heart of the inferno, the behemoth sprang free and shuddered into the night sky riding a column of fire. Two hundred eighty tons of Russian metal, kerosene, and liquid oxygen were heading for space.

The bulbous missile with its four flanking boosters soared aloft at nearly four miles a second. One hundred sixteen seconds after launch the boosters jettisoned, drawing a fiery cross thirty miles high as they fell aside. The central core flexed and barely slowed its journey toward the heavens. At four minutes and fifty-five seconds it shuddered again as the liquid propellant ran out and the engine shut down. It was a second early and five miles lower than intended, but momentum carried the craft another hundred miles through the atmosphere and into the blackness of space.

Twenty seconds later, pneumatic pistons nudged the nose cone away from the spent rocket. It sprang off to reveal the payload: a metal sphere the size of a beach ball, polished to shine like a star. Four spidery antennae whipped into position, and *Sputnik 1*, the rocket casing, and the cone began their maiden orbit around Earth.

It had taken just over five minutes for the Space Age to begin, and it began in the Soviet Union.

As the little orb headed to the East Coast of the United States, Americans were settling in to watch the premiere of a winsome suburban sitcom called *Leave It to Beaver*. On the news the big story was Eisenhower's decision to send federal troops to Little Rock, Arkansas, to escort nine black children to an all-white high school.

"We are bringing you the most important story of this century: mankind's breakthrough into space," the NBC radio announcer cut in. As word spread, families and neighbors drifted outside and stared at the evening sky. Astronomers peered through telescopes. The telemetry signal from the 184-pound ball was designed to be picked up by anyone with a shortwave receiver, and a ham radio station at Columbia University was first to broadcast the eerie sound: a chirpy *whoo-whoo-whee-whee*, gratingly repeated over and over again.

Visionaries had foretold the day when man would defeat gravity and leap above the earth's atmosphere. Now the dream was a reality, and a new epoch had dawned for humankind. Yet, to Americans' utter incomprehension, it had not dawned in the United States. It was as if the eeriest episode of *Science Fiction Theatre* had come to life, and the next day panic set in. Time and again America's leaders had boasted that theirs was the Number One Nation, light-years ahead of the Reds in technology. There was no chance of the Russians smuggling a suitcase bomb across U.S. borders, went one joke, because they were still working on the suitcase. Now Americans were laughing out of the other side of their mouths, and the headlines were bold, tall, and brutal:

REDS WIN SPACE RACE WITH MAN-MADE MOON

SIGHT RED BABY MOON OVER U.S.

ORB SPANS U.S. 7 TIMES A DAY

Pundits compared the moment to Columbus's discovery of the Americas or the splitting of the atom. Politicians thundered that *Sputnik* was a devastating blow to national prestige and security and proved that America was fast becoming a second-rate power. "What went wrong?" puzzled one television intellectual. "How did a nation of backward peasants forge so dramatically ahead of us in the race to space?" The unspoken fear: if central planning could achieve such wondrous feats, perhaps communism really was the wave of the future.

In an age of civil defense and air-raid sirens, when schoolchildren practiced crouching under desks or in dark basements while clasping their heads to keep their skulls from flying apart, people needed no help to be afraid. Men and women interviewed on the news asked the same question: if the Russians had *Sputnik*, what else did they have up there? The answer came four days after the satellite launch, when the USSR detonated an enormous twenty-megaton thermonuclear bomb. "This is a weight that our current rocket can carry anywhere," Soviet radio declared. "Our *Sputnik* proves to the world that we have the first ICBM, the ultimate weapon."

The moat of oceans that had kept Americans safe from mass destruction through two world wars had been leapt over in a single fiery burst. Bombers and submarines, they heard, were useless against missiles that could turn New York into a "slag heap" within half an hour of the enemy's pressing a button. "If Russia wins dominance of this completely new area," an air force general told a congressional committee, "well, I think the consequences are fairly clear: probable Soviet world domination." A poll revealed that 70 percent of Americans believed a nuclear war would happen and that, when it did, at least half the population would be killed.

The news was about to get worse. "In a masterpiece of propaganda timing," NBC reported thirty days after the first launch, "the Soviet Union announced it had launched a *Sputnik* number two, carrying a live dog. This is reportedly history's first space traveler." Moscow was talking about going all the way to the moon. From there, Communists could control the planet. How long before soldiers were sent up to attack America from outer space? Soon the airwaves filled with reports of strange objects sighted above Los Angeles and other cities.

For all the paranoia, the fear was real. The Soviet triumph was one of the greatest shocks in American history—as great in its way as Pearl Harbor. Until *Sputnik* beeped into their consciousness, Americans had owned the future. For many, the Nifty Fifties, with its drive-in restaurants, movie theaters, and churches (honk for amen), its Hula-Hoops and food blenders and beers and ball games on Saturday afternoons, was a decade of ease and prosperity and glitzy excess. Detroit was in the midst of its big tail-fin mania, grafting ever more outrageous protrusions onto the rear fenders of Cadillacs and their imitators, from the delta-winged Buick to the everyday Chevy and compact Rambler. "Suddenly, it's 1960!" cheered the advertising slogan for the 1957 Plymouth. Now automobiles took on the flowing shape of the R-7 and sprouted radio antennae modeled on *Sputnik 1*. The Soviet satellite was a wake-up call that everything was not as it appeared, that the nation had been partying toward a precipice. Politicians more used to telling voters what they wanted to hear admonished their fellow Americans to renounce their love affair with material goods and shore up their preeminence in global affairs. "The time has clearly come," declared Republican senator Styles Bridges, "to be less concerned with the depth of pile on the new broadloom rug or the height of the tail fin on the car and to be more prepared to shed blood, sweat and tears if this country and the Free World are to survive."

*   *   *

ON NOVEMBER 6, 1957, Nikita Khrushchev stood before the Supreme Soviet, the USSR's rubber-stamp parliament, to open the official celebrations for the fortieth anniversary of the Russian Revolution. He was in ebullient form, buoyed by bumper harvests and acclaim for his de-Stalinization campaign as well as by the new scientific triumph. "Our *sputniks* are circling the world," he boasted, flush with excitement. "Now, with America's failure, it will not be able to stop the forward march of communism." In fact, Khrushchev had been as surprised as anyone by the extraordinary impact of the little metal globe, but he was delighted to reap the political rewards.

Faced with a growing crisis and attacked for a failure of leadership, Eisenhower ordered the navy to bring forward its own satellite program. On December 6 the first Vanguard rocket carrying a satellite—a six-inch, three-pound sphere that Khrushchev laughed off as a grapefruit—was readied for launch at Cape Canaveral in the presence of the world's media. At home and at work, a huge audience watched the first live countdown to be broadcast nationally. The cameras rolled as the slender missile wheezed up four feet, then collapsed in billowing flames. The remainder of the nation's self-belief went up in smoke with it. OH WHAT A FLOPNIK! groaned one newspaper, while others came up with KAPUTNIK, DUDNIK, and STAYPUTNIK. At the United Nations a Soviet delegate asked whether America cared to receive aid earmarked for undeveloped countries. *Time* sealed Khrushchev's victory by putting him on the cover as Man of the Year. A golden, bejeweled Kremlin crowned his head; between his fingers he held *Sputnik 1* as if he were about to nudge it personally into Earth's orbit. "In 1957's twelve months," the editorial noted, "Nikita Khrushchev, peasant's son and cornfield commissar scorned by the party's veteran intellectuals, disposed all his serious rivals—at least for the time." He had also thoroughly confounded Western leaders, and nothing was scarier than an unknowable enemy.

Goaded by Khrushchev and spurred by *Sputnik*, Ike announced the establishment of NASA and signed the National Defense Education Act, which increased funding to schools and universities as a matter of national security. To many it seemed too little, too late. With Moscow firing off rockets and threats in every direction, and with conspiracy theorists muttering darkly about a vast fifth column of spies, Americans' confusion turned to near hysteria.

The *Sputnik* moment threw down a historic challenge to America and the West. They had been humiliatingly outplayed in their own game. Now, somehow, they needed to defeat the Soviets at theirs. People were desperate to rebuild their shaken faith in their way of life. The problem was they had no idea how to do it.

*　　*　　*

VAN WAS despondent for different reasons. In the 1956/57 season he had played twenty-three concerts, seven fewer than the previous year, and most were small-town recitals. In this, his fourth season, he was looking at three recitals in October, in McAllen and Graham, Texas, and Natchitoches, Louisiana, and then, after a three-month gap, two others, in Norwalk, Ohio, and Coldwater, Michigan. For the 1958/59 season he had a booking with the New York Philharmonic, which was rare for a pianist at his stage. Still, that was it.

There were two reasons for the trailing off, one simple and one more complex. The simple one was that the army had come calling. As required by law, Van had registered with the Selective Service System five days after he turned eighteen. A two-year academic deferment had run out that September. At any moment he expected to be called up for the statutory twenty-four months of active-duty service. He was perfectly open about it, and performance venues were therefore reluctant to risk a cancellation.

The other reason had to do with the structure of the American concert business. Of the two outfits that dominated it, CAMI was by far the bigger, which meant its artists had the lion's share of the work. Yet its Community Concerts division was notorious for bundling together an ever-changing roster of cheap new artists—and cheap foreign artists, mostly Frenchwomen of a certain age—with a few expensive star names. The system did give a chance to newcomers, but most had a promising first season, only to be passed over as their novelty wore off; a few built a following but were locked out when they tried to raise their fees; and only rarely did anyone become a headliner in regular demand. Gary Graffman, who was one of CAMI's battery of what it termed Outstanding Young American Pianists, or OYAPs, thought the firm's motto could have been "Wait and See If It Sinks or Swims." As a business model for market-testing unproven commodities, it might have been prudent, but for instilling confidence in sensitive artists, it was a bust.

Bill Judd was the firm's idealist, and he was undoubtedly keen to build Van's career. After his young client's tremendous early surge, Judd was happy to move him down a gear, giving him time to learn his trade and keeping him out of the way of critics such as the *Chicago Tribune*'s Claudia Cassidy, known in the trade as Acidy Cassidy. Yet Van was convinced he was ready for more, and with time on his hands he began feeling unloved and unwanted. His classmate John Browning seemed to be pulling ahead: after winning the Steinway Centennial Award in 1954 and the Leventritt on his second attempt in 1955, he had already toured Europe and signed a recording contract.

To his friends, Van appeared distraught and confused, even depressed. He talked with them on the phone for hours, trying to figure out what the problem was and what to do about it, and moped round his gloomy apartment until he looked peaked. One day his church friend Nola Rhodes enticed him down to Riverside Park, where he sat on the riverbank and peeled off his shirt. "Ugh, I look so white!" he groaned, wrinkling his nose. A cabin cruiser glided past. "I want a boat like that!" he exclaimed, then ruefully added, "I seem to want everything. I want to travel, I want to help my parents, I want to be a really great artist, I want to go everywhere, see everything, know everybody! And here I am—look at me. Going nowhere, fast!" Nola reassured him that faith and hard work would bring him everything he wanted, and he ran home to practice. When a concert was coming up he was wedded to the keyboard, but in between engagements he decried practicing as pointless drudgery and dragged friends out to the movies. Rildia Bee began calling them from Kilgore, imploring them to see to it that he practiced.

Reports began to filter back to his managers that his performances were getting erratic, and the state of things became clear one day when he was walking down Fifty-Seventh Street and saw two CAMI managers coming his way. As they neared, they suddenly crossed the street and resumed walking on the other side.

"You can't just sit on the tracks and pray; that won't stop the train," his parents had always taught him. "Cast thy bread upon the waters."

As a tither, Van was supposed to give 10 percent of his earnings to the church, but he gave more like 20. One day that year he was playing the organ in Mozart's Requiem Mass when it wheezed to a halt, and with the choir singing unaccompanied, he ran down from the loft and continued on the rickety old upright; the whole thing was broadcast live on the radio. Afterward he strode across to Steinway Hall and bought the church a concert grand. Even with his performer discount it cost as much as the Cadillac convertible he coveted, and he had to borrow the money from the bank. Unbeknownst to his parents, he was in debt to the tune of seven thousand dollars, a large sum at the time, and the monthly installments added to the burden. Anxiety got the better of him, and he began suffering from acute performer's stomach. Then a childhood ailment returned: late one night his nose poured blood for hours, and he called his friends in a panic, waking them up.

It was a year of accidents. That summer, he visited Mrs. Steinway and her family at her summer home in Plymouth, Massachusetts, and saw the ocean for the first time. "Oh!" he exclaimed: "The ocean!" It was in fact Cape Cod Bay. Later on, Schuyler Chapin and his kids invited him to take a dip. As a child he had been too busy for swimming lessons, but he stepped off the submerged shelf that dropped away a few feet from the shore and disappeared, until his hosts realized he was in trouble and pulled him out half-drowned.

In July his parents drove up from Texas to watch him play with the Cleveland Summer Orchestra, and while Rildia Bee was changing at the hotel, she slipped and landed heavily on her back. Van and Harvey called the house doctor, who gave her painkillers so she could attend the concert, and the following morning they got into the family Buick and headed east along the I-80 to New York. After seven hours she was in agony, but convinced it was just a sprain, she rested up so she could accompany Van to Billy Graham's Crusade. The thirty-eight-year-old evangelist's revival meeting had roared into town that May and filled Madison Square Garden (a venue more used to the sound of gloves thwacking jaws) with song and prayer and full-throated denunciations of communism. It was every Christian's duty, Graham thundered, to be constantly on guard against Red infiltrators, the fifth column of a godless religion that was "master-minded by Satan . . . I think there is no other explanation for the tremendous gains of Communism in which they seem to outwit us at every turn, unless they have supernatural power and wisdom and intelligence given to them." A close friend and adviser to the president, Graham preached his apocalyptic message to more than two million during the sixteen-week Crusade. Van sang in the bass section of the thousands-strong choir, belting out Baptist classics such as "Blessed Assurance," "I Love to Tell the Story," and "Wonderful Words of Life." He had a private box for the duration and dragged along Juilliard friends, including John Browning, Jimmy Mathis, and Jeaneane Dowis. Jerome Lowenthal, a studious, bespectacled pianist who had shared some classes with Van, met him one day coming home and was struck by how excitedly and emotionally Van enthused about the Crusade.

After several days of unremitting pain, Rildia Bee finally agreed to have an X-ray, which showed a broken vertebra that had narrowly missed paralyzing her. She was admitted to Doctors Hospital on East End Avenue and ordered to lie still for six weeks. After that, Van locked up his apartment, emptied his bank account to pay down several installments on the Steinway, and went back to Kilgore. Daddy had raised a bank loan to pay for the medical expenses, but there were Mother's forty-odd pupils to take care of, and while he waited for his army summons, Van took them on, often going way over their allotted hour until they begged to be allowed to go home. He still had time on his hands, though, so when the local Lutheran church sent over for a pupil to play during services, he volunteered himself and played there for several weeks.

Eventually the army called him to the induction center at Longview. The draft board evaluation went well until his nose started bleeding, and it was still pouring blood when he stood to take the oath. His hand was raised over the Bible when an orderly interrupted. An examination of Van's medical records revealed a history of chronic nasal hemorrhages and allergies beginning when he was eight. He was categorized 4-F, unfit for military service, and dismissed. He had been rather looking forward to a change of scene, especially as he had been preselected to join an Army Band tour of Africa. Instead he went back to Kilgore with nothing to do.

Bill Judd suggested throwing together a European tour, a possibility that Bill Schuman's Music Panel had already discussed: "He has won many awards in competitions, by competent judges, and is a first class pianist," the panel's minutes recorded, adding that he was approved in principle. His name had come up again when a letter was received "which backs up the Panel's opinion that he is terrific, brilliant, sensational. We shall try to see if a project can be worked out for him." Still, Van was reluctant. Nothing seemed to make sense anymore. It was the lowest ebb of his young professional life, and for the first time fear crept over him.

*   *   *

AMONG THAT year's Music Panel applicants was a striking young pianist from Los Angeles named Olegna Fuschi, who asked for a grant to take part in the Rio de Janeiro International Piano Competition. The psychological warfare people were keen to assist Americans in competing abroad, but Washington had vetoed it, in part because of the difficulty of identifying winners. Fuschi was turned down but went anyway. One of the Rio judges was a Russian pianist, Pavel Serebryakov, who had also been named as a judge for the forthcoming piano competition in Moscow. He had brought along a pile of brochures and application forms in various languages, and he gave a packet to Fuschi, saying he hoped she would come.

The large brochure was a luxury production that clearly heralded an important event. The royal blue cover bore a cameo of Tchaikovsky above the title INTERNATIONAL PIANO AND VIOLIN COMPETITION NAMED AFTER TCHAIKOVSKY. Inside were thirty-six pages lavishly illustrated with photographs of the composer, his birthplace, his house in Klin, his scores, his statue in front of the Moscow Tchaikovsky Conservatory, the Great Hall of the conservatory from various angles, and the large Moscow concert venue named Tchaikovsky Hall. There was no mistaking Russia's pride in its most famous composer, and there was no arguing with the stature of those behind the competition. Heading the Organizing Committee was Dmitri Shostakovich, now restored to first place in the Soviet pantheon. The always reliable Emil Gilels was chairman of the jury, which also included the highly unreliable but celebrated Sviatoslav Richter. After the programs for pianists and violinists, the brochure ended with a list of the eight prizes on offer, ranging from 25,000 rubles ($6,250 at the official 1957 exchange rate) and a gold medal to 5,000 rubles and a badge of honor.

Fuschi leafed through the brochure and then packed it in her bag. When she got back to New York, she brought it to the first lesson of the new school year and showed it to her teacher, Rosina Lhévinne. Rosina thanked Olenychika, as she called Fuschi, and turned over the pages. Still holding it, she walked slowly to the window and stared out. Very softly, half to herself, she said:

"Van."

Oblivious to Olenychika's interest in going herself, she dictated a letter to him. "I promise, they will love you," it ended. Then she consulted Bill Schuman. "Are you sure he's the right one?" the Juilliard president asked, and Rosina replied that he was, out of those in her class. Besides, she added, "I feel he vould make a *vonderful* representative of America in Moscow. He has the personality as well as the talent."

Around the same time, the handsome brochure arrived at the Fifty-Seventh Street offices of Steinway and Sons. Sascha Greiner, the veteran head of the Concert and Artist Department, picked up the phone and called Kilgore. A German-Latvian refugee from revolutionary Russia who had originally been hired to communicate with Vladimir Horowitz before the mercurial pianist learned English, Greiner was himself a graduate of the Moscow Conservatory. "You must go, Van!" he exclaimed excitedly. Van had already received the brochure from Rosina, but he hadn't given the idea much thought. The political situation held no fear for him: as Allen Spicer had berated him, beyond having a vague sense that world relations were strained, he barely knew what the situation was. Still, it was odd to think of dragging himself back to the competition circuit in his fourth year as a professional, with all the toil it entailed. Greiner got nowhere with Van, and when Rosina called two days later, Van told her he was truly grateful for the thought but wasn't interested.

"Oh Van, you must go!" she insisted. When she got no further, she wrote him a much longer letter in which she spelled out four excellent reasons for his taking part. First, he would have to work with great intensity, which would be good for him. Second, he would have to learn a great deal of new material. Third, he would meet the cream of the world's young pianists. Fourth, she believed he would win.

Bill Judd called her. "But you can't *do* that, Rosina!" he cried. The whole thing looked ridiculous. The program was heavily weighted toward Russian music, the jury toward the Eastern Bloc. Everything in Khrushchev's Soviet Union was political, and clearly an American had no chance: Van would lose and look like an amateur. Besides, Judd would have to cancel the dates he had been busy lining up for Van in Europe. Rosina listened but refused to concede. Privately she must have known it was a long shot; Russia had changed incalculably since she left it a lifetime ago. On the other hand, Soviet Russians were still Russians, and if Van somehow pulled it off, it could be the boost his flagging career and confidence needed.

Van wrote back. He still didn't think he would go, he said, but he would be in New York in early November, and they could discuss it then. Despite his reluctance, memories began to crowd in: memories of Christmas in Shreveport and the book with the pictures of St. Basil's Cathedral, of Rildia Bee's stories about Rachmaninoff, and Rosina's about the conservatory where Tchaikovsky taught and where she and Josef triumphed. There was also the curious fact, which Van was superstitious enough to heed, that a psychic he consulted in the spring revealed in a séance that within a year he would travel to "an agrarian country" and win a gold medal.

In November he went to dinner at Rosina's. As they leafed through the brochure, talked over the requirements, and sized up his chances, Van began to get agitated. "The gold medal!" he exclaimed. Yet he was still far from convinced. A campaign got under way, in the course of which Sascha Greiner took him to lunch three times. "Dear Van, I beg of you, *please* go," he wheedled. Eugene Istomin, the pianist who had been on the Leventritt jury, took him to lunch at Reuben's, a celebrity hangout on East Fifty-Eighth Street. They both seemed convinced that Van could win. Mark Schubart, the Juilliard dean, began looking for sponsorship; the brochure explained that Moscow would take care of accommodation, maintenance, and return transportation but not the outbound airfare. First Schubart tried the Music Committee of the president's People-to-People Program, another Eisenhower initiative aimed at fostering international understanding. The committee referred the matter to the State Department and came back with the information that State favored American participation and would place no restrictions on travel but also would provide no funds. Schubart wrote to Van informing him of the situation and then turned to the Martha Baird Rockefeller Aid to Music Program. Its administrator, the retired broadcaster César Saerchinger, indicated that the program was minded to offer a thousand dollars per contestant. Schubart was keen to avoid a repetition of the row that had roiled the music world when his boss, Bill Schuman, fought tooth and nail to send the Juilliard Orchestra to the upcoming Brussels World's Fair with government funds Schuman had voted for as a member of the Music Panel. Rather than propose Juilliard alumni to the Rockefeller program, Schubart spoke with David Wodlinger of the Institute of International Education and suggested that the IIE form a committee to choose the contestants itself. He followed up with a letter recommending that there be no preliminary trials or publicity, since the only hope of being well represented "devolves on our being able to send to Moscow, not students, but young professionals, preferably with a good deal of concert experience. This caliber of young artist would undoubtedly not wish to participate in a competition to take part in a competition." The IIE duly invited Schubart to be a member of the special committee, and on December 10 he called Bill Judd to tell him that Van had been nominated. Judd requested a formal letter, presumably so he could get Van out of the commitments he had made on his behalf, and Schubart obliged. The only other contestant chosen was Juilliard violinist Joyce Flissler, who had toured South America with the backing of Schuman's Music Panel. A few Americans who were already abroad, including Van's former classmates Daniel Pollack and Jerome Lowenthal, sent word that they would enter under their own steam; otherwise, no one else was both talented enough and willing to go.

Van, more in debt than ever, told Schubart he didn't need the money. "Take it," Schubart insisted. "You're crazy if you don't." Van was still wavering, but he decided to get ready just in case. There was a vast amount of music to prepare, and though he had already mastered some, a lot was new. The first round took in Bach, Mozart, Chopin, and Liszt as well as Scriabin, Rachmaninoff, and Tchaikovsky, but the second-round program consisted almost entirely of music by Russian or Soviet composers, some barely known in the West. The finals, if he reached them, required a concerto by Tchaikovsky, a specially commissioned work by a Soviet composer that would be circulated two months prior to the competition, and another concerto of the contestant's choice. There was never any doubt that Van would choose Tchaikovsky's Piano Concerto no. 1, but for the other concerto, he settled on perhaps the most demanding piano work of all: Rachmaninoff's Orientally rich Third Piano Concerto. When Van was fifteen he heard a recording of Rachmaninoff playing the piece, which was notorious for its technical challenges and struck fear into many pianists. Though Rildia Bee had given Van the music, and he had taken it everywhere with him, he had bided his time learning it until 1954. Then, without telling Rosina, he finally began, first humming and singing his way through, as Mother had taught him. It was a daring and dangerous choice.

Rosina gave up her Sundays, which were usually reserved for rest and trips to the country. "I won't charge you now, but you can pay me back after you win in Moscow," she half-joked. They worked together for three, sometimes four or five hours. "We have only three months in which to get ready," she prodded him at the start. "You must live as though you really were in training. See nobody and go nowhere five days of the week and be in bed by eleven." Remember the Russian proverb, she said, "Without hard work you can't even pull a fish out of the pond." When he got going, his ambition flared up again, and he practiced as much as ten hours a day. Still, he refused to commit.

The application form carried the instruction that it must reach Moscow no later than December 31, and on the day Rosina left for California to spend Christmas with her children she convinced Van to send it off. He could always pull out later, she reasoned, but if he delayed any longer all their work would be wasted. The required information about his schooling, awards, and chosen program had already been typed in, but at the last minute he dithered over the music, crossed out three pieces, and wrote in three more. As instructed, he attached three nine-by-six-centimeter photographs, a certified copy of his Juilliard diploma, and a negative of his birth certificate, which came complete with tiny hand- and footprints. Then he rushed to the post office. Even by express mail, it was impossible to predict whether the package would get to Moscow on time during the holiday season, and he followed it with a telegram to Shostakovich:

HAVE JUST MAILED MY APPLICATION TONIGHT DECEMBER
TWENTIETH HOPING IT REACHES YOU IN TIME.

A few days later Van headed out of town for his two scheduled community concerts in Ohio and Michigan. By the first he was feeling feverish, but he played both dates. The fever worsened as he flew back to New York, and when he stepped into a grocery store, he dropped to the floor in a faint. The doctor diagnosed a bad flu—in other reports, a flare-up of colitis—and prescribed bed rest, though months of anxiety had undoubtedly contributed to his collapse.

Probably it would not have helped his recuperation to know that one foreign competitor had already arrived in Moscow and was working even more single-mindedly than he.

*   *   *

LIKE VAN, Liu Shikun started learning the piano at age three, though he had even less choice in the matter. His businessman father, who had trained as a singer and was determined to see his son succeed as a classical musician, sat him on his knee and taught him, getting him to memorize each piece by singing it out. By six, Liu was performing Mozart concertos in his hometown of Tianjin, a treaty port near Beijing then under Japanese occupation, and at ten, the year the Communists won the Chinese Civil War, he took first prize in a national piano competition. Liu entered the conservatory and progressed so fast that he represented China at the prestigious Liszt Piano Competition in Budapest when he was seventeen. Politically savvy from growing up amid war and clashing ideologies, he was convinced it was a fix when first prize went to a Soviet pianist named Lev Vlassenko and Liu placed third; that year, 1956, relations between China and the Soviet Bloc had dramatically soured when Mao angrily denounced Khrushchev's Secret Speech and rebuked him for revisionism.

A gaunt six foot two with a crew cut and thick glasses, Liu was still four months shy of his nineteenth birthday when the Chinese Ministry of Culture entered him for the Tchaikovsky Competition. Artistic accomplishment fitted with a Maoist slogan, "Both Red and talented," and this time the ministry was taking no chances. As a backup, it selected pianist Gu Shengying, the delicate daughter of an entrepreneur who was in jail after being convicted of espionage during Mao's campaign against counterrevolutionaries, and in November it sent both pianists to Moscow to prepare. Liu was assigned to Samuel Feinberg, a veteran teacher and joint head of the Moscow Conservatory's piano department, who was alarmed to discover that Liu knew virtually none of the required literature.

The Chinese pianist had been given a large room at the Central Hotel, with a grand piano, thick walls, and the usual double windows to keep out the extreme cold. Eating out was a waste of time, so he bought bags of bread, butter, sausages, and cheese, silently thanking his old family cook for accustoming his stomach to Western food, and stashed them in the gap between the windows. He raided his supplies when he was hungry, drank water from the tap, and practiced eleven or twelve hours at a stretch. For four months he kept up the same routine, seeing nothing of Moscow except the route between the hotel and the conservatory, a dozen minutes' walk away.

When he was a boy, his father beat him when he ran away from the piano, and all his life he had hated practice. Yet he had no choice. The authorities back home were watching, and he knew the competition would be fierce; especially when the name of Lev Vlassenko, his bête noir from Budapest, was suddenly announced among the entrants.

*   *   *

THE TCHAIKOVSKY Competition was fast approaching, and the Soviet Ministry of Culture was in a quandary. It was proving bafflingly hard to find qualified native pianists who were willing to take part.

Soviet musicians had a stellar track record in competitions, in part because a central board strictly vetted all entrants. For this first international competition on home ground, the process was writ large. An all-union selection marathon had evaluated seventy musicians from conservatories in Baku, Erevan, Gorky, Kiev, Kishinev, Leningrad, Lvov, Moscow, Novosibirsk, Odessa, Riga, and Vilnius, putting them through preliminaries, semifinals, and finals in a dry run of the main event. Nine violinists and nine pianists were selected to go forward;

all but one from the Moscow and Leningrad conservatories, which caused the authorities a good deal of soul-searching about the state of regional teaching. Yet the ministry was far from convinced that a surefire winner had been found. The problem seemed to be that the Soviets' very dominance of the field had bred a kind of competition fatigue. Several international prizewinners in their late twenties with flourishing careers—among them violinists Igor Bezrodny, Rafael Sobolevsky, and Eduard Grach; and pianists Yevgeny Malinin, Dmitri Bashkirov, and Lazar Berman—had flatly refused to put in the necessary months of preparation. The bureaucrats approached Vladimir Ashkenazy, who was just twenty but who two years before had won the prestigious Queen Elisabeth Competition in Belgium, narrowly beating Van's old classmate John Browning. Ashkenazy refused, too, so they turned to Lev Vlassenko.

Solidly built like a football coach's dream tackle, with an erect bearing, beetling brows, and a Beethovian head of hair, at twenty-nine Vlassenko was only just within the upper age limit. A fitness fanatic who was often found standing on his head and who thought nothing of swimming the freezing Moscow River, he was known among the conservatory crowd, not always admiringly, as "Iron Lev." He was already an assistant professor at the conservatory and had little to gain from putting himself through another competition, especially when he still had raw memories of the rancor in Budapest, where a cabal of Hungarian students started whistling every time a Soviet competitor came onstage. Besides, he had never played the Tchaikovsky concerto and had no particular desire to do so now. Still, the authorities kept insisting, and though Vlassenko was no party stooge, he was cautious by nature and caved in.

By then it was January, and time was short. For bureaucratic reasons, he and his wife, Ella, both of whom came from Tbilisi, Georgia, were ineligible to be registered in Moscow, so they lived beyond the northern city limits, in one half of a bright green dacha bought by Lev's parents. Water came from a well in the garden, near the outdoor toilet; heat from a stove that an old woman helped them light. It was a big step up from his first two years at the conservatory, when he rented a corner of a room and slept on a chair, but it still had no piano. Each morning, he woke in the early hours and set off for the conservatory, where even in midwinter he arrived at 7:00 a.m. as it opened and practiced until lessons began. This winter the snow was especially high, which made it challenging to get in at all, but luckily the authorities made special arrangements for the important event. The Soviet contestants were bused first to the Composers' Union House of Creativity at Ruza, a peaceful compound of little dachas a couple of hours from Moscow, where Vlassenko spent two weeks learning the Tchaikovsky concerto, and then to Malakhovka, an area of historic dachas nearer the city, where Chekhov and Gorky once lived. The garage at the Malakhova resort home was turned into a rehearsal room, and two grand pianos, one a Steinway, were brought in. Day after day, Vlassenko played through the repertoire like Stakhanov at a coal seam, more or less up to tempo, intent on not missing a single note, concentrating so closely that he was spent after an hour. With his old teacher, the renowned Jacob Flier, there to support him, his confidence surged, which was just as well, because Iron Lev had a fatal and unpredictable flaw. Sometimes before a performance he was so nervous that he tensed up and played with sharp accents and exaggerated fortes or suffered memory lapses, and it scarcely helped when it was made clear that nothing less than the prestige of the Soviet state and of socialism itself rested on his shoulders.

Vlassenko was a voracious learner, and many evenings in Moscow he took courses at the Institute of Languages. Thanks to those classes, he could read English fluently, and shortly before the start of the competition he came across some laudatory articles about Van Cliburn. He was surprised. The lengthy official press releases had drawn attention to Roger Boutry and Annie Marchand of France and to Juilliard's Daniel Pollack and Jerome Lowenthal as exemplars of the foreign talent about to arrive, but there had been no mention of a Van Cliburn. When he took the articles to the Organizing Committee, he was told they were American hype and meant nothing.

He wasn't so sure. Alone among the Soviet contestants and jury, he suspected that a challenge lay in store.

The whole Soviet Union was abuzz with news of the Tchaikovsky Competition. The names of Shostakovich, Gilels, and Richter were everywhere. A national audience tuned in to a radio series called *Heading Toward the Competition*, which spotlighted the participants and their recordings, explained how the event would work, and interviewed leading Soviet musicians, who shared their hopes for its success. *Pravda* and *Izvestiya* devoted columns of print to the great event, running biographies of the contestants alongside their photographs: fifteen one day, fifteen the next. Muscovites reading the papers on street corners parsed the profiles for political meaning. The Soviet entrants typically made a play for sympathy by stressing that they came from a large family in a poor area such as Dagestan, while an Australian violinist attracted the wrong kind of attention by boasting that he was bringing a Stradivarius with him. All the foreigners volunteered that they were delighted to be coming to the Soviet Union, loved the country, and were enraptured by Tchaikovsky's music. To readers used to attacks on imperialist aggression, this was intriguing: not so much that many Westerners were yearning to visit, but that the regime had decided to make them say so.

*   *   *

BY THE time Rosina returned to New York in mid-January, Van was getting up from his bout of flu. "Oh, thank goodness you're back!" he cried when she called. "I must come right up and see you. Wait'll I tell you what happened to *me!*" Minutes later he showed up at her door paler and skinnier than ever, shrugged off his overcoat with its permanently missing buttons, and sank into a chair. Three precious weeks had been lost to his illness, but a wonderful doctor had put him on a regimen of "vitamins, shots, raw eggs, and six envelopes of Knox gelatin a day." The doctor conditioned Olympic athletes, and he had cut Van a deal: no win, no pay. The patient was feeling better already.

Rosina tried the gelatin and felt energized. Van resumed his daily practice and Sunday sessions, sometimes going into Juilliard to play. Before long, a cable from Moscow announced that sheet music for the special composition for the finals, "Rondo" by Dmitri Kabalevsky, would be sent "par avion your address." It was signed "Shostakovich," and on February 5 a letter arrived from Shostakovich. "Dear Mr. Van Kleeburn!" it began; presumably someone had translated his name into Russian, and someone else had translated it back again. The letter confirmed Van's place in the piano competition, gave details of the dates and how to get a visa, and asked for a brief biography and an itinerary so he could be met at the airport. The "Rondo" sheet music was enclosed. The letter was dated January 18 and had taken two and a half weeks to arrive; with time wanting, Van immediately sat down and learned the piece in a few days. On February 12 he replied as requested, to acknowledge receipt of the music; meantime, he had begun agonizing again over his choice of pieces, and he dragged Shostakovich into the dilemma:

A question has been posed as to whether La Campanella of Liszt is considered an Etude. Or would you prefer one of the Transcendental Studies? Also, would it be possible for me to include—or substitute, as the case may be—on the second preliminary program, the F Minor Fantaisie of Chopin and the Liszt Twelfth Hungarian Rhapsody, in place of the Chopin B Minor Sonata. Or might I use all three of these compositions? Of course, I still will be using the Beethoven Op. 57 and the Brahms-Handel Variations.

After congratulating the composer on the great success of his Eleventh Symphony in Leningrad, which he explained he had read about in the magazine *USSR*, Van expressed his eagerness to meet him and the rest of the Organizing Committee.

A little flurry of cables followed:

POSSIBLE USE "CAMPANELLA," LISZT TWELFTH HUNGARIAN
RHAPSODY AND CHOPIN F MINOR FANTAISIE IN PLACE OF CHOPIN
B MINOR SONATA ARE INCLUDED ON YOUR SECOND PRELIMINARY
PROGRAM. REGARDS,

COMITÉ D'ORGANISATION

CHOSTAKOVITCH

THANK YOU SO MUCH FOR YOUR CABLE WOULD APPRECIATE YOUR
CONFIRMING AGAIN TO AVOID ERROR THAT ACCEPTABLE TO
PRESENT BEETHOVEN APPASIONATE SONATA PROKOFIEF SONATA 6
FANTAISIE F MINOR AND LISZT 12 HUNGARIAN RHAPSODY AS PART
B OF SECOND PRELIMINARY WARMEST GREETINGS = VAN CLIBURN

COMITÉ D'ORGANISATION CONCOURS TCHAIKOVSKY ACCEPTE
VOTRE DERNIER PROGRAMME ET PRIE AVERTIR DATE ET
ITINÉRAIRE VOTRE ARRIVÉE MOSCOU

RESPECTS

CHOSTAKOVITCH

Moscow's English translators were clearly overstretched, but it was worth entering the competition just to correspond with the greatest composer of the age.

On Mark Schubart's recommendation, Van dropped by Cosmos Travel Bureau on West Forty-Fifth Street. A Mr. Reiner in the office negotiated contracts with the Soviet Union, and it turned out that he, too, had had a letter from Shostakovich, in his case asking for advice about how to publicize the competition; the *New York Times* had obliged by publishing a notice. Reiner booked Van on SAS flight 912 to Copenhagen, departing on the twenty-fourth, but Van went back and switched to Air France via Paris to Prague, even though it meant leaving a day earlier. He was getting nervous about taking such a

long trip without anyone to confide in, and he began wheedling people to go along. First he tried Rosina, but she had to teach. Then he
asked Sascha Greiner, but he had to work. Finally, he attempted to
convince Rosalie Leventritt. In her no-nonsense way, she told him
to go alone; it would be the best experience of his life, she said, if he
stood on his own two feet. Happily, a compromise presented itself
when the State Department summoned Mark Schubart to Washington. The Juilliard dean presented himself at its Foggy Bottom headquarters and sat in an empty interview room. After some time, an
officer walked in and began obscurely explaining how the day was
split into three periods, and activities that overlapped more than one
day were to be entered in the second period. Eventually Schubart
worked out that the State Department wanted an observer to travel
to Moscow and file reports; the bureaucratese was standard protocol
for submitting expense claims.

Van's three scuffed suitcases were packed, one stuffed with jars of
vitamin capsules and boxes of Knox gelatin, accompanied by detailed
instructions from the Olympian doctor whose wages were riding on
Van's success. His bills he left unpaid. Only one thing remained: a
visa. He kept pestering Mr. Reiner, who explained that doing business
with the Soviets required patience. "Look," he finally offered when
Van dropped by yet again, "I know the president of the Intourist Bureau; I'll call him in Moscow and see if he can help." The Intourist
president turned out to be a member of the competition's Organizing
Committee, and the visa came through on March 22, Van's last day in
town. Cosmos Travel had already sent Shostakovich a letter announcing that its client "Mr Harry La Van Cliburn Jr" would soon arrive "to
take part in the Violin Contest," and despite Mr. Reiner's deep Russian
connections, Van resolved to send his own cable with the details of his
Czech Airlines flight, for the Prague-to-Moscow leg of his trip, number OK502. That, too, got a little scrambled along the way:

ARRIVING OKAY 502 MARCH TWENTYFIFTH VANCLIBURN

That night he had one last engagement: a concert at the Leventritts' Park Avenue apartment for thirty of Rosina's favorite students and Rosalie's wealthy friends. After turkey and champagne for the guests, he began at eight o'clock, playing straight through his repertoire for the competition. From the Steinway came the familiar style, perfected. Every piece had been polished until the details shone and the whole gleamed, yet his playing was freer, more poetic than before. All those present realized they were witnessing something truly exceptional, and when he finished at midnight they were more drained than he. "Mrs. Leventritt made a graceful little farewell speech," noted Mark Schubart, "whereupon Van, with no encouragement from an absolutely bushed audience, played encores for a solid hour. I've never been so exhausted in my life."

Van had been strong-armed into entering the Moscow trial, and he had told everyone he was going only so he could see St. Basil's Cathedral and the Kremlin, the sights that had enraptured him as a child. If that had ever been true, it no longer was. A few days earlier he had flown home. "I could tell that he meant business," Harvey later recalled. "Then one night he told me, 'I'm going to win. The Russians will like my style.'" Even closer to his departure he went round to the Chapins' and announced very simply, "I'm going to win." Just in time he had rediscovered his faith in himself: that essential performer's belief that no one else can play the way you play; that others might have a sounder technique, a bigger repertoire, vaster experience, but they cannot sing a phrase the way you can or find such a delicate shade of sound; that confidence in the depth of your soul that you are capable of performing a tiny bit better than anyone else.

The next day, Van headed to Idlewild Airport, where the Lockheed Starliner with its distinctive triplet tail was idling on the runway. As he prayed the flight would be safe—in those days, there were at least a couple of crashes a year at the New York airport alone—the plane took off via Boston for Paris. When he reached

Paris's Orly Airport, he mailed home a letter he had written during the fifteen-hour flight and sent a final cable to Shostakovich:

ARRIVING MOSCOW TUESDAY MARCH 25TH FLIGHT 502 AEROFLOT

845 EVENING REGARDS VAN CLIBURN

*   *   *

THE DAY after twenty-three-year-old Van Cliburn left America with no one to wave him off, twenty-three-year-old Elvis Presley was processed into the U.S. Army with a frenzied media pack in attendance. "The Army can do anything it wants with me," Elvis patriotically declared. Washington was equally keen to show that the King of Rock and Roll was being treated like any other draftee, and he was sent to Fort Hood, Texas, for basic training before serving the remainder of his two-year stint at the Third Armored Division base in Friedberg, West Germany. His fans were distraught, and teachers' groups and parents were ecstatic, but the real news was that there was no end in sight to the draft of America's young men to combat the Communist threat. Nearly thirteen years after the end of World War II, American and Soviet tanks still stood barrel to barrel across the lines that divided Berlin, Germany, and Europe.

As contestants arrived in Moscow for the Tchaikovsky Competition, tensions between the world's two thermonuclear-armed superpowers had never been higher. With the weapons race shifting into space, voices on both sides chillingly called for preemptive strikes before it was too late. Risky maneuvers constantly threatened to escalate into full-blown conflict: in the latest incident, that Christmas Eve Soviet fighters had shot down a U.S. Air Force B-57 over the Black Sea, with the loss of all its crew. At any moment, fear and mistrust threatened to unfix the stays of civilization, of human feeling and sanity itself, to the point where a handful of men could envisage destroying the world rather than allow opponents whom they had never met to win. Not for a moment did anyone suppose that classical music would make a particle of difference.

SECOND MOVEMENT

Volante

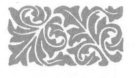

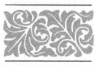

· 7 ·

To Russia, with Love

IN THE evening the landscape coming into Moscow looked flat, like Texas.

That was his first thought. The grassy plains and the cutout farms and the trees, the virgin forests overflowing the horizon, reminded him of home—which was not what a young American was supposed to think on first approaching the headquarters of world communism in the bleakest years of the Cold War.

The Aeroflot Tu-104 thundered away from the setting sun and began its final descent. The Soviet plane was the world's only working passenger jet, a product of the same futuristic technology that had stunned America five months before, when *Sputnik* whizzed far over their roofs. But to the tall Texan staring from the aircraft window, Russia represented something entirely different. The music he had been practicing for months played in his head: the glorious Romantic music from a bygone age of painted czarinas, glittering balls, and pealing church bells. He had loved it since he could remember, and to his exquisitely painful excitement he was here to play it in its birthplace.

Dusk had fallen when the jetliner taxied to a stop near the low terminal building. The passengers extinguished their pipes and cigarettes, which stewardesses had passed round to help with air pressure. A stony-faced militia boy came on board and worked his way down the rows.

"Passport," he levelly demanded. At the center of his cap band was an enameled red star badge bearing a hammer and sickle.

Van Cliburn handed over his documents and flashed him a smile. The young functionary was caught off guard and smiled back.

Out on the air stairs, the subzero cold sliced through Van like a flush of shame. Klieg lights reflected mistily off banks of dry snow, casting a pallid glow in the evening sky. There were dozens, maybe hundreds of planes parked around. Van scanned the waiting faces and unexpectedly saw someone he knew: Harriet Wingreen, a fellow Juilliard pianist, who had been out here accompanying an American violinist. He made for her, arms akimbo, and stooped down to draw her in; at five feet, she was a good sixteen inches shorter than he.

"Is everything all right?" he asked in his soft southern slide, looking searchingly in her eyes. His perpetual smile was thinner than usual, she thought.

"Everything is just fine," she reassured him, and he brightened up.

It was true up to a point. Harriet's husband had emigrated from the Soviet Union as a small boy and had stayed in touch with relatives back in Moscow. When she arrived, she had telephoned them, but they were too scared to come to her hotel, and eventually they agreed to meet her in a busy public place. It was all very hush-hush and unsettling, and she was glad to see another American face.

Before she could say more, a young Soviet woman came up. "Is this Van Kleeburn?" she asked. She was small, thin, and drably dressed, with short dark hair and thick horn-rimmed glasses that intruded like exclamation marks on a gentle face.

"What?" Van said, smiling at her askance.

"Mr. Van Kleeburn, welcome to Moscow," she said, introducing herself as Henrietta Belayeva, Van's designated interpreter from the Ministry of Culture. She had been told to look for the tallest boy getting off the plane, though not that he was so cute or had such resplendently buoyant hair.

"Ma'am," Van said with an elaborate politeness that seemed perfectly sincere, "wherever may be the hotel where I am staying, can you take me first to the Church of St. Basil?"

The Russian looked at him in surprise. "Oh yes, sure," replied Belayeva. "We can drive you there."

She stared hard at the young American, trying to make him out. He was so open, and he seemed to float rather than walk—as if he hadn't quite landed yet. That was it, she thought; he looked *happy*.

Outside the terminal, a porter loaded Van's three battered suitcases into the trunk of a black government car. The driver introduced himself, also in good English, as Yuri Klimov. He was Van's age, twenty-three, and was his appointed driver for the duration of the competition. He, too, seemed remarkably agreeable.

Everyone piled in, and the automobile pulled away from the curb. A minute later it turned onto a highway that led through gloomy pine forests punctuated by open fields and small hamlets. Soon a dull glow filled the sky ahead, and the road widened into a grand avenue. On either side, rows of Khrushchev's identical boxy apartment buildings were going up, five stories high and bolted together from the same prefabricated concrete sections. Farther on, the new construction yielded to much grander Stalinist blocks adorned with decorative arches, balconies, and overhanging roofs. Like the concentric rings of a tree trunk, Moscow's sprawl marked the succession of its Soviet overlords, each with his own bold blueprint for the future.

The car bounced across a vast open space and toward two immense curved apartment buildings that funneled traffic into the city's heart. From here, more monolithic blocks lined the avenue, interspersed with old single-story mansions, small parks, and the occasional monastery or church. Minutes later they trundled across a great beltway, an asphalt moat inaptly named the Garden Ring, built in anticipation of a time when Muscovites with enough money would not have to wait years for a car. Around it, silhouetted against the snow-bright sky, rose several of the Seven Sisters, imperial highrises that Stalin had commissioned after the Second World War to compete with American skylines. Topped with pinnacles and spires in a riot of Gothic, Renaissance, and Baroque, these atheistic cathedrals were as visionary and ungainly as Soviet Russia itself: built by forced labor using pirated American technology, they were heavily overengineered and housed precious little accommodation for their cost and bulk.

The car jolted across the Moscow River, and moments later Van saw the magnificent square of his childhood dreams. The Kremlin, with its ring of towers and ranks of white-topped firs facing a sea of dark cobbles, was vaster and more stirring than he had imagined. That night, Red Square and St. Basil's Cathedral were festooned with lightbulbs, like strings of stars twinkling against the pale, snowy sky. He had never seen snow like it, not even when he played in North Dakota. It was drifting down now, and as he stepped from the car he had the great stage virtually to himself. Before his eyes a half-century of history dissolved, and the czar of all the Russias came riding through the wooden gate in the Savior's Tower on a white horse. To Van this was not the menacing seat of an adversary bent on world subjugation; it was the most beautiful place he had ever seen.

*　　*　　*

THE PEKING Hotel, where Van was billeted, was a minor relative of Stalin's Seven Sisters. A striking stucco-and-stone confection, it stood at the intersection of the Garden Ring and Triumphal Square, with its new statue of the poet Vladimir Mayakovsky, who committed suicide in disgust at the revolution he had supported. Construction of the hotel had begun as a symbol of Sino-Soviet friendship in 1949, the year of Mao Zedong's victory, but in true Stalin style, there was not a hint of China about it. Two seven-story wings met at a squat corner tower crowned with a columned belvedere that featured a blue baroque clock and allegorical stone figures and supported a smaller structure from which rose a gold spire surmounted by a gold hammer and sickle on a bed of leaves. Above the entrance, Soviet heroes in life-size stone walked confidently into the future: a shot-putter with an intellectual, a teacher and a wrestler, a farmworker and a builder wielding a pneumatic drill. The hotel had finally opened in 1956, shortly after Khrushchev's Secret Speech infuriated Mao, and it now stood as a prominent reminder of the growing rift between the two Communist powers.

Henrietta Belayeva helped Van send a cable home—ARRIVED SAFELY EVERYTHING WONDERFUL—and settled him in. Upstairs, the spacious landings were guarded by a professionally surly *dezhurnaya*, the duty woman who kept hold of room keys when guests were out and kept an eye on them when they were in. Those who came back after she had nodded off could expect a mouthful of abuse. Long hallways with dark wainscoting and doors led to rooms with high ceilings and elaborate moldings. Van's suite had a bedroom, bathroom, and living room with a telephone, television, and shortwave radio. After Henrietta left, he was too jet-lagged and wound up to sleep, and there was a sheaf of competition papers to contemplate. Three large sheets were ready to be filled in with the pieces he would offer in each round. One small booklet with a blue cameo of Tchaikovsky on the cover contained photographs and biographies of all the entrants, and another turned out to be a handy guide for contestants. Following photographs of the conservatory and the hotels—the venerable Metropol, overlooking the Bolshoi Theatre, also housed some competitors—a note advertised that Shostakovich and his deputy chairman, Professor A. B. Goldenweiser, would receive visitors with questions for an hour daily, beginning at 1:00 p.m. There were jury lists, full timetables, and details of the hotel mealtimes, which were generous—dinner from 1:00 to 4:00 p.m., supper from 7:00 p.m. to midnight—to accommodate different performance schedules. Everything seemed to have been thought of. "Should you desire to visit a theatrical performance, concert, museum exhibition or cinema," the booklet concluded, "please apply to your interpreter in good time." Finally, Van pulled a nylon stocking over his head, stretched it tight as a bathing cap to train down his springy curls, and drifted off to sleep.

In the morning, Henrietta came to take him to the conservatory. She was so sweet and charming that he would have found it hard to believe she had to file regular reports on him for the KGB, like every government employee dealing with foreigners. Nor did he suspect for a second that his driver, Yuri, was a trainee diplomat specializing in English who, as was the custom in those times, most likely worked for the KGB. He might have been even more alarmed to know that the Peking was notorious as the KGB's official Moscow hotel. Visiting or newly employed secret agents were regularly quartered there, and an entire wing was reserved for them. The place was crawling with trained eyes, and secret monitoring rooms were said to be hidden throughout, including in the top of the tower and spire. Then again, urban myth also held that the much taller spire of the Hotel Ukraine contained a nuclear launching device. Some of the foreign contestants whispered knowingly about concealed microphones, but it was all part of the game.

It was another bone-chilling day; at the weekend the temperature had plummeted to a low of minus twenty-three Celsius. Along the route small domes and golden spires gleamed dully through snowy branches. An ancient house with turreted chimneys looked as if it had wandered in from a fairy tale. Across the street from the house, three wings of an imposing neoclassical pile enclosed a large courtyard, and seated in front on a granite pillar, caught in a flight of inspiration, was Tchaikovsky. The Moscow State Conservatory named for P. I. Tchaikovsky had been gussied up for the great occasion with long banners and a large cameo of the composer above the main entrance.

"Henya!" a voice called across the snowy courtyard; Henrietta often accompanied visiting musicians and was a familiar face at the conservatory. The voice belonged to a young assistant professor named Sergei Dorensky.

"Seryozha, come and meet my friend," she said. Dorensky was struck by how tall and shy the young man was and, when he came over, by his beautiful manners. Dorensky asked how he could help, and Van replied that he needed to play the piano. The young teacher led them through a door in the building's left wing and up some stairs to the control room, where he asked an official for the best available studio. More stairs led to a hallway lined with pairs of large white double doors. This was the piano empire, and Dorensky ushered them into a room, explaining that it would be Van's for the duration. It had two full-length windows, two grand pianos, and a motley collection of furniture. Van sat down at one of the pianos and gently touched the keys as if he were a child again, overwhelmed by thoughts of the geniuses who had played and taught in this very place.

*   *   *

AT LUNCHTIME Henrietta came up behind and touched him, and he jumped. She pulled him away and took him to the cafeteria, where there were a few familiar faces. Daniel Pollack, whom Van hadn't seen since Rosina's class, had come by train from Vienna, where he was studying on a Fulbright scholarship. He was in a foul mood. Since December he had been practicing ten hours a day, and it was only when he and his young wife, Noemi, arrived in Moscow and were dining with some fellow contestants that he discovered he had prepared the wrong pieces. His Austrian professor, who had read him the required repertoire, had apparently gotten in a muddle, and Pollack had come to Moscow armed with too many modern Soviet pieces and no Tchaikovsky concerto at all. After a sleepless night, he attended Shostakovich's daily surgery, where he explained the situation and offered to withdraw. The composer was terrified of provoking an international incident and called an emergency meeting of the Organizing Committee, which suspected Pollack was making some kind of political statement and shunted the matter to the jury, which had yet to pronounce.

Also unofficially representing Juilliard in the piano competition was the studious Jerome Lowenthal, who was studying on a Fulbright in Paris. The three had not been friends, and amid the tensions of the competition they exchanged little more than pleasantries. There was a third American pianist whom Van knew: twenty-six-year-old Norman Shetler, originally of Dubuque, Iowa, had briefly been part of the same set of young New York pianists that included Jimmy Mathis and John Browning. The son of a self-taught all-round musician and band organizer, Shetler had enrolled in Juilliard, but before he could attend, he was drafted into the army, where he served mostly as a typist. He was also currently a student in Vienna and had become infatuated with Europe; a trip on the wild side paid for by the Soviet government had seemed just the ticket. Besides, ever since he heard a record by Sviatoslav Richter, he had dreamed of studying with him, and he had brought along a gift in the hope of pinning down the elusive virtuoso.

With most of the other foreigners, including several pretty French girls whom everyone noticed, there was a language barrier. But the Soviet contestants were eager to befriend the visitors, and did their best to overcome it. They and Van began pointing at objects and teaching one another the words in their respective languages, cigarettes twirling in their hands. Russian proverbs turned out to be very similar to Texan sayings, and Van began to feel surprisingly at home.

Back in his rehearsal studio there was a knock at the door, and a tall, handsome young man entered. He had curly black hair, fleshy lips, and large brown eyes behind semi-rimless glasses.

"Welcome to Moscow!" he said in English, smiling warmly. "My name is Eduard Miansarov, but call me Eddik." He explained that he was originally from Minsk, in Belarus, but had studied at the conservatory and was also a competitor. They spent two hours playing and singing together until a second Soviet pianist joined them and introduced himself as Naum Shtarkman. A mild, romantic character whose mother worked in the conservatory cloakroom—his Ukrainian Jewish father had died in the war—Shtarkman had made his debut in the Great Hall at twelve and, the previous year, had won first prize in a competition in Lisbon. At thirty he was older than the upper age limit for the Moscow competition and was already an assistant professor, but the organizers had slipped him in as a backup in case Lev Vlassenko self-destructed. Van and his two new Soviet friends were soon inseparable.

That evening there was a commotion outside as the eighty-one-year-old dowager queen of Belgium arrived in a mink coat. A famed patron of the arts who lent her name to the prestigious Brussels piano competition, Elisabeth was known as "the Red Queen" for her penchant for visiting Communist countries. The guest of honor was welcomed by militiamen, students, and women in headscarves as she placed a huge bouquet at the base of Tchaikovsky's statue.

Back at the Peking Hotel a dining room had been set aside for the use of the contestants. Russian restaurants were not for the impatient, and this one was no different: The waiter carefully inscribed the order on his pad and informed the bookkeeper, who made her own entry and issued a slip to be passed to the kitchen. The kitchen staff then made an entry in their book, after which the food could be prepared. When the dish was ready, its appearance was recorded on a slip that was handed to the waiter, who took it to the bookkeeper, who made a new entry confirming that the ordered food had been prepared and then gave another slip to the waiter, which he took back to the kitchen and exchanged for the dish, which he was then permitted to serve, though not before endorsing his notepad to the effect that the item previously entered was now on its way to be eaten. When it arrived, the food was often surprisingly good, though invariably stone cold. Luckily there was caviar. Thorunn Johannsdottir, a statuesque young Icelandic contestant, gave Van her portion every day, and he slurped it happily down. She had already heard the other contestants gossiping about him. "My God, you know he's Texan," they said. Unlike nearly every other competitor, he had never been to Europe before, which made him even odder.

*   *   *

THE NEXT day it was snowing again, and a biting north wind had set in. The news on the street was that Nikita Khrushchev had finally consolidated his grip on the machinery of state. Bulganin, the last remaining June plotter, had been ousted as chairman of the Council of Ministers and demoted to his old job of running the state bank. Like Stalin, Khrushchev was now both first secretary of the Communist Party and premier of the Soviet Union, which gave him virtually dictatorial powers. With his hands on both main levers, he appointed himself commander in chief by creating a Defense Council and installing himself in its chair.

Back at the conservatory, Van ran into the tall, thin figure of Liu Shikun, who took his lessons on the same floor as Van's studio. They recognized each other from the booklet of competitors and shook hands. Van showed him his room, and they played for each other, Liu starting with Chopin's Polonaise in A-flat Major, op. 53. He had a big sound, played with attack on a large scale, and was brilliantly fast and precise. Van applauded, and hugged him, gesturing that Liu's technique was much better than his own. Then Van played Liszt's *Liebestraum*, and Liu applauded, too, thinking that Van was strangely innocent for someone four years older, like a big cute kid.

With some practice behind him Van had a little time to look around. In the conservatory's main entrance hall, modeled after the Parthenon, with cloakrooms to either side of the columns, there was an exhibition on Tchaikovsky, a showcase of handcrafted Soviet violins, and kiosks selling sheet music, books, and special editions. The violin competition was now coming to an end, and Van slipped in one night to listen. Of the eight finalists, six were Soviets, one was Romanian, and one, Juilliard's Joyce Flissler, was American. After the last performance, on Saturday March 29, word spread that the winner was Valery Klimov, a regular soloist with the Moscow Philharmonic, who was originally from Kiev; Flissler came in seventh. Klimov's teacher was the great David Oistrakh, who was chairman of the violin jury, which also included violinist Efrem Zimbalist, who was Russian Jewish by birth but had moved to the United States before the Bolsheviks came to power. A Soviet composer spread rumors that Zimbalist strongly disagreed with the jury's decision and had refused to sign the protocol and diplomas. He also claimed that Zimbalist had sent a telegram to the distinguished French pianist Marguerite Long warning her not to come to Moscow to serve on the piano jury. Controversy and scandal ensued.

Overnight the temperature dropped to minus seventeen Celsius.

At 9:30 a.m. on Sunday, the piano competition commenced with a meeting of the jury and contestants. There was some confusion about the number of entrants—for the good reason that the organizers wanted to deflect attention from the true figures. Twenty-five violinists had taken part instead of the anticipated twenty-nine, and of the fifty expected pianists, only thirty-six were present. The absentees included three Americans: Denver Oldham, a Juilliard graduate who was studying in London; Gladys Stein, who had studied at Columbia and was now in Vienna; and Trudi Martin, who had studied at UCLA. It was not clear whether they had been deterred by the required repertoire, the cost of travel, or the reputation of Red Moscow. Besides the four Americans who had made it, the contestants came from Argentina, Bulgaria, Canada, China, Czechoslovakia, Ecuador, France, Hungary, Israel, Japan, Mexico, Poland, Portugal, Romania, the USSR, and West Germany. Six were excused from the first round because they had won first prizes in international competitions, among them Lev Vlassenko, Naum Shtarkman, and, strangely, Danny Pollack and Jerry Lowenthal, who did not meet the criteria but who were perhaps given a pass on the supposition that the Fulbright was evidence of superior attainment. Since the Soviets did not recognize the Leventritt Award, Van was required to play. The thirty contestants drew lots, skipping number thirteen, and Van drew number fifteen.

As for the judges, they comprised perhaps the most formidable piano jury ever assembled. Alongside the sturdy Gilels and the lugubrious Richter was their teacher, Heinrich Neuhaus; and Vladimir Ashkenazy's teacher, Lev Oborin. The Russian Dmitri Kabalevsky and the Englishman Sir Arthur Bliss represented composers, and the other judges came from Austria, Belgium, Brazil, Bulgaria, Czechoslovakia, France, Hungary, Italy, Poland, Romania, and the USSR. All told, there were twelve judges from the Soviet Bloc and five from elsewhere, the latter carefully chosen from different countries and schools of playing to prevent them from forming a cabal.

By now the authorities had decided that Danny Pollack should stay in the competition, playing the pieces he had prepared, with the stipulation that if he reached the finals, he would be obliged to play a Tchaikovsky concerto. He spent the five days excluded from the first round learning one, though he was more remarked upon among the other contestants for constantly French-kissing his new bride in the conservatory hallways.

Van's turn did not come until the morning of Wednesday, April 2, which gave him more precious days to practice. Amid the novelty and excitement, he remembered to take himself to the International Post Office and Telephone Exchange in the Artists' Foyer upstairs in the main building and send a telegram to Rosina Lhévinne, who was playing a concert at Juilliard that night:

LOVE AND THOUGHTS WITH YOU TONIGHT FIRST PRELIMINARY APRIL 2 MORNING HAPPY BIRTHDAY INDESCRIBABLE JOY EXCITEMENT

Public interest was so intense that the preliminary rounds had been moved from the conservatory's small hall to the Bolshoi Zal, the Great Hall whose roof rose high above the main buildings. The evening before Van was due to play, he was given a midnight slot to try out its piano. As he climbed the wide, deep staircase, Rachmaninoff's big E-flat Minor "Étude-Tableau," op. 33, drifted out of the hall like the voice of Russia itself. He listened as if he were hearing it for the first time. At the top he crossed the broad foyer with its heavy rugs and peered into a dark anteroom. The glow from a pin light spilled over a bust of Mussorgsky. Through the open door he could see the stage; at the piano was Nadia Gedda-Nova, a French pianist of Russian parentage who cut a glamorous figure with her upswept curls. A great proscenium arch framed her, and behind, in front of a huge pipe organ, was a blown-up photograph of Tchaikovsky garlanded with flowers. Under the high clerestory windows, roundels of Russian and Western composers dignified the walls, and apricot velvet drapes and seats, elaborate plasterwork, and brass light fittings in the form of two trumpets and a lyre completed the fairy-tale scene.

Outside the door Van sat down, got up, and paced back and forth, thinking of the greats whose music these walls contained: Tchaikovsky and Rubinstein, Rachmaninoff and Scriabin, Josef and Rosina Lhévinne. The beauty in his mind was not just a dream now: it was all around. An intoxicating rush of bliss swept through him, and his last nerves dissolved away. Here he was, a twenty-three-year-old American, having the time of his life in Moscow at the height of the Cold War.

Back at the hotel he placed a call to Kilgore. The local operator connected him to the long-distance operator, who flatly stated that it was impossible to patch him through to the United States for at least another day. Foreigners quickly learned that there was a trick to this, as to everything else in the Soviet Union. If the caller was a man and the operator a woman, a few minutes of outrageous flirting dramatically reduced the wait to an hour. The phone duly rang, and the operators handed along the call from Moscow to London to the exchange in White Plains, New York, which rang through to the Cliburns. Van told his parents when he would be playing and asked them to pray for him. They prayed for him to do God's will and for the strength to cope with success or failure. Afterward, Harvey called the local Baptist, Methodist, and Presbyterian ministers, and soon they were asking the whole town to pray, too.

*   *   *

AT AN ungodly hour on Wednesday morning, Van buttoned his sole dress shirt and attached a wing collar lent him by a friend. He tied his white tie, pulled a ratty gray Shetland sweater over his head, and shrugged on his dress jacket.

Outside, the daytime temperature had finally crept above freezing, but a brisk east wind was blowing. Ducking inside the conservatory, he headed straight for the Artists' Foyer, and at 9:30 a.m. he walked onstage.

He was all arms and had a slight swinging gait. The nylon stocking treatment had done nothing to tamp his mop of curls. His head looked too small for his body, and the expression on his round, boyish face was disarmingly bashful. Smiles broke out among the assembled conservatory students, officials, and ordinary Muscovites.

Van sat down quietly at the piano. He tried not to look at the jurors, who were seated in front of the stage behind a row of green baize tables. But Rildia Bee had taught him to pay attention to the number and placing of the audience and the length and ambient noise of the room, and to his surprise, he saw that both levels of the hall were almost full.

He slid his long fingers onto the keys, straightened himself, and froze in position. The audience tensed with him: suddenly the boy was an artist, focusing his body and mind on his instrument. He started with Bach and the suffering tones of the Prelude and Fugue in B-flat Minor from Book I of *The Well-Tempered Clavier*, which he had learned as a child. The stern, spare sound tolled somberly through the hall. After a round of applause, he followed with the Mozart C Major Sonata, K. 330.

Mozart makes a pianist naked. There are few notes and no places to hide. The music either has meaning or is just a collection of sounds. Some pianists can play it as children; some never can. Most Russians, Richter included, found its pregnant simplicities temperamentally uncongenial. Van played unconventional Mozart. His tempos were slow, and his tone burnished; his phrasing broad and sculpted, weighing every note. Norman Shetler, who had played on the first day and was watching now, sensed an almost electrical connection between the audience and this young American. A mesmerized Sergei Dorensky thought Van seemed to be talking to the hall and each person in it. When the last short chord came emphatically down, they paused, and then burst out in a tumult of applause. Van stood up to take a bow, revealing his mangy gray sweater, then sat down and waited for the commotion to die away. To his surprise it carried on, and he had to stand up at the piano three more times. The tension broken, now he dared to sneak a look at the jury.

Next he played four études, by Chopin, Scriabin, Liszt, and Rachmaninoff—the last the piece he had heard swirling at midnight from the hall—which brought more concentrated bursts of applause. No one seemed to care that he fumbled a few times in Liszt's gallopingly difficult "Mazeppa."

The final piece was compulsory: Tchaikovsky's Theme and Variations in F Major, op. 19, which the audience knew and loved. You could hear the young American's love, too, and see it. Rocking from the waist into an expansive theme, he arched back from the keys and rolled his head to the ceiling, shaking it slowly as if in wonder, his eyes half-closed in pained ecstasy. Hunched down for an intricate passage, he frowned at his fingers as they flew across the keys. Sending stormy chords crashing around, he tensed and flexed as if he were about to spring off his stool. His playing was ecstatically lyrical, thrillingly Romantic, and symphonic in scale—and tears glistened in many eyes. In the Marxist-Leninist worldview, Americans were boorish materialists exploited by rapacious Wall Street monopolists and were doomed to be crushed by the engine of history. Next to that diablerie, Van Cliburn looked like an angel, a vulnerable, six-foot-four, mop-haired angel in a plastic wing collar and stringy bow tie. When the last chord stopped echoing, the hall took a collective deep breath and then thundered its approval. The clamor was unabated after Van left the stage, and amid it, two words were heard more and more:

"Vanya! Vanyusha!"

The first was a diminutive of Ivan, the second a diminutive of the diminutive, the kind of pet name a mother might whisper to her child.

Also in the audience was Ella Vlassenko, Iron Lev's wife. She liked Van's playing but thought some of it was exaggerated. Still, she couldn't help seeing that most people were beside themselves—very happy, she thought, that a pianist who wasn't one of their own was playing well. She began to worry for her husband.

*   *   *

THE JURY had been given a huge room for its deliberations, with a big table in the center. As the jurors filed in they disposed themselves round it—all except Sviatoslav Richter, who dragged his brooding form to a piano in the far corner. With his chiseled chin, thinning hair brushed forward, and almost comically morose expression, at forty-three Richter cut a striking figure. It was the first time he had been roped into a jury, and he was even less inclined than usual to be complaisant.

The unenviable task of managing Richter fell to his fellow Odessan Emil Gilels, who was far from a detached observer. The younger man by nearly two years, the prickly Gilels resented Richter's first rank and often sulked around him. Worse still was the obvious collusion between Richter and their teacher, Heinrich Neuhaus. Now a few days shy of his seventieth birthday, Neuhaus was like a father to Richter; as a young man, Richter had often slept under the piano in Neuhaus's tiny living room, and the two instinctively understood each other. Both were of German extraction and had been suspected of spying during the war; Neuhaus was carted off to the Lubyanka and almost certain death, but his students dangerously appealed to Stalin, and instead he was sent into exile. Gilels was convinced that Neuhaus preferred Richter's playing to his and had deliberately set Richter up in opposition to him, a suspicion that assumed such paranoid proportions that Gilels wrote to Neuhaus and the newspapers denying he had ever been his student. To Gilels, their joint presence was a torment, which only grew worse when the pair turned up late several times during the competition, completely missing one morning session. Nor were these the only tensions in the room. Neuhaus was no admirer of the composer Dmitri Kabalevsky, whom he termed the "poor man's Prokofiev." Richter, outdoing him, called Kabalevsky "deeply unpleasant" and declared that it had never occurred to him to play his "threadbare music." Kabalevsky had been quick to turn his back on Shostakovich when he was denounced at the Union of Soviet Composers, with which he was heavily involved. Just now he and its first secretary, Tikhon Khrennikov, an unreconstructed Stalinist who was also on the organizing committee of the competition, had ganged up on the composer Nikita Bogoslovsky for the crime of inviting a diplomat to a comedy soiree at the Central House of

Art Workers without proper authorization, and despite extracting a groveling letter, they had expelled him from the Composers' Union.

Immediately the judges began to argue, and the main subject was Van Cliburn. His Mozart was deeply unorthodox, and while some judges found his clear, pure lyricism charmingly generous, others dismissed it as tasteless and naive. Lev Oborin, inscrutable and composed, wanted to know why the young American swayed about the whole time and kept gazing toward the ceiling. "I don't like this," he frowned. "Lyova, you don't get it," retorted Alexander Goldenweiser, at eighty-three the leonine dean of Russian pianists: "He looks up because he is speaking with God."

Richter stood restlessly by the piano, wearing a pained expression. When the others passed their slips across the table, he handed his down the room. He was convinced that Van had played miles better than the others and gave him the full twenty-five points, as did another Soviet judge and a Bulgarian. Gilels and two others gave Van twenty-four. The lowest marks came from the Frenchman Armand de Gontaut Biron and the Portuguese pianist José Carlos de Sequeira Costa, at twenty-eight, much the youngest judge; both gave Van eighteen. Liu Shikun was close behind, with marks ranging from twenty-four to eighteen, and running a close third was Toyoaki Matsuura of Japan, whose imperturbably aristocratic demeanor belied a fiery temperament and a frenetic, impulsive style that departed by some distance from composers' intentions but delighted the audience. Richter gave many of the others scores as low as seven.

Van had to wait two days before the results were announced, at 10:00 p.m. Friday in the conservatory's White Hall. Twenty competitors went forward. Norman Shetler was not among them; he did get to meet his hero Richter and present the gift he had brought for him, the Dietrich Fischer-Dieskau recording of the Schumann *Dichterliebe*, but discovered that Richter never took students. Nor was Liu Shikun's countrywoman Gu Shengying. The Australian who had bragged about his Stradivarius was sent packing. So were two pianists who appeared to have arrived at the Tchaikovsky Competition by accident and had given performances varying from bizarre to ridiculous. One, from South America, played all his pieces nonstop with no pauses in between—whether out of nerves or ignorance of the conventions, no one could say.

To grumbles from the tired jurors, the second round began at nine thirty sharp the following morning. In the afternoon it was Liu Shikun's turn, and a packed audience admiringly applauded the nineteen-year-old sensation. Van's slot was not until Monday, three days later. That meant more time to practice, now with his Russian admirers crowding in to the last note. Naum Shtarkman gazed at Van with puppy eyes; he had fallen madly in love and admitted as much to Norman Shetler, who was also around Van a lot, now that he had time on his hands.

With the fuss surrounding the competition mounting daily, even the losers were treated like rock stars. The one sticky moment, when an interpreter lost her temper with her charge and railed against the misconceptions "you Westerners" had about Soviet people, stood out for its rarity. That Saturday, the Central House of Literary Workers hosted a friendly get-together with Soviet writers; Joyce Flissler attended, looking American with her heavy lipstick and eyeliner. There was also a visit to the nearby town of Babushkin, where contestants toured the Soviet Institute of Transport Construction and were welcomed by the director and locals with baskets of flowers and presents. Sunday there were no heats, and excursions to theaters and concert halls were laid on for everyone. Most popular was an outing to Tchaikovsky's house at Klin, two hours' drive from Moscow through forests of white birch, followed by a reception organized by the Ministry of Culture and the Executive Committee of the Klin Town Council of Working People's Deputies. Alternatives included heavily chaperoned meetings with students from Moscow universities and a soiree organized by the All-Russia Theatrical Society, during which laureates of the violin competition played in front of projected clips from Charlie Chaplin movies. Since it was Easter Sunday back home, Van attended a Russian Orthodox service, its ancient liturgy and ceremony a world apart from the relaxed Baptists with their shirtsleeved ministers. He prayed for peace of mind and the strength to continue, whatever was meant for him.

At the conservatory a bespectacled young man with thinning hair introduced himself: "Hello, I'm Slava Rostropovich." Van was taken aback by the young man's simplicity; ever since he was a boy, he had read about the great cellist to whom Prokofiev and Shostakovich dedicated their works. "In the next three days before the next stage," Rostropovich said, "maybe you'd like to have dinner with us. Let me invite you to my place and introduce you to my wife." To Van's shock and delight, she turned out to be the great soprano Galina Vishnevskaya. The three talked about opera and piano, which Rostropovich also played. Van told them about his mother and her studies with Arthur Friedheim. Rostropovich reminded Van of Chopin's saying that a piano is not ten fingers but ten beautiful voices. They had so many interests and views in common that Van felt like a younger relative visiting his family; he said so to his hosts, and they decided to adopt him.

The competition press officers hovered around, interviewing the contestants and asking their views on the Soviet Union. Van diplomatically stuck to music. "I have walked where Tchaikovsky, Rachmaninoff, Scriabin and other great musicians have walked," he dictated. "I am touched by the cordial reception that was given to me. It is a great pleasure to play for the Russians who are such fine lovers of music. The friendliness of the audience inspired me, and one felt as if one was playing better than usual. This is my first trip outside the United States, and I am very happy to be in the homeland of wonderful Russian composers for whose work I have great respect."

Everywhere he went, people recognized him. Bolder Muscovites began gathering outside his hotel; others came up to him in the street and seemed excited to talk to him. The whole city was talking about the tall, handsome young Texan with the charming manners and the romantic style of playing. Across the nation, millions tuned in to a daily radio program called *Diary of the Competition* and followed

Van's story, weighing up his chances against those of his chief rivals. News of a brilliant American pupil of the legendary Rosina Lhévinne reached the ears of Vladimir Ashkenazy, who decided to go listen for himself. He was lucky to have the chance. "No tickets left," the box office *prodavshchitsa* told callers asking for tickets to the Monday sessions. "Kleeburn is playing." It was a delightful surprise that an American could so enchant Russian ears. Still, no one really thought he could win.

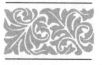

· 8 ·

"Vanya, Vanyusha!"

MOSCOW WAS a moody city, full of character, mysterious and exotic. Built atop the fissure between two worlds, the seat of a vast multi-ethnic empire, it had grown up piecemeal, with buildings of different eras and ranks jumbled together. Abandoned for two centuries as the czarist capital, it had triumphantly reemerged as the command center of international communism. Stalin had plowed under narrow medieval streets to create avenues wide enough to land a plane, surpassing invaders and fire in sweeping aside the past. His magnificently pompous high-rises, testaments to the aspirations of Soviet communism even as they mocked its egalitarianism, were towering proof of a new imperium. Yet a more colorful Moscow still peeked out between the monumental grayness: pastel mansions and gingerbread cottages, domes and bell towers, elegant boulevards and unexpected islands of greenery.

As with its architecture, so the city's life was an odd blend of old and new. Gaunt men silently skated through the halls of public buildings, waxing the floors with bristle brushes strapped to their bare feet. In the hotel laundry room, the man who pressed the clothes dampened them with a squirt of water from his mouth. Outside, a platoon of old ladies raked the square with bundles of twigs tied to broom handles. Policemen twirled batons at major intersections to direct trickles of traffic, mainly flatbed trucks and Victory taxis resembling cut-down versions of 1939 Chevrolets. The sidewalks were crowded and clean, beggars almost nonexistent. Vendors walked round in the freezing cold with trays of ice-cream cones, but on Red Square hundreds lined up at GUM, the State Department Store, to buy eggs. Nearby, like a sick secret policeman's joke, a vast branch of the department store Children's World had risen in the baleful shadow of the Lubyanka prison. A marble-lined cavern of toys intended to deliver on Khrushchev's promise of increased consumer choice, the store was permanently encircled by parents waiting in line for scarce children's clothes.

That week, the official newspapers were full of the progress of the Red Queen. Elisabeth of the Belgians traveled in a cortege like a czarina as she visited the Kremlin, the Metro, the "Red October" confectionary factory, Lenin's mausoleum and his museum in Gorki, and the Bolshoi and its ballet school. Cameramen filmed her every step, and the contestants were briefly left alone to explore the city, supervised of course. Van dipped his head into the impossibly grand Metro at Mayakovskaya station, with its Art Deco columns and ceiling mosaics. He went to art galleries and took walks along the Moscow River with his interpreter, Henrietta, and his new Soviet friends. Everyone seemed to have a tragic story. Eddik Miansarov, the handsome young pianist who had knocked on Van's door, had followed his childhood sweetheart, Tamara, to the conservatory and married her, but because of the accommodation shortage, they had been forced to stay in their bunks at the student hostel, he on the second floor, she on the fourth. Tamara soon realized that Eddik was more wedded to his music than to her: "If you have a baby, I'm gone!" he threatened not long after the wedding. Shortly afterward, his roommate shot himself, and as the scandal spread across Moscow, it was revealed that he and Eddik had been experimenting with creativity-enhancing drugs. Eddik begged the now-pregnant Tamara to persuade the rector not to expel him, and instead he was sent off to a clinic. The marriage did not last.

The companionship was welcome, because politics had finally caught up with Van. After talking to his fellow foreign contestants, he had become convinced that a Westerner could not win the competition. His nose had started to bleed again, he was too anxious to sleep, and once again he had been given the first morning slot. He asked for some sleeping pills, and whatever was in them knocked him out flat. He woke up mercifully refreshed, plastered down his curls with hair cream, and headed back to the hall for the second round.

*   *   *

OVERNIGHT THE temperature had stayed above freezing for the first time that winter. The first thaw was turning the snow to *slyakot*, the famous black sludge that made sidewalks an obstacle course and slowly laid bare all manner of things buried during the winter. Inside the hall every seat was taken, and an expectant hush settled before Van emerged. Playing in the first round had turned out to be an advantage: as well as allowing him to show off his range, it had given him a head start with the public.

He had an hour to play his way into the finals, and though he gave no sign of it as he sat down, afterward he told everyone that he thought his heart might stop. He steadied himself and began with the technically tricky Prelude and Fugue in G-sharp Minor by Sergei Taneyev. The piece had been recommended by the New York Philharmonic's music director, Dimitri Mitropoulos, and was well chosen: Taneyev had been the first winner of the conservatory's Great Gold Medal and later its director. Van pulled the piece off and then played another obligatory work of Tchaikovsky's, the first movement of his Sonata in G Major—not very securely, he thought. It was all becoming a blur when Chopin's Fantaisie in F Minor brought the audience to its feet.

The next piece was his old favorite, Liszt's Twelfth Hungarian Rhapsody. To the audience it was almost unrecognizable in the American's hands. Its folk themes came free and poetic as songs, sending up vivid images of rural villages and revealing unexpected depths: now reserved and stern, now dramatic and impulsive, now dashing and inflamed, as if he had somehow penetrated the essence of Hungary and was unfurling its national epic. His fingers stirred feelings latent in Russian breasts during the strict Soviet decades; memories of the golden age of Russian piano playing with its sweep and its passions, its rich gorgeousness and its forceful personality. Last, he played the fugue finale of Samuel Barber's virtuosic Piano Sonata, which highlighted something else: though his rhythms were rock solid, he had an uncanny way of making a phrase seem improvised. The applause lasted for nearly a quarter of an hour, and by the end, even members of the jury were applauding.

Yet the big beasts who had won first prizes were still to come. Eddik Miansarov played straight after Van and was inspired by his estranged wife's presence in the audience. Naum Shtarkman's turn came the next day. Van listened to him play Schumann and Prokofiev and discovered a soft, Romantic pianist in the Chopin mold, with a pearlescent technique. He told the press officers that he fervently wished Naum could play one day in America.

Finally, on Tuesday evening, it was Lev Vlassenko's turn. For once Lev took a taxi to the conservatory, and no sooner had he given the address than the driver began talking about the competition. "Well, how's that long one getting on?" he asked, referring to Van. In the Great Hall, Vlassenko's teacher, Jacob Flier, hid behind the organ, furiously smoking, though he had just given it up, nervous that his best student might implode. Sometimes he could tell from the way Lev came onstage and walked to the piano that something was wrong.

The favorite stepped out, pale in his dinner jacket and forcing a smile as he turned to the audience, making Flier's heart jump. Yet the weeks of seclusion and the months of obsessive concentration had paid off. Vlassenko's playing was brilliant and flawless, the epitome of the fearsomely virtuosic Soviet pianist. Not for nothing did one Western musician despair that behind the Iron Curtain "they had nothing but golden monsters with twenty-four fingers."

Ella was there to cheer him on. She was pleased, but she had also watched Van a second time, and now she had a new cause for concern. Outrageous gossip had reached her ears about Lev's background. His family had long concealed their roots in the nobility and czarist military, hiding papers, portraits, and medals in their cellar back in Georgia. But that was not at issue. "Is it true that Lev Vlassenko is Khrushchev's nephew?" Ella was asked, to her astonishment, and suddenly she realized the suggestion of nepotism was a thinly veiled threat. Rumors were rife that the competition was a stitch-up; the word was that a poster had already been printed announcing government protégé Lev Vlassenko as winner of the first prize.

*　　*　　*

MARK SCHUBART had now arrived in Moscow, his State Department expense forms at the ready, pretending, as instructed, that he was present in a private capacity. On his first evening, he attended a reception given by Richard Davis, counselor at the American embassy, and found Van the center of attention. Schubart asked some musicians what had happened, and they told him that "Vanya" was the toast of Moscow. Schubart immediately set out to track down Max Frankel, the young Moscow correspondent of the *New York Times*, to tip him off.

"Is this kid really so phenomenal, or is this just another case of Frank Sinatra bobby soxers?" the owlish Frankel skeptically asked, his serious glasses and steady expression belying his twenty-seven years.

"No, he's a hell of a musician," Schubart assured him. "He's well in line to win this thing, if the Russians ever let him."

Frankel scented a scoop and wangled himself a pass for the finals. American ambassador Llewellyn Thompson also decided to attend. A diplomat from a modest Colorado Baptist background who was universally known as "Tommy," Thompson had fully intended to stay away. With the sense of inevitability that infected all Western diplomats in Moscow, even one just a year into his post, the soft-spoken Thompson had explained that he was "tired of coming in second or third against the Russians."

The next day, Schubart took himself to the conservatory and caught some of the last semifinalists, including Danny Pollack, who had chosen the same Barber concerto as Van and played it with scrupulous finesse. Afterward the competition press people got hold of the Juilliard dean, who made a big play of Rosina Lhévinne's renown as the school's leading teacher. By the time he was through it was almost midnight, and he was trying to leave when Van emerged from his studio. "Come on, you've got to hear me," he said, and dragged Schubart in to listen to Kabalevsky's "Rondo," the piece written specially for the finals. Van played it through, and then played it another three times. "He would have played all night," Schubart said, "if I'd let him."

The last semifinalist performed Wednesday evening, and for a second time the judges retired to their room. Some were patently nervous. The young Sequeira Costa had quickly gathered that Lev Vlassenko was the "chosen one." It was far from clear what would happen if an American won instead. Many of the judges were guests in the country, and Khrushchev was as unpredictable as a wounded bull. As for the Soviet judges, they could only guess what kind of retribution the Union of Soviet Composers might dream up if they denied their compatriot first prize.

Sviatoslav Richter could not have cared less. He was convinced that most of the other judges were either idiots or craven stooges in thrall to the state. To his mind, there were only three real pianists in the competition, with Cliburn clearly first. Again he sent over his marks from the piano. Sequeira Costa watched Gilels's face as he went through the sheets, stopped at Richter's, and looked up at him.

"Why do you do this?" he asked. "Because this is not good for the general marks."

"For me," Richter answered, "people either make music or not music."

Kabalevsky chimed in, accusing Richter of the crime of "individualism," and other members of the jury protested, too. Richter drew a conclusion: "It was the first international competition to be held in Moscow, and it was vital that it should be won by a Soviet pianist."

The story was later put about, in part by Richter himself, that he had given all but his three favored competitors zero points. This evolved into a legend that he had awarded Van twenty-five points (or one hundred, in wilder versions) and all the others zero in order to leave only Van standing. In fact, Richter gave Van twenty-five points, Lev Vlassenko twenty-four, and Liu Shikun twenty-three, but he also gave four contestants (Nadia Gedda-Nova of France, Milena Mollova of Bulgaria, Naum Shtarkman, and Daniel Pollack) fifteen points each. All the others, including Eddik Miansarov and Jerome Lowenthal, got zero. The converse theory later spread that there was nothing to the gossip and that Richter had not given any zeros at all. Someone certainly wanted people to believe that: Richter wrote his marks in purple ink, but the zeros were later crossed out and carefully changed in blue ink to threes. Maybe Gilels, who used the same blue ink, doctored the sheets, worried that his handling of the jury would be criticized. Possibly a faceless bureaucrat did it. Or perhaps it was Richter himself, responding in a typically insolent way to a scolding from Gilels or another official; after all, to give thirteen competitors three points each was no less dismissive than giving them zero.

When the marks were tallied, Lev Vlassenko was in the lead, with 411 points. Second was Liu Shikun, with 404. With 393, Van was tied for third place with Naum Shtarkman. Danny Pollack was fifth, with 345. The result was a relief for the more nervous jurors, who hoped that an awkward and potentially dangerous conflict with the authorities would be headed off. Still, several excellent Soviet pianists had been eliminated, and after more discussion the jury decided to address the Ministry of Culture, asking permission to add an extra prize. The request was granted, and to fit in Eddik Miansarov, the field of finalists expanded from eight to nine. Late at night the contestants were finally called together and the names were read out:

From the Soviet Union, Lev Vlassenko, Naum Shtarkman, and
    Eduard Miansarov.
From America, Van Cliburn and Daniel Pollack.
From China, Liu Shikun.
From Bulgaria, Milena Mollova.

From France, Nadia Gedda-Nova.

From Japan, Toyoaki Matsuura.

*   *   *

YET THERE was also the public to worry about. Vanya-mania, a mostly female phenomenon, was seizing Moscow with indecent haste. It had little in common with the Tarzan cult or the previous summer's wild alfresco couplings. Van brought a different ideal of a man and attracted a different type of admirer: the nice Soviet girl. Well-behaved young Soviet women were not supposed to smoke or drink, frequent nightclubs, wear lipstick, or paint their nails. They studied hard, spoke seriously, dressed conservatively, were strongly patriotic, and thought the West was deeply decadent. Still, it was impossible to see Van, with his curly blond hair and beautiful long fingers, as the enemy. He was kind, and sensitive, and charming, and modest, and very tall, and a bit of a mama's boy. He disliked rock and roll and espoused Russian virtues such as sentiment and nostalgia. The more they heard about him, the more they found him "just like us." Girls bearing flowers began pursuing him for autographs. They carefully cut out his photograph from the papers and slept with it under their pillows. Suddenly they had a Westerner they could safely adore. Their mothers could hardly complain, since they, too, had fallen in love with the sweet, vulnerable American. Jerry Lowenthal, who had time on his hands after failing to make the finals—perhaps because his more intellectual style was swept away in the Cliburn wave—had trouble containing his cynicism when women approached him wanting to talk about Van. "He reminds me of my son," the older ones said with sighs, while their daughters wanted to know if Van was married. Tarzan haircuts were for the chop: suddenly a bushy, curly coiffure was the rage for men and women alike.

The competition continued without pause, and the finals began Thursday evening. This time every moment was to be beamed to television sets across the USSR.

Van's turn came Friday at 7:00 p.m. That morning, he had rehearsed with the renowned Moscow State Symphony, and now he was sitting in the Peking Hotel dining room in full concert dress, staring like a condemned man at the meal spread in front of him. He decided he wasn't hungry and instead downed in one gulp his preperformance booster of three raw eggs cracked into a glass, yolks intact. A journalist named Paul Moor snapped him in the act. Ten years older than Van, Moor had been around since the start of the competition, which he was covering for *Life* and *Time*. He came from El Paso, Texas, had briefly studied at Juilliard, and had been involved with the composer Aaron Copland. Van's cousin Mrs. Lillian Reid was his old algebra teacher, and when it turned out that Moor, too, had been taught piano by a pupil of Arthur Friedheim, Van must have wondered if there was anyone in the world he could trust more. When it was time, they headed to the conservatory together.

A picture of pandemonium met their eyes. For three nights, students had camped outside the box office, hoping for a spare seat. Favors had been called in to procure tickets reserved for officials, but even those with high connections had been turned away. Thousands had come to try their luck or witness the event, and they had jammed the courtyard and narrow streets, bringing pedestrian traffic to a standstill. The police were struggling to keep order as ticketless fans tried to rush the line or slip quietly behind it. Those who were caught were roughly dealt with, and as the chaos worsened, KGB guards materialized to keep order. This was not just a musical event; it was a national festival that had taken on the fervency of a mass demonstration.

In his dressing room, Van downed an assortment of vitamin pills and applied drops to his nose. He sat up straight and put his hands on his knees. His right index finger was bandaged after a cut had opened into a full-length split from too much practicing. He closed his eyes, inhaled in four gulps through his nose until his chest filled out, and exhaled in four bursts. Then he prayed.

Max Frankel jostled through the crowds, headed up the great staircase, and found his seat near the flower-bedecked stage. Looking around, the journalist saw many familiar faces. Virtually the entire Soviet *nomenklatura* seemed to be there with its wives, instantly recognizable by their government-store garb copied from the pages of Western fashion magazines. At stage right, the dowager queen Elisabeth sat in the government box alongside Khrushchev's daughter. Besides the seventeen hundred seated ticket holders, scores stood shoulder to shoulder down the aisles and lined the backs of the balconies. Harriet Wingreen was waiting to watch her fellow Juilliard alum, and Norman Shetler was in the front row. Paul Moor was ready with his camera, and Ambassador Thompson was in place with his wife, Jane.

Onstage the orchestra tuned up. The jurors took their seats at the front. Richter was especially restless; perhaps he was still thinking about the poor French girl who had made such a mess of her concerto the previous night that he had felt physically ill.

Van entered, and the roar seemed to swell the walls. The audience stamped their feet and yelled the now-familiar "Vanya! Vanyusha!" With a sheepish glance of gratitude, Van picked his way between the violas and cellos to the piano. Culture Minister Nikolai Mikhailov, seeing him for the first time, was surprised by both his height and his demeanor: the American was, he thought, "a shy boy, somewhat angular, with a naïve, childishly touching expression on his face; precisely a boy, not a young man."

The conductor rapped his baton ineffectively. With gentle hazel eyes set in a sensitive face and eloquent hands that clearly expressed his emotions, Kirill Kondrashin was a man of simple origins who was evangelical about bringing great art to the people. At the morning rehearsal he had bonded in a fatherly way with the young American, while Van had felt miraculously in tune with Kondrashin, as if he were born to play with a Russian conductor.

Van nodded, Kondrashin raised his stick, and the hall went quiet to hear what the Texas wonder boy would do with their Tchaikovsky First.

*   *   *

HE LEANED back, eyes half shut, lips pursed to sing, and played to himself the scenes set in the Moscow of his imagination. As he plunged his hands fearlessly into the crashing opening octets, the sound ringing out full and rich as a Russian bell, he was transported back centuries to the old Kremlin, with its Byzantine intrigue and pomp. The czar and czarina entered, followed by their boyars, and took their seats. With the dashing barbarity of the first theme, a grand ballet began. As the melodies weaved together, the mood was bitter-sweet, like *Anna Karenina.* The architecture was lucid, the rhythm propulsive, the tone massive but mellifluous, the nuances and shades of sound infinite. There was no affectation; like an actor breathing unsuspected color into a writer's words, Van felt every movement of the music, bringing out each detail in dazzlingly sharp colors and blending it into the mounting emotional drama.

The ballet ended, and he was in the second movement, telling the simple story of a peasant women with her baby, his hands tenderly rising and staying suspended for long moments, seemingly weight-less. In the middle, at the prestissimo section, he sketched a dream sequence, a fleeting memory of bygone youth. Then a hullabaloo: the baby has woken up. Van's hands flew abruptly from one side to another, as if he were pushing away heaps of sounds that threatened to engulf him, but his face was a picture of absolute ease.

Now the last movement was reeling from his fingers: a drunken Russian folk dance, punctuated with explosive hiccups. Here, of all places, where Tchaikovsky had first played his concerto to a horrified Nikolai Rubinstein, Van could feel the sadness-in-happiness of the Russian heart. The tempo was unhurried, the tone lullingly song-like. Imperceptibly the drama intensified, until the gathering energy broke like a thunderstorm that fused together the flashes of scenes and images in one great curtain of sound, a triumphant, exulting cli-max of freedom and happiness and the glory of life.

A final furious dash up and down the keys, and applause thun-dered through the hall. Van bowed, repeatedly. Kondrashin bowed.

The orchestra stood up and bowed. The conductor left the stage, and when the buzz finally died down, Van played the tricky "Rondo" by Kabalevsky, who was sitting directly in front of him at the jury table. This time the audience jumped to its feet. The regulations required Van to remain seated and wait for Kondrashin to come back out for the second concerto, an arrangement that would never have stood under professional conditions. Yet, to Van's embarrassment, he had broken a piano string during the "Rondo," which his fans took as further proof of his terrific emotional intensity. He was given a five-minute break while the technician attended to the piano, allowing him to get a glass of water and the audience to murmur with bated breath.

When Kondrashin finally came out, the hall had reached an almost unbearable pitch of emotional tension. Only Van was serene. He felt that God's blessing had descended on him, and he sat down to play as he had never played in his life.

Gently he picked out the first muted notes of Rachmaninoff's Piano Concerto no. 3 in D Minor. To his mind, the liquid work was a one-act opera in which the soloist took all the roles. His tempos were slow, his phrasing generous, and the piano merged with the orchestra to sing a nostalgic lament of remembrance and loss. The sweep was symphonic, but the tone was chastely confiding, as if the powerful swells and delicate shades and sudden avalanches and belligerently ardent lyricism were the inward drama of a searching soul. He heaved upward in electric surges toward the stormy first movement cadenza—and suddenly the audience let out its breath. For the first time in living memory Van was playing the "Ossia" cadenza, the big one that even Rachmaninoff had found too difficult and had substituted with a shorter, simpler passage that nearly every other pianist adopted. His huge hands hurtled into the hard-driving chords, the relentless outburst under complete command. The audience barely noticed the stunning technique: they were transfixed by the experience of watching a boy from Kilgore, Texas, play Russian music more like a Russian than their own musicians. If you'd closed your eyes, though few did, you could have imagined yourself in a time before Stalin's Terror, before Lenin himself, when, in this very building, Tchaikovsky composed and Rachmaninoff played music that echoed the greatness of the Russian soul. Where did an American get to divine the subtleties of their spirit, the inmost essence of their sacred, scarred culture? To a people so long cut off from the West, it was dizzying and devastatingly moving.

Already Van was playing the final movement, his long fingers climbing to a farseeing height of divine generosity, reaching still further for an expansive moment of transcendent calm, played out of time. Then the gradual descent to the coda, where the first theme returns, humbler and wiser, the cascading emotions crashing down in a single exhalation until it ended in a joyous surge of sound.

For a moment, as he bowed his head over the piano, there was absolute silence. Then, like a sea swell, the audience rose as one, as stamping and cheers echoed and reechoed. Next to Max Frankel an elderly Russian musician jumped to his feet. "Just like Rachmaninoff!" he cried. "Just like Rachmaninoff!"

"Did I hear you right?" Frankel asked.

"Maybe even better," the man exulted.

Van effusively thanked the orchestra and embraced Kondrashin with a hug and a kiss on both cheeks, Russian-style, which drove his fans wilder. Ignoring the regulations, the jury stood up and applauded. Richter was crying. Neuhaus and Goldenweiser, who had always been at odds on every issue, hugged one another. Around the hall, groups of students set up a chant of "First prize!" It caught on, even though six of the nine finalists were still to play. Tearful women pushed to the front, proffering huge bouquets of roses. Van shyly took the flowers and slanted offstage to renewed sighs and screams.

The white-haired Goldenweiser, an old friend of Rachmaninoff's, labored down the center aisle muttering, "Genius! Genius!" The orchestra players were smiling and joking, tiredness forgotten in the knowledge that they were part of a red-letter day in Soviet music.

Gilels made his way backstage. He had always been careful to play the consummate party loyalist, but now he walked straight up to Van and threw his arms round him. So did Kondrashin. The veteran English composer Sir Arthur Bliss bustled over: "Oh my dear boy, you played wonderfully today," he said with a sigh. "I admire your gift and I will go down on my knees in front of you, I would give you the biggest, highest prize possible, but, alas, I cannot do this." They hugged each other, and both cried.

The applause showed no sign of letting up, and after a hasty consultation the judges agreed on a blatant violation of the rules. Gilels took the young American by the hand, led him out a second time, and kissed him in full view of the party bosses. As Van demurely bowed, a salvo of precious pictures, historic program notes, and old diamond jewelry flew toward him. Dazed, he picked his way through heaps of flowers. There were flowers inside the piano and flowers falling from the air. He caught some and pressed them to his heart. Finally, the orchestra abandoned all restraint, stood up, and joined in the celebration.

The clamor reached the ears of the crowds still pushing outside the conservatory. "Vanya! Vanya!" they shouted. "Kleeburn! Kleeburn!" the audience returned. Now they were clapping rhythmically in unison, a peculiarly Russian compliment.

Frankel looked around in disbelief. The standing ovation lasted eight and a half minutes. No one could remember anything like it in the ninety-two-year history of the Moscow Conservatory.

Finally, the stage was reset for the night's second finalist, Eddik Miansarov. By the time he came on, a large part of the audience had walked out.

Outside, the police and military cordons collapsed. Fans climbed up fire escapes and across roofs, and riots broke out as the authorities tried to restrain them. Van stayed safely inside, venturing out only at midnight, still surrounded by admiring friends. Teachers came up and told him they had believed only Russians could really feel Rachmaninoff and Tchaikovsky. "We were mistaken," they said, half in wonder and half in chagrin. Inside the doors, he glanced at the billboard where posters advertising forthcoming concerts were pinned up. A large sheet announced a solo recital to be given by the winner of the piano competition the following Friday. Space had been left for the name, but students had already written in "VAN CLIBURN" so many times that there was no room left. As always in the Soviet Union, there was a political message behind the mischief making. Vladimir Ashkenazy, who had managed to squeeze into the concert, was in no doubt that Van had to win. Yet he and his fellow students half-feared that the conservatory's party functionaries might get a call from the Central Committee Secretariat and that it would all be hushed up as if it had never happened.

Across the Soviet Union millions had gathered in front of television sets to watch the broadcast. Van was the first American most had seen live, and they were taken aback. In Leningrad, two piano-mad schoolgirls named Elena and Natasha were mesmerized by his ardent, soulful performance and the way his whole body seemed fused to the music. In Egorievsk, in the Moscow region, tenth-grade student Tanya Kryukova watched shaken and sobbing. She cried through the break in the performance and, afterward, sat down and wrote to Van, "Oh if only I had been in that hall that evening! If only I could get close to the stage, close to you, and join the mad applause to you, to your talent. Of course you wouldn't even have noticed the seventeen-year-old girl, mad with happiness and admiration, but I could have kissed and kissed your hands, the wonderful hands of the wonderful musician . . . My dear, dear Van Cliburn, I cannot describe my admiration for you. I have no words to prove that I am in love with you as a pianist and a musician." A maid at a Moscow institution was equally transfixed. "You know," she tremulously told a friend, "I always turn off the TV or switch channels when they start playing this kind of music, an orchestra or something. But this time there was a young lad playing, really just a boy, and I was sitting there in tears. I don't know what happened to me, I never listened to this kind of music, but I couldn't tear myself away. I could have sat there forever." Van's tender Romanticism had unlocked feelings pent up for decades by the programmed pragmatism of Soviet life, and barely knowing why, countless Russian hearts reached out to him. That night, a young American less than a month into his first overseas trip was the most beloved individual in the Soviet Union.

No one, least of all the psychological operation experts, could have foreseen it, because it could have been no one else. Out of a bleak world of enmity and despair had come a tall, blond, blue-eyed Texan who loved Russia and its music with humble reverence. He had old-fashioned courtliness, a touchingly eager manner, and a spectacular way with the piano that transported them to a half-remembered past. Music that depicted the many cruelties and brutalities of that past was not for him: the Russia he summoned up with his hands was a place of magnificence, beauty, and romance. How could anyone not have fallen for him?

He had one more quality, which more than anything else transformed the Soviet people's image of Americans: innocence. "He's a fourteen year old boy psychologically," Sviatoslav Richter gloated to Heinrich Neuhaus, who was starting to say the same thing but was relieved his friend said it first. It was meant, mostly, as a compliment: an intuition that Van possessed the forthright sincerity and originality common to great artists—the instinctive approach to music that Anton Rubinstein summed up as following "whatever your soul tells you." At this heady moment, with all Russia turned on its ear, it really seemed it could take something that simple to change the world.

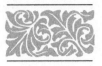

· 9 ·

"We Are in Orbit"

MAX FRANKEL had been stationed in Moscow for only a few months, but it was long enough for him to have grown frustrated with his lot. Like every newcomer, he had learned to read *Pravda* back to front, starting with the bottom of the last column, where the real news (about changes in the leadership) was buried. Most foreign hacks filled their quotas by moistening those crumbs and serving them up alongside gobbets of propaganda about harvests improving and industrial quotas exceeded, larded with the maximum skepticism they could muster and the censors would swallow. By diligent digging, Frankel had done better, landing a few carefully padded punches at bureaucratic absurdities, such as freight quotas reckoned by railcars not contents, which incentivized workers to trundle empty trains around Siberia; or shoe factories whose productivity was measured by the quantity of leather they consumed, which yielded footwear fit only for Frankenstein's monster. What he really wanted to know was what the Soviet people privately thought of the system they devoted their lives to gaming. Yet Western reporters were closely corralled in foreign ghettos, and it was almost impossible to meet any ordinary Soviets. So limited were his contacts that he counted Nikita Khrushchev as his best Russian friend.

The young *karespondent* had developed a sneaking fondness for the potbellied premier and his pugnacious banter, and though Frankel heartily despised the Soviet government, he also harbored grand dreams of saving the planet by helping the two superpowers over-come their mutual ignorance and fear. The moment he saw the pan-demonium at the conservatory, he knew it was the story he had been waiting for. In the safety of a concert hall, Russians had forgotten their fear of authority and had showered an all-American boy with love. Now the burning question was whether the leadership would let them have their way, or strike out the truth with the stroke of a party secretary's pen.

Frankel darted off to the foreign annex of the Central Telegraph on Gorky Street, where he did daily battle with the Glavlit censors concealed behind a curtained glass door. "A boyish-looking, curly-haired young man from Kilgore, Tex., took musical Moscow by storm tonight," he typed:

> He dazzled the audience with a display of technical skill that Russians have long considered their special forte. He added to it a majestic romantic style that his 1,500 listeners could not re-sist.
>
> Mr. Cliburn had emerged from the first two rounds of the competition as the rage of the town. Nothing has been so scarce here in a long time as a ticket to his performance . . .
>
> It is far from certain that Mr. Cliburn will win first prize in the competition. The nine finalists are all first rate and include another American, Daniel Pollack of Los Angeles. But Mr. Cli-burn is clearly the popular favorite and all Moscow is wonder-ing whether an American will walk off with top prize.

To drive home the extent of the furor, he added that the competi-tion had gripped Moscow the same way the World Series captivated Americans.

The journalist handed the long article to a sleepy woman, who disappeared behind the door. For once it passed the censors intact. To Frankel's equal surprise, his New York editors grasped its signif-icance. The story made the morning's front page, along with a publicity photograph of Van at the keyboard in his stringy bow tie. Such was the news value of the Cold War: less than four years earlier the *Times* had marked Van's Leventritt victory with a brief notice on page twelve. Yet not even Frankel suspected just how closely the competition was being followed at the highest levels of the Soviet government.

*   *   *

ONCE AGAIN Khrushchev's strategy of opening up to the world had had unforeseen consequences, and his bureaucrats found themselves in a bind. On the one hand, the mass adulation of the American pianist was so fanatical that it amounted to a provocative political statement; to sanction his victory was not just to admit defeat in a musical contest, but also to acknowledge a popular hunger for freedom. On the other hand, snubbing him risked ruining the reputation of the brand-new competition, exposing it as a propaganda exercise and squandering the international respect it had been designed to reap. Yet Marxist-Leninist ideology taught that it was impossible for a bourgeois to outperform a Communist; to diehards, any suggestion to the contrary was counterrevolutionary. The officials began to quarrel over what to do.

The day after Van's triumph every member of the Central Committee received a long dispatch marked "URGENT—SECRET" from Deputy Culture Minister Kaftanov. It recounted Van's success, the standing ovation from all members of the jury "contrary to the provisions of the competition," and the audience chant of "First prize, first prize!" The foreign jurors, Kaftanov reported, had asked that a request be sent to the government to establish a special "Big Prize" for Van Cliburn. "The rules of the Competition do not envisage such a prize," he noted. "There is a great frenzy around Cliburn's performance, an erroneous attitude among a certain part of the musical public, there are discussions of the allegedly possible non-objective evaluation of his work . . ." Nevertheless, he added, the Soviet comrades on the jury believed that Cliburn's talent "deserves very high praise and that awarding the first prize to him would be very fair":

Moreover, Comrades Kabalevsky and Gilels think that even sharing two first prizes between Van Cliburn and Vlassenko would be unfair. If this is the case, the voting could result in some very serious complications. The foreign members of the jury could, while trying to secure the first prize for Cliburn, unjustly and artificially mark down the marks for other Soviet musicians.

The Ministry of Culture thinks, in connection with the above, that the first prize should be awarded to Van Cliburn. It seems to us that the forthcoming performance by Soviet musicians L. Vlassenko and N. Shtarkman in the third stage will not cause any important changes to the situation.

A decision to award the first prize to Van Cliburn can in no way diminish the authority of the Soviet school of piano as all the first prizes at the violin competition were awarded to Soviet violinists. The second prize at the piano competition can be awarded to the Soviet pianist Lev Vlassenko.

Such a decision can be received with approval by the broad circles of the musical public and raise even higher the authority of the Tchaikovsky competition.

Please give us instructions.

Whether or not Gilels and Kabalevsky really believed that the foreign judges would revolt at the prospect of splitting the prize, they had decided to stand up for the young American. Consequently, the Culture Ministry, having pressured Lev Vlassenko to take part, and having selected him as the winner of the competition, demoted him to second place before he had even played.

*   *   *

LEV AND Ella had stayed overnight with relatives in Moscow, and as in every household, the radio was tuned to the broadcasts from the conservatory. When Van started on the Rachmaninoff, Lev had stopped to listen. "That's good playing," he said, and he followed it to the end. The third movement convinced him less than the first two, but the ever-protective Ella was sorry he had heard it.

His chance came the next evening, between Naum Shtarkman, who clenched up and played listlessly, and Toyoaki Matsuura. Vlassenko performed his signature piece, the Liszt Piano Concerto no. 2 in A Major, enveloping the audience in its soft sounds before thrilling them with a cascade of octaves in the Tchaikovsky. On Sunday it was the turn of Danny Pollack, who was playing the Tchaikovsky with an orchestra for the first time and, by common consensus, fared less well than in the second round, and Liu Shikun. "Apart from brilliant musical gifts," the conductor Kirill Kondrashin said afterward of the Chinese contestant, "he stands out for the incredible diligence that is typical of his people. During the day one literally had to drag him away from the instrument." Even onstage, Liu took advantage of the lengthy applause to check passages from the piece he was about to play.

That night, the jury convened one last time. Richter assumed his customary stance, but this time the others objected sharply. They wanted no more mischief with the marks, they insisted; the decision had to be collective. Gilels proposed a new voting system: each juror would simply write his choice of winner on a slip of paper and sign it. Richter reluctantly complied, and Gilels read out the slips one by one. Of the seventeen judges, fifteen voted outright for Van. Two hedged their bets, and both were foreigners. Despite his fulsome praise, Sir Arthur Bliss bracketed Van joint first prize with Liu Shikun; and Lajos Hernádi of Hungary bracketed him with Lev Vlassenko.

The ballot for second place was more surprising: because of further hedging, it was tied between Vlassenko and Liu. Yet again the Ministry of Culture's plan had spectacularly backfired. It was scant consolation to the Soviets that third prize went to Naum Shtarkman and fourth to Eduard Miansarov. Milena Mollova of Bulgaria came fifth, Nadia Gedda-Nova of France sixth, and Toyoaki Matsuura of Japan seventh, by default leaving Daniel Pollock with the eighth and last prize.

Despite the brave stand taken by Gilels and Kabalevsky, this was not the end of the process. Five years after Stalin's death the old thinking still clung on: toe the line, avoid responsibility at all costs. In a system where all decisions went through the party, there was only one way to avoid blame: refer it upward.

Gilels spoke to Culture Minister Mikhailov, who seemed petrified by the American's popularity and went to Khrushchev. The premier had just returned from an official trip to Hungary.

"We don't know what to do," the minister began.

"What?" Khrushchev replied curtly. "What do you mean?"

"We now have a Tchaikovsky Competition and an American pianist who plays very well," the minister quavered, "and we don't know what to do."

Very likely Khrushchev eyed him with withering patience. "What do the others say about him? Is he the best?"

"Yes, he is the best."

"In that case," the premier grunted, "give him the first prize."

If you cannot catch a bird of paradise, Khrushchev was fond of saying, better take a wet hen. The outcome was not really so bad for him. It helped prove that the Soviets were not afraid of comparison with the West, even if that meant losing occasionally. And it gave a useful credibility boost to his calls for peaceful coexistence, which, for all his missile rattling, were essentially sincere. Besides, Khrushchev liked classical music only slightly less than he liked folk music, and his favorite piece was the Chopin F Minor Fantaisie. While he was in Hungary he had heard Van playing it on the radio.

The stars were aligned for Van in Moscow. The matter was settled.

*　　*　　*

THE ANNOUNCEMENT was due at 11:00 that night, but to give the system time to sort itself out, it had been pushed back to the following afternoon. After Liu's performance the foreign contestants had drifted back to their hotels, and in the small hours those staying at the Peking were still sitting in their private dining room having a snack and a glass of tea when Eddik Miansarov burst in.

"Van, you've won!" he cried, sweeping him up in a bear hug.

"You can't know that, Eddik, not yet," Van demurred, shaking his head. "Nothing's official till tomorrow noon." He was still objecting when Naum Shtarkman ran in, panting heavily.

"Vanya, you've won!" he said. "There's no question about it. I just heard the news." Van shook his head and began explaining the situation again when a uniformed conservatory official rushed in.

"Vanyushka," he said, grinning knowingly, "you'd better go up to your room and put on your white tie and tails."

Van stopped talking, smiled shakily, and headed to the door. "Everyone is going back to the conservatory now," the official was saying as the winner walked heavily up the stairs.

*   *   *

OUTSIDE THE conservatory, hundreds of hard-core fans had refused to go home and were loitering in the cold night, scrutinizing the comings and goings for clues to the results. When they saw Van and his friends approaching, they flocked over, applauding excitedly.

In the Great Hall, the lights were dimmed and covers were draped on the chairs. Kondrashin was at the podium, the orchestra was tuning up, and technicians were setting up movie cameras to film the winning program for the many Soviet citizens without access to television. Van strode up to the piano, whipping off his crumpled sweater and throwing it to the floor, and sat down flexing his fingers. A few silent beats of Kondrashin's baton, a few introductory bars from the orchestra, and Rachmaninoff's great concerto once again poured from his hands. But a few minutes in, he stopped, unhappy with the way he was playing. Kondrashin tried to persuade him there was nothing wrong with it, but he shook his head, placing his huge palm on the damp back of the conductor's white shirt. "Okh no," he said in a plaintive Russian accent, "one more time." They began again. After a minute of near-perfect playing, he banged his fists on the keys and started replaying some passages to himself, as if he were quite alone and there were no orchestra waiting. The musicians sat back and rested, their eyes, hands, and lips sore after four days of rehearsing all day and performing all night. Van's friends drew near as he thumped his knees in frustration, as tense as fans whose team was losing. They groaned at the slightest flubbed note and guffawed when the exhausted brass players made a silly mistake. After four hours the cameramen got the concerto on film. With morning light streaming in through the clerestory windows, everyone took a short break and prepared to record the Tchaikovsky. No one was surprised when the orchestra started several times in a muddle, but everyone was startled when the piano rang out as crisp and clear as a fresh-washed spring day.

*   *   *

IN MARK Schubart's hotel room the phone woke him at 4:00 a.m.

"Van's won!" Max Frankel shouted in his ear. He, too, had lingered at the conservatory long enough to catch a glimpse of the recording session before rushing off to the censor's office. Schubart threw on some clothes, hurried downstairs, and sent a four-word cable to Bill Schuman at Juilliard:

WE ARE IN ORBIT.

This time Frankel's piece ran across four columns of the *New York Times* front page, directly beneath the masthead. U.S. PIANIST, 23, WINS SOVIET CONTEST, proclaimed the headline. A large photograph showed Van shaking hands with juror Lev Oborin, with a beaming Henrietta Belayeva between them and a flashbulb about to pop. A second piece, entitled TALL AT THE KEYBOARD, profiled Van as a Man in the News and drove home its sheer unlikeliness:

A native of the American Deep South who is the son of an oil company employee and a beneficiary of the Rockefellers: that is who stands as the cynosure of Moscow today.

His name is Van Cliburn, and he now lives in New York.

In the first days of the Tchaikovsky International Piano and Violin Festival, when he emerged from among forty-nine contestants here as the darling of the serious listeners and bobby-soxers alike, they called him "the American genius."

Now that he has won the contest, the Russians have dubbed him "Malchik [little boy] from the South."

Both titles seem apt. Despite his slender six-foot four-inch frame, Mr. Cliburn, who is 23 years old, is boyish in appearance. He has a small face, with a sharp nose and clear blue eyes tucked under a thick head of blond, curly hair.

He was born in Shreveport, La. His speech betrays the fact that he has not been away too long from his "daddy," who lives in Kilgore, Tex., where Van spent his early years . . .

Mr. Cliburn brought to the stage of the Tchaikovsky Conservatory a formidable talent, combining great technical skill with a robust and crowd-appealing emotional style. And that is comparable to bringing a copy of Marx to the Kremlin.

In Morningside Heights, Allen Spicer stared wonderingly at the papers. A few years ago he had berated Van for never reading them, and now the boy was the lead news. He called out to Hazel: "That's great," they agreed. "At last he can afford that piano he bought for the church." Yet, as he read on, the Old Princetonian might have begun to wonder what his former roomer had gotten himself into. In the same issue, the *Times* ran an editorial headed THE ARTS AS BRIDGES that suggested that artists such as Van might succeed where politicians had so conspicuously failed in spanning the gulf of hostility and misunderstanding between the superpowers. It was a noble sentiment, but in a world of *sputniks* and ICBMs, it placed a crushing burden on tender shoulders.

As Van's victory became a lead story on every global outlet, many eyes turned to watch his next step. At the State Department, Secretary Dulles ordered officers to report on the young pianist's personality, attitude, and reliability. In the Kremlin, the Central Committee began a detailed investigation of his case. The KGB opened a file on him, and so did the FBI. Journalists knocked on the Spicers' door, interviewed Harvey Cliburn's bank manager, and camped out on the Cliburns' little lawn.

In Van's Moscow hotel room, the phone kept ringing, though he was hardly ever there to pick up. Sol Hurok had swung into action, sending one telegram to his friend Max Frankel asking to be put in touch with the young hero and another to Mark Schubart congratulating him on his signal service to American culture. Rather than wait, Hurok cabled Van, who had fruitlessly pursued him for so long, with an offer of management that somehow leaked to the American press. RCA Victor, America's leading classical label, also cabled Schubart, asking "that he use his good offices to explain to Van Cliburn" that they had made a formal proposal for his services as a recording artist. When Columbia Records and every other major label joined the chase, Van briskly instructed Bill Judd to play them off against one another—so that "if I go in one day and want to play 'Clair de lune,' they'll have to record it."

He had come to Moscow to marvel at St. Basil's Cathedral, indulge in the music he adored, and perhaps, just perhaps, revive his floundering career. Instead he had become a worldwide phenomenon and had been handed an opportunity, and a responsibility, that no classical musician in history ever had. The prize giving that was about to take place was not the end of a crazy adventure: it was only the beginning.

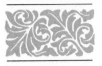

· *10* ·

"American Sputnik"

AT THE Peking Hotel, Harriet Wingreen had gone to sleep when there was a tremendous banging on her door. She opened up to find Van in a fluster.

"Let me in, Harriet. Let me in fast! I've gotta get in!" he blurted.

"What's the matter, Van?" she mumbled.

"The girls are all after me!" he exclaimed. They were following him everywhere, and one had mysteriously appeared in his room in the dead of night.

Harriet closed the door and considered the situation: Van's six-foot-four frame, her five feet, the couch, the bed. "Van, all right, you take the bed, and I'll sleep on the couch," she said sleepily. He spent the night and left the next morning, slipping out early and looking anxiously around.

It was a bright Monday morning, the spring sun suddenly flaring like a match struck in the dark. Later on, the mercury was expected to scale the unfamiliar heights of six degrees Celsius, and the lilac and apple were flowering ahead of time. At midday Van gingerly emerged beneath the stone shot-putter and wrestler and attempted to head off for the official announcement of the results. As soon as he was spotted—which was, after all, not hard—the cry went up, and a crowd of devotees swarmed over holding out hand-knitted socks and hats and jars of jam. Some had heard reports that he had lost ten pounds while in Moscow, and in a country where fruit was a great luxury, his fans shyly proffered bags of oranges.

At the conservatory most of the students had missed the night's activity and were milling round in confusion. "So Cliburn didn't win first prize after all," a young Soviet violinist ruefully thought as he arrived for class, noting the tense atmosphere. It turned out that the rumor had reached them several days late that the first prize was to be split so "Iron Lev" could come out on top after all. When the doors opened, they piled into the White Hall, which was soon crammed with contestants, judges, officials, students, fans, musicians, guests, photographers, and reporters, all noisily swapping the latest news.

"Dear comrades and guests," Emil Gilels began. "We have all come here on this sunny spring day in order to announce the joyful news with which we have been preoccupied for a long time." He praised the competitors, lamented the jury's difficult job, and began to read out the results:

"First prize, which includes twenty-five thousand rubles and a gold medal, to Van Cliburn, USA."

At Van's name, screams of joy, wild applause, and chants of "Vanya!" burst out. The two men hugged and kissed, the flashbulbs popped, and Van blew a kiss to the room. Eventually Gilels was allowed to continue. The second-prize winners received twenty thousand rubles and a silver medal; the third-prize winner, fifteen thousand rubles and a bronze medal; and the rest, cash awards of descending value. As a mark of the exceptionally high level of playing, Gilels added, five violinists and five pianists who had failed to reach the finals were to receive diplomas and cash. Six semifinalists, including Jerry Lowenthal, collected honorary certificates. Then a series of judges stood up to praise the courage and talent of the winners, give a few career tips, and wish the losers better luck in the future. All declared that for quality of artistry and technique, there had never been a competition like it.

As soon as the speeches were over, the press set upon Van.

"What is your father?" asked a reporter from *Trud*, a mass-circulation trade union newspaper. "Is he a worker?"

"He is a worker," Van replied, not mentioning the word *oil*.

"What is your mother?"

"She teaches piano."

"Ah yes, good," the reporter said, nodding.

A journalist for the United Press wire service pointed out that, under Soviet law, Van might not be able to take home his winnings. "Money doesn't mean anything to me," he cheerfully replied. "There are so many things you cannot buy with it. Winning just means a great deal to me as an American. I would not take a million for this trip." The reporter asked what he wanted to do next. "I would really like to go back to Texas," he said. "I'm just about to break down." Max Frankel thought Van was basking in the attention, and he was not altogether wrong. For all his shyness, Van finally had a leading role that he was being allowed to play. It took the journalist and his friends more than an hour to drag him away for a snack. Afterward, Van sneaked in an hour's practice, watched by Naum and Eddik, the other Soviet competitors, and the press. Paul Moor snapped him kissing the matronly babushka who cleaned his studio, which was filled with fresh blossoms sent by admiring girls. The photojournalist was now acting as Van's unofficial manager, at the request of his parents, who trusted him because he was from Texas. Norman Shetler watched Moor and decided he was busy inveigling his way into Van's confidence for his own purposes. Shetler resolved to stick by Van and help where he could.

As the news spread, passersby stopped anyone who looked American to congratulate them on their victory. Across the country, people gathered round TV sets and avidly swapped rumors about what kind of political influence had been brought to bear and by whom. The possibility that the public's wishes had had an effect was almost too much to hope for; the likelihood that the decision had been made purely on artistic merits was not taken seriously.

Back at the hotel, Harriet Wingreen knocked on Van's door to see if he had survived. No one opened it, so she kept knocking. Eventually Norman Shetler peeked out and said, "Oh it's you—come in quick." Fans had tried to storm the room in their enthusiasm to see and touch Van. Record companies and managers had been calling nonstop, and all the while, Van had been trying to put a call through to Kilgore.

"Have you heard the news?" he asked when he was finally connected. Rildia Bee assured him that they had; first from a friend in Shreveport, where it arrived on the wire service, and then from CBS, whose representative called from New York and offered to patch her and Harvey through to Moscow.

"It's official," Van proudly stressed. He reassured her that the Russians were being wonderful and asked if she had told a lady across town who ran the Community Concert Association about his win. "Honey, she already knows," Rildia Bee replied, and when he ascertained that a family friend in the next town also knew, he felt he had finally made it. He had to ring off then, because at five he was due at the Kremlin for a diplomatic reception for Queen Elisabeth of Belgium. Ambassador Thompson had offered to take him, but at the last minute Jane Thompson called and apologized, saying her husband had to be out of town. "But I'll be taking you to the Kremlin for the reception," she said brightly, adding that she had just heard Khrushchev was still away, so unfortunately Van wouldn't get to meet him. Van was excited enough to meet a queen, and Jane sped over in her car. A few minutes later they drove under the Borovitskaya Tower and up into the red citadel whose jumble of palaces, churches, and barracks seemed to breathe the chivalrous and brutal, civilized and archaic, materialistic and spiritual epic of Russian history. It was a curious thing for a Westerner to enter these precincts, though the towers topped with red stars brought back half a memory of Kilgore's derricks with their Christmas lights.

At the top of the hill, several historic buildings were being razed to make way for Khrushchev's vast new Palace of Congresses, but the car headed for the wedding cake yellow and white of the Romanovs' Great Kremlin Palace. The double eagles had long been ripped off and replaced with hammers and sickles, but the reception halls had lost none of their jaw-dropping extravagance. A host of officials, including Deputy Premier Anastas Mikoyan and new foreign minister Andrei Gromyko were in attendance, but all eyes flowed toward Van, even when Voroshilov, increasingly doddery but still the nominal head of state, entered with the queen. When Van was presented to her, she lavished praise on his performance and invited him to play at the Brussels World's Fair, which was opening that Thursday.

Suddenly a short, rotund man in a baggy suit waddled out of a side door and caught Jane Thompson's attention. "Van!" she whispered in surprise, "Khrushchev is here." The premier's tall, blond son, Sergei, and small, dark interpreter Viktor Sukhodrev followed him into the hall. A functionary approached Van. Officially, Comrade Khrushchev was to greet the contestants at a reception the following afternoon, the man explained, but as a most highly esteemed guest, would Van like to meet him now?

Before Van could properly respond, Khrushchev bore down on him, grinning so broadly that he exposed a mouthful of steel, and threw his arms round him. The Soviet leader stood five foot three, and his belly was in the way, so he had to jump a little to kiss Van on one cheek and jump again to kiss him on the other, even though Van subtly bent his knees. Cameras greedily snapped.

Khrushchev righted himself, still grinning.

"Why are you so tall?" he asked, with Sukhodrev translating.

"Because I am from Texas," Van returned.

"You must have a lot of yeast in Texas," Khrushchev said with a chuckle, introducing a subject close to his heart. His favorite snack was a double-yeasted dough that he liked best fried as *pirozhki*.

"No, just vitamin pills," Van managed, perhaps thinking of his fast-depleting supplies.

"How old are you?" the premier asked.

"I am twenty-three," Van replied, with all the dignity his sweet child's face could muster.

"My son is also twenty-three," Khrushchev said, pushing Sergei forward.

"What month was he born?" Van asked.

"I must ask his mother about that," the Soviet leader said, grinning. Sergei was his favorite, but he had never been the most doting of fathers.

"Was it July?" Van suggested.

"Probably July," Khrushchev agreed. He neglected to add that Sergei was a rocket scientist engaged in building missiles that were designed to pulverize Western cities.

The situation was unreal; politics aside, one only had to imagine the likelihood of an incumbent American president dropping by after a music competition and going out of his way to engage the winner in banter. It was about to get stranger.

"I was listening to you in the second round on the radio in Hungary," Khrushchev said. "I loved the way you played the F minor Fantasy opus 49 of Chopin."

Van was stunned into silence. He looked at the warty, gap-toothed premier, suspecting he was being tricked. He turned to the smooth Sukhodrev, wondering if the interpreter had made it up. But Sukhodrev was only two years older than Van, and it seemed unlikely that he knew such an obscure piece, either.

"What did he say?" Van asked.

"He said he was so thrilled that in the second round you played the F Minor Fantasy by Chopin," Sukhodrev repeated.

No American musician thought of being part of the mainstream of national life. Yet here was a superpower leader, treating Van as an equal and speaking appreciatively of a piece as delicate and refined as the Chopin F Minor Fantaisie. Van began feeling he was in a musical paradise.

The reception over, the entire party moved on to the conservatory for the formal award ceremony. Onstage, the competition officials were ranged behind a long table. Shostakovich opened the session. Reformers were convinced the composer was a secret dissident, his music a subversive commentary on the sins of Soviet society, but as usual he made a safe speech, praising the talented artists who, he said, held aloft the banner of true art, and declaring that the competition would take its place in the history of music. Nervous, fidgety, and tetchy, he chewed his nails and fingers, twitched his chin, wrinkled his nose to push up the thick glasses that veiled his eyes, stuttered as he spoke through tight lips, and with an expression on his pallid face unfathomably balanced between courage and doubt, irritation and moroseness, betrayed no hint of what he was thinking. Van had no idea of Shostakovich's past troubles and merely thought the composer was very kind, interesting, and nice.

Dmitri Kabalevsky handed out the prizes, to a ringing ovation. Minister of Culture Mikhailov took the podium to declare Moscow the world capital of music and announced that the Tchaikovsky Competition would henceforth be held every four years. Efrem Zimbalist was dragged on to make a short speech, presumably to quash rumors of his rebellion. Valery Klimov, the winning violinist, thanked the government and the Communist Party, on behalf of the Soviet participants, for their unswerving commitment to the training of young talent. Finally, Van tried out a few lines in Russian. "Dear friends," he said, "I'm very grateful to the audience for inspiring me. Thank you very much." Everyone laughed and cheered. He felt thrilled of course, as if he had been rewarded for twenty years' hard labor, given a passport to explore new places and meet wonderful people. Yet, at the same time, he felt strangely guilty and discomposed. He had heard and so admired the beautiful performances by some of the other participants, including the three Soviet winners. It was so much easier to praise others than to bear the responsibility of winning. As Mother always said, when it came down to it, the stage was a lonely place.

Besides, the Soviets were his friends now. Even Iron Lev had turned out to be all warmth and enthusiasm. When he approached Van, his face lit up with childlike candor, and his booming voice and infectious laugh made it impossible not to like him. Lev had brought along Ella and their young daughters, Irina and Natasha, and during the prize giving, Irina clambered onstage. She was ordered down and started crying, so Lev gave her his silver medal to play with and Van took her on his knee.

After the presentation the top winners of the violin and piano competitions performed, the latter clearly at a higher level than the former, with Kondrashin again conducting the Moscow State Symphony. Van was last, with the first movement of the Tchaikovsky. For the first time, Liu Shikun listened properly, his heroic months of rehearsal finally over, and he was stunned. He had never heard anyone play the piano as if he were making it up, freely ignoring the markings and sending opposites—dark and light, fast and slow, strong and gentle—into spiraling collisions. He vowed that from then on he would liberate his own style. Soviet pianists, among them young Sergei Dorensky, also fell under Van's spell, realizing that Russian music could be more melodic and dramatic than the Soviet school, with its intense focus on virtuosity, allowed. Not all praised Van unreservedly. There was a drop of bad taste in his unabashed Romanticism, sniffed Heinrich Neuhaus, even though he had voted for him and publicly called him a genius. Lev Vlassenko privately agreed, though he, too, had much to think about. "The competition has demonstrated that one should not be afraid to sincerely express the feeling which is dormant in one's soul," he reflected to a journalist. "Sometimes I feel too embarrassed to show it." The musical unbuttoning echoed what millions of ordinary Russians already felt.

At the end, cheers rang out and Van played one encore after another. Khrushchev and the leaders left, but the audience shouted, "More! More!" in English. Van's bandaged finger was now blistered from overuse, and he raised his hands. "Bol'shoye spasibo," he called out: "Many thanks." No one moved, and his fans were still shouting as the house lights were extinguished. Numerous young women were lying in wait outside the main entrance, so officials shepherded him through a back door.

On the way out, a Western diplomat turned to an American guest: "Now you really have a sputnik," he said. In that combustible atmosphere it did not seem far-fetched to liken piano playing to the first space launch: Moscow Radio itself had dubbed Van "the American Sputnik, developed in secret." Within hours, as images of Van and Khrushchev in a mutually admiring grip flooded the world's front pages, it seemed even more apt. The effect was electric. In a flash, the unfathomable leader of world communism stood revealed as an approachable human being.

*　　*　　*

THERE WAS no time for rest. An hour after the hall was emptied, Van was back onstage for another nocturnal filming session, this one lasting till 3:30 a.m. The next day, Tuesday, came Ambassador Thompson's lunch in honor of the American contestants. Then Van was back at the Great Kremlin Palace for the Ministry of Culture's reception. It was held, with full pomp, in the vanishingly vast St. George's Hall, the Kremlin's grandest. Van stepped onto a sea of intricate parquet and saw Khrushchev heading for him with outstretched arms. The premier proudly presented his son, daughter, and granddaughter, and then caught sight of Lev Vlassenko.

"Why did you let the American chap take first prize?" he demanded of Vlassenko, the levity underscored with a whisper of menace.

"Look at me, and look at Van," Vlassenko joked, pointing up at his rival.

Khrushchev spotted Liu Shikun, who was nearly as tall as Van, and leaped up trying to pat the top of his head.

"Great man!" he said. "You and Van Cliburn are the most talented pianists at this event. But of course Van Cliburn is the number one talent and you are the number two talent." Liu murmured in agreement and chose not to notice Khrushchev's rudeness to Vlassenko.

"I'm very, very pleased that you have made your Chinese people proud," Khrushchev continued, perhaps hoping the honor might help paper over the widening Sino-Soviet split: "It's a big surprise for the Soviet audience that China has such a talented pianist." Liu expressed his thanks for the encouragement and promised he would strive for a higher artistic outcome.

"After a few years why not have another competition between you two and see who's the winner and who's the runner-up?" Khrushchev added, grinning.

"For now I think Van is better than me," Liu modestly replied. "I definitely learned a lot from him." The Chinese ambassador stepped in and thanked the premier for his inspiring words. The two countries talked so little these days that Soviet citizens had eagerly questioned Liu about daily life in China.

Bulganin, deposed as premier just eighteen days earlier, was on show so the press could see he was in good shape. Inadvertently hitting on the real reason for his demotion, Van mistook him for the leader of the June plot against Khrushchev and, "with grave courtesy," addressed him as Mr. Molotov. No one seemed to mind.

Mikoyan approached Van with his versatile mix of vibrancy and self-control. "You've been a very good politician for your country," he said, smiling seriously. "You've done better than all the politicians." Khrushchev nodded energetically and swept his arm to take in Van, Liu Shikun, and the Soviet winners. "Here we are without a round table," he noisily declared, "having an ideal example of peaceful coexistence." From the back a voice suggested the musicians might be better off running things without any governments. Khrushchev genially agreed.

Waiters appeared with Soviet champagne for the toasts. Van hesitated, shifting from foot to foot. "I really don't care for any," he murmured, but he took the glass and brushed it over his lips. There were more speeches, and the winners played before the Belgian queen left for home. Paul Moor slipped out, too, asking Norman Shetler to accompany him; he had overheard the word *karespondent* and was afraid he was about to be arrested.

A final official press release disclosed some remarkable telegrams and letters written by students, workers, soldiers, and pensioners, all praising the competition for its outstanding contribution to world music and international friendship. "It is hard to express your feelings when listening to the beautiful performances of the musicians," Comrade Chebotaryova from Moscow had written: "You feel again and again how lovely it is and you want to listen to the composers' melodies for ever and never hear the stamping of soldiers' boots or the clicking of tanks' caterpillars." And from a group of young construction workers:

> Dear Friends, we are proud that the International Music Competition is held in Moscow, the capital of our motherland, and that it's named after Tchaikovsky. Here in Pyotr Ilyich's home region close to the ancient city of Votkinsk we're building one of the largest hydropower stations of the five-year period, the Votkinsk Hydropower Station. Our workers' settlement is named after the great composer. We are sure that the competition will contribute to improved international relations and may it resonate as a joyful anthem of peace and friendship.

These remarkably articulate builders may have had the same help as Shostakovich, who signed a piece for *Pravda* that extolled Van's "phenomenal musical talent and brilliant, inimitable individuality" but pointed out that the United States had heretofore relied on European imports for its music and was evidently uninterested in celebrating its own talent. "We on our side," the piece concluded, "are sincerely glad that this outstanding young American artist first received the broad and full recognition which he deserves here among us in Moscow."

This was a workable spin. The state media never tried to downplay Van's talent; not only was he too popular at every level, but it would also have made the competition look ridiculous. The composer Khachaturian declared his performance of Rachmaninoff's Third "*better* than Rachmaninoff's; you find a virtuoso like this once or twice in a century." Yet, increasingly, they downplayed his Americanness, reminding readers and listeners that his teacher, albeit an émigrée, was Russian and that his mother's teacher had been Russian, too. To their deep satisfaction, they discovered that Van was really a great Russian pianist after all. From there it was only a step to anointing him their own Soviet pianist.

Even so, the authorities had had a sharp shock, and a postmortem got under way that was conducted partly in public. When the secretary of the jury complained in *Sovetsky Muzykant* of a lack of tact and objectivity among the audience—"I dwell on these points," he darkly warned, "because I have seen the elements of frenzy and clamor among the conservatoire students"—a leading critic boldly declared in *Sovetskaya Kultura* that the Soviet training system placed too much emphasis on technical excellence and none on fostering individuality, with the result that Soviet players all sounded alike. Minister of Culture Mikhailov revealed his intentions in a lengthy report to the Central Committee. As well as criticizing "the erroneous behavior of member of the jury S. Richter," he admitted that the results had not met expectations and suggested that many young players had become both cocky and out of practice by spending too much time playing abroad on propaganda tours. His good socialist prescription was even more state control of performers' schedules and selection procedures.

In its own way, Van's victory really was a *Sputnik* moment for the Soviet Union; the jolt to its belief that its People's Artists were the world's finest was comparable to America's loss of faith that it was first in technology. Yet thanks to Van's extraordinary popularity, a first remedial step was already being taken. Across the Soviet empire, piano teachers were suddenly beset by people of all ages wanting to begin lessons.

*   *   *

AT 808 South Martin Street the phone was ringing off the hook. A small avalanche of letters and cards overwhelmed the mailbox; the overspill, tied in bundles, had been taken back to the post office. A steady parade of florists stepped up the short drive, passing the local, state, and national media camped out on the sidewalk and lawn.

Three reporters from *Life* magazine announced they were gathering material for a possible spread and crowded into the small house, snapping away. A journalist from *Time*'s Dallas bureau introduced himself as Tom Martin and took a good look round before filing his impressions. "The best single word that we can use to describe the Cliburn home would be 'unpretentious,'" he wired New York. "Possibly, 'nondescript' would be a better word . . . It sits among a bunch of other houses in a definitely lower middle class neighborhood." With its "imitation mahogany" décor, he added, it almost nullified Harvey's executive status, as did his personal appearance. As for the Cliburns' social stratum, it was "peculiar":

> They move in no social circle except the music and church group. Their church, of course, comes first above all. They frequently entertain, or attend entertainment provided by the music club. They are by no means members of the elite of Kilgore society and aren't even members of the Kilgore Country Club. They are present there when there is some musical event in progress, but do not participate in the club's activities. To sum up: they are middle class, socially speaking, and because their church takes up so much of their time, they might properly be classified as lower middle class.

The journalist's prejudices were confirmed when Rildia Bee, who cooed to the gentlemen of the press that she was "so overwhelmed with joy and gratitude I hardly know what to say," went ahead with her regular church prayer meeting.

The Cliburns had no experience in dealing with the press, and nothing to hide; Harvey asked only that any story acknowledge that Van was a strict tither. They readily admitted that they had literally mortgaged the farm to finance Van's education; specifically, eighty acres around Moody that Rildia Bee inherited from her mother, all that was left of grandfather Jack McClain's twelve thousand acres of Central Texas blacklands. "That's one of the things Van has already

told us," Rildia Bee confided: "He wants to come back and clear the
books and get all the debts out of the way. We don't owe much anyway, and it's something that has never worried us. We're both in good
health and I have my lessons so we don't think it's much of a problem."
They balked at giving the exact amount of their debt, so Martin went
off to pin down their bank manager. George Hayes, executive vice
president of the Kilgore National Bank, asked not to be quoted but
revealed that the Cliburns "borrowed from time to time, but never
heavily. He says the biggest loan never exceeded twenty five hundred
dollars . . . Hayes says that most of the money the Cliburns borrowed
has been paid back and that there is only a 'small amount' still left to
be paid." The *Time* name opened every door and cut through every
duty of confidentiality. In New York a researcher named Serrell Hillman interviewed the Spicers, Chapins, and Steinways; Mrs. Schuyler
Chapin compared Van to Marilyn Monroe for the way his personality shone through his performances. Hillman tracked down Donna
Sanders, now the not very happily married Mrs. Steve Roland, who
gossiped with her former roommate Jean Heafner and nosed around
Juilliard.

Bill Schuman, Juilliard's president, was euphoric. He was convinced that Van's victory was set to make the school the preeminent
institution he had always wanted it to be, especially when senators J.
William Fulbright and Lyndon B. Johnson, the majority leader, read
into the Congressional Record glowing accounts of the young pianist's global impact. The next day, April 15, he sent a night cable care
of the Peking Hotel:

ALL OF US AT THE SCHOOL ARE GLOWING WITH PRIDE FOR
YOUR WONDERFUL SUCCESS. WE SEND YOU CONGRATULATIONS
AND MUCH LOVE AND LOOK FORWARD TO YOUR TRIUMPHANT
RETURN.

Here, in spectacular action, was the East-West rapprochement
that Schuman had argued for in numerous Music Panel meetings.

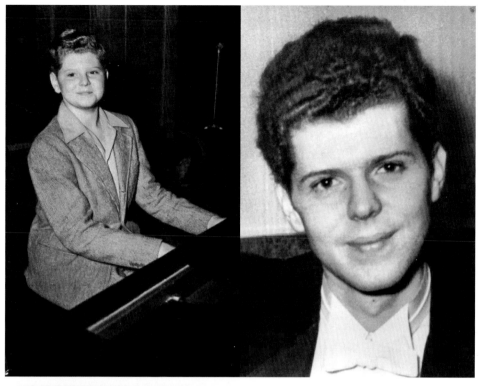

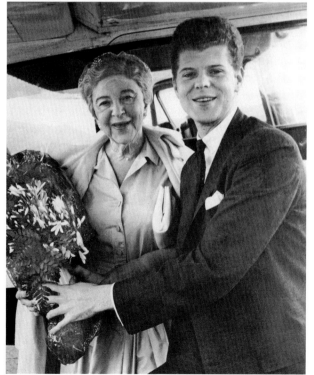

Above: Van at age nine and later as a young professional concert pianist. *(Courtesy of Cliburn Foundation)*

Left: Van with his teacher Rosina Lhévinne around 1954, the year he graduated from Juilliard. *(Courtesy of Juilliard School Archives)*

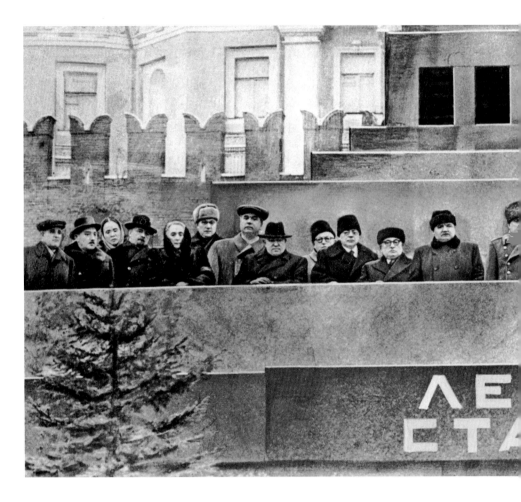

The Soviet and international communist leadership at Stalin's funeral in March 1953, atop the newly renamed Lenin-Stalin Mausoleum in Red Square. At the microphone is the new premier, Georgy Malenkov. Left of Malenkov are Kliment Voroshilov, soon to become head of state; reinstated foreign minister Vyacheslav Molotov; and Nikolai Bulganin, soon to become minister of defense. To the right of Malenkov are Nikita

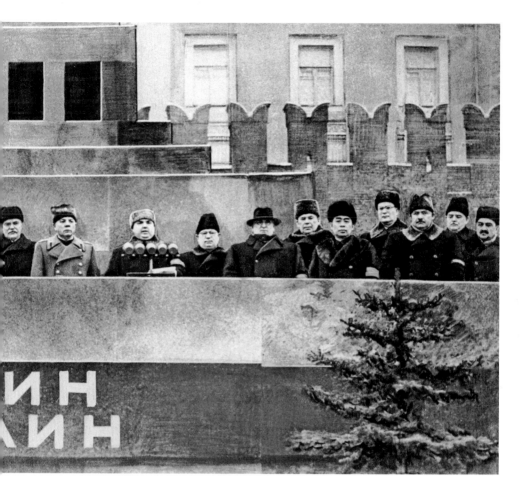

Khrushchev, who retained his Politburo membership but had been stripped of special responsibilities, and feared security chief Lavrenty Beria. At far right is former and future trade minister Anastas Mikoyan; third from right is vicepremier Lazar Kaganovich. Among the other mourners are representatives of foreign communist parties, including Chinese premier Zhou Enlai, fifth from right. *(Keystone-France/Getty)*

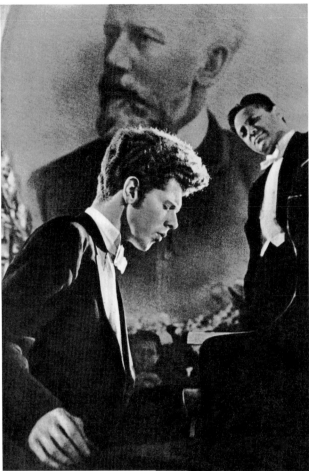

Left: The last Romantic. Van readies himself to play in the finals of the Tchaikovsky Competition as conductor Kirill Kondrashin watches. Behind him is a giant portrait of Tchaikovsky.

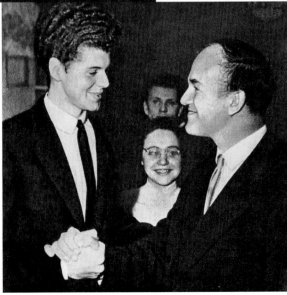

Below: Van with celebrated pianist (and rogue juror) Sviatoslav Richter during the Tchaikovsky Competition. In the background is Van's devoted interpreter, Henrietta Belayeva.

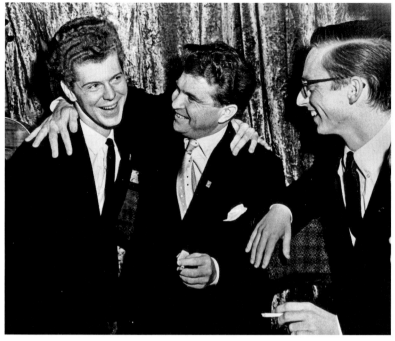

Above: Van and chairman of the Tchaikovsky Competition piano jury Emil Gilels embrace as American competitor Norman Shetler looks on. *(Courtesy of Emil Gilels Foundation)*

Below: Van receives his gold medal from Dmitri Shostakovich in the Great Hall of the Moscow Conservatory on April 14, 1958. *(Nikolai Rakhmanov/TASS)*

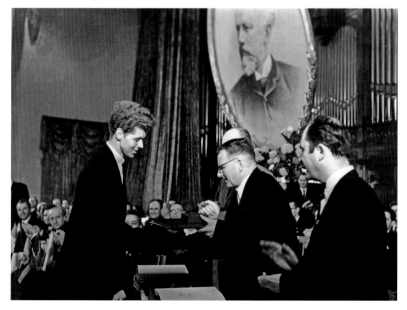

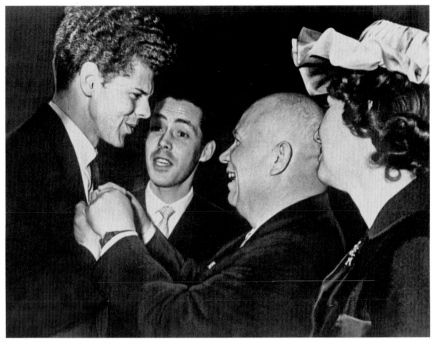

Above: Premier Khrushchev congratulates Van at a Kremlin reception on April 14, 1958. Interpreter Viktor Sukhodrev is between them; at right is Jane Thompson, wife of the American ambassador. *(AP)*

Below: From left to right, medalists Naum Shtarkman, Van, Liu Shikun, and Lev Vlassenko. *(Courtesy of Irina Vlassenko)*

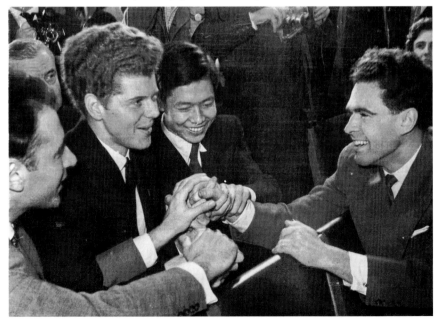

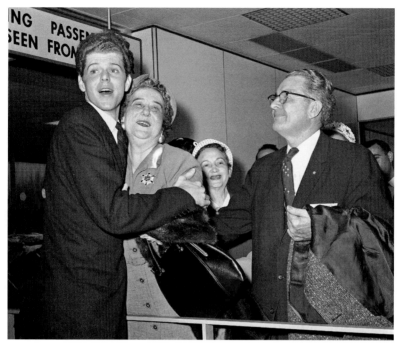

Above: Van with Rildia Bee and Harvey Cliburn at Idlewild Airport on Van's return from Moscow. *(AP)*

Below left: Snatching a bite and a haircut in Van's suite at the Pierre. *(LIFE/ Getty)*

Below right: Mother and son, teacher and student, photographed at the piano in the Pierre suite. *(LIFE/Getty)*

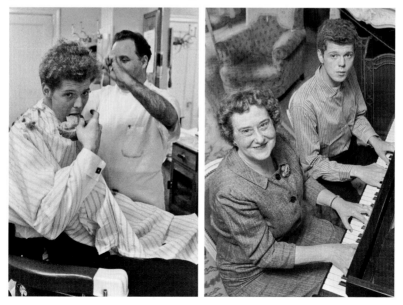

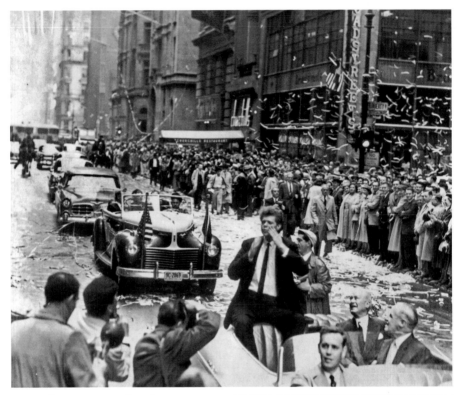

Above: New York welcomes
Van home with a ticker-
tape parade on May 20, 1958.
(Courtesy of Cliburn Foundation)

Below: President Dwight D.
Eisenhower receives Van at
the White House on May
23, 1958; also present but out
of sight are Van's parents
and Soviet conductor Kirill
Kondrashin. *(National Park
Service/Dwight D. Eisenhower
Presidential Library & Museum)*

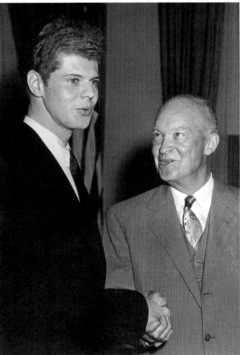

Granted, it was somewhat surreal that the agent of international understanding was the gangly Texan who was chiefly remembered at the school for always being late. Two days later, still giddy with excitement, Schuman wrote Mark Schubart in Moscow:

> The biggest problem of all, of course, is to keep Rosina on the ground. At the moment she is having a picture taken with her current crop of students for *Life Magazine*. The room is, of course, the room in which she taught the great Van Cliburn. Incidentally, can you get any good rates in Europe on the engraving of Van Cliburn plaques. I am planning several for the outside of the building and am even thinking of taking one home to New Rochelle.

Rosina had also received letters of congratulations from senators and congressmen, but not a word from the most important person: "Rosina is crushed and I am afraid hurt," Schuman wrote, "that Van has not been in touch with her since the contest." The nearest she got was when a friend phoned and held the mouthpiece against a shortwave radio. Crackling down the line came the unmistakable sound of Van's Rachmaninoff, followed by a Soviet announcer who remarked that the pianist's teacher was Russian.

Both Rosina and Bill Schuman were distressed by news that Van was rushing into major commitments. They urgently tried to warn him to hold off until he got home, but it was impossible to get through—besides, it was already too late. "I am afraid," Schuman told Schubart, "that he has made some foolish moves." Van had already agreed to appear on *The Steve Allen Show*—the presenter had moved on from *Tonight* the previous year—staying loyal despite a flurry of rival bids. More worryingly, the New York Philharmonic had instantly upped their bid for his services from a second-rate slot in their Saturday-evening children's series to four prime dates in December, with Leonard Bernstein conducting. Now Bill Judd picked up the phone and spoke to the orchestra's assistant manager, who was also his brother. "Georgie," he said, "I think we have to renegoti-ate Van's contract." Judd pushed the fee up from a paltry five hundred dollars. Still, the temptation to capitalize on Van's sudden celebrity was too great, and CAMI booked the Symphony of the Air, the re-incarnation of Toscanini's disbanded NBC Symphony, for a string of concerts in May.

"I want Kondrashin," Van said when Judd called to tell him.

"Oh fine, fine, sure," the manager murmured, not taking him too seriously. No Soviet conductor had ever made a guest appearance in the United States, but Van sounded out Kondrashin and the Soviet Ministry of Culture, which made encouraging noises even though the conductor was booked to tour Bulgaria at the same time. And when Judd called the State Department, to his surprise the official raised no objections and asked only if an "interpreter" (which every-one knew was code for a KGB minder) would be coming with him. The U.S. government appeared to be caught unprepared as much as everyone else, because the same department was playing it decidedly cool toward Van himself.

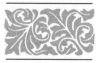

The Last Romantic

IN VAN'S hotel room a large bouquet of spring flowers arrived from Khrushchev's wife. This was deeply gratifying, and made the silence from the American government all the more puzzling. Reporters had begun asking about it, and Van confided to an American embassy official that he was disappointed not to have heard from the U.S. president. Two days after the news hit the front pages, the embassy received a cable from the State Department that was so perfunctory it almost made matters worse:

> PLEASE DELIVER FOLLOWING TO PIANIST VAN CLIBURN:
> "HEARTIEST CONGRATULATIONS. SPLENDID PERFORMANCE.
> SIGNED WILLIAM S. B. LACY, SPECIAL ASSISTANT TO THE
> SECRETARY OF STATE."

John Foster Dulles had signed the order himself, but the hawkish secretary of state evidently preferred not to associate his name with the Soviet event. Finally, the following day, the White House woke up and sent a telegram in which Dulles's boss went straight over his head:

> DEAR MR. AMBASSADOR:
>
> WILL YOU PLEASE EXTEND MY OFFICIAL AND PERSONAL

CONGRATULATIONS TO VAN CLIBURN. I KNOW THAT ALL
AMERICANS JOIN WITH ME IN PAYING TRIBUTE TO HIS ARTISTIC
TALENTS AND ARE PROUD THAT HE WAS AWARDED FIRST PRIZE
IN THE INTERNATIONAL TCHAIKOVSKY PIANO CONTEST. WHEN
HE RETURNS TO THE UNITED STATES, I HOPE HE CAN COME
TO THE WHITE HOUSE SO THAT I CAN CONGRATULATE HIM
PERSONALLY ON HIS TRIUMPH. IT IS GOOD TO SEE ARTISTIC
TALENT RECOGNIZED, AND I BELIEVE SUCH CONTESTS ARE GOOD
FOR A BETTER UNDERSTANDING BETWEEN PEOPLES OF ALL
NATIONS.

WON'T YOU ALSO EXPRESS MY BEST WISHES TO DANIEL POLLACK
WHO TOOK NINTH PLACE IN THE COMPETITION.

DWIGHT D. EISENHOWER.

Tommy Thompson, now back in Moscow, wrote pointing out that Pollack had in fact placed eighth, and Joyce Flissler had come in seventh in the violin competition and had been completely overlooked. The message was duly amended, though since Flissler had already left Moscow, the embassy sent a cable to New York to await her upon her return.

Van quickly composed a reply, accepting the invitation. The Soviet propaganda machine was determined to get value from the winners, and he had precious little time to himself—just enough to call home for forty minutes and visit Kondrashin's house to see his new baby. There were tapes to make for Moscow Radio, for which Van and Daniel Pollack were paid two hundred rubles a minute. Conservatory officials gave Van a private viewing of their prized collection of original manuscripts; among them was Tchaikovsky's Piano Concerto no. 1, which Van handled like a holy relic. They asked him to visit the studio of the sculptor Bachic-Serbien to have a life mask made for its collection. On Thursday he and fellow gold medalist Valery Klimov made a pilgrimage to Tchaikovsky's museum-home at Klin. As they approached the large blue-and-white dacha, the composer's great-great-nephew came forward to greet them and then gave them a guided tour. When the movie cameras were ready, they took turns performing, Van playing Tchaikovsky's own piano and perspiring under the klieg lights, until most of the day had gone by. Even then, newsreel cameramen and reporters followed his every step, but it was hard to complain when everyone was so kind and hospitable.

To give Van a break, Paul Moor took him to a concert, which turned out to be one of his most memorable experiences. Sviatoslav Richter had not played in Moscow for nearly a year—he preferred to turn up on short notice and perform on bad pianos in small halls in obscure towns—but he had decided to burn off the grime of judging by giving a recital and two concertos. The recital opened with Schubert's great last Sonata in B-flat Major, which made Van weep unabashedly for minutes. After the Schumann Toccata, Richter launched into three Prokofiev pieces and finished with the Seventh Sonata, building up with unfathomable subtlety to a thrilling finale. The audience shouted so vehemently that he came back and played it even better. "I really don't think I'm in a daze or anything," Van said, turning to Moor, "but I honestly believe this is the greatest piano playing I've ever heard in my life." Moor, who agreed, reported that the feeling was mutual: Richter had called Van a genius—"a word," he had added, "I do not use lightly about performers." Hearing that, Van cried again.

Friday evening a "wildly pushing crowd" jammed the conservatory for Van's prize recital and demanded seven encores. With Shostakovich listening, Van boldly played a teenage composition of his own called "Nostalgia." Afterward, Tommy Thompson hosted a buffet supper at his residence, Spaso House. The event was nearly derailed when Van asked if he could invite several of the leading figures from the competition. The sticking point was not the Soviets but Liu Shikun: the embassy could hardly welcome the Chinese pianist as the representative of a government the United States did not recognize. With the State Department's cognizance, the supper was declared to be a purely informal affair, and a diplomatic incident was averted. In the end Liu stayed away, perhaps on his own embassy's advice, as did Emil Gilels, Lev Vlassenko, and the Soviet violinists. But Shostakovich brought his wife and his son, Maxim; Kabalevsky and Kondrashin also came with their wives; and Richter, who had been in the audience, briefly put in a rare social appearance. Danny Pollack had left to play a tour of southern Soviet cities before returning to Vienna, but Jerry Lowenthal was present, and overheard Van talking with Tommy Thompson: "I said to Mr. Khrushchev," he was explaining to the ambassador, "that in this post-Sputnik age we have to love each other." How about that, marveled the earnest Lowenthal; the mad-looking kid had turned out to be a natural diplomat.

Thompson was fully aware of the impression Van had made on the Soviet Union. When Secretary Dulles sought his opinion of the young pianist, the ambassador wired back that his victory had done much to disabuse the Soviets of the impression that the United States was a nation of Philistines. He added a caveat, though: "Because of his immaturity and some personality traits, there is some danger that public and official adulation will go to his head and I took occasion of [a] luncheon which I gave for contestants to give him some friendly advice." More alarm bells rang when Van found time to write a short article for United Press that was reprinted across America. "There are no political barriers to music," he boldly began:

The same blood running through Americans also runs through the Soviet people and compels us to create and enjoy the same art.

I've become even more aware of this since I have been in Moscow. What has thrilled me so much is the great spirit of musical unity achieved here at the Tchaikovsky Competition by the different peoples of the world whose governments are at political loggerheads . . .

Russian reaction to my playing has been a wonderfully heartfelt one. These people have long felt that America has a fine culture but until recently have had not much proof of this. I helped to show them that their feelings are right.

They are so pleased to learn that America loves their music—
Tchaikovsky, Rachmaninoff, Shostakovich and other Russian
composers—as much as they do.

In his enthusiasm to build bridges, Van also made a big fuss about
his friendship with Eddik Miansarov and Naum Shtarkman, recount-
ing their first meeting and emphasizing that they had stuck together
ever since. Apparently it never crossed his mind that, for their sake,
such a show of warmth to a Westerner might have been better kept
out of the world's press.

As Van left the next day, with Henrietta and Paul Moor, for a victory tour of Leningrad, Riga, Kiev, and Minsk, the U.S. embassy in
Moscow kept up its dispatches to the State Department. "Among
Moscow teenagers he appears to have somewhat the same appeal
which Elvis Presley has in the United States," Minister-Counselor
Richard H. Davis reported. "On the occasion of his recent departure
by train for a concert in Leningrad, a crowd of approximately 200
teenage girls saw him off, showering him with flowers, requests for
autographs, and chanting in English, 'we love you.'" In the old czarist
capital, there were fevered scenes as scalpers prevented students from
getting tickets, and Van spontaneously opened his rehearsal to thousands of disappointed fans. Among them was the schoolgirl who had
watched his finals on TV; she had since gone Van-mad and felt she
was in heaven witnessing this mysterious messenger from a distant
country in the flesh. Some who had obtained tickets to the evening
concert had waited in line for three days and nights, and halfway
through the concert, one woman fainted; others openly wept. Afterward, strangers ran up and hugged and kissed Van, shyly holding out
presents. He hugged them back, picking up one girl and twirling her
round, and he endeared himself still more when he made a pilgrimage to Tchaikovsky's grave, dug up a handful of earth, and took it
away in a jar. Equally moved, Van called Rildia Bee and told her that
he had performed on the stage where her teacher Arthur Friedheim
had played.

*   *   *

SOMEHOW BILL Judd managed to get through to his most famous client, and after they spoke he contacted the State Department, which cabled the embassy in Moscow:

NEW YORK AGENTS OF VAN CLIBURN REPORT FROM TELEPHONE
CONVERSATION WITH HIM THAT HE MAY BE UNDER
CONSIDERABLE RUSSIAN PRESSURE AGAINST HIS WILL TO EXTEND
HIS TOUR OF RUSSIA AND THUS JEOPARDIZE FIRM US CONCERT
COMMITMENTS. HIS AGENTS REQUEST THAT YOU EXTEND
APPROPRIATE ASSISTANCE TO HIM.

The embassy tracked Van down while he was still in Leningrad, and he explained that he was trying to finish his tour in time to give one last concert in Moscow and then rest for three or four days before flying home. He added that he hoped to return to the USSR afterward, in late May or June. This did not sound like a man who was under duress, and soon another telegram arrived from the State Department, this one marked SECRET:

DEPARTMENT HAS RECEIVED REPORT THAT MANAGER OF VAN
CLIBURN, WHO HAS BEEN IN TELEPHONIC COMMUNICATION
WITH CLIBURN IN MOSCOW, AND ANOTHER FRIEND OF CLIBURN
ARE CONCERNED OVER WHAT THEY CONSIDER TO BE DECIDED
CHANGE IN ATTITUDE OF YOUNG PIANIST. IN ONE CONVERSATION
CLIBURN REPORTEDLY STATED HE WAS PLANNING TO RETURN
TO MOSCOW FOR LONG VACATION. IN ANOTHER CONVERSATION
WHEN QUERIED AS TO HIS PLANS WHEN IN WASHINGTON,
CLIBURN STATED THAT IF PRESIDENT WANTED TO SEE HIM
WHITE HOUSE COULD GET IN TOUCH WITH HIM. ADDITIONALLY,
THESE FRIENDS NOTE THAT CLIBURN HAS BECOME QUITE
LAUDATORY OF HIS RECEPTION AND STAY IN SOVIET UNION.

UNDER CIRCUMSTANCES, THEY ARE PARTICULARLY
APPREHENSIVE AS TO WHAT MIGHT HAPPEN WHEN CLIBURN
FIRST RETURNS TO US AND MEETS PRESS. THEY BELIEVE HE IS
LIABLE TO MAKE SOME VERY UNWISE STATEMENTS IF QUERIED
ON POLITICAL MATTERS, ABOUT WHICH HE KNOWS VERY LITTLE,
PARTICULARLY IN VIEW OF HIS REPORTED CHANGE IN ATTITUDE.
THEY SPECULATE IN THIS REGARD THAT CLIBURN MAY HAVE
BEEN "APPROACHED" BY SOVIETS.

The information, which was doubtless obtained by listening in on Van's calls, had first been passed to the office of FBI director J. Edgar Hoover. According to the report, Van had told Judd that he intended to stay in Russia indefinitely "and further stated 'If Eisenhower wants to see me, he knows where he can find me.'" The informant added that Judd was "very much concerned in that he believes when Clibern [*sic*] returns he will make a fool out of himself with his pro-Soviet attitude." Hoover suggested that the president's press secretary, James Hagerty, be alerted and added, "Also suggest Johnson (Senator) be *confidentially* advised." The two men were duly informed; Hagerty replied that the president was committed to meeting the young pianist, but the White House "would play it very cautiously from now on."

Fears that Van's enthusiasm might convert a cultural triumph into a propaganda debacle were bad enough, but the suggestion that Soviet recruiters might have turned him was deeply grave. When he finally returned to Moscow on May 10, somewhat rested after swallowing another potent Soviet sleeping pill on the night train from Minsk, he was met by a party of U.S. embassy officials who protested that they hadn't spent any real time with him and declared that this was to be his embassy day. Two days later Minister-Counselor Davis replied to Foggy Bottom with a lengthy telegram, also marked SECRET. Van was planning to bring his parents to the Soviet Union that summer and to return for three months the following spring, he noted. But he had "so far kept away from any political comment and I would judge from my talk with him today he will continue to do so." While the young pianist was undoubtedly naive and politically unsophisticated, Davis concluded, "I would doubt that he has been 'approached' by Soviets or that he has any idea other than pursuing his musical career in US and abroad in fashion normal to life of an international artist."

Between his triumph and the traditional heated Russian hospitality, Van would have been hard-hearted indeed if he had not lost his head a little. During his absence, hundreds of letters and boxes of pink floral telegrams had piled up in his hotel room, some simply addressed, "Conservatory, Vanya Kleeburn." Many came from students: not only musicians but entire classes at the Faculty for History and Philology of the Ivanovo State Pedagogical Institute and the Faculty of Soil Science and Biology of Moscow State University, who signed themselves, "Your friends forever." Others came from a forestry engineer, a geographer, and a telegraph operator named Saida Nurmukhamedova, who asked Van, "on behalf of all Soviet telegraph operators, to pass our friendly greetings to the American telegraph operators. Our telegraph operators will always be happy to hear your exceptional playing." She added, "When I have a son I shall definitely name him after you." Many declared undying love, sometimes in the form of tearful verses written on paper adorned with roses or lilies of the valley. "Vanyusha my dear," one simply read, "please stay in Moscow and the USSR. Nowhere else would people value and love you more." Two girls in the seventh grade told him, "You set our hearts on fire." Other letters were anonymous, including one from a pianist, a graduate of the Moscow Conservatory, who had been reduced to tears by Van's Rachmaninoff. "How hard it is going to be to say good-bye," she concluded. "You will probably never know about me, but I want you to know that when you leave you will take with you a piece of my heart, and that I will be with you till the end of my days. Don't forget me. I won't tell you my name. What for?" Occasionally there was a hint of distrust for the West—one writer asked Van to pass on his best wishes "to all honest Americans"—or a brave barb at the Soviet Union. The students of the Vilnius Conservatory wrote saying how delighted they were that he had won and how sorry they were to be "living in this nasty place that isn't one of the cities that you will visit." Yet many letters, some very long and earnest, voiced hopes that Van's triumph would improve world relations. "I would like to express my deep gratitude to our compatriot Rosina Levina who has instilled in you the love for Russian music and the Russian people," wrote twenty-year-old medical student Klara Gribanova. "I would like the friendship between the young people all round the world to become even stronger." In comradely fashion, she signed off, "With a warm handshake."

Gifts had also piled up uncontrollably, many treasured heirlooms that had been hidden from the authorities and uncovered, polished, mended, and passed on to the young visitor as secret tokens of lives unlived. An unnamed family gave him a porcelain platter decorated with a troika that they had cherished for seventy years: "Look at it in your bad moments," read the accompanying card, "and think there are people who love you and always will." Most moving of all was a lilac shrub that a group of students had clubbed together to buy after they heard he wanted to plant one on Rachmaninoff's grave in New York.

If he had stolen the Soviets' hearts, they had equally stolen his. "I tell you," he confided to Paul Moor, "these are my people. I guess I've always had a Russian heart. I'd give them three quarts of blood and four pounds of flesh. I've never felt so at home anywhere in my whole life." He was speaking in the heat of the moment and never expected his words to appear in print, even when Moor mentioned that his *Time* article might become a cover story. "Oh sure," Van thought, not taking it too seriously. He that expecteth nothing is never disappointed.

*   *   *

THERE WAS no chance of any rest before leaving Moscow. He was invited to ballets and operas at the Bolshoi and visited the Central Music School, where he played a duet with a young pianist while yet another film was shot. There were more recording sessions, one lasting until half past five in the morning. By the time of his final marathon with the Moscow State Symphony, they had shared the stage for three concerts and forty-five hours of recordings. "We have something for you," the players said as he entered the hall, and they presented him with an album containing pictures of every place he had visited during his stay. With it was an enamel box of chocolates decorated with scenes from Pushkin's fairy tales, an enamel cigarette case for his favorite Kents, and a poster for their final concert, signed by every member of the orchestra.

The next day, he walked out to take his place in the Great Hall one last time. He picked up a letter from the keyboard, used it to brush off some petals, read it, and put it on the floor, then thought better of it and slid it in his pocket. The orchestra players craned to see what he was doing, and laughter rippled through the hall. The accumulated tension dissolved, but the moment he began to play, the audience and the seventeen million watching on state television hung forward and let his poetry flow through them. At the end, the rhythmic clapping echoed and reechoed like thunder. Women rushed up to present flowers, and a man handed up a balalaika. After three encores, Van stepped forward and read a message in Russian. Pronouncing the words with great effort, he said that he had come to love Soviet audiences and would try to be worthy of his gold medal. Since he could take only half the prize money out of the country (and none of his earnings), he asked the Ministry of Culture to establish two memorial prizes at the Moscow Conservatory in the names of Josef Lhévinne and Sergei Rachmaninoff. He also asked that Lev Vlassenko, Naum Shtarkman, and Eddik Miansarov be sent to perform in America. "Today," he ended, "when I have to tell you 'goodbye,' my heart is full of memories and sadness. Until the end of my days I cannot forget your kindness. Thank you!"

Then he went back to the piano. Earlier in his visit he had heard the melancholy strains of "Moscow Nights," the hit song from last summer's World Festival of Youth. Now he improvised his own version, gently, ardently, a tribute to the city and its people. The audience melted in delight and love for this romantic stranger who loved them. They cried, and the viewers at home cried, and the next day they talked about nothing but their feelings and their tears.

In the morning a reporter for *Sovetskaya Kultura* tracked Van down in his hotel room, where he was exchanging photographs and embraces with the violinist Valery Klimov while a team from Moscow Radio recorded his parting message to the Soviet people. The journalist managed to get in a question when a call came in from Van's parents. "I'm so sad to leave Russia," he overheard Van say to them: "I would love to come to Russia with you." As the interview went haltingly on, an artist sketched Van's portrait, and when it was finished Van looked and decided he liked it. He took it, thought for a moment, and wrote on it: "To the readers of *Sovetskaya Kultura* newspaper, I would like to express my deep satisfaction about being able to visit Russia and play for such a captivating audience and to fall in love with the Soviet people. My most heartfelt greetings, devotion and gratitude. Van Cliburn."

Halfway through the conversation the news came that a third Soviet *Sputnik* had been launched. Van broke out in an admiring smile and exclaimed, "Bravo! Bravo! Bravo!"

*   *   *

THE FOLLOWING day, he headed to Vnukovo Airport with many new friends, fourteen extra suitcases, and one six-foot lilac shrub. The Intourist officials refused to let him pay the surcharge for overweight baggage, which at 4,800 rubles approached a fifth of his winnings. As the cameras whirred and crowds of fans, officials, and students pressed in, he made a little farewell speech, again in Russian, and backed toward the waiting plane, his cheeks wet with tears. Henrietta Belayeva glowed with pride. She had lived Van's triumph every day and was as madly in love with him as was Naum. They and Eddik and everyone else waved as the SAS plane took off for Copenhagen.

When it could no longer be seen, the crowd drifted thoughtfully apart. For many people, life had perceptibly brightened, but it was far from clear that the mighty gears of state would shift to match.

Two weeks earlier, on May 1, Labor Day, Khrushchev had watched from the Lenin-Stalin mausoleum's viewing balcony as vast squads of troops goose-stepped in unison and bulky military hardware rolled past. Heavy rain had turned Red Square into a black lake, but nothing could dim the premier's grin. Standing stiffly at his side, a reminder to the West of its clumsy meddling abroad and (so Khrushchev thought) the talismanic power of Soviet missiles to check its ambitions, was the hero of Suez and his new ally, Egyptian president Gamal Abdel Nasser.

Later in the month, the premier changed tack. Heeding scientists' warnings that years of nuclear tests were poisoning the atmosphere, Khrushchev announced a unilateral moratorium just as the United States was about to begin a new round. To his fury, America went ahead. A few weeks later, Imre Nagy, the leader of the failed Hungarian anti-Soviet revolution of 1956, was executed after a secret trial: in a cynical ploy worthy of Stalin, Khrushchev allegedly ordered his death as a lesson to aspiring rebels. When protests broke out round Soviet embassies in the West, busloads of Soviet demonstrators arrived at the American embassy in Moscow and lay about the building in tit-for-tat revenge.

Spinning and kicking, barracking and blustering, Khrushchev continued his ungainly *gopak* on the international stage. His embrace of the young American pianist had stunned the world, but it remained to be seen if Van and his beloved music would prove to be partners in peace or pawns in a brutal game.

· *12* ·

"He Played the Piano and the World Was His"

ON BOARD the departing SAS flight, Van watched Russia recede for a long while before looking down at a card that a spokesman for Soviet musicians had slipped in his hand at the last minute. It was another touching paean to an unforgettable few weeks and a heartfelt plea for him to return soon. Yet again he choked up, but during the short flight to Copenhagen there were plenty of thoughts waiting to crowd in. Could anything in his life match up to this feeling he was carrying away? What did his extraordinary stroke of fortune signify? How was he ever to live up to it, when the Leventritt Award had seemed an onerous responsibility? And what did it mean that if the piano competition he'd won had been in Berlin, scarcely anyone would have noticed?

The plane was late arriving, and Van missed his connection to New York. While he waited for the next flight an enterprising reporter tracked him down, and he gave a telephone interview. "I'm going home with the most exciting memories of my life," he gushed. "There are moments I will never forget. Of course I will go back to Moscow one day to play there again. Russian audiences inspire me. All Russians are very warm. They're sweet people. The only thing that the Russians want from the Americans, English or Scandinavians is to meet them in an atmosphere of friendship, sincerity, and mutual understanding. I'm glad to be going home but still I'm going to miss Russia. I have friends there in the world of music and this friendship will live forever."

Eventually the new flight began boarding, and the hostess came over.

"Oh!" she said, "you're the one on the magazine!"

"What magazine?" Van asked.

"*Time* magazine," she replied. "Your picture is on the cover." She fished out her copy, and there he was, drawn with a pained expression and reddish hair waving like a sea anemone. A banner across the masthead read: THE TEXAN WHO CONQUERED RUSSIA. On the reverse, unpromisingly, was a full-page advertisement for the "CONVAIR-*Astronautics*' ATLAS . . . the free world's first ICBM," with a color picture of a giant rocket rising into the night amid furies of fire. The U.S. Air Force had just conducted a successful test flight of the burly missile, which was touted as "a vital weapon for our national security and a key to ultimate peace."

Van turned to the lengthy cover story, "The All-American Virtuoso." After reading a few words, he shuddered with dismay. "Ah swear to goodness, ah just can't believe all this is happenin' to li'l ole Van Cliburn from the piney woods of East Texas!" it began, purporting to quote him, Van. It made him out to be a comic rustic, "as Texan as pecan pie."

He read on. There was private information about his failed relationship with Donna, his health troubles, and his debts, which were said to be so heavy that he "took to such money-saving devices as playing classical music for his supper in Manhattan's Asti Restaurant." There were lines about his childhood being hell and his schoolmates thinking him queer, things he had never intended people back home to read. There were intimate descriptions of his preconcert routine and his fits of sobbing, including at Richter's recital, which made him sound kooky. Over and over, there were private words spoken to just one person: a cynical aside about the prospect of "all those people making money out of me" as offers rolled in; moments of elation after his Moscow concerts. "I tell you, these are my people," he read himself quoted as saying. "I guess I've always had a Russian heart. I'd give them three quarts of blood and four pounds of flesh. I've never felt so at home anywhere in my whole life." Paul Moor, his purported protector, had betrayed his confidence. Or, rather, Van realized to his chagrin, he had trusted in Moor's discretion. He would never make the same mistake again.

The plane banked through dense clouds and landed at Idlewild at 9:45 a.m. on Friday, May 16, four hours late. The crew let Van off first, and as he climbed down to the wet tarmac, photographers came running. Flashbulbs flared, movie cameras whirred. Like a pro he stopped and smiled, stretching his arm out to wave.

An official diverted him to a packed conference room. He glimpsed his beaming parents in the last row, but reporters surrounded him, shouting questions. One brandished a copy of *Time*.

"Why does this say, 'These are my people?'" the man demanded.

"Who put those words in my mouth?" Van retorted. He had brooded all the way home and had steeled himself for an inquisition. "I actually said, 'These all remind me of Texas people.'" His welcome in Moscow had been so warm, he explained, that he was certain there "must be a little bit of Texan in the Russians."

"And I told them so," he brightly added, spotting a group of hometowners who had come up from Texas to welcome him back. Mrs. Leo Satterwhite Allen's speech and dramatics training was finally coming in handy.

"You said Khrushchev was a nice man," a journalist stated accusingly.

"He was to me," Van evenly replied. "I only saw him socially. He was nice to me, and I was nice to him."

"You must think you're a big success," another taunted.

"Oh no, I'm not a success," he politely demurred. "I'm just a sensation."

How did he feel, asked another reporter, about playing Carnegie Hall before some of the biggest names in American music?

"In general, I wish I didn't have to do it," Van drawled.

He scanned the faces in the close, low-ceilinged room. They looked mildly disappointed. Clearly they had come expecting a flaming Red sympathizer or at least a self-important upstart, and all they got was a prim young man who was dying to hug his parents. The *New York Times* noted that the pianist looked even younger than he was and acted correspondingly: he called his father "Daddy" and his mother "Honey" or "Sweetie."

The Cliburns set off for Manhattan in a limo, with Van's luggage following—except for the lilac shrub, which had been impounded by the plant quarantine authorities. The family's destination was not Van's little apartment on Fifty-Seventh Street but the Pierre Hotel on Fifth Avenue, one of the city's most elegant addresses. The elevator whizzed them up to the plush calm of a twenty-second-floor suite overlooking Central Park. Van's eyes opened wide, especially when he discovered that his parents had an adjoining suite. In one of his two living rooms his eyes fell on a Steinway parlor grand, and he shot over, his hands eagerly sweeping up and down the keyboard.

The sun pierced the blanket of clouds and flooded the tower suite with spring light. Porters began wheeling in luggage, and Van fell on it, eager to show off his souvenirs and tell the stories behind them. Soon the piano and every piece of furniture were piled high with an astonishing twenty-five hundred items, among them samovars, silver spoons and tea services, medallions, woodcuts, etchings, oil paintings, music scores, albums, photographs, and leather-bound books. Some were intended for Rildia Bee, including "a gold and white satin evening bag with matching white kid gloves, amber and silver jewelry, beautifully packaged bottles of perfume, samples of modern Russian ceramics and antique Russian enamels, and cigarette boxes fashioned of malachite." Several moved Van to tears, including a little plate painted with Tchaikovsky's portrait that a boy violinist in Riga, who had received it for his birthday, had shyly proffered.

People arrived. Bill Judd was there with Van's new press agent, Elizabeth Winston, trying to settle him down. A *Life* photographer was snapping away, and a *New York Times* reporter looked on, making notes for a piece that was splashed over the morning's paper along with photographs of some of Van's loot, including a sculpture of his head:

"He hasn't had one bite to eat since 8 o'clock," Mr. Cliburn said, talking pure Texan. "I carried him out to the doctor just to see if he was all right. He was, but he's got to have some rest."

Meanwhile, Van was inviting stragglers into the suite, hugging his mother again and assuring her that he really was all right and that there was every reason to celebrate.

"Honey," he said, "let's learn where we are."

He warmly greeted everyone who got near him, and when one man offered to spare him another handshake, remarked, "Oh, stop it."

As he became convinced that the visitors showed no tendency to harass his son, the elder Mr. Cliburn shyly pointed out some of the gifts Van had brought back.

"Just look over there," Mr. Cliburn said, almost in a whisper, pointing to the corner of a sofa. "That little top and those dolls."

After a few hours' sleep and a visit from the hotel barber for a much-needed haircut, Van was back at Idlewild to greet Kirill Kondrashin, honored artist of Soviet Russia and winner of two Stalin Prizes, whose visa had been rushed through just in time. The Russian emerged into brilliant sunshine and said a few words to an AP reporter about Van's Moscow triumph. Then the two hurried to the waiting limo and went directly to Carnegie Hall, where the Symphony of the Air was already assembled.

Outside the hall, Van's cornflower-blue eyes peered from a large poster advertising his concert the following evening. A green-lettered banner partly obscured his face and announced: SOLD OUT. A growing crowd of disappointed fans was trying to convince the doorman that they should be allowed into the rehearsal, and when they spotted Van they swarmed round him. "Are you Harvey Kilgore?" asked one man, thrusting out his hand. After the rehearsal, another crowd surrounded him as he made his way toward Sixth Avenue and dropped into a diner for a Coke and some American cigarettes for Kondrashin.

Back at the Pierre, the Cliburns and Bill Judd conspired to restrain Van for the rest of the day. The drapes and blinds in the living room were drawn against the sun, and in the half-light Van and Kondrashin sat down at a lunch table with a record company boss, a concert manager, and a conductor, who talked business in somber, hushed tones. Van was more interested in making Kondrashin feel at home, and they communicated in a mix of hugs and gestures, cigarettes in hand. Abram Chasins, the chairman of Van's Leventritt jury, dropped by with his pianist wife, Constance Keene, who as always was dressed head to toe in red, and Chasins thought he had entered a wake. Van got up and showed them into the other living room, where the Russian booty was arrayed. "Isn't it wonderful?" he whispered, as if he half-believed there would be a knock on the door and it would all be carted away—though the bigger risk came from Chasins, a notorious kleptomaniac, who carried a card signed by a psychiatrist to prove it. Every so often, Manhattan hostesses caught him in the act of palming the spoons at dinner and firmly told him to hand them over.

Three penguin-suited waiters wheeled in wagons piled with sizzling steaks, chops, and cutlets. Judd wrote Van's name on the check and added a large tip. Van jumped up, looked over his shoulder, and turned white. "Can we afford this?" he murmured.

In the Liberty Music Store a life-size model of Van sat at the grand piano. Down on Broadway, the *Time* sign blazoned his story in tall neon letters. That night, its subject was back among the pipes and strip lights of the Steinway Hall basement. He had an audience even there, and the *Life* photographer never stopped snapping away.

*   *   *

THE NEXT evening, scalpers were unloading tickets outside Carnegie Hall for one hundred fifty dollars a pair, compared with the regu-

lar prices of fifty cents to five dollars. The advance demand had been
the heaviest in the hall's history; hundreds, probably thousands, had
been turned away. An enormous crowd was milling around in every
conceivable manner of dress, from voluptuous ball gowns to jeans
and sneakers. The music pack was out in force, but there were also
people who had never been to a classical concert and had been drawn
by the excitement.

Inside, it was punishingly hot. Every one of the 2,760 seats was
taken, and there were far more standees than the regulation eighty.
Rosina was there, anxious and still a little peeved at Van, with Mark
Schubart and Bill Schuman. Mikhail Menshikov, the elegant, ebullient Soviet ambassador known among the diplomatic corps as Smiling Mike, was watching. So was Rachmaninoff's daughter, Princess
Irina Volkonsky. The New York City mayor was present, along with
nearly every notable critic. Only one important person was missing:
Sascha Greiner, the Steinway veteran who had lunched with Van until he agreed to go to Moscow, had died a week after Van won.

Backstage, Van's only pair of shoes was distracting him. A sole had
come loose, and he fastened it with a rubber band. He said a prayer
with old Benny, the faithful Carnegie Hall artists' attendant, before
striding toward the low doorway that led onto the stage. On his way
through he thumped his head on the lintel, but he quickly recovered
with a rueful smile and bowed modestly to a polite, expectant ovation. His tails looked enormous, the trousers billowing round his
skinny frame. He sat down and got up again. The seat was too high,
and he tried to wind it down. It jammed, and he sighed, shrugging to
the audience. He tried twisting the knobs again and shook his head.
If he was aware that he, a twenty-three-year-old not yet four years out
of Juilliard, was about to be measured against the greatest pianists of
the age, he gave nothing away.

He stilled himself, lifted his hands, fixed his gaze on Kondrashin,
and played Tchaikovsky's Piano Concerto no. 1. A few nervous
smashes caused an anxious ripple, but he settled into a restrained,
bravura performance. Unorthodox ovations broke out between the

movements, just as they had at his debut four years ago, and at the end the audience leaped, shouting, to its feet. As Van embraced Kondrashin, the orchestra joined in the ovation. Only two people, sitting in a first-tier box, were silent: Harvey sat with his hands folded in his lap, and Rildia Bee kept her gloved arms placidly crossed. "She really is bursting," said a friend seated nearby. It was, thought the *Times* critic, "tremendously moving . . . They seemed not so much bursting with pride—and perhaps disbelief—as transfixed by it."

Van headed backstage and changed his sodden shirt. Moscow had been something else, but there was a reassuring fixedness to this place he knew well. "I'm so happy to be home again," he said, and minutes later he emerged to play Rachmaninoff's Third. Another roaring standing ovation brought him back six times for three encores, and while he was still bowing, half the audience rushed the backstage doors. For the first time in the hall's sixty-seven years the green room became a dangerous crush, and the orchestra's huge instrument room was opened up. Even that grew so full that photographers climbed on tables to get a clear shot. To the ushers' horror, Van looked each fan in the eye, gratefully shook each hand, and gravely autographed the proffered programs. "What do you play?" he asked teenage musicians. "Who is your teacher? What are you studying now?" A journalist who was writing an article titled "Van Cliburn at Home" for the popular Soviet magazine *Ogonyok* shook the hero's hand but was swept away before he could ask for an interview. He wrote the piece anyway, and did manage to tell his readers that Van's friends were now calling him Ivan.

Rosina scribbled her congratulations on her program, sent it upstairs, and headed back to Claremont Avenue. Outside Carnegie Hall, on Fifty-Sixth Street, a cordon of policemen with locked arms were struggling to restrain a throng of ticketless fans. "Jeepers, I wouldn't even wish this on me mudder-in-law!" panted a young cop.

"We can all breathe easily now," the papers reported the next morning: "The Russians were right." The note of relief was unmistakable, but the thought behind it was unspoken. If Van had disappointed, why would the Russians have given him the prize? Surely it would have meant there was a political stitch-up at work? Even now, some Americans found it easier to believe that Eisenhower's office had talked to Khrushchev's office than that one of their own was the deserving winner, though it would probably have been the first time in history that two government heads had discussed the arts, let alone a music competition that had been well off their radar till Van won. "Over and over again," a reporter noted shortly after Van's victory,

> the question last week has been: "Is this Van Cliburn really that good?" It was asked by people who were delighted with his triumph in Moscow and were eager to believe the best. It was asked by a skeptical few who cannot rid themselves of the prejudice that a foreigner is somehow automatically superior as a virtuoso to a tall young man from Texas. It was asked rhetorically by some who were convinced that this was just another example of Russian duplicity.

Yet, if he really was the best, why had it taken the Russians to tell them so? A letter to *Time* pointed out the irony that the flap over a Soviet competition winner "would seem to indicate that the U.S. is the latest country to become a Russian satellite . . . Are we to understand that American artists will henceforth have to pay their obeisance to Khrushchev before they can hope to be recognized in their own country?"

The fact was that the Old World's blessing had always helped aspirants to make it as artists in America. The fascination with Van's victory, though, went far beyond music. After the shock of *Sputnik* it was the first sign that America could rise to the Soviet challenge and win—win, moreover, on the Reds' home ground, in a contest of their choosing. Perhaps it ran still deeper. Cultural insecurity, along with manifest destiny and a Protestant work ethic, had made America the powerhouse of the world. Yet, at this point in U.S. history, with the country's dominance far from guaranteed, Americans were desperately in need of reassurance. Van had given it to them, in the very field where the nation felt most inferior to the Old World, and no one could have been more American than a blue-eyed blond Texan who loved big cars, mouthed folksy wisdom, and crooned "Blue Moon." In 1958 he was a hero from central casting, to teenage girls the perfect bachelor, to their parents a squeaky-clean role model, an anti-Elvis who was said never to drink or smoke and who drew crowds like a musical Billy Graham with his message of spirituality and greatness from out of the heartland. As for the fact that he adored Russian culture, preached a gospel of friendship not victory, and was trailing a Soviet conductor everywhere he went—these were minor snags in the thick canopy of satisfaction.

*   *   *

VAN HARDLY had time to read the morning papers, because he was getting ready for his very own ticker tape parade. May 20, 1958, was Van Cliburn Day in New York City.

Despite the damp weather, there was a carnival atmosphere downtown. The mayor had asked schools and colleges to declare a holiday, and on Beaver Street and Stone Street a thousand junior high school band members and students assembled at 11:30 a.m. alongside a combined band of Boy Scouts and Cubs. The main group formed into four units of two hundred students, each headed by a band, and arrayed themselves in marching order, eight abreast. Mounted police led them into Bowling Green, and shortly after noon the cacophonous cavalcade set off along Lower Broadway. Majorettes twirling batons led the way, page boys drummed, fifers tooted, cheerleaders yelled, and the massed colors of the New York City Fire Department brought up the rear. Two open-topped cars followed. Van perched on the trunk of the first, his legs on the backseat, wearing a dark suit, white shirt, and narrow dark tie. City officials sat at his feet. Bill Schuman and his wife traveled in the second car, with Harvey and Rildia Bee, and members of the press drove alongside in two trucks provided by the Department of Sanitation. As Van glanced up he saw ticker tape twirl down from office buildings draped with banners and flags, and people hanging out of windows thirty and forty stories high, all the way to the skyscrapers' mist-shrouded tops. On the ground, cheering crowds stood three or four deep, a dozen in places, waving signs reading WELCOME VAN CLIBURN. Some climbed on car roofs to get a better view. The front row consisted almost entirely of girls, and as the car approached, their hands stretched out in a rippling wave of flesh. Van leaned over to touch as many as he could reach. A few girls broke free and dashed up for a handshake or hug. One girl stood on tiptoe for a kiss, and Van planted some of his excitement on her lips. "He's cuter than Tony Perkins!" another screamed. "You showed them Russians!" older spectators shrieked with pride. A few hollered something about youths needing a haircut; the rest shouted them down. Van smiled and waved.

The sun broke through and bathed the procession in light. Just above Trinity Church a man ran up: "How does it feel?" he shouted.

"How does it feel?" Van repeated, gasping, shaking his head, crossing his hands over his heart, and blowing kisses to the world. "I wonder who it's for." The only thing that kept him together was Mother's parting entreaty to be thinking what he would say on the stand.

The head of the parade arrived in City Hall Park at around 12:30 p.m. A lectern was waiting on the steps, facing VIP tiered seating decorated with bunting and UN flags. The Department of Sanitation Band and the United Nations Chorus were waiting with four hundred more students and the Texas Club of New York. The marchers took their positions, the Fire Department colors arranged themselves behind the rostrum, and the assembled five thousand waited.

Van climbed out of the car with his mind still a blank. His parents joined him. When he spotted Kondrashin among the waiting dignitaries, he dragged him onto the platform. The band played the national anthem with the crowd singing along, and the United Nations Chorus followed with four selections. Speakers, including the pastor of Calvary Baptist, sang Van's praises, and New York City mayor Robert F. Wagner presented him with the city's Scroll for Exceptional and Distinguished Service. They shook hands, and as Van moved in front of the microphone the words finally came. The victory, he declared in a strong, soft voice, did not belong to him but to classical music, a universal language that he hoped the win would help more people speak. "It was a wonderful thing to go to the Soviet Union," he added, "and I wish you could have been with me and seen the wonderful, heart-warming love and affection given." At his side, Harvey put an arm round his back: whether in support or warning, it was hard to tell.

From City Hall a limousine mounting a blaring klaxon took them to the Waldorf-Astoria, with a police escort clearing the way. In the Empire Room five hundred guests had been seated for more than an hour; the more impatient had begun to dip into their halibut flakes "Antoine." Finally Van strode in, nearly tripping over his flapping sole as the mayor struggled to keep pace and an orchestra, furnished by Local 802 of the Musicians' Union, struck up the national anthem. When it finished, half the room surged forward to receive hugs from the returning hero, have autographs signed, or simply be in his orbit. Van blew more kisses. On the dais, Rildia Bee smiled graciously while Harvey looked about in disbelief. Bill Schuman spoke of Juilliard's pride in its now-famous alumnus. Abram Chasins made a speech, allowing his tablemates to check if the silver service was still intact. Rosina Lhévinne received the city's first annual Van Cliburn Award, in the form of an inscribed vase. The composer Richard Rodgers praised "this young, this very old diplomat." The mayor toasted Van's mother and daddy with Georges de Latour Cabernet '48—Van demurely raised a glass of Vichy water—then toasted Van and presented him with another decoration, the medal of the city. Van shook his head, scattered some kisses about, and rose unsteadily to his feet. Reported *The New Yorker*, he

wished all his friends would say an occasional prayer for him to enable him to live up to all that had happened. He knew, he said, that it could have happened to somebody else. "Ah appreciate everything," he said. "You will never know. Ah love you." He blew kisses to all, and strode to the piano. A hush fell over the Empire Room, the waiters stopped serving dessert, and Van Cliburn, transported now, played two numbers.

As a bonus, when he discovered that one of the dignitaries was heading to Moscow that afternoon, he sat down and wrote long introductions to his Soviet friends, including Premier Khrushchev and ex-premier Bulganin, and before handing them over, he read them to the room. Somewhere toward the back was Joyce Flissler, the New York–born violinist who had placed seventh in the violin competition. She had been included at the last minute, and no one paid her the slightest attention—but then, no one had treated her a jot differently since she had returned from Moscow a month earlier. She was fond of Van and admired him, but her claret came in a bitter cup.

"He's the Eggheads' Elvis Presley!" chortled the *Sunday Daily News*, outdone only by *Time*, which dubbed Van "Horowitz, Liberace and Presley all rolled into one."

"It's a dream!" Van kept saying. "And if it is, I hope I never wake up."

The police estimated that a hundred thousand had cheered Van on, perhaps the most since Charles Lindbergh was rapturously welcomed home thirty-one years earlier. The city had hoped the event would be even bigger, an American Music Day involving all New York's music students and teachers, but one by one the music schools and university music departments had cried off. Most explained that it was exam week or that they were not equipped for marching, but some publicly aired gripes: they were suspicious of the sudden official interest in their existence, suspected they were being used for political ends, thought it unfair to single out one competition winner when others had been ignored, and found it ripe that the authorities left it to private charity to fund American emissaries and then jumped on the bandwagon when they won. Others, demonstrating why classical music was not more popular, sniffed that an academic procession in caps and gowns would have been all well and good, but a ticker tape parade was undignified for a musician. More than a few schools had not even bothered to respond to the city's invitation. PARADE FOR PIANIST LAGS, the *New York Herald Tribune* had headlined six days earlier.

There was also a nasty whiff of sour grapes that followed Van round. More than one prominent pianist was insanely jealous of his fame: "I could have gone to Moscow, too," one repeatedly scoffed. Another rival took the time and trouble to mail a "shockingly scurrilous and green-eyed poem" to thousands of musicians, alleging that the Tchaikovsky Competition had been rigged. The author of the low doggerel was of course anonymous, but in the catty music world, this was far from the only intimation that the Russians had "arranged" Van's victory as a propaganda stunt. Some of the claims were not so much paranoid as batty, including a tip-off received by the FBI, which was continuing to keep tabs on Van, from an informant who had been in the Soviet Union during the competition. In a report marked TOP SECRET, an agent noted that the source "advised she had watched the concert on television and the director of the concert was only a third-rate conductor. The source expressed the opinion the reason a third-rate conductor had appeared could be that the director was a homosexual and Cliburn must be one also. The source further advised she considered another contestant much better than Cliburn and was of the opinion Cliburn must have been given the prize for some purpose of the Russians."

*   *   *

THE DAY after the parade, Wednesday, the Van Cliburn Show moved on to Philadelphia. Van's performance at the Academy of Music was cheered so loudly that he repeated the last two movements of the Tchaikovsky, and as his Cadillac finally pulled away hours later, screaming groupies gave chase and tore off one of the door handles. The next day, he disrupted the sedate Wanamaker's department store when he tried to buy a few new clothes. "Van Cliburn is here!" girls shrieked. "God bless you, son!" called an old man on an escalator, leaning dangerously over: "Bless you always for what you did for America!" At 2:00 a.m. on Friday, the cavalcade of pianist, parents, manager, press agent, conductor, and reporters arrived in Washington, DC, and Van, Liz Winston, and the chauffeur went looking for hamburgers and coffee. At an all-night snack bar, a nightclub pianist who had just come off duty slid into the booth and regaled Van with his life story. Van listened intently, chipping in to ask for more details, and it was nearly dawn when the Cliburn contingent wandered back to the hotel to catch a few hours' sleep before setting out for the White House.

An invitation to the Executive Mansion was a rare honor for an American artist of any age, let alone one who was unknown only a few weeks earlier. Van's immense popularity had made such a visit politically desirable, and though the government had declined to sponsor his travel abroad, Eisenhower had invested a good deal of political capital in cultural exchange programs. Yet the invitation had been for Van alone, not his parents, and certainly not for the Soviet conductor who was now standing alongside them in the Oval Office. Kondrashin good-naturedly passed on his best wishes on behalf of the Soviet people, thus becoming the first private Soviet citizen to meet the American president. Texas-born Ike cordially showed off his family snaps and posed for photographs, but he explained that his helicopter was waiting to take him to his Gettysburg farm and he would unfortunately miss the evening's concert at Constitution Hall. So would Mamie, who had already left for the weekend, and Vice President Richard Nixon, who was otherwise engaged. Still, Ike said, he was sure the concerts were a breeze for Van "after coming out on top in that kind of ordeal over there."

The chat lasted twelve minutes, after which the visitors were escorted out and the new Afghan ambassador was ushered in. At a press conference, during which Van ducked more loaded questions about his opinion of the Soviet Union, one reporter asked if the president had congratulated him on winning the contest. "Yes, I think so," he answered carefully. "I think he did it elliptically, if nothing else."

Another pointedly inquired whether Khrushchev had attended his concerts, and taking the bait, Van replied that he was very greatly disappointed not to have the chance to play for Ike.

Culture enjoyed an official status in the Soviet Union that it had never had in America. Yet Eisenhower's coolness could also be ascribed to what looked very much like presumptuousness on Van's part. Ike's press secretary had doubtless passed on J. Edgar Hoover's intelligence that, while in Moscow, Van had spoken dismissively about meeting the president; perhaps it was Ike himself who decided to "play it very cautiously." Then the young pianist had insisted on turning up with his Soviet friend in tow. Now he had come very near rebuking the president for not attending his concert, which could only increase the administration's caution in dealing with the headstrong young man. Lyndon B. Johnson, the Senate majority leader, had also seen the FBI report, which perhaps explained why he and his fellow Texas senator, Ralph Yarborough, also contrived to be out of town that Friday. Nor was there any mark of recognition from the powerful Texas State Society, though some members of the Texas delegation held a luncheon in the Senate Dining Room and presented Van and Kondrashin with gold cuff links enameled with the opening phrase of Tchaikovsky's First.

The official aloofness left the stage to the Soviets. That night, as a society audience filled Constitution Hall, the Cliburns pointedly took their seats in the box of Smiling Mike Menshikov, the Soviet ambassador, who had already sent a gargantuan basket of flowers backstage. Afterward the Soviet embassy in Washington hosted a gourmet supper for fifty guests, with Van and Kondrashin at the top of the horseshoe table and the first-desk members of the orchestra ranged on either side. Glasses were set for champagne, brandy, wines, and vodka, and Smiling Mike began toasting Van, Van's parents, and Kondrashin, the "number two papa of Van Cliburn." Menshikov could match any Bolshevik in verbosity. When he had presented his credentials that February, the president cordially asked about his background. His answer, the State Department memorandum recorded, ran "through his entire employment record" and "consumed 15 minutes of the 33 minute appointment." Three weeks later Menshikov contrived another lengthy meeting with Eisenhower, who was forced to explain that if he personally heard out all eighty ambassadors he would have no time to run the country. As soon as he could, Van sprang at the piano and played into the small hours. Between the music and the vodka, the normally somber embassy swam with warmth and camaraderie and light.

The next morning, General Robert Cutler, the president's national security adviser, asked Pat Coyne, an FBI veteran on the NSC's intelligence staff, to call the agency and find out what it had in its files on Van Cliburn and Kirill Kondrashin. "According to Coyne," noted J. Edgar Hoover's assistant A. H. Belmont, "Cutler advised that following the ovation that Cliburn received at his concert in Constitution Hall here last Friday, Cliburn gave Kondrashin two 'European kisses' and then kissed him on the lips." The inference was clearly that such unhealthy behavior might be a sign of unpatriotically effete tendencies.

· 13 ·

"He's Better Than Elvis by Far!"

BACK IN New York, Van was too keyed up to sleep, and he kept Liz Winston and Bill Judd talking into the early hours. Harvey, who didn't much like the big-city habits his son had picked up, came in rubbing his eyes. "You've got to let this poor boy have some sleep," he scolded them. They would have been only too glad: Liz had lost thirteen pounds in the nine days since Van's return; Bill, eight. Van himself had grown so thin that he had had his clothes taken in. But he pulled the two friends back: "Oh *please*," he implored. "Please don't go. Not yet. Let's have just another cigarette." They were still talking at dawn.

He had coasted on nerves through parades and speeches and concerts played under pressure that few musicians had ever experienced. Acting as if nothing had changed was his way of coping, but the next day the cracks began to show. That night, he was to appear on *The Steve Allen Show*, and during a rehearsal, the host held up a dummy sleeve of Van's yet-to-be-recorded first album, mocked up with a color photograph taken in the Soviet Union.

"What is that you're holding?" Van burst out. "This is unauthorized. I never authorized this." Color was for pop sensations, not serious musicians, who on album covers remained as black-and-white as piano keys and concert garb. He grabbed the sleeve, ripped it to pieces, and stormed off to his dressing room, slamming the door. A soberer album cover was quickly concocted, while Allen rehearsed his next guest, the great Louis Armstrong, and Van emerged his usual self in time to play the last movement of the Tchaikovsky and banter gamely. His fee was three thousand dollars, thirty times the sum he had received the previous time, but there was no complaint about that or his tantrum. He had the package: talent, youth, congeniality, fame, and photogenic looks, his rapt absorption especially striking in close-up.

At the Pierre, Van suddenly stood up at midnight. "I'm going back to my apartment to practice," he declared drastically. "I can't go on like this. Do you know, I haven't really worked in two months? I've just been playing, playing, playing." He grabbed his coat, ran out the door, and returned at 5:00 a.m., again too wired to sleep. But on May 26 he was back in remarkable form for a reprise of his program at Carnegie Hall. "A great event in the history of music in America is taking place tonight," intoned the announcer on WQXR, which broadcast the concert in full. At the beginning of the second half, Van brought on Kondrashin and turned to the audience. "I do hope you will forgive me," he politely drawled, "for departing from concert procedure and decorum to express one thought of appreciation to you for being so very kind to me." It came across as a charming mark of youthful gregariousness and the novelty of the occasion, though some may have felt he was taking his new role as a public figure too seriously. Afterward, he introduced Mayor Wagner, who expatiated on Van's impact in the worlds of music and international relations; then Van played the Rachmaninoff, to another raucous ovation. With cheers still echoing in their ears the Cliburns entertained a throng of guests until 3:00 a.m., when Abram Chasins noticed they had been too busy being hosts to eat, and proposed a trip to Reuben's. "Y'all go along," Harvey said with a grimace. "I'm *daid.*" Van, Rildia Bee, and the others traipsed down the street. Cabdrivers honked and waved. Cops walked over to slap Van on the back, doormen stepped out to pump his hand, and passersby thanked him "for doing what you did for us over there." Small shrieks met their entrance to the restaurant. As they made their way to their table, a drunk staggered up to shake the hero's hand and then slid to the floor. As the man babbled his congratulations, Van gently lifted him up and pulled up a chair. Putting an arm round him, he asked, "Do you *really* mean it? Did I do *that* much?"

Four days later, following an all-night recording session of the Tchaikovsky First with Kondrashin and the Symphony of the Air, Van was the featured guest on CBS's *Person to Person*, the hit show that peered into the homes of public figures. In his case, "home" was the rococo suite at the Pierre, where multiple television cameras had been set up. Trademark cigarette in hand, Edward R. Murrow introduced the guest from the studio, then swiveled toward a big screen showing Van and his parents seated on a couch. After calmly explaining that beneath the "Hollywood glamor type of sensational publicity," music was "really quite nerve-wracking, tedious, and quite demanding," Van stood up to give Murrow a tour of the suite and of his Soviet souvenirs. When Rildia Bee talked about her son's early fondness for playing, Van interrupted to say that it was true he was always famous for it, but "if it interfered with any of my outside activities or my friends, I never quite enjoyed it." Harvey began to speak, but Van overrode him to tell America that his father's great love was medicine and "he would have been a most fantastic doctor." He broke into Russian to recount his acceptance speech in Moscow, then sat at the piano and dashed off a few bars of "Nostalgia," which he described as "a mood picture after a short story I had read when I was fifteen, by Jack London."

The next morning, Van rented a white-and-baby-blue Lincoln Continental convertible and drove with the top down to Valhalla, a commuter hamlet twenty-five miles from Midtown Manhattan. In the backseat was the lilac shrub, which had finally emerged from quarantine, and the jar of soil from Leningrad. Drivers banged their horns and shouted, children leaned out to wave, and Van grinned and waved back. In the cemetery, he planted the sapling on Rachmaninoff's grave and laid a floral piece before the Russian Orthodox cross, the flowers red, white, and blue for the Soviet Union and the

United States. As the press looked on, Kondrashin scooped up some soil to return to Tchaikovsky's grave, while Rachmaninoff's daughter gave Van her father's lucky coin, a small Czar Nicholas five-ruble gold piece.

After that, the Soviet gifts were packed off to Steinway Hall, where more than two thousand of them went on public display. The Cliburns were moving out of the Pierre, and Rildia Bee and Harvey were heading home, but the question was where Van should go. Fan letters and telegrams were still pouring into his Osborne apartment, engulfing the tiny rooms, but to landlords, pianists were worse than dogs. Several rejected him the moment they heard his name, and for the time being he squeezed back into the old place.

It was a strange life he had begun leading, half American and half Russian, half homey and half grand. One day he stepped out to a Horn and Hardart automat for a dollar dinner and found his neighbor reading a newspaper article headlined VAN CLIBURN SIGNS MILLION-DOLLAR CONTRACT. Nor was his the only life that had changed. Before she left town, Rildia Bee was a guest on the legendary CBS panel game show *What's My Line?*

*   *   *

ON JUNE 1, Kirill Kondrashin flew back to Moscow laden down with Van's parting presents: a silver Tiffany table service and a life-size FAO Schwarz Russian bear. But Van was unable to manage without his number two papa, and less than two weeks later, Kondrashin rejoined the Cliburns in London after Van cabled a personal request to Khrushchev. "I wish you the greatest success in your remarkable creative work," the Soviet premier wired back. On June 15 the two musicians brought seven thousand cheering Londoners to their feet in the presence of the American and Soviet ambassadors, and after thrilling Amsterdam, Van went on to the Brussels World's Fair.

A town-size conglomeration of exhibition halls and national pavilions had been erected on a plateau outside the Belgian capital, with the adjacent American and Soviet displays vying to create the biggest stir. The Soviets had already asked Van to perform with them, which added to the worries of Bill Schuman and his Music Panel that the USSR was saturating the fair with talent. But America got in first, and on July 5, Van appeared with the Philadelphia Orchestra in the expo's Grand Auditorium. It was lunchtime, an inauspicious hour in Belgium for anything but lunch, but the arena was sold out. In the audience was a leading student of Rildia Bee's Russian teacher Arthur Friedheim, who knew nothing about Van beyond what he had seen in the headlines. When Van began to play, the man was sure he had heard the identical sound before: the same poise and great, rich sweep; the same uncanny pedaling and mastery of detail. Then he sat up with a start. "I listened to Cliburn with my eyes open," he later wrote, "and I knew that Arthur Friedheim was playing again, as Liszt played before him."

After a performance in Paris, Van flew home to fulfill one of the few engagements he had made before Moscow: two concerts in Chicago's Grant Park—at his old fee of eight hundred dollars, for the pair. When he arrived in the Windy City on July 15, a waiting troupe of Kilgore Rangerettes draped themselves over him. A wailing police escort whisked him to his hotel, where the brass band of the Moolah Temple in St. Louis serenaded him with "The Eyes of Texas Are upon You" and its interpretation of Tchaikovsky's First, while teenagers who had mounted a vigil in the lobby flew at him. The following evening, hundreds of policemen struggled to hold back the crowds as Van's motorcade nosed through. Seventy thousand turned out to watch him, spilling far into the distance beyond the twelve thousand seats; the previous season's record was eighteen thousand, for *Carmen*. Two days later Van played to eighty thousand, wearing long johns under his tails and nursing a fever of 103 degrees Fahrenheit; it was after that evening that the Elvis Presley Fan Club of Chicago forsook the King of Rock and Roll and voted to relaunch itself as the Van Cliburn Fan Club.

The mega concerts kept coming. July 31, it was the Hollywood Bowl, whose twenty-two thousand seats Van filled two nights running. This time he netted eighteen thousand dollars, but his biggest thrill was the chance to mix with the stars. Noted anticommunist Cecil B. DeMille and his niece Agnes lent him their piano for practice and threw him a lavish post-concert party. Norma Shearer asked him to play at her dinner soiree, where the guests included Clark Gable, Joan Fontaine, and Arlene Dahl. In his first semester at Juilliard he had played at Dahl's wedding reception to make some extra money, and he reminded the flamboyant actress that she predicted he would become a big star. Shearer set up movie screenings for Van at MGM, and he ate with Danny Kaye and visited with Jack Benny, Merv Griffin, Greer Garson, and Ingrid Bergman. Van loved Hollywood with its tinsel glamor, and Hollywood pressed him to its well-padded bosom.

Three days after the Bowl, he was back in New York for a benefit to rescue the indebted Lewisohn Stadium, a colonnaded amphitheater on the City College campus that was the summer home of the New York Philharmonic in pre-air-conditioning days. With tickets at double the regular price, a record audience of 22,500 crammed in, and hundreds more lined the windows and rooftops of nearby apartment buildings. A watching critic sensed an enormous hunger for beauty: "Going toward the back for the slow movement of the Rachmaninoff," he wrote, "one heard the romantic strains which were being gratefully received by thousands of upturned faces. One needed a Cinemiracle eye to take them all in, yet hardly one of them stirred." At the end they went wild, and made Van play seven encores. But if confidential reports were true, the concert nearly ended in tragedy. The next day, two FBI special agents were interviewing "a prominent individual in New York City," also described as "a wealthy real estate operator," about a separate matter when he told them that Van had come to his apartment at four o'clock that morning in a state he described as "extremely emotionally upset." The developer added that his family physician had been with Van, and the two had explained that following the Lewisohn concert, Van's father "came backstage and caused a great disturbance" by pulling a gun on the physician and threatening him for influencing his son with "liberal ideas." The man described Harvey as "very conservative, politically, and possibly a Ku Klux Klan member." The whole scene, he added, "was observed by Soviet Diplomatic officials, and Van Cliburn is greatly upset over the incident." The developer had notified his contacts in the NYPD's Nineteenth Precinct to see if they could pick up the gun; the reason he was telling the FBI, he said, was because "he felt that a 'valuable piece of propaganda' like Cliburn should be protected from any type of emotional or physical upset." The reliability of the information was clouded by the fact that Van's father was referred to as "Frank," but J. Edgar Hoover was sufficiently concerned to pass the information on to the State Department's director of security.

*   *   *

ONE OF the transfixed faces in Lewisohn Stadium that evening belonged to the Moscow Conservatory's Sergei Dorensky, who had arrived July 7 as part of the first group of Soviet exchange students since World War II. Wearing plaid shirts and floored by New York's summer heat, the students had visited the United Nations, taken in Broadway shows, and gone on a Circle Line boat tour during which the guide pointed out a large building near Grant's Tomb as Van Cliburn's school. When Dorensky returned to Moscow, Khrushchev bustled up to him after a concert and asked how Van was. News also reached Van of a conversation between Khrushchev and an American in Moscow. "I felt very sorry for your young musician, Mr. Cliburn," the premier reportedly told the visitor. "He never had a minute's rest the entire time he was in our country. We were so enthusiastic about him, he was so acclaimed, so much in demand, that we doubt that he ever slept." Khrushchev added that Van was "a very warm, friendly young man who absolutely captivated the Soviet people" and had drawn the two nations closer together.

Van was still hoping to reappear at the World's Fair, this time with a Soviet orchestra. He had already cabled his acceptance when he told the press that he was unsure if he could go, almost certainly because he had been warned that the U.S. government had taken an interest in the issue. By then the Soviets had already put up posters announcing his arrival, and in early August they brought the matter to a head by tipping off the American press. Van had been looking forward to escaping the New York heat at a series of swimming parties, but instead he flew to Washington to seek official blessing for the Soviet linkup.

There had always been tension at the heart of Cold War cultural diplomacy between joining hearts and winning minds. What to peacemakers was the art of fostering friendship was to warriors a tool for demonstrating their side's superior values and diminishing the enemy's credibility and appeal. The psychological warfare approach was dominant, and from that perspective, Van was a mixed blessing. Certainly he proved that an American could play the piano as well as any Soviet, which was no mean thing. Yet, rather than promote avant-garde music (as the CIA advocated) or American music (as the State Department advised), he loved Russian culture, believed it was the greatest in the world, and said so, loudly. Besides, he kept blurting about the Soviets wanting peace, which to foreign policy professionals was dangerously naive. When Van finally got a hearing, State Department officials made it clear that they disapproved of him playing at the Soviet pavilion on the USSR's showcase National Days. Amid hurried consultations, that hurdle was overcome when the concert was recast as a commercial enterprise sponsored by a Belgian impresario in a Brussels concert hall. Still, after several days Van returned to New York deflated and defeated by bureaucracy. "Officials here said that it was not up to them to say whether a concert artist could perform," the press reported. "They said only that the United States had no objection to his playing at the commercial concerts."

Van flew to Brussels for the unsanctioned concert, which took place on August 17 in the presence of Elisabeth, the Red Queen. Along with the rest of the audience, she loudly applauded the determined efforts of orchestra and pianist to cede the limelight to each other, as did the *New York Times*' Howard Taubman. "A young American and 100 Russians made music together stirringly tonight," he reported, "showing an audience of Western Europeans on holiday that at least on this one thing the United States and the Soviet Union were in perfect accord . . . There have been intimations in certain quarters that it was wrong of Mr. Cliburn, an American, to appear with a Soviet orchestra in the World's Fair forum, where competition in the performing arts between the two major powers is keen. But the pianist's willingness to appear and the Russians' to have him is a credit to both." The Soviets scarcely lacked virtuosos of their own, and by intimating that nationalism had no place in music, once again they occupied the moral high ground ceded by the U.S. government.

Whether at the State Department's instigation or in response to its concerns, Van went on to Heidelberg, in West Germany, and played for the servicemen of the U.S. Seventh Army. Photographers snapped him scanning the jukebox at an airport snack bar, where he eventually spent a nickel on Vaughn Monroe's "There's No Piano in This House." Afterward the army flew him back to Washington, and the navy flew him on to New York. Van quietly dropped his idea of taking his parents for a vacation by the Black Sea, but he was not about to abandon his Russian friends, and he began to plan a tour of the Soviet Union for spring 1959.

*   *   *

BY NOW he had gained back seven of his ten lost pounds and was thinking of having his clothes let out again. Yet having returned from Moscow with just two of the efficient Soviet sleeping pills, he had not slept two nights together for months. A cigarette was constantly in his hand except when he was playing, and for breakfast he nibbled at hamburgers washed down with coffee. The nerves, the diet, and the absurd schedule were beginning to take their toll. Throughout the summer, he was plagued with toothaches and carbuncles, and spent hours a day at the doctor and dentist.

Audiences at home and abroad were still clamoring to hear his prizewinning program, but the critics were beginning to gripe about the lack of a new repertoire. Even though he had turned down far more engagements than he had thought of procuring before Moscow, it was impossible to find time to practice, polish, and perfect.

There were lawyers, accountants, record company executives, and agents to deal with. Tributes kept coming: one made him an honorary citizen of Minnesota; another, the Lotus Club's youngest honoree. Accepting an honorary doctorate from Baylor University, he returned his four-thousand-dollar fee to make endowments to the departments of religion, law, drama, and music in honor of his great-grandfather, grandfather, grandmother, and mother, and jointly with Harvey donated ten thousand dollars to establish a fund for the orchestra. There were offers of movie and TV appearances; he accepted a guest spot on *What's My Line?* but with some reluctance turned down most, including the lead role in two Hollywood biopics of Liszt. There were press conferences to give, such as the one he called that September—he was no slouch at publicity—to announce he was donating his remaining Moscow winnings to New York City's cultural program. Even when he took time off to attend the opening night of the Metropolitan Opera, eyes were as much on him and Rildia Bee as on the stage. Amid it all, he somehow found time for acts of remarkable altruism. When he heard that a New Yorker with whom he shared a doctor was dying of cancer, he asked the man's family to hire a piano and lend him an apartment key and he turned up late, once in white tie and tails and another time in plaid shirt and jeans, to play Rachmaninoff. He played through the nights until, one morning, he was softly crooning along to Gershwin's "Someone to Watch over Me" when the sun came up and the patient was gone, borne away on a soulful tide.

When the new season began, he practiced from midnight until at least 6:00 a.m., back in the Steinway basement for fear of annoying the neighbors. His weight dropped again. In desperation, he tore out his precious phone. Messages left with the Osborne switchboard piled up unanswered, provoking accusations of bigheadedness from old "friends" that leaked to the press. He was disloyal to no one, just completely overwhelmed. For one thing, he had a demanding young fan base to tend to that was unknown to other classical musicians. That summer, his RCA Victor recording of Tchaikovsky's

Piano Concerto no. 1 hit the top spot on the *Billboard* LP chart, beating Johnny Mathis's *Greatest Hits* and the *South Pacific* sound track, and stayed there for seven weeks. "At Victor these days they mention the names of Presley and Cliburn in one breath," *Billboard* reported. Teenagers played the Tchaikovsky down the phone to each other, puzzling their parents by running up huge bills. Parties of girls waited patiently until a restaurant table Van had once sat at became free. One girl refused to wash for weeks when he signed her arm. When a girl in Minneapolis wrote asking if he could play at reduced prices for teenagers, he opened all his rehearsals to children and students, for free or at a low price set by the orchestra or school board. Hundreds, including dating couples, turned up to the first, in New Haven, Connecticut, and afterward some wrote to thank him "from the bottom of our hearts." In Scarsdale, New York, eighteen hundred teens cheered as he walked in, tossed his jacket onto a chair, and sat down to rehearse Schumann's Concerto in A Minor. Outside, the police caught two fans trying to climb in through a restroom window and held back nearly five hundred more, who stood in freezing autumn rain craning to catch the faint strains through the doors. "To watch Elvis I could understand," a traffic patrolman marveled. "But for this crowd to sit quiet and listen to Van Cliburn play it straight— this is a revelation." Afterward the fans swarmed up for autographs; whenever Van grew tired he remembered he was only a few years older than many of them. Appreciating classical music no longer meant being derided as a longhair: that was the Soviets' gift to the Americans. The music of Tchaikovsky and Rachmaninoff was now more popular than ever before. Van had claimed it back, reminding the nation of the bond it shared, if not with the Soviet Union, then with the Russian people.

He pushed on, crisscrossing the country from Newark and Pittsburgh to Waco and New Orleans, performing benefits for orchestra pension funds in New York, where he played three concertos in a row; Boston—two on consecutive days, at the highest prices ever charged—and Philadelphia, where his costar was Maria Callas. On a November morning he motored into Austin, Texas; stole an hour's sleep; played a dress rehearsal attended by twenty-two hundred children and students, followed by afternoon and evening concerts that drew fifteen thousand; and was made an admiral of the Texas Navy. He was, they said, Texas's proudest brag, even bigger than oil. On another trip home he pushed through a fever and proudly escorted his mother to a dinner thrown in her honor by the Fort Worth Piano Teachers Forum. During the meal, Irl Allison, founder of the National Guild of Piano Teachers, stood up and waved a check for ten thousand dollars, to be awarded to the winner of a new piano competition named for Rildia Bee's little boy. Van, still modestly aware of his youth and inexperience, dropped his fork in horror, and Rildia Bee reassured him it would never happen.

Kilgore, small in size but not in heart, responded on December 2 with "Van Cliburn Day in Texas," the second-ever state day in honor of a living person and the first for an honoree younger than ninety. Driving down Main Street, he came face-to-face with his portrait on a giant billboard fronting the oil derricks that bore the legend KIL-GORE, PROUD HOME OF VAN CLIBURN. At a press conference, he received another key to the city, this one nearly as tall as he; luncheon for five hundred followed at the National Guard Armory, which was bedecked with Rangerettes and flags. "He's better than Elvis by far!" a love-struck girl said with a sigh when Van played an afternoon matinee for students. Texas governor Price Daniel attended that, the evening concert, and the closing reception for two thousand. Two weeks later Shreveport, ever the bridesmaid, followed with its own Van Cliburn Day. That month, the State Department had asked Van to play in India, which had developed close relations with the Soviets since Khrushchev's visit there three years earlier. The thinking was probably that Van's enthusiasm for Russia could do little harm in the subcontinent, while his youth and talent could earn America some kudos, but he pointedly refused, citing the engagements in his hometowns.

For eight months there had been no letup, and still he had only one pair of shoes. It all reached a pitch of ridiculousness one after-noon in New York when he ducked into a modest restaurant to es-cape some especially persistent fans and found himself in the midst of a wedding ceremony. The rabbi abandoned the bridal couple, "rushed up with the marriage certificate in hand, and thrust it into the unex-pected guest's palm, urging him on with excited little cries to sign it." Reviewing the phenomenon, one critic, an admirer, seriously advised Van to withdraw from concert activity for several years and return to study. Another bluntly warned that he was in danger of becoming "a flesh and blood juke box which at the insertion of the proper coin always plays the same tune." Even friends began to fret that without time to himself, he might never secure his status as an important artist.

So it ever was, from the time of the first virtuoso. But it was not conceit that kept Van repeating his prizewinning program: quite the reverse. With no false modesty, he called himself a service profes-sional, like a waiter, and he felt obliged to give listeners what they wanted and to thank each personally for his or her custom. The outreaching spirit, the reverence for beauty, the love of people, the duty to serve—the same qualities that made his art speak to millions drove him on, together with a dash of fear that soon it might all van-ish. It was not for himself but for a greater cause: for classical music, which to Van was the breath of God that could heal the soul. Har-vey's dream for his son to be a missionary had rubbed off after all, just not the way he had expected. There was, though, a price to pay for ministering to others so publicly. Accepting his responsibility, he also accepted that he must always be above reproach. He was thrilled, humbled, and grateful for his success. Yet, haunted by the fear of scandal, he became guarded in public and yearned for quiet times with close friends. Few if any of them thought he was truly happy.

As the most improbable year in the history of classical music drew to a close, the utter impossibility of escaping the spotlight became clear when Van headed off to Tucson, Arizona, ready to play a con-cert on January 4. Three days after the concert he was still there, apparently to have emergency dental surgery connected with the earlier removal of a wisdom tooth—so, at least, said a "Tucson minister friend of Cliburn, acting as his spokesman." The minister, Reverend Newton H. White III, a Juilliard graduate from a wealthy family who had organized the city's Northminster Presbyterian Church, added that the dentist "foresees emergency treatment in the next few days," and as a result, "Cliburn's nationwide concert tour would be canceled on a day-to-day basis until the dentist allowed Cliburn to travel." The *Tucson Daily Citizen* was unpersuaded. "It's pretty hard to get your teeth into what's keeping Van Cliburn in Tucson," it punned in a front-page piece headlined "What's with Cliburn's Teeth?" The dentist in question, it noted, vigorously denied Reverend White's statement: "There's no question of any surgery or anything," he said. "He's simply suffering from a local dental problem. It's not something that's going to take very long. Nothing indicates he won't be better real soon. He could have the work done anywhere."

In fact, it appears that what kept Van in Tucson when he should have been playing in Texas and Georgia was Newton White, who had perhaps encouraged him to play hooky for a few days and recharge his energies in the sun. The two men were seen dining at the Cliff House; the *Arizona Daily Star* reported that the skinny pianist had three bowls of turtle soup, beef Stroganoff, and a filet mignon, toothache notwithstanding. Van eventually left, but was soon back in Tucson for a vacation. This drew the attention of the FBI, which noted in Van's file that the figure from Northminster Presbyterian Church who met him on arrival had been "arrested at Phoenix, Arizona, on October 22, 1955, for violation of the Municipal Code relating to indecent acts and during interrogation revealed a long history of homosexual activities commencing at the age of sixteen or seventeen years." Van returned to Tucson later in the year, attending a concert with White and White's beautiful new thirty-two-year-old bride, Marjorie, and began house hunting. Eventually he bought a large adobe complex with a pool and mountain views on a dirt track called North Indian House Road, which was about as far away from the world as he could get. But his escape to the Arizona sun would be tinged with tragedy. Reverend White had agreed to organize a new church, St. Andrews, and on October 25 the first service was held at his spacious new marital home on Casas Adobes Drive, with Van playing the piano for the hymns. Less than two months later, just before Christmas, Marjorie White went back to her former home with her eight-year-old son and six-year-old daughter from a previous marriage. Later that day, the girl found her mother and brother drowned in the backyard pool. Van kept his house, but in 1961 he rented it out. Two years later, Newton White died, aged forty-nine, of a weak heart. Van made a handsome donation to Juilliard in his memory.

· 14 ·

In the Heat of the Kitchen

WHILE VAN Cliburn was belly flopping like a blue whale in the American musical pond, Liu Shikun was making a small but significant impression on a reservoir outside Beijing.

Classical Marxist theory held that revolution could never take hold in a nation of peasants. Mao had solved that problem by the simple expedient of declaring peasants to be proletarians, but once in power, he embarked, like Stalin, on a crash program of industrialization driven by an emperor-size cult of personality. One of the chief projects of the Great Leap Forward, which began in 1958 with orders to farmers to melt down their tools into unusable steel, was the construction of the vast Ming Tombs reservoir. On Liu's return from Moscow the reservoir was under breakneck construction by hundreds of thousands of "volunteers," and Premier Zhou Enlai extended the young pianist the signal honor of inviting him to help dig the dam. Zhou dug beside him the first day, and one day Mao himself came and dug, too. Liu shoveled dirt for two months and was paraded on the front page of the *People's Daily* as a national hero, complete with his own stirring slogan: "Learn from Liu Shikun."

In July, while Liu was still digging, Khrushchev arrived for a summit organized to try to patch things up with Mao. The Chinese chairman approached the meeting with an ineffable smugness born of the conviction that he, not his lily-livered revisionist comrade, was now the lodestar of communism, "making him the historical pivot around which the universe revolved." There was no red carpet or honor guard to welcome the Soviet leader at the airport, and no air-conditioning at his dingy hotel to deal with the airless humidity of a Beijing summer. At their first meeting, Mao repeatedly leaped up and jabbed his finger in Khrushchev's face, and the next day, he invited him to a pool party at his government mansion, aware no doubt that the portly premier could not swim. Mao famously bobbed up and down in the polluted Yangtze like a blubbery seal—according to his propagandists, breaking several records. When Khrushchev arrived, the chairman covered his hair with a knotted handkerchief, dived in, and energetically splashed up and down, displaying various inelegant but effective strokes while interpreters scurried along the edge trying to relay his splashy sermonizing. Khrushchev donned an enormous pair of green Chinese trunks and stood delicately in the shallow end until a swim ring and water wings appeared and Mao beckoned him into deep water. The rotund Bolshevik energetically dog-paddled and drifted far enough to get in a few words. If Mao was determined to treat him like a barbarian paying tribute to a Chinese emperor, Khrushchev had a gift that could make the chairman sit up and beg. Mao was desperate to get his hands on an A-bomb, but Khrushchev, having promised one complete with full documenta-tion, had yet to deliver. Meanwhile, he had an even more powerful device to wave in Mao's face. "Now that we have the transcontinental missile," Khrushchev boasted, "we hold America by the throat. They thought America was beyond reach. But that is not true."

The summit went so badly that on his return Khrushchev pulled hundreds of Soviet scientists and advisers out of China. Kremlin-ologists read their tea leaves and decided his de-Stalinization project was not going as planned. While Khrushchev had gone too far for Mao, he had not gone far enough to entice Yugoslavia back into the Soviet Bloc as he'd hoped; and while many neutral countries were leaning toward Moscow, expansion of the Soviet sphere was too slow to satisfy hard-liners outraged that NATO's European members were talking of basing U.S. missiles on their soil. In September, Bulganin, the demoted premier, was removed from the Central Committee, stripped of his Central Bank job, and sent to Stavropol as chair of the Regional Economic Council. Yet unlike Stalin, Khrushchev was not fully the master of his world, and little by little the screws were tightened again.

"There was a pleasant period of thaw last spring when Moscow applauded Van Cliburn," the *New York Times* reported. "But the freeze is on again." A pair of cultural edicts signaled the changing winds as clearly as a weathervane. Two weeks after Van left Moscow, the Central Committee had unprecedentedly confessed to "blatant errors" in its past judgments of musicians, including those "gifted composers" comrades Shostakovich and Prokofiev. Suddenly Soviet composers were free to look West to innovators such as Boulez and Stockhausen, while Shostakovich, going his own way as usual, put the finishing touches to an operetta called *Cheryomushki*, which some thought glorified Khrushchev's new housing projects and others thought satirized them. Five months later, though, the authorities furiously hit back at suggestions of another misjudgment when the Russian writer Boris Pasternak unexpectedly won the Nobel Prize for Literature. The honor should have been ample recompense for their losing the Tchaikovsky Competition, but for the awkward fact that two years earlier Khrushchev had banned Pasternak's great symphonic novel *Doctor Zhivago* on his censors' advice that its story of lost aristocratic freedoms was anti-Soviet. Since then, the book had been smuggled to Europe and published in numerous languages, including a Russian edition printed with CIA funds that was handed out from the Vatican pavilion at the Brussels World's Fair. Desperate attempts to halt its spread had merely created more of a sensation and had been called off, but Pasternak's Nobel inflicted a propaganda defeat too humiliating to let stand. As the propagandists spun into action, *Pravda* trashed the book as "low-grade reactionary hackwork," prompting many of Pasternak's friends and fellow writers to denounce it unread. Secret policemen arrived at the author's dacha, threatening to return his mistress to the Gulag and send him into exile. Begging Khrushchev not to sever him from his beloved Russia, Pasternak turned down the award. On October 29, 1958, Komsomol leader Vladimir Semichastny, soon to be head of the KGB, tore into the sixty-eight-year-old writer before an audience of fourteen thousand, decrying him as a "mangy sheep" who "went and spat in the face of the people . . . If you compare Pasternak to a pig, a pig would not do what he did," Semichastny exploded, adding for clarity that a pig "never shits where it eats." Khrushchev sat prominently in the audience, enthusiastically applauding the words he had dictated down the phone the night before about the book he had never read. It was one thing for artists to grapple with Stalin's ghost and air intractable social issues; it was quite another to contravene the will of the party, or of himself.

In the wake of the *Zhivago* affair, every whisper of dissent was agonizingly debated at the highest levels for fear that one heresy let slip would spawn a thousand more. A general clampdown ensued, and among its more unpleasant episodes was a gay witch hunt at the Moscow Conservatory.

It was scarcely a revelation that some Russian and Soviet musicians were homosexual—Tchaikovsky may have ended his life when his "subversive passion" threatened to trigger a political scandal—and as usual, politics rather than morality was the issue. Like every Soviet institution, the school was riddled with KGB informers: even Vladimir Ashkenazy had been pressured into signing up, though he was fired after being reported for devouring *Doctor Zhivago* on an overseas tour and refusing to help entrap a gay foreign pianist. Others were keener to curry favor, and when rumors spread that an assistant professor of piano had seduced one of his students, they quickly reached the student's father, an influential second-tier official with access to top government figures. To rein in the conservatory, the authorities rounded up more gay piano teachers and made an example of them. Among them was Naum Shtarkman, Van's close friend and admirer, who was arrested as he was about to perform at a factory in Kharkov, in northeastern Ukraine, and sentenced to eight years in prison. Sviatoslav Richter, who lived with the soprano Nina Dorliak but was known, like her, to take same-sex lovers, refused to play in Moscow for so long that even the flintiest officials got the message.

Van had hoped to bring Naum over to perform in America, and he must have heard about his gentle friend's ordeal. Perhaps it gave him pause for thought about his own impending return to the Soviet Union. If so, however sad the news, he was in no personal danger. During the competition, teachers and students had suspected from the start that he was gay, and at some point the FBI appears to have received intelligence that a Soviet agent "knew that Van Cliburn was a homosexual," though not whether any use was made of the knowledge. It seems inconceivable that any was. Like Richter, Van was politically valuable to the Soviets and had friends in the highest places, which made him untouchable. When Deputy Premier Anastas Mikoyan gave the traditional anniversary of the revolution speech that November, he hailed Van as an example for foreign political leaders to follow in their dealings with the Soviets.

*   *   *

IN JANUARY 1959 the sixty-three-year-old Mikoyan arrived in America on a two-week visit that he described to the press as a "holiday." The Kremlin number two was the first senior Soviet official to visit since 1945, and the mystery deepened further when his vacation plans turned out to include two meetings with President Eisenhower and five with John Foster Dulles, who was bedridden and dying from cancer. The emphatic Armenian had become Khrushchev's foreign policy troubleshooter, and his mission was to downplay his boss's startling recent ultimatum that the Western allies had six months to get out of Berlin, which had been quartered between the U.S., Britain, France, and the USSR at the end of World War II but was stranded in Soviet-backed East Germany. In public, he lost no opportunity to stress that the Soviets wanted peace and an end to the Cold War, and as part of his one-man charm offensive, he hosted a lavish reception at the Soviet embassy in Washington, to which he insisted Van be invited.

Late as usual, Van arrived just before the reception was due to end. As he leaped up the red-carpeted steps of the Beaux-Arts mansion in downtown Washington, Smiling Mike Menshikov, the ambassador, sprang out to kiss and embrace him. A moment later the five-foot-five Mikoyan ran up, pulled Van down for a bear hug, and, to furious applause, kissed him on both cheeks in front of portraits of Stalin and Lenin. Half of the four hundred guests had already left, and the mounds of beluga caviar on ice were severely depleted, but Mikoyan hustled Van to the grand piano in an adjoining room. "Play, please play," he implored Van in Russian, standing inches behind him as he sat. Van launched straight into "Moscow Nights," and Smiling Mike started singing in a strong voice. Mikoyan joined in, and the other Soviet officials and their wives followed suit. When Van tried to get up, Mikoyan pushed him back down and whispered in his ear a request for the Twelfth Hungarian Rhapsody. The deputy premier listened in a trance, tears welling in his glittering eyes. Afterward he took Van into the private VIP room and sat talking with him on a satin-covered divan for an hour.

In the morning's *New York Times* the headline was gloomy: MIKOYAN ANGRY AS U.S. SPURNS BID FOR FREER TRADE. The next page carried the sunnier news of Van's starring role at the fete, suggesting that the undercurrent of fellow feeling was still flowing strongly. Yet to Americans allergic to the color red, the second story raised more hackles than the first. One outraged housewife fired off a letter to Mark Schubart at Juilliard, expressing "consternation, anger and indignation" at Van's embassy performance. "It is a pity," she fumed, "to see an artist become embroiled in politics when he doesn't know what the score is and, as in this case, when he accepts the patronage of people . . . who have stunned the civilized world with their unabating and wholesale criminal acts." Probably much of official Washington agreed. Mikoyan had, after all, been one of Stalin's intimates, while his younger brother, Artem, was co-designer of the Soviet Union's most famous warplanes: the "Mi" in MiG stood for Mikoyan. Suspicions only grew when the deputy premier flew on to Cuba, where Fidel Castro had seized power during Mikoyan's stay in America. The

USSR had rapidly recognized Castro's government, but in reality, no one in the Soviet leadership had heard of the bearded revolutionary; Khrushchev suggested contacting the Cuban Communist Party, who replied that Castro was a bourgeois in the employ of the CIA. Mikoyan's task was to find out what on earth was going on in Cuba, but American hawks surmised that something sinister was afoot. As usual in the Cold War, they were convinced that their rivals exerted a diabolical grip on world events, a belief that flattered the other side's attempts to catch up with the chaotic reality.

*   *   *

IT IS not clear whether Van had heard of Naum Shtarkman's fate before he met Mikoyan, but in any case there was little he could do. Standing up for his Soviet friend would have meant exposing himself, and however high his stock was, it did not license him to meddle in internal Soviet affairs, especially in an area where America had no claim to the moral high ground. In any case, his love for Russia ran too deep to be easily shaken, and his plans to return to Moscow that spring were derailed only when his career hit an unexpected bump. In February he was manicuring his nails in a San Francisco taxi when the vehicle went flying over a pothole and the nail file sliced into the middle finger of his right hand, which turned red and painfully swollen. He bandaged it up and played with his left hand for an audience of twelve thousand at the American Association of School Administrators conference in Atlantic City, but five days later he was admitted to New York's Hospital for Special Surgery and underwent a delicate operation to drain an abscess. Journalists speculated about whether he would be able to play again, reporting that he had been days from losing the finger, and possibly his right hand and forearm as well. On doctors' orders, he canceled three months of concerts and recuperated in Tucson before returning to New York to attend the Bolshoi Ballet's debut at the Met on April 16. As in piano playing, the Soviets considered they were "ahead of the entire planet" in ballet, and the night, masterminded like most Soviet cultural visits by Sol Hurok, was the most glamorous that New York City had known in

years. The capacity crowd of nearly four thousand included Marlene
Dietrich, Greta Garbo, and Noël Coward; the orchestra played the
American and Soviet national anthems; the troupe performed Prokofiev's *Romeo and Juliet*; the audience stood and cheered; and the
dancers applauded back. Yet many eyes, including those of the FBI,
were on Van, standing in Smiling Mike Menshikov's box surrounded
by Soviet and American flags.

On May 4, Van was presented with the prize for best instrumental
performance with an orchestra at the inaugural Grammy Awards,
which were handed out at simultaneous ceremonies in Beverly Hills
and New York. His hand had finally recovered, and he was practicing hard. In June he set out on a whirlwind European tour, bringing
down the house in such august settings as La Scala, in Milan, before
returning to New York in time to attend the Soviet exhibition that
had opened at the Coliseum as another manifestation of the new cultural exchange program. He toured the stands as an honored guest
of the exhibition's director-general, Aleksei N. Manzhulo—another
fact the FBI duly recorded—and was astonished to see his face in full
color on a piano-shaped box of chocolates. "My goodness, it's me,"
he said as a Soviet press officer explained that it was the best-selling
candy in the Soviet Union. Elsewhere there hung a huge photograph
of Van receiving his gold medal from Shostakovich. He sat at a Soviet-
made "Estonia" grand piano, which he obligingly praised, and then
played as the flashbulbs popped: first Schumann and Chopin, and
then "Moscow Nights." "All right, Van, go through one more routine," a cameraman demanded, and he rattled off a Chopin ballade
before recording a message for Soviet state radio, which broadcast it
along with the whole impromptu concert.

He was eternally obliging. The *bon viveur* in him loved the life of
a concert pianist: the meetings with old acquaintances and new, the
rehearsals and performances and parties, the famous friends and the
attention. Yet the loner in him yearned for the self-communion of
solitary practice. A few weeks later a *New Yorker* journalist ran into
him under the marquee of the Plaza Hotel during a downpour, and

they retreated to the Oak Room for onion soup. In an age of relentless publicity, the journalist asked, how did Van continue his struggle to master music?

"Divine indifference," said Van, happily slurping the last of his soup. "Swami Vivekananda says it is divine indifference that urges men to qualify for building an ideal. The Buddhist says '*Neti! Neti!*'—'Not this! Not that!' I suppose one could call it unconcern. Prestige or simple recognition is often mistaken for success. Nothing could be further from the truth. For me, the greatest possible success would be to be utterly alone without feeling the need to talk to anyone."

*   *   *

WITH VAN absent from Moscow, Leonard Bernstein and the New York Philharmonic filled the gap on a State Department–sponsored tour. "Your music and ours are the artistic products of two very similar people who are natural friends, who belong together and who must not let suspicions and fears and prejudices keep them apart," Bernstein rousingly told Russian musicians. He ended his last concert with Shostakovich's Fifth Symphony; in the audience, the first time he had appeared in public since his censure, was Boris Pasternak. The effect was sensational, but it was quickly eclipsed when, on July 23, another American visitor became embroiled in the most famous verbal sparring match of the Cold War.

Vice President Richard M. Nixon had come to open the American National Exhibition at leafy Sokolniki Park, in suburban Moscow, the counterpart to the Soviet exhibition at the New York Coliseum. Futuristic glass-and-steel pavilions displayed chrome-finned automobiles, pleasure boats, heavy tractors, hi-fi sets, model railways, and modern art. A multiscreen film by Charles Eames called *Glimpses of the U.S.A.* played alongside fashion shows and dancers from Oklahoma. Muscovites flocked to have Polaroids taken of themselves and to munch on corn on the cob. At the permanently mobbed Pepsi-Cola stand—Coca-Cola had cried off—one woman complained that the brown liquid smelled like benzene, while men wanted to know if it could get them drunk. Most popular of all was the "Typical American House," a full-scale replica of a six-room ranch-style suburban home furnished by Macy's. The house was cut away for easy viewing, which, together with its shock value, earned it the nickname Splitnik. To its fifty thousand daily visitors, the most mind-boggling part was its kitchen.

On a hot summer's evening, Khrushchev gamely accompanied the famously Communist-hating Nixon to the official opening. The Soviet leader sported a roomy light gray suit and white homburg; Nixon, a dark tailored suit and dark tie. After the vice president cut the ribbon, they moved to a mocked-up RCA color television studio, where the cameras rolled and Nixon took the first jab by extolling the wonders of videotape. "This indicates the possibilities of increasing communication," he said, grinning toothily, "and this increasing communication will teach us some things and it will teach you some things, too. Because after all, you don't know everything."

"If I don't know everything, you don't know anything about communism—except fear of it," Khrushchev shot back. Nixon was on the defensive; if anyone had told his opponent that a Soviet émigré founded Ampex, the firm that made the video recorder, he might have been floored. Khrushchev followed with a sharp cross, grunting that the Americans would doubtless use the video of the exchange for propaganda purposes and would not translate his words. Nixon slipped past this by promising that every word would be broadcast on American television. Khrushchev beamingly pumped his hand, and Nixon hit back that he hoped *his* words would be broadcast across the Soviet Union. "Da," Khrushchev barked, slapping Nixon's hand and going for a combination of punches. Jabbing his finger, the premier bragged that the Soviets were ahead in most things and would soon be saying "bye" as they overtook the United States. Taken by his own turn of phrase, he chortlingly repeated it in English, vigorously waving his hand to the delight of the crowd. Then he goaded a glum Nixon into congratulating the Soviets on their achievements in rocket science and astronomy. The first round ended in a draw.

The Nik and Dick Show moved on to the model house, where Nixon scored some points by going on about how advanced America was. Standing by the railing in front of the kitchen, he aimed an uppercut at his opponent by boasting that capitalism alone could produce a comfortable home filled with laborsaving devices. "We don't have to have one decision made at the top by one government official," he explained. "We have many different manufacturers and many different kinds of washing machines so that the housewives have a choice." He ended with a low left hook: "Would it not be better to compete in the relative merits of washing machines than in the strength of rockets?" Khrushchev bobbed and weaved, scoffing at the electric lemon squeezer and insisting that most Americans could ill afford these "typical" luxuries. Nixon gestured to a built-in panel-controlled washing machine, which a young Russian-speaking American was demonstrating, and found his mark. "In America," he said with a smirk, "these are designed to make things easier for our women."

Khrushchev was on the ropes, and he knew it. In the Soviet Union, he weakly parried, women worked in every field, shoulder to shoulder with men.

"I think that this attitude toward women is universal," Nixon hit home. "What we want is to make easier the life of our housewives." The vice president was not at all sure he had won. "I felt like a fighter wearing sixteen-ounce gloves and bound by Marquis [sic] of Queensbury rules, up against a bare-knuckled slugger who had gouged, kneed and kicked," he later admitted. But in 1950s America, his blow for housewives' convenience was decisive, and he was hailed for standing up to the Soviet bully. The bruising encounter burnished Nixon's credentials as a statesman, and to Khrushchev's dismay, it helped him win the Republican presidential nomination the following year.

Ignoring the embarrassment as usual, Khrushchev bullishly maintained that it had been worth exposing his people to shiny appliances if it prodded the economy into producing desirable consumer goods. It was no use leaving faceless bureaucrats to decide what style of shoes people needed, he lectured perplexed party cadres; workers would only be more productive if they could vote with their wallets for things they actually wanted to buy. The exact mechanism by which that would happen was unclear, but when his experts calculated that the Soviet Union's command economy could overtake the United States' free-market economy in twenty years, he put his full faith in the figures. Khrushchev feverishly began to reorganize the Soviet bureaucracy and economy from top to bottom, impatiently demanding drastic improvements in impossibly short time frames. Soon a new national slogan was plastered on walls everywhere: CATCH UP WITH AND OVERTAKE AMERICA.

Ever the believer, Khrushchev was convinced that communism could win on the terms set by Nixon, and he was ready to take his message to America itself.

· 15 ·

Khrushchev in the Capitalist Den

EISENHOWER HAD forbidden Nixon from mentioning the biggest news of all while in Moscow: just before he set off, Khrushchev had accepted the president's invitation to visit the United States. The Soviet leader had been angling for an invitation for some time, and although his highly publicized embrace of Van the previous year certainly did not bring it about directly, it undoubtedly contributed to the modest warming of relations that made it possible.

Khrushchev was secretly amazed and proud that he, a mere worker, should be embarking on a state visit to the capitalist superpower. Pride also made him prickle at the mere semblance of a slight, fret about behaving correctly, and resolve to be thoroughly unimpressed by what he saw. Yet in the few weeks between Nixon's departure and his own, he was boosted by new triumphs of Soviet technology: that September, *Luna 2* became the first spacecraft to reach the surface of the moon, while the icebreaker *Lenin*, the world's first nuclear-powered ship, sailed on her maiden voyage to clear sea routes in the Arctic Ocean. "Only people who refuse to look reality in the face can doubt the boundless possibilities for human progress offered by communism," he rejoiced in a rallying speech before he left. Americans, meanwhile, contemplated the visit with a little hope and more hostility. To conservatives it was as if the Antichrist were dropping by Rome for eschatological talks with the pope.

On September 15, 1959, Khrushchev touched down at Andrews Air

Force Base in his brand-new Tu-114, a turboprop beast that was the largest and fastest passenger plane in the skies. He had been bursting to show it off and refused to back down even when engineers found cracks in the fuselage. Standing fifty feet from the ground, it was also the world's tallest aircraft, a fact that was gratifyingly demonstrated when the airport steps proved too short to reach the forward hatch. Instead, Khrushchev, together with his wife, Nina; his son, Sergei; two of his daughters, a son-in-law, and accompanying officials and bodyguards had to clamber down the emergency escape ladder, thus presenting their rears to America.

Khrushchev beamed at his welcome, which included a one-hundred-twenty-strong military honor guard, a twenty-one-gun salute, and the president waiting with three thousand members of the public and press. Under his gray Stetson, Eisenhower was tight-lipped. He had intended the visit to proceed only if Khrushchev backed off his ultimatum on Berlin, but his diplomats had not made the link clear, and the threat stood. As the president delivered a muted homily about universal peace, Khrushchev's attention drifted. He held his homburg over his face to ward off the sun, fanned himself with it while mugging to the crowd, and playfully waved it to all and sundry. When the hat ran out of uses, he stage-winked at a young woman and took a dramatic interest in a butterfly that fluttered past. It was all done, noted a reporter, "with the studied nonchalance of an old vaudeville trouper." Ike's demeanor did not soften when Khrushchev took the stand and began crowing about the icebreaker and the unmanned rocket, which he made sure to mention had landed on the moon bearing the emblem of the Soviet Union.

The motorcade sped into downtown Washington along a route lined with sparse crowds of curious onlookers, flag-waving Soviet embassy staff, and more than four thousand police and armed forces. Back home, *Pravda* reported that three hundred thousand turned out in the American capital, with hands swaying and shouts rolling like waves, adding that "not even the end of World War II brought such a sea of people onto the streets of Washington."

After talks at the White House during which Khrushchev presented as his official gift a model of the much-touted Soviet rocket, Ike proposed a helicopter sightseeing trip. The Soviet leader initially declined, fearing an assassination plot, but relented when he realized the president would be in the same copter. They took off at rush hour so Khrushchev could see the bumper-to-bumper cars heading to suburban houses just like the one he had pooh-poohed in Moscow. He remained studiedly silent throughout, though he certainly admired the helicopter: when he got home he ordered three for his own use.

That evening, the Khrushchevs were the guests of honor at a White House state dinner. Ike wore white tie and tails; Nikita Sergeyevich, a dark suit pinned with medals. In his speech, Khrushchev acknowledged that America was wealthy but predicted that tomorrow the Soviet Union would be just as rich. "The next day? Even richer!" Music was provided by Ike's favorite band, "a jazzy pop combo called Fred Waring and His Pennsylvanians," whose biggest hit was "I Scream, You Scream, We All Scream for Ice Cream," but the *Washington Post* noted that the president had missed striking a note of harmony by not booking Van Cliburn. Van was disappointed himself, and wondered whether he would be invited to one of the Soviet receptions for Khrushchev. He placed a call to a Russian contact, with the FBI listening in, and was assured he would be included. Heartened, he announced that he was going to send three dozen roses to Madame Khrushchev at Blair House, the presidential guest residence.

The day following the dinner was taken up with more tours and meetings, including a trip to the Agriculture Department's experimental farm at Beltsville, Maryland, where Khrushchev declared the pigs too fat and the turkeys too thin. Photographers snapped away; luckily American editors were not as undiplomatic as the one in a well-known Soviet joke who struggled to find a suitable caption for a photograph of the premier with some prize hogs before settling on "Third from left, Khrushchev." Still, a National Press Club dinner that evening, broadcast in prime time on the three major networks, threatened to turn into a turkey shoot. The first questioner asked why Khrushchev had remained silent while Stalin committed atrocities; red-faced and scowling, the Soviet premier refused to answer. Another pressed him on Hungary: the question, he fumed, "stuck in some people's throats like a dead rat." A third raised the topic of his infamous remark to a group of Western diplomats three years earlier: "We will bury you!" he had blustered, which many Westerners took as a threat to launch a nuclear strike. Khrushchev patiently explained for the umpteenth time that he had not alluded to an actual burial but to the inevitable historical triumph of communism predicted by Marxism-Leninism. Another reporter asked if he had plans to launch men at the moon, but unfortunately Khrushchev's interpreter used a word for *launch* that was closer to *throw*. "What do you mean?" the Soviet leader thundered. "Do you mean abandoning them?" His voice mounted. "We don't throw anyone anywhere, because we value our people highly. We're not going to throw anyone to the moon." Every so often the roller-coaster performance righted itself when Khrushchev's plain, persuasive language drew applause from the hardened hacks, only to go for a loop into another cultural chasm.

Still smarting, the premier took the train to the capitalist den of iniquity. Out in New York Harbor a Hungarian refugee had blindfolded the Statue of Liberty to spare her eyes the sight of the "murderer," but Khrushchev soon had his revenge. On the way up to the presidential suite, on the thirty-fifth floor of the Waldorf-Astoria, the elevator jerked to a halt. The operator, security men, and officials looked at one another in horror, but the Soviet leader beamed. "So what?" he crowed. "The elevator broke down. Here's the famous American technology. So it happens to you as well." He chortled away for ten minutes until the car bumped up halfway to the next floor, and Henry Cabot Lodge, America's ambassador to the United Nations, helped the Soviet premier out with a shove to his broad backside. Khrushchev referred to the incident throughout his trip, though he left out the last bit.

A cocktail party for rich financiers brought no meeting of minds, and Khrushchev headed back to the Waldorf-Astoria for an Economic

Club of New York dinner in his honor. Inside the great ballroom, several guests quizzed him about how Marxism, which foresaw total victory for communism, could accommodate peaceful coexistence. When they kept pushing, he lost his temper. "If you don't want to listen, all right," he shouted. "I am an old sparrow and you cannot muddle me with your cries. If there is no desire to listen to me, I can go! I did not come to the USA to beg! I represent the great Soviet State!" The next day, he addressed the United Nations and surprised everyone with a plan to abolish nuclear weapons within five years, but afterward, as he toured Manhattan, he erupted at the sight of placard-brandishing protestors, whom he assumed had been stationed by the authorities just as at home. Taking the elevator (this time without hitches) to the top of the Empire State Building left him unplacated. "If you've seen one skyscraper you've seen them all," he later declared. When he pointed out that the "conical shape of A-bomb waves made tall buildings situated even at great distances from ground zero more vulnerable to destruction" and observed that the Soviets were building only four or five stories high, an American aide suggested they would all soon be living underground.

Khrushchev left New York complaining that he had not seen a single worker and flew to Los Angeles, where he had specifically asked to visit Disneyland, meet John Wayne, and tour an aerospace plant. He was irritated to discover that he was instead booked for lunch at Twentieth Century-Fox with three hundred movie stars, though several, including Ronald Reagan, had refused to come. Between the Sahara-like heat and the TV floodlights, the long, low studio commissary was unbearably close, but there were compensations. Following orders, Marilyn Monroe was wearing her tightest dress, and Natalie Wood, whose parents were Russian, had been coaching her. "We the workers of Twentieth Century-Fox rejoice that you have come to visit our studio and country," she said breathily, in passable Russian. Khrushchev squeezed her hand so hard and long she thought it would break, they chatted about *The Brothers Karamazov*, and the premier invited her for a tête-à-tête at the Kremlin. When he met

Shirley Temple "his eyes lit up like a pinball machine," and grabbing her hands, he placed them on his stomach, which she reported was firm, and not soft as she had expected.

The wine flowed, and Elizabeth Taylor stood on a table to get a better view.

During the meal, Khrushchev heard that his visit to Disneyland had been canceled. The given reason was safety concerns, but Walt Disney was famously right-wing, and the visitor detected a snub. He stood up to make a long, rambling speech and, at the end, started shaking his fists. "Just imagine, I, a premier, a Soviet representative . . . told that I could not go!" he shouted. "Why not? Is there an epidemic of cholera or plague there? Do you have rocket-launching pads there? Or have gangsters taken over the place? If you won't let me go to Disneyland I'll send the hydrogen bomb over!" Between the weather and his choler, he almost seemed heated enough to blow Mickey Mouse to smithereens along with the rest of Southern California.

"Screw the cops," Frank Sinatra said loudly to David Niven, who was sitting next to the matronly Mrs. Khrushchev. "Tell the old broad you and I'll take 'em down this afternoon." Unbeknownst to Sinatra, the "old broad" understood English.

Luckily John Wayne was there to discuss the relative merits of vodka and tequila.

"I'm told," Khrushchev said through Victor Sukhodrev, the young translator whom Van had met in Moscow, "that you like to drink and that you can hold your liquor."

"That's right," Wayne drawled, and they went to work, the first secretary of the Communist Party matching the Duke shot for shot. Neither mentioned the actor's well-known anticommunism, or his meetings with army chiefs to discuss how to insert "Militant Liberty" into the movies.

After lunch, Fox president Spyros Skouras took his guest into a separate room with Kim Novak, a famous beauty who had starred in Hitchcock's *Vertigo* the previous year. "Kiss him," Skouras said quietly to Novak. Sukhodrev translated, whispering into Khrushchev's ear. The premier's coarse features melted into a broad grin. "Why is it necessary to ask her?" he said. "I'll kiss her myself with great pleasure." He took her tenderly by the shoulders and did the honors on both cheeks. Presumably Novak was more susceptible to power than Marilyn, who told friends she thought Khrushchev was "fat and ugly and had warts on his face and growled."

Khrushchev moved on to the set of *Can-Can*, starring Shirley MacLaine. His face darkened when he saw the high-kicking chorus line, but he applauded politely, chatted with the actors, and posed for pictures with the scantily clad showgirls. Having survived the sustained seduction, he retreated to his armored Cadillac and toured Los Angeles under a dazzling sky, with four hundred photographers and reporters in pursuit. The stars' mansions with their manicured lawns were a poor substitute for the canceled Disneyland visit, and as the car tour wore on, Khrushchev's demeanor grew glummer.

That evening, the Soviets attended a plush civic banquet hosted by Los Angeles mayor Norris Poulson, who had decided to shore up his vote by taking a hard line. "Mr. Chairman," he sternly said, wagging his finger, "we do not agree with your widely quoted phrase, 'We shall bury you.'" If necessary, Poulson pledged, America would fight to the death to preserve its way of life. Khrushchev turned scarlet and ordered Alexei Tupolev, the son of the designer of his mammoth plane, to stand up. "We can always turn round and go home," Khrushchev barked, his veins bulging. "It will take us ten hours, and we can leave at any moment." Jane and Tommy Thompson were in the audience, and Jane burst into tears as she watched all their cocktail diplomacy at endless Moscow receptions unravel before her eyes. "I am the first head of either Russia or the Soviet Union to visit the United States," Khrushchev darkly ended. "I can go. But I don't know when, if ever, another Soviet premier will visit your country."

Los Angeles had been an unmitigated disaster, and the next day, there was no official to see off the visitors as they left by train for San Francisco. Khrushchev's mood brightened as he toured the bay

and city, but nose-dived again when he got into a shouting match
with union leaders. When they prodded him about cultural values,
he retorted that the Soviet people would never want to see what he
had seen: honest girls forced to hitch up their skirts and show their
bottoms to satisfy the corrupt tastes of rich consumers. He pushed
back his chair, turned round, bent over, lifted his coattails, and did an
impression of an "honest girl" dancing the cancan. "A person's face
is more beautiful than his backside," he declared, wiggling his ample
derriere as evidence. In America, he decided, even union bosses were
traitors to the working class.

After a more relaxing sojourn inspecting hybrid corn in Iowa,
Khrushchev returned to Washington to host a reception at the Soviet
embassy. Van had finally received an invitation, and for once he was on
time for the receiving line. When he walked in, the orchestra struck
up Tchaikovsky's Piano Concerto no. 1, and Khrushchev, instantly
perking up, gave Van a bone-crushing hug. "When you come to Moscow again, you'll be our guest," he promised enthusiastically. Van expressed his gratitude and kissed Mrs. Khrushchev's hand. "Did you get
my flowers?" he asked. Nina beamingly explained that they had not
been back long enough to know if anything had been delivered.

The next morning, all the papers ran photographs of the two
men smiling at each other with unreserved affection as Khrushchev
reached up to clasp Van's face. It was another iconic image that once
again permeated the political frost. Khrushchev, too, was warmed
by the encounter, and he made space in his packed schedule to spend
more time with his young American friend. He was still itching to
show off his prized airplane, and early in the day, the two set off for
Andrews Air Force Base. Khrushchev proudly gave Van a tour of the
metal beast, with its luxurious cabins for six and full kitchen and dining room. Afterward they went back to town in time for a luncheon
at the Soviet embassy, and as Van arrived, reporters peppered him
with questions about the mysterious plane. When lunch was over
Van accompanied the Soviet leader to his rooms at Blair House, and
after they had visited some more, Khrushchev walked him out to

the porch. They shook hands and kissed each other on both cheeks in full sight of the press, which leaped on the un-American display of affection.

Van was not being deliberately brave or courting controversy. His childhood had accustomed him to the company of older people; at sixty-five, Khrushchev was two years older than Rildia Bee. Good manners and natural affection prompted Van to return a kindness, his infatuation with Russia roused him to adopt its customs, and his lack of worldliness prevented him from calculating the political cost of his loyalty. Now more than ever, though, the price of trying to straddle the Iron Curtain became clear. That day, the *Chicago Sun-Times* ran a piece in which friends of Van complained that security agents were investigating him, and a journalist on the rival *Chicago Daily News* called a contact at the FBI. The agent refused to comment but drew up an internal memorandum. "Stick to 'no comment,'" J. Edgar Hoover scrawled on the bottom in his emphatic hand, adding, "The 'kissing bout' Cliburn & K. had together at Soviet Embassy last evening was disgusting." With his patriotism under fire, Van was forced to state publicly that he was not a Communist or a Soviet agent, though he refused to apologize for his taste in friends. "These are my kind of people," he defiantly said of the Russians.

As the backlash continued, the Cliburns received a call in Kilgore. "Rildia Bee, this is Sam Rayburn," rang the firm voice of the veteran Speaker of the House; her father had been Rayburn's first campaign manager, and he was an old family friend. "Now listen. I want to tell you. I just heard about Van and I called J. Edgar Hoover and told him that he's no more of a communist than I am. I've known him since before he was born."

As the most unlikely state visit in American history neared its end, Eisenhower took Khrushchev to Camp David for the weekend. When the Soviet leader received the invitation, he had flown into a rage on the assumption that being shuffled off to the presidential dacha was an insult to him and the Soviet Union, but when he understood that it was an honor, he calmed down. Eisenhower had a cold, so they skipped the first bout of talks and went straight to dinner, followed by a screening of a Western. Over breakfast the next morning, they reminisced about the wartime alliance before moving on to the mainsprings of disagreement: Germany, disarmament, propaganda, and ideological conflicts involving third countries. As usual Berlin was a sticking point. "Berlin is the testicles of the West," Khrushchev once gloated. "Every time I want to make the West scream, I squeeze on Berlin." Yet with free movement between its Soviet and Western sectors, it was also a gash in the Iron Curtain that bled large numbers of professionals and skilled workers whom the Soviet Bloc could ill afford to lose. Khrushchev was convinced he could eventually reverse the flow by building a socialist paradise in the East, but he was also afraid of a resurgent West Germany and eager to conclude a peace treaty that would decouple it from NATO. The discussions got nowhere, and the mood grew so dark by lunchtime that Khrushchev felt he was at a wake, or at least the bedside meal of a terminally ill patient. Irritated, he flicked barbs at Nixon, who had flown in, lampooning the vice president's behavior at the Kitchen Debate. Eisenhower was astonished: the Soviet premier was making himself feel better by insulting the vice president during a social occasion in the presidential retreat.

White House aides had begun to worry that the summit would worsen relations rather than improve them, and to break the ice, Eisenhower suggested a helicopter ride to his Gettysburg farm. There, the Soviet premier played with the president's grandchildren, invited them to Moscow, and took a lively interest in the Black Angus cattle. Eisenhower offered him one as a gift, and Khrushchev heartily accepted, offering to send Russian birch trees in return. The next day, Khrushchev agreed to abandon his ultimatum for Western forces to leave Berlin while they worked toward a permanent solution, and Eisenhower pledged to attend a four-power summit in Paris followed by a visit to the Soviet Union. At lunchtime the aides were occupied with drafting the communiqué, and there were only nine at the table, including Khrushchev and Eisenhower and their ambassadors

Tommy Thompson and Smiling Mike Menshikov. Thompson later drafted a memorandum of the conversation:

> Mr. Khrushchev produced a box of chocolates which he said had been given to him by Van Cliburn with the request that he and the President eat them together. These were passed around the table and Mr. Khrushchev remarked about the high quality of American chocolates. Ambassador Menshikov said in Russian that Russian chocolates were better. Mr. Khrushchev turned to the interpreter and said "Don't translate that remark." Then, having noted that I had heard it and that the President was waiting for a translation, he explained what Ambassador Menshikov had said and said he had asked the translator not to translate the remark because it was so tactless. Ambassador Menshikov's only reaction was to say rather sourly that at least he personally preferred Soviet chocolates.
>
> With respect to Van Cliburn, Mr. Khrushchev said either on this or an earlier occasion that Van Cliburn had expressed disappointment that he had not been able to play for Mr. Khrushchev on the White House piano which he said was possibly the best instrument in the world. The President said he had not realized that the White House piano was so special. Mr. Khrushchev went on to remark about the great success which Van Cliburn had had in the Soviet Union. It was not quite clear to me whether Mr. Khrushchev was fully aware of Van Cliburn's presumptuousness in attempting to needle the President through him about failure to use him to entertain Mr. Khrushchev.

After lunch, tempers flared again when Khrushchev vowed to support Mao if he attacked the ousted Chinese nationalists in Taiwan, whom the United States still recognized as the legitimate rulers of China and was committed to defending. When they reverted to Berlin, and Khrushchev insisted on a fixed timetable for negotiations,

Eisenhower angrily rescinded his agreement to attend the Paris summit and visit the Soviet Union. After hurried discussions, a compromise was reached in which Eisenhower would state his point of view at the coming press conference and Khrushchev would not contradict him.

The Soviet leader's trip had been utter chaos, with any number of diplomatic incidents that could have resulted in a dangerous fiasco. In light of that possibility, it had to be counted a success. Little concrete progress was made, but both sides accepted the need for a nuclear test ban treaty, a German solution, and a permanent means to lowering tensions. Eisenhower found Khrushchev as verbose and ebullient as Stalin was enigmatic and controlled, but he decided he could talk to him. His advisers concluded that the Soviet premier was a very difficult but remarkable man who was open to new ideas so long as they could be reconciled with Communist ideology and who wanted and needed peace in order to carry out his vision. For all his panting and steaming, Khrushchev had relished being the star of his own American show. He had put a very human face on the Soviet Union, and many Americans had responded. "Nikita, come again!" crowds chanted as the Tu-114's huge propellers started up and the vast plane lumbered down the runway. One last tragedy was narrowly averted when the plane barely managed to clear the treetops as it began the five-thousand-mile return flight to Moscow.

*   *   *

BACK HOME Khrushchev reflected on his trip and grew increasingly euphoric. He praised Ike's "wise statesmanship" and, in January, announced that the peace dividend enabled him to slash the Soviet armed forces by 1.2 million personnel, a third of the total. His detractors, who complained that his one-man diplomatic offensive was erroneous and reckless, were aghast. To hedge his bets, he told the Presidium that Soviet ICBMs made the cuts possible because "Main Street Americans have begun to shake from fear for the first times in their lives." Secretly he had been astonished by America with its endless cornfields and self-service cafeterias, its unsubtle power and raucous debates, and he was newly determined to free up funds to provide for his people. He commissioned the first Soviet golf course so Eisenhower could play his favorite sport, and despite his outrage at *Can-Can*, he kept hold of the photos of himself and a scantily dressed Shirley MacLaine.

Having reported home, Khrushchev headed to Beijing to fill in Mao. Again there was no honor guard at the airport, and this time there was no microphone, either. Khrushchev insisted on speaking anyway, and made pointed comments about Eisenhower's hospitality. The leaders' meeting turned into an exchange of insults. Khrushchev took offense at some comments by the Chinese foreign minister, a marshal in the People's Revolutionary Army: "Look at this lefty!" he scoffed, and when the minister persisted, the Soviet premier lost all restraint. "Don't you dare spit on us from your marshal's height!" he screamed. "You don't have enough spit!"

In Los Angeles, John Wayne shouted with pleasure when he received a crate containing several cases of premium Russian vodka. The accompanying note read, "Duke, Merry Christmas. Nikita." Wayne sent a couple of cases of Sauza Conmemorativo tequila to his Moscow drinking buddy, with an equally terse reply: "Nikita. Thanks. Duke."

Despite all the bumps in the road, a new era in superpower diplomacy had dawned. Many Soviet citizens dared to dream that the Cold War would soon be over; most Americans, too, yearned to cast off their deepest fears. As both Ike and Van prepared to take up Khrushchev's invitations, hopes built that this was the breakthrough the world had been awaiting.

· 16 ·

Back in the USSR

NEAR THE Osborne Apartment House on Fifty-Seventh Street, an old lady was neatly arranging the fruit on her stall when a group of twelve young men and women halted indecisively in front. She glanced at them and rolled up her long jersey sleeves. "It is clear to me," she said, "that you are Russians and you're going to visit my neighbor Van Cliburn. You don't need to ask how much these apples cost. I'm not going to bargain with you. I also love Russia and Russian people."

Rather shaken by her shrewdness, the group carried on. They had been trying to track Van down for three weeks since arriving in December on a student exchange. Among them was Van's old foe turned friend Lev Vlassenko, and while he was waiting for news of Van's whereabouts, he had breakfast with Rosina Lhévinne, who cleaned most of his plate as well as her own. He also watched her teach, noting that she adhered to the Anton Rubinstein school and that a quirk in Van's playing of the Chopin F Minor Fantaisie derived from Josef Lhévinne, intelligence Vlassenko later passed on to readers of *Sovetsky Muzykant*.

Finally, the appointed day arrived, and the group waited with a gaggle of news agency photographers. Vlassenko looked around nervily and was the first to spot the tall figure in a gray coat, his head hatless and hair resplendent as ever. The cameras clicked as the two medalists excitedly hugged on the corner of Sixth Avenue and Fifty-

Seventh Street. Upstairs in the Osborne, the visitors crammed round the Steinway, remarking on a stern portrait of Rachmaninoff hanging on the wall next to a picture of the composor's enormous hands. Van explained that they were two of his most precious objects. Atop the chest of drawers was another prized possession, a model of *Sputnik 1*. One of the Soviet group later reported the scene in loving detail for the party youth paper:

> Wonderful sounds fill the small room on the ninth floor of an ordinary building on 57th Street. Van Cliburn played, and probably he saw millions of Soviet people in front of his eyes, people who fell in love with the modest Texan boy with his amazing talent and his pure soul. When the last notes died I asked Van to express in words what he had wanted to tell us with his music, and here is what he wrote for the readers of *Komsomolskaya Pravda*:
>
> "I was happy to receive representatives of the Soviet youth. My heart is still full to the brim with memories of the days that I spent with you. They are precious to me. I want to use this opportunity to pass my most ardent feelings and gratitude to the Soviet youth. It won't be long before I'll be with you again, before I will play for you again. I will preserve for ever my gratitude and sincerity. Van Cliburn."

A few weeks later, on February 14, 1960, Van sent a Valentine to his beloved Russia when he joined the Moscow State Symphony to play Prokofiev's Piano Concerto no. 3 at Madison Square Garden. Kirill Kondrashin was back to conduct, Van's fellow gold medalist Valery Klimov played the Tchaikovsky violin concerto, and an audience of 16,100 hung on every note. This reunion was also widely reported in the Soviet media, but nearly two years after the competition, it made Van's absence from the Soviet Union all the more conspicuous. The problem was not just the heavy concert schedule Bill Judd and CAMI had lined up for Van, but also the politics, which were far trickier than Van had imagined. He badly needed a wise head and steady hand to guide him, and that November he had finally found one. Seven years after he swooned at the romance of *Tonight We Sing*, Van signed with Sol Hurok.

The switch had been coming ever since the stout impresario swept the young pianist into his offices at 730 Fifth Avenue straight after the ticker tape parade and announced he was taking him under his wing. For more than a year Van dithered while Hurok pursued him with champagne and caviar and grew increasingly irate: "Get rid of the bum," the manager growled when Van turned up unannounced at one of his parties. When Van did eventually sign, the news came as a terrible blow to Judd, and engagements had to be worked through. Yet Van had always dreamed of seeing the words "S. Hurok Presents" above his name, and now the legendary impresario was both a sentimental ideal and a practical necessity. Hurok was Russian and the biggest name in the business, the manager of Isaac Stern and Marian Anderson, Feodor Chaliapin and Anna Pavlova, as well as the celebrated pianist Arthur Rubinstein, who was heard complaining that he had worked all his life to earn top dollar only to be overhauled by a pipsqueak. "What's the matter?" Rubinstein groused when an orchestra pursued him for an engagement. "Can't they afford Cliburn?"

Throughout the Stalin years, Hurok had fought a losing battle to bring Russian artists to the West, and his deep connections made him uniquely qualified to preside over the new cultural exchanges. With his fedora rakishly pulled down over the fur collar of his topcoat and his silver-topped cane in hand, he was a regular sight at Bloomingdale's while splurging on the latest Soviet ballerina. Now he saw an unmissable opportunity in the first state visit of an American president to the Soviet Union. The plan was for three of his stars, the soprano Roberta Peters, the violinist Isaac Stern, and Van, to play an intimate recital for the top leaders at the Kremlin before performing across the country. Peters was under the impression that Ike himself had personally requested all three, but given official attitudes toward

Van, the initiative may have been Hurok's alone. His new recruit was the key to the plan: after all, Van had received Khrushchev's personal invitation. He was to go for three months, leaving enough time to take the Black Sea vacation he had promised himself two years earlier. Finally, it seemed, he would be back at the heart of the affair.

So he would—but in a very different way than he envisaged.

*   *   *

AT 6:25 a.m. local time on May 1, 1960, a spindly black plane took off from the U.S. base in Peshawar, Pakistan.

For four years the CIA's top-secret U-2s had crisscrossed the skies far above the Soviet Union. Soviet radar detected many of the twenty-four deep-penetration overflights, but their missiles and planes were not able to reach them. Project Dragon Lady reaped America an information bonanza, including confirmation of the Soviets' meager ICBM capacity. By 1959 the arsenal that Khrushchev had brandished at the West turned out to consist of six R-7s, mostly sited in a swamp south of Arkhangelsk. The huge rockets needed twenty hours' preparation for firing, and because the liquid oxygen had to be supercold, they could be kept fueled for only a short time. Since the Americans now knew the locations of the launch pads, their B-52 bombers could take them out before the tanks had even been filled.

The Soviets did, however, have an improved antiaircraft missile. "The way to teach these smart-alecks a lesson is with a fist," Khrushchev vowed. "Just let them poke their noses in here again."

In the cockpit of the plane leaving Peshawar, Gary Powers, a former U.S. Air Force captain, pulled back hard on the controls and soared up into the sky. The single-seat, single-engine aircraft was notoriously difficult to fly: wearing a spacesuit and breathing oxygen, the pilot had a margin of just ten knots, or twelve miles per hour, between the stall speed and the critical Mach number, a gap known as the coffin corner. Worse, in Powers's case, his regular plane was grounded and its replacement had a history of malfunctioning. Yet Powers had notched up twenty-seven missions across the Soviet

Union and Eastern Europe, making him the most experienced of all U-2 pilots. The plane leveled off at seventy thousand feet, and the huge camera in its slender belly clicked and whirred into action.

Since it was a holiday on the ground, the skies were unusually clear of traffic, and the Soviets began tracking the intruder before it entered their airspace. It continued on a northwesterly heading until it was over the Baikonur Cosmodrome, the launch site of *Sputnik* and home to the two latest R-7s, and then turned north toward Sverdlovsk, more than thirteen hundred miles inside the border.

Above the city the autopilot broke down, but since he was halfway to his destination, Powers decided to fly the plane manually and complete his mission. Two hundred seventy minutes into the flight, he heard a dull thump and saw a bright orange flash as an antiaircraft missile exploded nearby. The U-2 lurched forward and began whirling toward the distant ground. A Soviet MiG-19 appeared on its tail and then blew up, hit by friendly fire. Powers was forced into the U-2's nose and prevented from ejecting, which may have saved his life if, as was later claimed, the seat was rigged to explode when the Eject lever was pressed. Instead, with the plane spinning halfway to the ground, he dragged the canopy open and unbuckled his seat belt. The plane fell beneath him, but his oxygen mask was still attached and yanked him down after it. His visor frosted over in the ice-cold air, and he was struggling blindly to get free when suddenly the hose broke, the chute opened, and he floated down next to a chunk of the plane gliding to earth on its long wings.

In Moscow, Khrushchev was watching the May Day celebrations from the balcony of the Lenin-Stalin mausoleum. This year he had ordered that the usual military display be replaced with athletes, children, and white doves. There were two weeks left before the Paris summit, and he wanted to send a signal that the cooperative spirit was alive and well. When he received news of the U-2, he was in equal measure horrified at the international consequences if he reacted publicly, worried about appearing weak in his generals' eyes if he did nothing, and electrified at the prospect of exacting revenge for the years of infuriating intrusions.

By the time he was captured, Powers had not used the needle tipped with a lethal shellfish toxin that he carried concealed in a silver dollar. The map showing his course survived the crash, along with large parts of the plane, including the camera and its contents, and blew away his prepared cover story. From his interrogation, the KGB learned that the CIA believed it was impossible for a pilot to survive an accident at seventy thousand feet, exploding seats and poison pins aside. Khrushchev kept quiet, waiting to see what the Americans would say.

After four days, NASA issued an elaborate cover story explaining that a plane had been lost during a high-altitude weather research mission above Turkey and might have drifted off course. Setting a trap, Khrushchev ordered the release of information that a spy plane had been shot down—without any mention of a pilot. As he expected, the Americans assumed that Powers was dead and fatally embroidered their story.

On May 7, old Voroshilov retired as the ceremonial head of state and was replaced with Khrushchev's protégé Leonid Brezhnev. Khrushchev and the eternal Mikoyan were the last of Stalin's henchmen to survive in power, and Nikita Sergeyevich held a card that, if played well, could further strengthen his hand, and if not, irreparably weaken it. That day, he appeared before a session of the Supreme Soviet and sprang his trap. "Comrades, I must tell you a secret," he announced, his veins bulging with a heady cocktail of rage and self-righteousness. "When I was making my report I deliberately did not say that the pilot was alive and in good health . . . And now, just look how many silly things they [the Americans] have said."

Khrushchev had the Eisenhower administration on a hook, but in public he was careful to blame the U-2 program on CIA director Allen Dulles. Probably he believed it: privately he told Tommy Thompson that he "could not help but suspect that someone had launched this operation with [the] deliberate intent of spoiling [the] summit meeting," again suggesting that that someone was Dulles. Then he sat back and waited for Eisenhower to apologize for his out-of-control subordinates.

In Washington, Ike quietly read Thompson's cable. He had always been nervous that the U-2 overflights could be represented as acts of aggression justifying war. He understood that Khrushchev was giving him a way out that could salvage the summit, perhaps was even asking for his help. Yet he faced an impossible choice: blame Dulles and hand his political opponents false evidence that he had lost control of crucial decisions in the federal government, or take responsibility and risk blowing up the summit.

There was a third choice. "I would like to resign," he told his secretary. But abandoning his post was unacceptable to an old soldier. On May 11 he personally revealed the scope of the U-2 program and his direct authorization of each flight. He declared the program on hold but reserved the right to restart it in future, if it were deemed necessary to prevent a surprise attack. In response to questions, he said he was still going to the Paris peace conference, which was now just three days away. Privately he did not have great hopes but was clear that he had to give it his best shot. "My feeling is that the world is headed toward an arms race of such magnitude as can culminate only in unbearable burdens on our peoples at best, or general war at worst," he wrote to a critic of the talks. "No efforts should be spared to find some way out of this grim prospect." But by placing his political capital above his relationship with the Soviet premier, he had booby-trapped an already tortuous path.

In his Kremlin office, Khrushchev flew into a rage at Ike's broken faith, but he recovered enough to wait and see whether the president would make amends at the summit. At a final press conference, the premier pledged to work to improve relations.

The first meeting of the principals was scheduled for the morning of May 16, a Monday. As he prepared to fly to Paris, Khrushchev, too, was in a corner. He had been trying to exorcise the ghost of war from the Soviet machine to free up funds for his domestic programs. Yet now his antiaircraft rockets had forced him to concede that the Americans knew his missile-rattling was a feint. Undoubtedly the hard-liners would agitate for a return to the old ways, and the generals would demand that their shorn budgets be restored. During the flight, he reviewed the facts and felt humiliated. Here he was, flying to meet the Americans as if nothing had happened. Why would they negotiate in good faith if they cared so little about sabotaging the talks? He had been duped by American perfidy, the Soviet Union's dignity insulted once too often. Worried that the other leaders might try to ambush and outgun him, he made a decision. On Monday morning he arrived at the Elysée Palace with just one objective.

In the conference room with Ike were France's president, General de Gaulle, and Britain's prime minister, Harold Macmillan. Khrushchev took the floor and loudly declared that he would not discuss any of the issues on the agenda until the president of the United States did three things: apologize to the Soviet Union and condemn the deliberate provocation, guarantee that no more flights would violate Soviet airspace, and punish the individuals responsible for those to date. If any more spy planes dropped in on the Soviet Union, Khrushchev added, he reserved the right to carry out missile strikes on U.S. bases. Meanwhile, the president was no longer welcome to visit the Soviet Union the next month.

Eisenhower was equally furious at Khrushchev for delivering a drubbing in front of their fellow leaders. He could scarcely repudiate his own actions or, at the Soviet leader's bidding, punish subordinates carrying out his orders. Nor could he give Khrushchev a veto over U.S. intelligence gathering. He undertook again to suspend the flights.

The Soviet leader stalked out. The next day, he went home. He and Eisenhower would never meet again.

Thanks to what Ike called "that stupid U-2 business," a rare chance to make the world safer had been squandered. The Soviet press filled with anti-American propaganda calling for vigilance and readiness to repel the imperialist aggressor. Mao was invited to Moscow. The armed forces received standing orders to repel all intrusions into the airspace of the Soviet Union and its allies. Jets were scrambled with alarming frequency on both sides. On July 1 the Soviets shot down a U.S. Air Force B-47 over the Barents Sea, and four crew members drowned.

The world held its breath. The Cold War had dramatically heated up again.

*   *   *

"WELL, I'M not going," Van said when the Paris summit spectacularly misfired, though as usual he volunteered no political opinion of the crisis. Then the State Department called. The cultural mandarins had lined up a selection of performers to coincide with Ike's state visit. "Well, we canceled everybody," the official said, "but Mr. Khrushchev told us he wants you to continue." Van readily agreed, but to avoid any new misunderstandings, he flew to Washington and, the day before he was due to depart, made a round of courtesy calls, including one on Ambassador William S. B. Lacy, the State Department's director of East-West exchange agreements.

Van arrived in Moscow on May 26. Two years had passed since he flew tearfully away, and the political environment was so hostile that another American pianist concertizing in Moscow that year was mock-machine-gunned in the streets and greeted with shouts of "U-2" from the audience. Yet the moment Van emerged from the airplane, he was surrounded by hundreds of yelling teenagers and older women tossing red and white flowers. Henrietta Belayeva was waiting, still madly in love. A girl handed him a huge bouquet of lilies of the valley, and a white-haired babushka wrapped him in a motherly hug. He was amazed and touched, and when a journalist from *Teatr* magazine got hold of him, Van panted out elated thoughts:

> I have a feeling that I've come home. Of course you know I have always loved Russian music, but when I first got to know your country it was as if I got a second Russian soul. I fell in love with Moscow and the Russians at first sight. But it was

especially often at home in the USA that I remembered the Russian woman who I met on my last visit, and who as you just saw I was so happy to see now. When I first met her back then she showed me a photograph of her son who died in the war. He was like my twin—he was really terribly like me, it was amazing. He was also my brother by profession; he was a pianist too. She asked me, "Can I call you my son?"

Then he was off, swept away by adoring fans. The *Teatr* journalist listened to the excited chatter and had a sudden insight: the more the Soviet people reviled America's leaders for jeopardizing peace, he thought, the more they yearned to give their respect and love to this American who they believed had a pure soul and heart.

Hurok had booked Van into the National, which looked out on Red Square and was the least bad hotel in town. The room filled with friends old and new, and Van eagerly welcomed them all. When the *Teatr* journalist turned up, Van carried on where he had left off two hours before:

He was probably a good musician, that pianist who was killed, about whom I feel like a brother. There is an amazing amount of musical talent in Russia. Once I was so captivated by the playing of Sviatoslav Richter that I kissed the hand of this wonderful musician, and the fact that the lovers of music received me here with such warmth and care fills me with joy and a feeling of responsibility. If you ask me what I would like to see here first of all, I reply: A grand piano. I need to practice properly before the concerts, as this tour is a great responsibility for me. I need to pass examination by the audience once again.

Khrushchev stayed true to his word and arranged a dacha where Van could rehearse. Leaving the city, the government car headed through the prettiest part of the Moscow region, passing forests of white birch and firs and little dachas and churches. After a couple of hours, it turned off the main road and down a country lane. Here, through a pair of hand-forged metal gates with a lyre motif, was something that could only be Russian: a forest full of composers. Van had been allotted a simple green wooden dacha in the leafy, meandering compound known as the House of Creativity at Ruza. Next door was Shostakovich's dacha, where Prokofiev had also lived. In Van's, an enclosed veranda with a folding bed led to a few small rooms, one with wood baffling and a Weinbach baby grand. The bathroom facilities were rudimentary, and the sole fireplace was made from roughly stacked bricks, but the silence was startling and the air was soft with the perfume of grasses and flowers. The *Teatr* journalist found his way here, too, and remembered a line from "Moscow Nights": "Not a rustle is heard in the garden." Local lore held that the song was composed in this very house, and as the music wafted from Van's piano it seemed it had been written for this very night.

With the last notes still lingering, Van struck the opening chords of his concert program. Composers out for a stroll slowed their footsteps and listened. A ten-year-old pianist who had already played his exam pieces to the tall, friendly visitor hovered outside. The piano gathered strength, but suddenly it stopped and Van burst out of the cottage. "Isn't this paradise?" he cried, flinging his arms wide open and stretching his tired fingers. An unseen cuckoo called from the trees. "How many times will I come back here?" he called back, and silently he counted its long series of notes, wanting to believe in the prophetic bird.

In the daytime, he ambled down the paths with his friends, Henrietta of course, and Lev Vlassenko and Sergei Dorensky, who came down to see him. The group sat smoking in the canteen, a simple one-story barracks that was light and airy inside, with starched cloths covering the round tables, each piled with a dish of apple *piroshky* or fluffy rolls or a large jam tart. A low antique sideboard from a merchant's house bore two samovars and stacks of glasses in metal holders. Between meals, they played table tennis and went down to the wild shores of the Ruza River, a tributary of the Moskva, where they rowed in a little boat. Van, casual in a T-shirt and zippered blouson, knelt down to talk to a little girl and helped a boy wearing a baggy coat, heavy boots, and a beret with his fishing rod. Photographers swarmed after him, and he obligingly posed lying in the grass. Peace and quiet were never long his Russian companions.

During Van's week in Ruza, Boris Pasternak died, humiliated and enfeebled by his persecutions. Sviatoslav Richter kept vigil beside the open coffin, playing the works of Pasternak's piano teacher Scriabin on a battered upright; his own teacher, Heinrich Neuhaus, had made him memorize the music after Pasternak eloped with Neuhaus's wife Zinaida. Handwritten notices of the writer's funeral spread through the Metro, and thousands braved KGB surveillance to attend along- side squads of foreign journalists. In the crowd, a young voice recited Pasternak's banned poem "Hamlet" in grievous tones. More voices denounced his treatment by the authorities and his fellow writers, and party officials rushed to close and bury the coffin. "We excom- municated Tolstoy, we disowned Dostoevsky, and now we disown Pasternak," a last protestor bitterly lamented. "Everything that brings us glory we try to banish to the West." Within weeks, Paster- nak's mistress was arrested with her daughter for collecting foreign royalties from *Dr. Zhivago*. She wrote to Khrushchev begging to be re- leased and reminding him how she had cooperated with the security agency, and three years later she was quietly freed.

*   *   *

DESPITE VAN'S welcome and Pasternak's send-off, there was no mis- taking the nationalistic mood among most Russians. Roberta Peters and Isaac Stern had also arrived to fulfill their concert dates, and Pe- ters felt the tension crackling. They had been warned not to speak in the hotel, in case it was bugged, so they went for a walk in Gorky Park, only to run into a public display of the U-2 wreckage. The spoils included the camera and a selection of its photographs, together with Powers's maps, false IDs, bills in a range of currencies, the poisonous silver dollar, and (despite the CIA's carefully checking the planes for clues to their origin, even scrutinizing the pilots' underwear) Powers's personal credit card. A party of young Soviets, sixteen or seventeen years old, approached the musicians and spoke in English. They explained that their families had moved to Moscow from Massachusetts, and they were desperate to get to the United States, but friends and relatives who had applied for help at the American embassy had been arrested on their way out, slung in jail, and never heard from again. Unnerved, Peters and Stern went to the embassy themselves to check that it was safe to stay. When they performed, the Russian love of music poured out in cheers and applause, but afterward the concertgoers swarmed backstage, always asking the same question: "Does America really want war?" There was never a suggestion that the Soviet Union might begin hostilities—always the fear of being invaded again.

Van, meanwhile, was busy renewing more friendships. Naum Shtarkman was still serving time, but Eddik Miansarov was there, as was his ex-wife, Tamara, now on her way to becoming a major Soviet pop star. Van brought her a bottle of French perfume and her son a plush toy kitten. Other foreigners from the competition were in town, too. Thorunn Johannsdottir, the Icelandic pianist who had given Van her caviar, had come to the conservatory for postgraduate study and found the Soviet students incredibly kind—until it became common knowledge that she and the out-of-favor Vladimir Ashkenazy were an item, after which they looked right through her. Liu Shikun was back, too. The businessman's son had recently joined the Chinese Communist Party, a timely step when Mao's regime had nationalized the arts, and he had composed a piano concerto for youth, accompanied by traditional Chinese instruments, that met with official approval. In return, the government had sent him to Moscow for further study, giving him respite from a country deeply scarred by the loss of tens of millions of lives during the Great Leap Forward. Van hugged and chatted with them all, over meals in restaurants where he ordered caviar sandwiches, licked the eggs off the top, and left the bread, a luxury version of his Carnegie Hall student pot roast.

CBS anchor Walter Cronkite, who was also in the Soviet capital, was crossing Red Square when he saw a mob milling around. He went to investigate and found Van hemmed in by women proffering flowers, silver vases, and cuff links and clutching at his clothes. "Aw, look at that," Van said with a sigh, kissing them. "It's so beautiful—thank you." An all-women fan club, called the Van Club, had grown around a nucleus of admirers who'd met one another while standing in line all night for tickets to his competition bouts. Its unofficial leader was Irina Garmash, a simple-seeming young woman who wrote Van heartbreakingly beautiful letters every two weeks. The devotees socialized regularly, swapping news about their idol, and now they followed him down the streets and stood outside his hotel, waiting for a friendly wave from his window. When he left the hotel to play his first concert on June 3, they were ready with huge bouquets of flowers.

Outside the conservatory thousands once again filled the courtyard and the surrounding streets. Squads of militiamen were struggling to keep order. Students wearing red armbands directed ticket holders inside. The few spares sold for more than ten times their face value. From the loudspeakers a voice barked at the crowd to move along, but no one paid any heed.

In the Great Hall the aisles and stairs were packed solid. Tommy Thompson was present, as was an array of Soviet officialdom, including the magisterial "Madame" Furtseva, a former weaver who was now the minister of culture. By the time Van came out, his fans had spread a thick layer of flowers over the stage apron and piano bench. Roberta Peters looked on in awe. Four years older than Van, she was already famous when he started at Juilliard and had starred in the Hurok biopic *Tonight We Sing* while he was still a student, but she had never seen anything like this. Van bowed over and over to ringing cheers and shouts of "Vanya" and "Vanyusha," removed some flowers, and sat down to play Prokofiev's Third and Brahms's Second Piano Concertos, with Kondrashin conducting. At the end, the audience clapped in thunderous unison, and dewy-eyed girls surged down the aisles. In Van's dressing room Prokofiev's widow embraced him, saying in Russian, "Wonderful, wonderful." During

the encores, including "Moscow Nights," women at the front propped
their elbows on the stage and stared up in a reverie. Van bent down
to shake their hands and talk to each of them, and when he finally
made to leave, they climbed up and dragged him back to sign autographs. As the house lights went off, he was still there, standing amid
a frenzy of flowers in front of Soviet and American flags, saying in
broken Russian, "I will never forget your wonderful welcome."

"Strained relations between the Soviet Union and the United States
over the U-2 spy plane incident did not discourage hundreds of cheering Muscovites from pelting the 25-year-old Texan with flowers and
nearly mobbing him with affection as he emerged from the conservatory," the *New York Times* reported. At a post-concert dinner, "Soviet
cultural officials were extremely courteous and carefully avoided political subjects." On the embassy lawn sat an abandoned jet-powered
speedboat with a silver plaque on its dashboard inscribed, TO NIKITA
S. KHRUSHCHEV FROM DWIGHT D. EISENHOWER. As a satire on the stalled
summit and state visit, it was priceless, but a monument was scarcely
needed when Khrushchev was busy grandstanding at press conferences and heaping invective on Ike and America. The Soviet leader
was still livid about the U-2 imbroglio. On top of everything else, a
great deal of money had been spent preparing for the president's now-
canceled visit: as well as the golf course, a shoreside mansion had
been built on Siberia's unspoiled Lake Baikal, complete with costly
new roads and communications.

In America, where newspapers were still giving saturation coverage to the squall of Soviet denunciations, reaction to Van's ecstatic
welcome was far from universally positive. A reader wrote to the *Chicago Tribune* to suggest that the pianist "could do his own country a
great service by canceling his tour and leaving Russia because of the
attacks on this country and its President by Mr. Khrushchev. This
step might cause Mr. Cliburn some inconvenience, but in the long
run he would have the satisfaction of making a widespread protest
against such an unsavory character as the Russian leader." Those
who thought that with diplomacy in crisis it was more important

than ever for artists to step into the breach, or who were reassured that the Soviets still loved at least one American, stayed silent.

To his Soviet fans, Van transcended politics as a kind of ideal American-Russian hybrid, an exotic but beloved adopted son, and nothing short of outright war would have kept them away. Two days later the Great Hall was equally jammed for his second concert. "In the summer heat," UPI reported, "two spectators fainted during the first number of Mr. Cliburn's program and had to be carried into the lobby. Many youngsters, as adoring of Mr. Cliburn as some American youth are of Elvis Presley, rushed down the aisles at the end of the Chopin program to thrust armfuls of lilacs and tulips at the tall, smiling pianist. Other music lovers pelted Mr. Cliburn with sprigs of lilies of the valley as he stood bowing and clasping his hands to his chest in gratitude for the reception." Swept up in music and love, Van was overwhelmed and utterly alive, and he saw no reason to trim his sails to the political winds. He had grown especially fond of Deputy Premier Anastas Mikoyan since their divan chat in Washington, and now he met Mikoyan's son Stepan, a test pilot, and Stepan's wife, Ella, a classical music aficionado, who sat at the symphony with her head in the score. After each of his ensuing concerts, he slipped through the back door of the conservatory and crouched in the rear of Stepan's Buick, a 1956 eight-cylinder monster, concealed under a mound of flowers. They then sped to the House on the Embankment, a grim monolith with five hundred apartments and twenty-five entrances, which housed many members of the upper echelon. In the courtyard, Van emerged from the blooms and hastened to the Mikoyans' fourth-floor apartment, where Ella had a library of three thousand records, scrupulously cataloged and stored in a huge glass-fronted cabinet. Close friends came for dinner, and afterward they sang "Moscow Nights" and other sentimental songs round the piano till the small hours, while Ella mended Van's frayed concert clothes. In this private world he was in his element, roaring with infectious laughter, telling preposterous stories about opera divas, and doing wicked impressions. His keenest fans quickly cottoned on to the ruse and threw flowers at the car as it left after subsequent performances, and at four in the morning Aschen Mikoyan, Ella and Stepan's eleven-year-old daughter, looked down from her bedroom window and saw some of them sitting on a bench in the courtyard, gazing up.

Sol Hurok arrived and installed himself in Lenin's old suite at the National. He invited Van, Roberta Peters, and Isaac Stern for dinner, and they reminisced about the past while digging into cans of caviar. Van spoke glowingly of Rildia Bee and everything she had done for him. The flamboyant Hurok basked in his wealth and status, but at heart he was a closet socialist who had come to the United States with a handful of rubles and got his start arranging concerts for labor organizations. He never stopped scheming to bring great artists to the greatest number of people, an obsession for which he had an uncanny instinct. Van, though a lifelong Republican voter, was utterly in sympathy with him. He had come to love the impulsive impresario, with his thick Yiddish accent and his lurking humor, which always threatened but never quite managed to burst into a smile.

*　　*　　*

DURING A break between Moscow performances, Van, Kondrashin, and Henrietta set off on a tour of Riga, Minsk, Kiev, Sochi, Leningrad, Yerevan, Baku, and Tbilisi. In Leningrad's Philharmonic Hall two thousand fans swarmed down the aisles to present Van with souvenirs, including a pigeon that "bounced out of his arms and flew to the ceiling." A thousand followed him to his hotel, cheered when he stepped onto the balcony to appeal for "Russian-American friendship," and continued cheering long after midnight. In Tbilisi he was asked to don the Georgian national costume and sit at the piano while his photograph was taken. He gamely agreed and gave permission for the pictures to be published, which in Russia was interpreted as a political statement, much as his innocent words in Leningrad had been at home.

On July 4 he was back in Moscow playing for the Independence Day celebrations at Spaso House, the U.S. ambassador's residence. Khrushchev was in Austria, but Mikoyan attended and sang lustily along as Van played Russian songs. Afterward the Cliburn party moved south, and on the thirteenth it reached Sochi, on the Black Sea. At Adler airport, crowds pressed flowers and babies at Van in the warm sunshine, plump Sochi ladies with lovely smiles revealed gold teeth, and men wore plaid shirts and battered hats. He smiled back, hot in his dark suit, button-down shirt, and thin tie, his face nicked from shaving, while Kondrashin grinned in an airy white shirt and filmed the scene on his fancy cine camera. In another unprecedented mark of favor, Khrushchev had lent Van his state villa, an imposing mansion fronted by a two-story white portico set amid lush gardens with a swimming pool and badminton court. Van kicked around it for a week before returning to Moscow for his final concert on July 19. Twenty thousand fans filled the Lenin Sports Palace, which Khrushchev used for political rallies, to hear Van play Tchaikovsky's Piano Concerto no. 1 with Kondrashin and the USSR State Symphony. "More than 1,000 teen-age Russian girls stampeded down the aisles," UPI reported. "They crowded around the stage and threw bouquets at the lank, grinning pianist. Usherettes flanked the stage at the end of the concert to defend Mr. Cliburn from the showers of flowers, gifts and notes that were directed his way by the fans. At times during the concert, the teen-agers sighed in unison or wept. When it finished, the entire audience kept Mr. Cliburn coming back for curtain calls for at least half an hour." By the end, Van and most of the audience were weeping; so, no doubt, were many watching the broadcast on television.

His tour over, Van returned to the Black Sea for his long-delayed vacation. With its subtropical climate, the coast was the main resort for the whole Soviet Union, and it was especially famous for its medicinal spas. Every major institution had its own establishment where workers, gifted a voucher by their trade union, could get meals, treatments, and massages free or at cost. In the usual hierarchical Soviet way, the Council of Ministers' spa was rated the highest in several categories. Cottages were dotted round a large park, and Van moved into one that had been equipped with a piano. Henrietta stayed with him, and Ella Mikoyan installed herself in the main building. The three swam, walked, took trips to a mountain lake, and lazed in the sun. One day, Van went to the Mikoyans' nearby compound for a late lunch party. With mock solemnity Anastas Mikoyan warned Van not to divulge the address of Khrushchev's dacha, as it was part of the nuclear weapons research facility; Van replied that it made no difference to him as he could barely work a camera, let alone understand complex technology when he saw it. Young Aschen, who by now had developed a fierce crush on him, was sick in bed and missed the festivities, but at her mother's prompting, Van stopped in to cheer her up.

Khrushchev had not arranged to meet his young American friend, probably because it was politically awkward to be seen championing an emissary of the treacherous imperialists, even one as beloved as Van. Yet he undoubtedly approved Van's two final engagements. The first was a luncheon in his honor given by the Presidium of the Union of Soviet Societies for Friendship and Cultural Ties with Foreign Countries, at which speaker after speaker insisted that political tensions would not affect artistic relations. The second was at the Ostankino Television Technical Center on August 22 for the filming of a TV show called *We Will Meet Again*. In front of the cameras, Van posed with Belka and Strelka, two feisty stray dogs plucked from the Moscow streets who had trained at the Institute of Aviation Medicine and had just returned from a day in outer space aboard the latest Soviet rocket. Van grinned, and the dogs wagged their tails in canine proof of the superiority of the Soviet system. The program was broadcast across the Soviet Union, and three days later the photographs were plastered on page two of *Pravda*. Watching from Washington, the FBI was less impressed. "Cliburn, described as a 'Soviet matinee idol,' appeared on television in Moscow giving his impression of his recently concluded tour of the Soviet Union which program was reported as cleverly arranged to reinforce current communist propaganda images," an agent noted. "Cliburn was reported to have expressed appreciation for the 'wonderful hospitality' he had received." So he had, but before he left he proved his imperviousness to politics in a different direction by endowing Moscow's crumbling Central Baptist Church to the tune of eighty thousand rubles, the sum total of earnings from his recent Soviet tour. Russia's Baptists had been severely persecuted before the war, and that very year, a new campaign banned them from having prayer houses, publishing literature, and forming an association. There were mass arrests of Baptist activists, and they were forced to become an underground movement, meeting clandestinely and illegally disseminating information.

Van's triumphant return to Moscow had hurtled along at an even greater disconnect from political realities than his first breakthrough. At this point it was impossible to say whether he had aided America, the Soviets, the cause of peace, or himself. He headed for the airport accompanied by heaps of gifts, including a three-week-old puppy, who he later told the Soviet news service TASS was a relative "of the heroes of the cosmos: Belka and Strelka," and had been presented by their trainers. Amid teary farewells he boarded the plane for home. On board was Barbara Powers, the wife of the downed U-2 pilot. On August 17 her husband had been convicted of espionage and sentenced to three years in prison and seven years' hard labor. As to whether the most popular American in Russia and the wife of the least popular American in Russia spoke—and if so, what they said to each other—the record is silent.

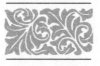

Sole Diplomacy

TWO WEEKS after Van left Moscow, Nikita Khrushchev set out for New York. In a typically unorthodox move, he had appointed himself head of the Soviet delegation to the United Nations, which allowed him to stroll into the enemy lair without an invitation. His plan was to advance the case for his nation's policies in plainspoken terms and expose the perfidy of America and the president whom he had called his friend. The intended audience was not just his own people or Americans but also the leaders of the nonaligned and Third World countries who were gathering for the opening of the fifteenth annual session of the General Assembly.

The Soviet leader's staff schemed to make him unwind and prepare himself by persuading him to sail on the SS *Baltika*, a midsize twin-screw steamship that had been known as the *Vyacheslav Molotov* before the former foreign minister's disgrace. The party leaders of Bulgaria, Romania, Hungary, Belarus, and Ukraine went with him, and after ten days of playing Warsaw Pact shuffleboard in choppy conditions, they watched the Manhattan skyline rear on September 19. As they approached, motorboats revved toward them, their decks packed with anti-Soviet protestors holding placards, chanting through megaphones, and hanging an outsize Khrushchev in effigy from a gallows. NYPD speedboats circled the liner and accompanied it to East River Pier 73, which was near the United Nations building but turned out to be an ancient structure half-rotting into the water.

Smiling Mike Menshikov had warned that it was expensive to rent a good pier, and Khrushchev had ordered him to find something cheap.

The ship came to a halt near the pier and waited. After much delay, news arrived that the longshoremen's union was refusing to service the enemy vessel, and the crew winched down a lifeboat and set off trailing a towing rope. When the leaders finally picked their way along the rickety jetty in pouring rain, there was no American welcoming party and no press pack baying questions to Khrushchev, who sulkily assumed that Ike had leaned on his media mogul pals to starve the premier of publicity.

Khrushchev took up residence at the headquarters of the Soviet mission, a large Federal-style town house on the corner of Park Avenue and Sixty-Eighth Street. Security considerations precluded him from going for a walk, and he bounced round the elegant rooms like a ball in an arcade game. One by one, reporters collected behind police barriers outside, and a small throng had gathered by the time he spied the cameras and notebooks through the glazed balcony door of the ballroom. Instantly he sprang to life, calling his trusty interpreter, Victor Sukhodrev, and ordering the reluctant guards to open the door. A chorus of questions met them, and he answered each one with gusto and at great length, gesticulating excitedly and hollering above the street noise, completely unfazed that no one understood his Russian. The dapper Sukhodrev was forced to shout as well, which tickled his boss. Pedestrians on Park Avenue approached and stopped to watch the Soviet leader hold forth. Passing drivers wound down their windows and booed. Khrushchev grinned, shook his fist at them, and booed back.

The next day, the press corps came prepared with microphones on long poles. Khrushchev looked slyly at his interpreter: "Okay, let's go get some fresh air," he said, "if we can call this New York air fresh. And we'll chat to the guys at the same time." The balcony became a vent where he blew off built-up steam until the United Nations gave him a better outlet.

The Soviet premier had decided to attend every morning and

afternoon session of the General Assembly, and the other Eastern Bloc leaders dutifully followed suit. Seasoned diplomats stared as they trooped in each day on the dot of eleven and took their places in the empty chamber, where sessions always started late. When they finally began, Khrushchev watched curiously, trying to understand why delegates were variously applauding, ignoring the proceedings, and wandering about with a freedom that no one would have dared adopt in the Supreme Soviet. During lulls in the proceedings, he stared balefully down the neck of the foreign minister of Fascist Spain, who was seated directly in front of him.

When it was his turn to speak, he ground on for two hours about the U-2 and imperialists. Soviet allies applauded loudly, and Khrushchev returned contentedly to his desk, but as soon as he realized that not all his suggestions were going to be adopted, he began shouting out objections. An official explained that the delegates could not hear him through their headphones. When the Philippines envoy took the lectern and made reference to the 1956 Hungarian Revolution and the Soviet annexation of the Baltic republics during World War II, Khrushchev banged his fists on the table and stamped his feet. The carpet deadened their impact, so he picked up his country's nameplate and swung it round. By coincidence, this was the correct etiquette when asking a speaker to give way, and the slight but phlegmatic Filipino stood aside. Khrushchev charged up, waving him away like a fly, and began a disquisition on a subject unrelated to the matter at hand. The president of the Assembly, an Irish diplomat named Frederick Boland, interrupted and explained the rules. Khrushchev threw off a few insults about American marionettes in the Philippines and then went back to his desk, which he continued to thump whenever a delegate said something that sounded like an insult to communism. When the Spanish foreign minister left his seat and took the podium, Khrushchev thumped so hard that his wristwatch stopped. "Dammit, I've even broken my watch because of this capitalist cad!" he growled, and he leaned over, pulled off his shoe, and thwacked it repeatedly on the table. The hall stopped, transfixed by the sight of a superpower leader behaving like a truculent child. Bounding to the front, Khrushchev grabbed the microphone and shouted that the Spanish people would soon rise up and overthrow Franco's bloody regime. The chairman interrupted to explain that the rules forbade insulting heads of state. Without his headphones, Khrushchev had no idea what the chair was saying, and he turned on Boland. "So you, chairman, you too support this dirty imperialist and fascist cad!" he roared. "Well this is what I have to say to you. The time will come when the Irish people will rise against their oppressors. The Irish people will overthrow imperialist lackeys like you!"

Boland turned crimson. "You have violated all the rules!" he shouted back. "I ban you from speaking and I am closing the session." He banged his gavel with such force that it cracked and the head went flying. The representatives of the world's nations looked on. Khrushchev was still bellowing, but his microphone had been switched off and few people could hear him. When Boland got up and stalked out, the premier reluctantly left the stage, but he and the Spanish delegate continued to exchange insulting gestures until the UN police intervened.

On October 11, two days before Khrushchev was due to fly home, banner headlines announced that an Estonian sailor on the *Baltika* had defected and was seeking political asylum. When reporters ambushed the Soviet leader, he declared that he would have helped the poor soul with his application if he had asked. "God bless him!" he said, ducking into his car. The defector disclosed that the ship was carrying a model of some kind of advanced spacecraft, and since Khrushchev had timed a lunar landing to coincide with his previous visit to America, rumors spread that a probe was about to reach Mars. Soviet officials denied the story, but it was not far off the mark. On October 14 a Soviet Mars vehicle blasted off with an expected arrival date of May 1961, but it failed during the booster's third burn stage and scattered debris across a wide swath of Soviet territory. The model went back on board the *Baltika*.

Had the details of the Mars shot been known, it would have lent an

irresistible analogy for Khrushchev's explosive year of personal diplomacy. The rambunctious premier went home characteristically un-
bowed, convinced that his robust defense of communism had taught
the imperialists a thing or two. The Soviet press praised his outburst
as heroic, and his popularity with ordinary citizens was undimmed.
Yet to many in the political class, including his own UN delegation, it
was the new peak in a string of mountainous debacles.

On October 15, Sviatoslav Richter arrived in Chicago at the start of
a ten-week tour of America. After being kept under wraps for years,
Richter was now being displayed everywhere as a flagship Soviet
product, though instead of the usual single KGB minder masquerad-
ing as a chauffeur or secretary—musicians called them gorillas—the
unruly pianist had two. His debut was a sensation, but it could not
erase the impression left by a shoe on a UN desk.

Incredibly, the worst was still to come.

*   *   *

THE 1960 presidential election was dominated by Democratic accusations that the Eisenhower administration had sat on its hands
while the Soviet Union built a commanding lead in stockpiles of
nuclear weapons. Nixon, the Republican nominee, was among the
few with access to the hard data from the U-2 missions, but to his
intense frustration he was unable to reveal it for fear of compromis-
ing intelligence sources, and in a tight election the spurious "missile
gap" helped John F. Kennedy win the presidency. Khrushchev, whose
barnstorming in New York did nothing to help Nixon's cause, was
delighted to see the back of the combative debater he referred to as
"the shopkeeper."

The new president was soon put to rights. The strategic balance
of power still favored the West, as it always had. The Soviet leader's
impression of a nuclear-armed madman was all too effective at suggesting otherwise, but in his quiet way Eisenhower had been playing
the same game. Privately he had been certain that America's triple
defense of nuclear bombers, submarines, and short-range missiles
was superior to any Soviet ICBM. He had been equally confident that

the Soviets would never risk a first strike unless their very existence were threatened. But he had made the case mainly to himself, and he ended his presidency warning of the dangers of a "military-industrial-congressional complex" in which politicians in the pockets of corporations funneled vast funds into unnecessary weapons programs.

Kennedy took his chips and bided his time. To change tune too soon after taking office would have been an embarrassment, and there was no shortage of those in his first year. In April 1961, Fidel Castro took three days to defeat fourteen hundred CIA-trained Cuban exiles who disembarked to overthrow him at the Bay of Pigs; Khrushchev had been informed about the invasion well in advance. The same month, the deep voice that had announced Stalin's death crackled from Soviet radios with news of another scientific triumph: Yuri Gagarin had become the first human to journey into outer space and orbit the Earth. As a propaganda coup, it outshone even *Sputnik*; it was also the clearest possible demonstration of the Soviets' confidence in the reliability of their ICBMs. And then there was Kennedy's first summit with Khrushchev.

On June 4 the graceful president and the portly premier sat down in Vienna to discuss Berlin and other pressing issues. "How old are you, Mr. President?" Khrushchev asked, throwing Kennedy off balance from the start; he was forty-four, younger than his opposite number by a quarter century. "My son would have been this age by now, or even older," Khrushchev added sadly; Leonid, a bomber pilot, had died during the war. Khrushchev then proceeded to give the novice his usual lecture on how socialism would replace capitalism just as capitalism had replaced feudalism. After several hours of statistics, historical parallels, and references to the classics of Marxism-Leninism, Kennedy shifted uneasily and borrowed a cigarette off his interpreter. When he got a word in, he ventured to dispute some points of ideology, which his advisers had specifically warned him against, and was felled by a thousand cuts. "He beat the hell out of me," the president later said. "He savaged me." On that, Khrushchev agreed. Kennedy, he wickedly suggested, was still in short pants.

"Yeah, well since the Americans have such a president now, I'm very sorry for the American people," Khrushchev said to Viktor Sukhodrev as they took their evening constitutional round the Soviet ambassador's residence. He hadn't meant to upset the sallow young man, he added later, but there was no mercy in politics. The West had a measure of revenge when Rudolf Nureyev, the young star of Leningrad's Kirov Ballet, defected in Paris—despite the KGB's efforts to entice him onto a homebound plane with the unlikely incentive that Comrade Khrushchev had requested a personal performance.

At home, Khrushchev's stock rose again. Andrei Gromyko, his foreign minister, told a party assembly that the summit had been "a meeting of a giant and a pygmy." The change of U.S. president seemed to have played into the premier's seasoned hands, and he renewed his ultimatum for Western troops to withdraw from Berlin within six months. Kennedy responded with a televised address in which he declared that any Soviet action against West Berlin would mean war, announced a sharp military buildup, and urged a national effort to construct shelters in case of an atomic exchange. Yellow Fallout Shelter signs appeared on schools and other public buildings, and homeowners dug up their backyards. *Life* ran a feature on a young couple who spent their honeymoon sealed inside twenty-two tons of steel and concrete buried twelve feet under their lawn. Yet there were never enough bunkers to go round, and the drive, which had the unfortunate effect of causing America to look scared, had the makings of a fiasco. In "The Shelter," a 1961 episode of *The Twilight Zone* set in a typical suburb, the only family with a suitable refuge barricades itself inside when the sirens go off by mistake, ignoring the desperate cries of neighbors who tear each other apart as surely as if an H-bomb had exploded overhead. The moral dilemma of whether a sheltering family could shoot an intruder was taken seriously enough that it provided a popular theme for Sunday sermons.

To Khrushchev, Kennedy's apparent weakness was a sign that power relations within the United States were in chaos, making accidental war more likely. The Soviet leader began to hanker after the old days of mutual nuclear bluff and pondered what to do about Berlin. He had threatened to sign a bilateral peace treaty that December with the German Democratic Republic (Soviet-controlled East Germany), thus tearing up the four-power agreement made at the end of World War II that guaranteed the West land access to its own quarters of the city. But the threat was hollow: he was not willing to risk military reprisals by acting unilaterally, and it was clear the West was not going to budge. Meanwhile, droves of East Germans were defecting by the simple means of going down the steps to the subway, which still served the whole city. Already three million had taken the train to freedom, threatening the East's economy and perhaps its existence. Even Khrushchev's aides joked that soon no one would be left in the GDR except its leader, Walter Ulbricht, and his mistress.

Kennedy and Khrushchev stared each other down across the German fault line. In the end it was Khrushchev who blinked first.

At midnight on August 12, 1961, GDR troops lined up across Berlin. The next morning, the streets along the Eastern side of the border were torn up and 124 miles of barbed wire was rolled out around the Western zone. Within a week, concrete blocks went up, and then guard towers. Western leaders did nothing; some wondered what had taken the Soviets so long. A broad gash running across the city was preferable to an East German offensive or an attempt to seal off West Berlin completely; besides, the wall had unlimited propaganda potential as a concrete symbol of Eastern Europe's captivity.

To regain the advantage, Khrushchev announced that the Soviet Union would end its self-imposed nuclear test ban by exploding the most powerful hydrogen bomb ever built, a 100-megaton monster with the combined force of six thousand of the bombs dropped on Hiroshima and Nagasaki. In response, Kennedy finally stepped out of his crouch and did what Eisenhower had never dared. Armed with compelling evidence from new spy satellites, he tore up his own election platform and called Khrushchev's bluff. Administration officials revealed that the Soviet Union had never come close to outstripping America's nuclear arsenal. "We have a second strike capability," explained the U.S. deputy secretary of defense, "which is at least as extensive as what the Soviets can deliver by striking first. Therefore, we are confident that the Soviets will not provoke a major nuclear conflict." Khrushchev retaliated by giving the go-ahead for the test shot on October 30. Last-minute adjustments cut the predicted yield by half, to lower the risks of widespread fallout and the fireball's consuming the delivery plane. Even so, windowpanes broke more than five hundred miles away. Yet the device, which became known as the Czar Bomba, was nuclear posturing: a white elephant that was too big and heavy to deliver by ICBM or carry very far by bomber.

As well as delivering a fiery riposte to Kennedy, Khrushchev had timed the bomb to explode on the penultimate day of the Twenty-Second Congress of the Communist Party of the Soviet Union, when more than four thousand delegates were assembled in his newly completed Kremlin Palace of Congresses. Among the diversions laid on for them was an exhibition at the Manezh, the old czarist riding school (next to the Kremlin), which had recently become home to the Central Exhibition Hall. Prominent among the contemporary Soviet artworks were "at least three busts of Van Cliburn." No other American could have sat comfortably amid the great Soviet jamboree of ideological reaffirmation, but for all his anger at America's leadership, Khrushchev had not lost his reformist zeal. The show of nuclear might gave him the cover he needed to shovel more manure over the corpse of Stalinism. Already he had pushed to retitle cities, factories, and landmarks named after the dictator: Stalinabad, Staliniri, and Stalino would henceforth be known as Dushanbe, Tskhinvali, and Donetsk. As new revelations flew and the state media luridly recounted a litany of "monstrous crimes" that cried out for "historical justice," the biggest acts of revisionism were left for the Congress's approval. On October 31, Stalin's embalmed body was removed from Lenin's mausoleum and reburied near the Kremlin Wall. Days later Stalingrad, the reborn symbol and proof of the dictator's victory in the Second World War, was renamed Volgograd. For the Chinese delegation it was the last straw. They walked out of the Congress and would never attend one again.

When the Czar Bomba went off, the United States immediately resumed testing with a series of small underground shots followed by larger-yield atmospheric and high-altitude tests, popping off dozens of nuclear devices like fireworks at intervals of two or three days. Kennedy's revelation had grabbed back the atomic advantage—with real deployable weapons, not hot air. Yet, as Eisenhower had suspected, the price was to humiliate the Soviets and play into the hands of Kremlin hard-liners.

* * *

MUSIC, JOHN F. Kennedy once remarked, was important "not just as part of our arsenal in the cold war, but as an integral part of a free society." Unlike Ike, he attended concerts regularly—Van played for him twice—relying on Jackie to tell him when to applaud. And unlike its predecessor, his new administration was intensely relaxed about using Van as a political weapon.

In February, with the Bay of Pigs invasion imminent, Van had made a goodwill tour of Mexico with spectacular results. His concerts sold out, he was mobbed in the streets, and when he attended a bullfight, the stadium shot to its feet chanting his name. He turned beetroot red and shyly waved, while in the ring, Mexico's foremost matador dedicated the doomed *toro* to the young pianist. Days after the Berlin Wall went up, Van had made his West Berlin debut with the Radio Free Berlin Symphony, earning the useful headline VAN CLIBURN PLAYS FOR FREE BERLIN. When *The Ed Sullivan Show* taped an episode at West Berlin's Sportspalast, with Van playing a Chopin polonaise to an audience of Allied military personnel, he was mobbed by screaming female fans like a chastely classical Elvis.

Musically as well as diplomatically, in 1961 Van charted a new course. For three years he had studied conducting with the venerable German-born maestro Bruno Walter: "I recognize the divine spark in your nature and musicianship," wrote Walter, who unsuccessfully tried to introduce Van to anthroposophy, the spiritual system founded by Rudolf Steiner. Walter became a cherished mentor, and their sessions proved invaluable when the New York Philharmonic invited Van to conduct Prokofiev's Piano Concerto no. 3 from the piano at a few weeks' notice. After he played an afternoon recital at Constitution Hall in Washington, DC, a police escort rushed him to the airport in time to make the flight to New York, where he headed straight to Carnegie Hall and pulled off the Prokofiev to good reviews.

Three years after his Moscow victory he was constantly on tour, playing the biggest arenas in cities nationwide and abroad. He performed with all the great orchestras and developed an especially strong partnership with the Chicago Symphony, recording Beethoven and Schumann with the great Fritz Reiner. His LP of Rachmaninoff's Piano Concerto no. 3, recorded at Carnegie Hall on his return from Moscow but long delayed while he agonized over a few wrong notes, reached the top ten and won him a second Grammy. At the end of 1961, RCA presented him with a gold disc for his Tchaikovsky First, which *Variety* noted marked "the first time that a long-hair artist has come up with a million-seller on an individual disk." His fees, starting at six thousand dollars per performance but often doubled by his share of the box office, were the highest in the business. Percentage takers attached themselves to him like remoras on a shark, but he had plenty left over to liberally endow orchestras and establish scholarships, including one at Juilliard in Rosina Lhévinne's name. She had been swamped with students since his victory made her the world's most famous piano teacher, and every New Year she received hundreds of greetings from Russians saying, "Thank you for sending us Van Cliburn!" The two remained affectionately in touch, though sometimes she wrote complaining that he was impossible to get hold of and had unaccountably deserted her, and once, she grumbled— perhaps while slurping the mound of caviar that she had taken to having nightly with dinner and never offered to anyone else—to Van's old friend Jeaneane Dowis, who was now one of her assistants, that she couldn't understand why he had never attempted to repay her for the free lessons she gave him before Moscow.

Van's life was spent in airports, hotel rooms, and halls, or traveling

between them. Stewardesses became his friends; on one flight the attendant turned out to be his old Latin teacher and childhood crush Winifred Hamilton. With the house in Tucson rented, he had no home of
his own and no intention of getting one. In 1961 the Osborne went co-op
after residents banded together to save it from demolition, but instead
of buying, Van moved along West Fifty-Seventh Street to the modest
Salisbury Hotel, which perched on top of Calvary Baptist Church. Gary
Graffman bumped into Van carrying his furniture down the block. One
room served as his combined office and living room, with the Steinway
lid piled with sheet music, a carved wooden troika, and a bronze-tinted
bust of Chopin that Rildia Bee had given him for an early birthday.
When he was away from New York, the hotel rented out his apartment
on the understanding that he could keep his piano there. Kilgore remained his legal residence until his parents moved back to Shreveport
for Harvey's work: Magnolia had now become part of Mobil Oil, and
Harvey was the area representative for its new crude oil and liquid gas
department. Van changed his permanent address to Shreveport.

Not having a home did not deter him from splurging on antiques.
Harvey panicked that his profligate son was going to fetch up in the
poorhouse, and on one visit he proposed various ideas for investments. "Oh, Daddy, I just don't have that much to invest now," he
demurred. "Did you buy something else?" his father said, frowning.
Van loved pretty things so much—Sheraton furniture and Russian
imperial silver were among his favorites—that he couldn't resist. Yet
he was cannier with money than he gave out. A financial adviser in
California purchased a good deal of West Coast property on his behalf, including strip malls and residential complexes that provided
a handsome return even if they failed to delight their tenants. One
struggling actor checked into the Halifax, a rat-infested pile owned
by Van off the crack alley section of Hollywood Boulevard, and described it as "the crappiest hotel in history." Most of the residents,
the man recalled, were "retired character actors who were living out
their golden years in Van Cliburn's dump."

Van would have been horrified. He was as modest as ever, an endearing mix of celebrity and small-town boy. He was friends with everyone, from Frank Sinatra to Placido Domingo, whom he introduced to each other, and ate at Club 21 and the Oak Room. Yet he also sat for hours talking to budding musicians at gatherings such as the Interlochen National Music Camp in Michigan, sharing ice creams and munching through heaps of hamburgers between rehearsing, playing, and sometimes conducting as often as three times in a day.

Fame had not spoiled him, but neither had it improved his concept of time. He became notorious for turning up late for rehearsals or recordings and for disappearing to make epic phone calls. Before concerts, he seemed oblivious to the waiting audience; beset by nerves, he would lock himself away in his dressing room, praying for the strength to play until he found the comfort he needed, or furiously chain-smoking for half an hour until the moment was just right. Increasingly he canceled engagements on short notice. Rildia Bee was the only person who could discipline him, and in 1962 Sol Hurok took her on as her son's tour manager. "Well he's a nice boy, but sometimes I could just wring his neck," she deadpanned, or something like it, while sitting backstage and following every note. Soon she was with him nearly all the time, which stopped Harvey from fretting about his wayward son—at the cost of being increasingly left on his own. Van gave in gracefully and loved having his mother there. He trusted her advice and, after putting up a show of independence, invariably followed it, and she cushioned him from the pressures of fame. Mother and son became famous for staying up all hours, wrapped in the quiet of night, which was comforting and cozy and put paid to any lingering thoughts that Van might have entertained of having a romantic life.

· *18* ·

Endgame

IN MOSCOW the Second International Tchaikovsky Competition got under way in April 1962. Since Van's victory, Soviet musicians had been furiously racking up awards, winning twenty-seven first prizes and thirty-five second and third prizes at thirty-nine international competitions. Yet being humiliated at home a second time was an intolerable prospect, and the rigorous selection procedures were quietly scrapped. Instead, "Madame" Furtseva, the all-powerful minister of culture, pulled seven leading pianists into her office and ordered them to take part. Among them was Vladimir Ashkenazy, who tried to explain that the Tchaikovsky concerto was not good for his small hands; he received short shrift. Ashkenazy had recently married Thorunn Johannsdottir, and the ministry had already warned him that his career would be finished if his foreign wife refused to become a Soviet citizen. Scared of getting more strikes against his name, he gave in, and to the authorities' considerable relief, he won joint first prize with British pianist John Ogdon, which was enough to save Soviet face. An American, Susan Starr, shared second prize with a Chinese pianist, Yin Chengzong, confirming an unsuspected depth of talent in both countries, but all but one of the remaining prizes went to Soviet competitors.

Van missed the contest. Unlike most musicians, he could not simply drop in on the Soviet Union, play a concert or two, and move on. A Cliburn visit was a national event in which critics pored over his

every note to detect minute changes in style, fans spent their savings
to join him at every stop, and journalists sought his views on the
state of the world. Even in his absence the Soviet media pestered their
American intermediaries to obtain interviews with him or information about his activities. One Moscow journalist commissioned a contact to procure Van's salutation to a conference of Soviet painters and
artists; another requested and received greetings "addressed to his
friends, the people in the USSR on the anniversary of the October
Revolution." Russian friends and officials kept in touch with him by
phone, and the FBI logged the conversations. One piano graduate of
the Moscow Conservatory told the Bureau that she was hoping Van
might urge Khrushchev to let her mother join her in America. For
all his political insouciance, he was aware that everything he did and
said concerning the Soviet Union had an impact. "Some politicians
maintain that the world of art and music is a closed isolated world,"
he told the Soviet news agency TASS in an interview from New York.
"I do not share this opinion. Arts and music play a tremendous part
in getting people of various nations closer and in establishing mutual
understanding and friendship."

In the spring of 1962, with relations between the Kremlin and the
White House plumbing new depths, Van embarked on a European
tour with no plans to visit Moscow. Yet when he reached Finland
he found, to his surprise, that the Soviet government was urgently
seeking him out.

*   *   *

THAT MAY, Nikita Khrushchev paced alone around a park on the
Black Sea with several puzzles on his mind. He was still itching to
repay the Americans for the U-2 imbroglio, which, by upsetting his
planned reforms, had loosened his grip on the party. Since then Turkey, which bordered two Soviet republics, had become host to American Jupiter-class intermediate-range ballistic missiles that could hit
Moscow, as could American missiles already in Britain and Italy.
Meanwhile, new glitches were plaguing his ICBM program, and
though Soviet scientists had tested a new antiballistic missile system,

it was a long way from being operational. Slowly but surely the balance of power seemed to be slipping to the West.

As he walked back and forth to the sea, Khrushchev hit on a possible solution. To deter further attacks on Fidel Castro, help spread revolution across Latin America, and give the Americans a taste of their own medicine, he would secretly install nuclear missiles in Cuba. Perhaps it also crossed his mind that Van had stayed in his Black Sea house, because it was only days later that the Ministry of Culture tracked Van down in Helsinki and invited him on short notice to a festival of modern music that was under way in Gorky, some five hundred miles from the Finnish capital. Rildia Bee, who had come along as Van's companion and handler, urged him to accept, and he cabled Anastas Mikoyan to make the necessary arrangements.

The Cliburns went directly to the vast Gorky Automobile Plant, home to a Ford assembly line that had been shipped from Detroit in the 1930s and reassembled by Americans fleeing the Great Depression. The venue was the plant's newly completed Palace of Culture, a monumental complex resplendent with marble columns, stained glass, and crystal chandeliers. Kondrashin was there to conduct the hastily arranged concert, and peeking at the audience from behind the curtain, Van experienced a rare moment of joy. "I saw the faces of people who understand every movement in a musical phrase, the subtlest tone," he explained to a journalist from *Moskva* magazine. "I heard that there were many workers in the hall and I wanted to play for them." None of the faces belonged to Americans: Stalin's regime had taken away the immigrants' passports, forced them to become Soviet citizens, and, during the purges, executed most and sent the rest to Siberia. Blissfully unaware of anything beside the music, Van sat in front of the massed ranks of autoworkers and played Prokofiev's demanding Piano Concerto no. 3.

After two days, he and Rildia Bee set off for Moscow, also at the government's invitation. It was late when they checked into the National Hotel, but Van walked over to Red Square and lost himself on the cobbles among the pigeons. Khrushchev naturally knew of his arrival and decided to make a fuss over one American he still counted as a friend. So that Van could rehearse undisturbed, the premier offered him use of one of the large new Politburo mansions on Lenin Hills. The Cliburns had no choice but to accept, but soon afterward Viktor Sukhodrev received an urgent call from the Ninth Directorate of the KGB, the department responsible for guarding Soviet leaders and sensitive facilities. The secret policeman explained that the visitors were thinking of moving back to their hotel, which could be seen as slighting Khrushchev; since Sukhodrev was friendly with Van, the KGB man asked, could he dissuade them?

Sukhodrev sped over to Lenin Hills and found the Cliburns dining with the composer Aram Khachaturian, who was eating strawberries wrapped in smoked sturgeon. The interpreter joined them and smoothed the way by revealing that Khrushchev had inquired after Van's health—a sign of favor, Sukhodrev marveled, that was not even accorded to foreign leaders—before making an eloquent plea that the guests should stay put. Van listened attentively and replied that he was very grateful for everything, but his mother had taken to the National and had already got to know the maids and staff. She was sad, and he missed the cozy hotel, too, with its lady admirers who brought him flowers and souvenirs and turned his room into a shrine to its resident deity. Sukhodrev reported his failure to the mansion commandant, and Van and Rildia Bee packed their bags.

It was sentimentally impossible for Van to open anywhere but the Great Hall of the conservatory. Awkwardly, though, his fellow American pianist Byron Janis was already booked to play there with Kondrashin as part of a State Department–sponsored tour of the Soviet Union. Even more awkwardly, Janis was also a client of Sol Hurok, who happened to be in Moscow at the time. Hurok professed astonishment at Van's presence, since he was supposed to be concertizing elsewhere, and Janis, who was of Russian ancestry and spoke the language, put in a call to the Ministry of Culture. In a syrupy voice, a Mr. Belotserkovney deeply regretted to inform him that Van Cliburn would be performing in the Great Hall with Kondrashin, that Janis would be moving to Tchaikovsky Hall, and that it was all a simple misunderstanding.

American reporters scented a story and asked Janis for a quote. "No comment," he replied sourly. The Stalin-era Tchaikovsky Hall, which was kitty-corner to the Peking Hotel, had famously poor acoustics, and Janis was slated to make a recording with Kondrashin that night. He irritably refused to budge. The last time he had played in Moscow, the U-2 row was raging and he walked onstage to hostile chants of "Kleeburn! Kleeburn!" This time round, he was finally feeling loved by his ancestors when Van had unexpectedly arrived to spoil things again.

Belotserkovney of the Culture Ministry called Kondrashin, who called the sulking pianist. "Janis, the recordings are in jeopardy. You must play in Tchaikovsky Hall or there will be no recordings," he said, and hung up. Janis devised a plan. He got Belotserkovney drunk, draped two girls on his knees, and threatened to back out entirely. A compromise was hastily arranged whereby Janis played a recital in Tchaikovsky Hall and moved to the Great Hall for a midnight recording session after Van had vacated it.

Once again Moscow welcomed Van as its own. After his first concert, on June 13, he sent his mother onstage to play two encores, to tumultuous applause. The next evening, Khrushchev sat beaming in the government box by the stage. At the end, he stood up applauding and gestured to Van to come back to the private reception room. The premier was already on his way when an aide ran after him and reported that Van had announced he was going to play Nikita Sergeyevich's favorite Chopin piece, the F Minor Fantaisie. Khrushchev reappeared, grinning and clapping. Afterward, Van soothingly told a journalist that he ascribed the plaudits "not to my humble person but to the American people as a whole, as a sign of respect for my people from the Soviet people and their wish to live in peace and honest cooperation with the United States." Peoples who respected each other's culture, he added, would never want to fight. Despite the glow of friendship, Van did have a minor falling-out with Kondrashin, who recommended a more academic approach to Brahms and Schumann, going even so far as to suggest that Van return to studying, and discovered that his young friend had a temper after all. Meanwhile, Janis received some compensation for his humiliation when Milan's Teatro alla Scala called and asked him to take over a concert canceled by Van at five days' notice. He thought it over and quickly decided the crumbs were too tasty to refuse.

Van had extended his stay to play at Khrushchev's vast Kremlin Palace of Congresses on June 19, and Khrushchev granted him the rare favor of an invitation to spend Sunday with his family at his dacha outside Moscow.

Stalin's villa at Kuntsevo had stayed shuttered since his death, and Khrushchev's new compound, which the KGB drably named Dacha no. 9, had been rebuilt for him at Usovo, on the Moscow River. Passing between lines of tall birch and pine, the car stopped before a twelve-foot concrete wall with two small guardhouses. Gray iron gates swung open onto a long drive leading to a handsome neoclassical structure of cream stone with a two-story portico, not unlike a scaled-down White House. Surrounding it were rose gardens, fountains, clipped lawns with yellow benches, and a pagoda overlooking the river. A green carpet ran up to the door between potted plants. Inside were forty rooms with old-fashioned furnishings, including a mahogany-paneled living room, a dining room with bright blue draperies, and a cozy billiard room.

It was a warm, sunny day. With Viktor Sukhodrev interpreting, Khrushchev took Van on a tour of his vegetable garden and prized cornfield before leading him down to the river. A public beach packed with local bathers could be seen a hundred yards away, but the dacha had its own beach and a dock where pleasure boats were moored. Khrushchev ushered Van into a rowboat and took the oars, giving Van the tiller.

"We've been watching you for two years," the Soviet premier said, heaving away. "You're very wise. You don't engage in politics."

"If I did," Van answered, "my grandfather would come back from the grave and kill me. He told me: 'Politics is a great art, but it is divisive. Great classical music is for everyone all over the world.'"

Khrushchev grunted agreement. "I'm proud of you because you love classical music," he said.

When they returned to shore, Van briefly played the piano and the party ate a late lunch under the trees. Khrushchev was keen to fatten Van up: "Because you are too skinny, Vanya," he said, grinning expansively. His son, Sergei, who was working on guidance systems for Soviet cruise missiles, whirred away with his cine camera. In summer the Khrushchevs always served *okroshka*, a cold soup made with *kvass* mixed with chopped meat or vegetables. Van asked what it was, sampled it, and requested more details of how it was made. Khrushchev started in on a long explanation of *kvass* (a fermented drink made from dark bread) that baffled his guest, which only made the premier more determined to make Van understand. Van politely pushed the bowl away none the wiser, and for the rest of the meal he studiously ignored the jugs of *kvass* in the middle of the table.

After lunch the party sped along the river in motorboats, Van in his suit and tie seated next to the premier in his loose shirt and homburg. They stopped for a shooting party, one of Khrushchev's favorite pastimes, which Van sat out with Nina Khrushchev and the other ladies. Afterward they went bathing. Viktor Sukhodrev stood stiffly on the bank while Khrushchev's youngest daughter, Elena, called him a Foreign Ministry fuddy-duddy and ordered him to jump in. He politely refused on the grounds that he was working, until Khrushchev needled him as well, whereupon the interpreter stripped off and splashed round with Van and the extended Khrushchev clan. Finally, Van and Khrushchev hugged and said their good-byes. "Wouldn't you like to take along a glass of *kvass* for the road?" Khrushchev asked. "*Kvass*, never!" Van replied in Russian, and the unlikely pair burst out laughing.

The premier and his family were deeply fond of the American pianist, and Van went on his way with indissoluble memories. But it is also possible that Khrushchev had engineered Van's entire visit and showered him with favors to give himself useful political cover for the greatest of all his foreign policy adventures.

Between Van's invitation to Gorky and his trip to the dacha, the Soviets had earmarked sixty one-megaton missiles for Cuba, and a military delegation had visited the island in disguise. Fidel Castro had needed no convincing about a proposal to combat "insolent American imperialism," but finding locations where the missiles could be concealed had proved trickier. After driving round for a while, the ranking Soviet marshal had decided that coconut palms looked uncannily like rockets, and back in Moscow he convinced Khrushchev that the missiles could be disguised by the simple expedient of attaching a crown of leaves to their nose cones. Missiles also needed launchers, trailers, and fueling trucks, which resembled vegetation even less. Yet the proposal had the merit of being extremely cheap, which was important because the cost of Khrushchev's scheme had already swollen alarmingly. Military advisers pointed out that troops were essential to defend the missiles against a possible American invasion: at least fifty thousand, with artillery and tanks. An air defense system had to be created, with antiaircraft guns and MiG-21 supersonic fighters. Shore defenses would need to include missile batteries, high-speed patrol boats armed with homing missiles, and bombers. Soviet submarines would have to be based in Cuba to patrol the U.S. coast. The biggest problem of all was how to transport and deliver so much military cargo undetected. The minister for the merchant navy reported that it could be done if the shipping plan for the entire year were scrapped. Khrushchev gave the order.

*   *   *

BACK AT the National, the Soviet newspapers were hard on Van's trail. A reporter for *Komsomolskaya Pravda* kept ringing the switchboard, but the receptionist explained that their star guest was too busy preparing for concerts and television appearances, holding official meetings, and taking walks round the city. The journalist cornered Henrietta Belayeva and enlisted her help, and the reporter climbed the staircase as if she were on her way to a royal audience:

The door is opened and I enter the room. Cliburn is in front of me. He's tall and slim, with a somewhat tired, pale face. His eyes are expressive and thoughtful and his hands are the hands of a magician, hands that touch the keys and make you fly away into the world of incredible heightened beauty and deep reflections.

Van introduced Rildia Bee, who was sitting in an armchair beside him. "We feel at home in the Soviet Union, we feel well here," she said. "Da da, ochen khorosho," said Van. "Ya lyublyu Moskvu." He continued in English: "It is a city that has given me wings." The reporter posed her most pressing question: "Van, can you tell me what you think about the forthcoming Eighth World Festival of Youth and Students in Helsinki?" He went red and apologized that he had had almost no chance to follow the young people of the world preparing for this exciting meeting, and then made some airy comments about there being nothing nobler than fighting for peace, which made flowers and music blossom. She solemnly reported these bons mots, adding that millions of Soviet citizens loved Van, were inspired by his brilliant art, and waited impatiently for his performances. In the same rapturous vein, Van told *Pravda Ukrainy* that he hoped to bring peoples together through his music. "I think the cultural exchange between our countries is the greatest achievement of our time," he declared. "They should develop it. It's through art that people come to friendship, that's my deepest conviction. Isn't it thanks to art that I found so many friends in your country? I would so like to see them all and hug them. But, unfortunately"—he stretched out his arms—"even my long arms won't be enough for that."

Van went on to Israel, where his press conference was the first in Israeli history to be attended by representatives of both the American and the Soviet embassies. The Israelis received him almost as warmly as the Russians. "Whenever he appeared on the teeming boulevards," a reporter noted, "he was swamped by admirers and autograph seekers and charmed them as well as the press by his Texan

courtesy and boyish naiveté." To all appearances Van had become a
supranational institution, floating above the political troposphere as
a celestial messenger of love and peace, while the dirty business of
superpower rivalry carried on far beneath.

*   *   *

THAT SUMMER, unprecedented numbers of Soviet ships sailed into
the North Sea and the Mediterranean, catching the attention of European security services. Surveillance planes buzzed the decks but saw
only agricultural machinery, while the ships' passengers appeared to
be technicians, tourists, and bearded Cuban revolutionaries. In September the CIA calculated that triple the number of Soviet ships had
arrived in Cuba compared to the previous summer, and overflights
soon revealed why. Columns of tanks, armored personnel carriers,
launchers, and trucks piled with khaki crates of missiles were crawling inland from every port. Cruise missiles resembling small planes
emerged from crates and were installed along the coast under camouflage, near antiaircraft batteries. MiG-21 fighters and Ilyushin Il-28
jet bombers were unpacked and assembled, and Soviet Komar missile
boats entered the ports under cover of darkness.

At the White House, President Kennedy received the troubling
reports. He warned the Soviets that installing offensive weapons
in Cuba would bring serious consequences but publicly refused to
countenance an invasion. Secretly he had already given the CIA the
go-ahead for Operation Mongoose, an aggressive covert operation
designed to help Cubans overthrow the Castro regime. The operation allegedly stretched to getting into Castro's hands exploding
cigars and depilatories to make the dictator's beard fall off. By a remarkable coincidence the Cuban revolt was intended to occur that
October, the same month the Soviet warheads were due to arrive.

*   *   *

ON SEPTEMBER 24 the first Van Cliburn International Piano Competition took over Fort Worth, Texas. Four students from the Moscow Conservatory took part, bringing photographs and gifts for
Van. With them were interpreters who were less interested in the

scores than in the bomber assembly lines at the nearby Lockheed Martin plant, a fact duly noted by the FBI, which amid the heightened tensions filled up a large file with intelligence about the Soviet visitors.

Out-of-town reporters delighted in telling readers that Cowtown, famous for its fat cats, fat cattle, and monster honky-tonk, had discovered there was more to music than "Willy, Waylon or Garth at Billy Bob's saloon" singing about "whiskey rivers, lyin' eyes or achy breaky hearts." Yet with well-heeled residents vying to host the fifty-four competitors, Rildia Bee and Harvey glad-handing at every event, and cowboy hats and ranch parties galore, the contest had a definite flavor of Texan hospitality. Otherwise it was blatantly modeled on the Tchaikovsky Competition, which, depending on how you read it, was either a compliment or a challenge to the Soviets. There were three rounds, with lots of compulsory Russian music. The judges used the same twenty-five-point system, though their habit of stopping performers in mid-phrase and telling them to move on disconcerted many, as did the decision, urged by Van, to re-audition three second-round losers at the end of the finals. At first he had hoped the contest would never happen, and when it was clear that it would, he briefly considered disassociating himself from it. Still, he came round, and it was his charm, elegance, and high standards that the thousand volunteers aspired to uphold.

Rosina was there as a guest, but Bill Schuman and Mark Schubert had evaded and finally refused entreaties that they join the advisory board, presumably not wanting to attach the Juilliard name to something untested, nearly provoking Van into backing out of a major Juilliard fund-raiser. On October 7, Rosina's student Ralph Votapek of Milwaukee, Wisconsin, won first prize, which undoubtedly caused Van mixed feelings. Soviet competitors Nikolai Petrov and Mikhail Voskresensky came second and third; in sixth place was a Portuguese pianist, Sérgio Varela Cid, who had gone up against Van in the original Tchaikovsky Competition. The prizes, some donated by Van, were generous, and the award included a Carnegie Hall debut and management by Sol Hurok. Van greeted each contestant, discreetly watched many performances, and announced the winners. He seemed to have been around for so long that it was strange to think that, at twenty-eight, he was barely older than many of them.

It was a busy time for cultural exchange. That September, Sol Hurok had brought the Bolshoi Ballet back to America for a thirteen-week tour. "For three hours," the *Times* reported, "East-West tension—the threat of nuclear warfare, missile shots and planetary probes—was forgotten." Meanwhile in Moscow, the New York City Ballet opened on October 9 at the Bolshoi Theatre, sharing the stage with the Bolshoi Opera, whose production of *Boris Godunov* with American bass Jerome Hines was rapturously received, with Khrushchev leading the applause. A week later Vladimir Ashkenazy began his second American tour in Washington, DC, his travel ban revoked after his victory in the Tchaikovsky Competition. Khrushchev was no doubt satisfied that the exchanges helped maintain the fiction of business as usual; perhaps he even hoped that the enthusiasm generated by ballet dancers, pianists, and singers might temper Americans' response to the appearance of Caribbean-based missiles that flew at four miles a second and could hit Miami in less than a minute.

*   *   *

ON OCTOBER 14, 1962, a U-2 flying over Cuba snapped several pictures that revealed clumsy attempts to camouflage launch sites for ballistic nuclear missiles. After processing, the photos were shown to the president the next morning. JFK assembled a circle of his closest advisers, including Tommy Thompson, newly returned from Moscow as Secretary of State Dean Rusk's adviser on Soviet affairs. The Joint Chiefs of Staff unanimously called for air strikes to wipe out the missile sites, followed by a full-scale invasion. Thompson argued for a strong warning. After fierce debate, Kennedy instead ordered a naval "quarantine" of Cuba; the term was deliberately chosen instead of "blockade," which under international law connoted an act of war. At the same time, he wrote to Khrushchev demanding the removal of the missile bases and all offensive weapons. On October 22 the president addressed the American public on television to explain his action, warning that a global crisis beckoned if the Soviets refused to heed his call. "It shall be the policy of this nation," he unequivocally stated, "to regard any nuclear missile launched from Cuba against any nation in the Western Hemisphere as an attack by the Soviet Union on the United States, requiring a full retaliatory response upon the Soviet Union." The readiness level of U.S. forces rose to DEFCON 3, and a naval force headed for the Caribbean.

Khrushchev ordered some vessels carrying weapons to turn back and the rest to sail on, including four diesel submarines armed with nuclear-tipped torpedoes and one ship carrying nuclear warheads that was close enough to reach port before the exclusion zone went into effect. Two days later he cabled the White House insisting that the nonblockade clearly amounted to an act of aggression and the Soviet ships would ignore the attempted "piracy." As the ships reached the five-hundred-mile line, U.S. naval forces intercepted them, searched them, and allowed them to continue when only food, fuel, and non-offensive equipment were found on board.

Spy planes returned with new images showing the missile sites nearing operational readiness, with fuel tankers and command trailers standing by. For the first time ever the Strategic Air Command's state of alert rose to DEFCON 2, one step below maximum readiness for nuclear war. B-52s carrying thermonuclear weapons took to the skies on continuous airborne alert, some patrolling near the borders of the USSR. Smaller B-47s were dispersed around civilian and military airfields, ready to take off on fifteen minutes' notice. More than one hundred ICBMs were readied for launch. In prospect was the first direct military confrontation between the two superpowers since the start of the Cold War.

Kennedy replied to Khrushchev that his hand was being forced after repeated assurances that no offensive weapons were being deployed in Cuba had turned out to be lies. Huddled in gruelingly long sessions with his advisers, Kennedy listened closely to Tommy Thompson, the only one with deep personal knowledge of the Soviet leader. Thompson was convinced that Khrushchev could be persuaded to remove the missiles, and stood firm against proposals for air strikes and amphibious invasions, warning that they could push the impulsive premier into making a move against West Berlin or Turkish bases that could lead ineluctably to nuclear war. Kennedy had begun to believe that an invasion was unavoidable, but he agreed to give diplomacy more time. As if to amplify the possibility, the previous night Van had played Rachmaninoff with the National Symphony at Washington's Constitution Hall, while that night, the twenty-fifth, the Leningrad Philharmonic began its first American tour at New York's newly opened Lincoln Center, the first foreign orchestra to play there.

The next afternoon, ABC News correspondent John Scali contacted the White House with startling information. A Soviet agent had tipped him off that the Kremlin would remove its missiles under UN supervision in return for an American commitment never to invade Cuba. The agent was the same Alexander Feklisov who had once listened to Rachmaninoff's choir at the New York baths, now promoted to KGB station chief in Washington. White House staffers were scrambling to verify the back-channel offer when a letter from Khrushchev clattered over the Teletype from the U.S. embassy in Moscow. Sent at 2:00 a.m. Moscow time, it was rambling and emotional but contained the seed of a solution that mirrored Feklisov's information. "If there is no intention . . . to doom the world to the catastrophe of thermonuclear war," wrote Khrushchev, "then let us not only relax the forces pulling on the ends of the rope, let us take measures to untie that knot. We are ready for this."

Intelligence experts pronounced the letter genuine, and Thompson's long game seemed vindicated. Yet the morning brought news that Radio Moscow was broadcasting a harsher message, demanding that the United States remove its Jupiter missiles from Turkey in return for the Soviet missiles leaving Cuba. The different style led analysts to question whether Khrushchev was still fully in command; at the least there was clearly dissent in the Presidium, if not outright chaos. The new proposal put Kennedy in an awkward position: it was hard to dismiss it as unreasonable when the United States was anyway planning to remove the missiles from Turkey, but to accept would make it look as if he had capitulated to blackmail. Soon a new letter from Khrushchev came through, essentially repeating the morning's offer, which now appeared to be the agreed-upon Kremlin position.

An hour later a Soviet surface-to-air missile launched from Cuba shot down a U-2, killing its pilot. Kennedy told the chiefs of staff to be ready to attack within days, but he also plied Thompson with questions about Khrushchev's likely intentions and state of mind and how far the premier might have to go to appease hard-liners in the Soviet government. Thompson suggested responding to Khrushchev's first letter and ignoring the second, and he sat down to help draft the reply. The letter, which was sent later that night, included a series of suggested measures for the removal of the Soviet missiles under UN auspices and a pledge that the United States would not invade Cuba. Thompson also suggested sending Robert Kennedy to meet secretly with the Soviet ambassador; given the Soviets' conspiratorial concept of American power, he argued, they would have more faith in the president's brother than in anyone except JFK himself. Coached by Thompson, Bobby passed on the message that the Soviets could either remove the missiles or watch the Americans do it, but that the president was keen to avoid war. As for the missiles in Turkey, he added, they were already obsolete and vulnerable to Soviet attack and would soon be gone anyway, but this could not publicly form part of a settlement.

Five hundred miles from Cuba a Soviet submarine skirted the exclusion zone. Only the objection of a single officer prevented the use of a nuclear torpedo when a U.S. Navy vessel attacked the sub with signaling depth charges. Far away over the east coast of the USSR, a U-2 pilot accidentally trespassed into Soviet airspace for ninety minutes. The Soviets scrambled a squadron of MiGs, and the Americans dispatched nuclear-armed F-102 fighters across the Bering Sea. The world was teetering on the brink of a potentially devastating nuclear exchange.

With no reply forthcoming from Moscow, ABC's John Scali arranged another meeting with Alexander Feklisov. Scali asked the spy why Khrushchev's two letters were so different; Feklisov unconvincingly blamed poor communication. Scali shouted that it was a "stinking double cross" and that the United States would invade within hours. Feklisov replied that Khrushchev would soon send a new response and that Scali should assure the administration that no deception was intended. No one would believe him, the journalist retorted, but after they separated, he delivered the message.

The next morning, October 28, Radio Moscow broadcast a statement from Khrushchev declaring that the Soviet missiles would be dismantled and repatriated. If Feklisov was acting on his own initiative, as it appears, his intervention bought desperately needed time.

The worst crisis of the Cold War had lasted thirteen days. Tommy Thompson took off for the funeral of his mother, who had died in its midst. Robert Kennedy and Secretary of Defense Robert McNamara later called him the unsung hero of the hour.

One by one the missiles were taken down, packed up, and loaded onto eight ships, which were scrutinized by the U.S. Navy as they crossed the never-declared blockade. The line stayed in place while the Soviets tried to remove their bombers, which required the cooperation of Fidel Castro. The Cuban leader was incensed at the Soviet climbdown. He had been minimally consulted on the weapons' installation and not consulted at all about their removal. At the height of the crisis, he had goaded Khrushchev to launch a preemptive nuclear strike on the United States, intimating that he was ready to die in a nuclear inferno. Even the Soviet leader, whose romantic attachment to Castro had blinded him to the folly of his scheme, thought he was crazy. "Can you imagine!" he marveled to Mikoyan's sons. "As if he doesn't understand it would mean a global catastrophe!" On November 3, Khrushchev dispatched their ever-reliable father to manage the delicate feat of getting the planes back while keeping Cuba as an ally. After meeting Mikoyan at the airport, Castro refused to see him for three days. A few minutes into their talks, Mikoyan received news that his wife had died. Castro suggested postponing the discussion, but Mikoyan demurred. The situation was too grave, and he asked for the funeral to take place without him. Finally, Castro saw the writing on the wall and agreed to the withdrawal of the forty-one Il-28 bombers; the rest of the armaments stayed in Cuba, though not the large cache of tactical nuclear weapons that the Soviets had secretly planned to leave until Castro provoked them into changing course.

On his way home Mikoyan stopped over in Washington and switched effortlessly from arm-twisting Castro to sweet-talking Kennedy. The Bolshoi Ballet had also arrived in town, after playing to empty houses in San Francisco, and for their first social outing after the crisis, the First Couple attended the opening night, which for lack of a suitable stage took place in an old movie theater. Reporters noted that the president "applauded louder and longer than anyone in his section." At intermission he accompanied the Soviet ambassador backstage to greet the dancers, who gave Jackie a portrait miniature of Tchaikovsky. She invited them to the White House and took young Caroline to watch a rehearsal with their star ballerina, Maya Plisetskaya. JFK's mother and his brother Teddy invited the whole company to Cape Cod for a dinner in honor of Plisetskaya's birthday, and Bobby Kennedy commenced an affair with her. The arts were useful for patching up broken friendships as well as making new ones.

Six months later the United States quietly removed its missiles from Turkey. His authority boosted by his handling of the crisis, JFK committed America to landing a man on the moon before the decade was out and traveled to Berlin to crow that the West had not had to build a wall to keep its people in.

* * *

THE FIRST sign that Khrushchev had ushered his nation into the world fold had been his hearty celebration of Van's victory. The first

sign that his tumultuous cavalcade had hit the skids came that December, at two cultural events. Touring an exhibit of avant-garde art
in the Manezh on December 1, 1962, Khrushchev furiously denounced
the paintings as "dog shit" and the artists as "faggots" whose "asshole
art" was fit only for urinals. Meanwhile, at his elbow, emboldened
hard-liners hooted for the artists to be arrested, or strangled. What
seemed like an intemperate outburst, or a cheap attempt to garner
support by playing the simple man taking on the cosmopolitan elite,
looked far more ominous when the authorities did everything they
could to sabotage the premiere of Shostakovich's Symphony no. 13
on December 18. The choral setting of poems, beginning with a
lament for a massacre of Jews by Nazis and collaborators at Babi Yar,
near Kiev, purportedly offended by putting Jewish suffering before
Russian. Two singers and a conductor backed out before Kirill Kondrashin took up the baton. Like Shostakovich, he had long nursed
deep contempt for the Soviet system.

Both events were roaring successes, and no one was arrested or
exiled, but the campaign escalated. The Central Committee set up a
commission to crack down all over again on "formalist tendencies."
Leading artists were hauled into the Kremlin and given stern lectures
that brought back unpleasant memories of the late 1940s. In March 1963
the intelligentsia was summoned to a Kremlin meeting with Khrushchev himself. "The thaw is over," he thundered. "This is not even a
light morning frost. For you and your likes it will be the arctic frost."
In case anyone doubted his resolve, he reminded them that his regime
had "helped smash the Hungarians." The echoes of Stalinism were unmistakable: "Society has a right to condemn works which are contrary
to the interests of the people," he warned. As for avant-garde composers, having allowed them access to Western innovations, he turned
on them. "We flatly reject this cacophonous music," he declared of
twelve-tone compositions. "Our people can't use this garbage as a tool
for their ideology." Once again, artists began to live in fear of intimida-
tion, but the about-face was a sign of weakness, not strength.

*   *   *

IN COLD War politics, there were no villains or heroes. Neither side was innocent or entirely to blame. Khrushchev and his opposite numbers in the White House did not have a fetish for needless confrontation: even as they authorized espionage, nuclear blackmail, subversion, and proxy wars, they knew how severely the rivalry drained their domestic programs. They knew the arms race was a nonsensical game of numbers; that regional conflicts could drag them into a tit-for-tat exchange that could escalate into nuclear war. Yet the revolving gears of international allegiances had their own inexorable logic. Every crisis averted created another. Public opinion, entrenched bureaucracies, and powerful interest groups exerted their pull, as did the same shifting forces in their allies and client states.

Of all the dangers, ignorance was the greatest. To cut through the confusion of voices that had bedeviled the Cuban crisis, the White House and the Kremlin established a telephone hotline. The two sides moved to prevent emerging powers from developing atomic technology; a test ban treaty was signed in August 1963, though it failed to stop China from exploding its first nuclear device the following year. The glimmer of hope that Churchill had foreseen in an equality of annihilation, that Eisenhower had understood when he insisted on planning only for total nuclear war, was enshrined in the theory of mutual assured destruction, or MAD, whereby the superpowers targeted each other's cities with first- and second-strike weapons of such destructive capacity that their survival depended on there being no war at all. The *Dr. Strangelove*–style acronym made the case that when humanity's propensity for violence had reached the point where annihilation rested on the flick of a switch, the only sane response was one that, to an average person, closely resembled insanity. Khrushchev knew this as well as anyone.

In September 1963, President Kennedy took the rostrum at the United Nations and proposed that the United States and the USSR join forces to reach the moon. Khrushchev categorically dismissed the idea, but over the following weeks he concluded that the Soviets might benefit economically and technologically from a joint venture.

He was on the point of changing his mind when the president was assassinated in Dallas. Khrushchev, on a visit to Ukraine, wired the usual protocol telegram to the White House, but he and his wife also sent personal letters to Jackie. The next day, they cut short their trip to visit Spaso House, passing through Soviet mourners gathered outside the gates, and signed the book of condolences with tears in their eyes. Mikoyan, who had carried Lenin's coffin, attended the American president's funeral. Jackie wrote touchingly to Khrushchev, saying that she was very moved by how upset Anastas Ivanovich had looked as he came down the line, and how much her husband had wanted to work with him for peace.

After Kennedy's vice president, the former majority leader Lyndon B. Johnson, took over the presidency, the leaders exchanged letters. Yet they never got to take each other's measure in person, which was perhaps a pity, because the ambitious Johnson, "cunning yet insecure, imposing yet ungraceful . . . the shrewd peasant come to shake up a nation and rule a superpower," was in some ways the American Khrushchev. After a decade in power the Soviet leader's overreaching had finally caught up with him. There had been no joyous explosion of energies to fire the USSR's economy into catching up with that of the West, let alone overtake it. His bureaucratic meddling had brought the economy to a virtual standstill, and after a promising start his grand agricultural schemes had proved an epic disaster. There were riots over food prices, and rebellions over radical reforms of party structures that weakened the powers of functionaries, whom Khrushchev belittled as "dogs peeing against curbstones." China finally broke off relations with the Soviets, and Mao took to insulting Khrushchev at every turn. Ten years of unrelenting activity had made an adversary of nearly every person he counted as a friend.

As so often, the protégé wielded the knife. On October 12, 1964, Leonid Brezhnev called his mentor at his Black Sea villa and notified him that a special Presidium session was to be held the next day to discuss agricultural issues. Khrushchev suspected the worst but flew back. At the meeting, his peers took turns denouncing him for fostering a cult of personality, flouting collective government, cozying up to the West, creating the Sino-Soviet split, embarrassing the state, behaving waywardly, governing incompetently, permitting nepotism, and nearing his dotage. That night, he called Mikoyan. "I'm old and tired," he said. "Let them cope by themselves. I've done the main thing. Could anyone have dreamed of telling Stalin that he didn't suit us anymore and suggesting he retire? Not even a wet spot would have remained where we had been standing. Now everything is different. The fear is gone, and we can talk as equals. That's my contribution. I won't put up a fight." He was glad, he later vowed in his habitual barroom language, that the party had advanced to the point where it could fire its first secretary: "You smeared me all over with shit, and I say, 'You're right.'"

The next day, the Presidium and Central Committee voted to accept his retirement. Shortly before his ouster, he had spoken with the Soviet cosmonauts aboard the *Voskhod 1* orbiter, during the seventh manned Soviet space flight, the first to carry an engineer and physician as well as a pilot and to dispense with space suits. At their homecoming ceremony there was no mention of the premier who had overseen the entire Soviet space program. Khrushchev was dispatched on a modest pension to his dacha, where he suffered from depression, cried a lot, and slept badly. The pension was later reduced, the dacha was exchanged for a smaller one, and the leader who for all his faults had saved his nation from the ravages of Stalinism was airbrushed from Soviet history.

Mikoyan, the great survivor, outlasted the latest upheaval and was appointed president of the Soviet Union before retiring the following year. The stolid Brezhnev became first secretary and put up the shutters on reform. His government spent vast sums on music, literature, and art in the same way that it invested lavishly in gymnastics and weight lifting, as ideologically useful tools. "In order to be victorious," the reempowered Composers' Union leader, Tikhon Khrennikov, commanded his troops, "we must strictly obey the party line and guide our youth." Those few Moscow nights that had transfixed the world in 1958 now belonged to a less predictable, more innocent age.

THIRD MOVEMENT

Pianoforte

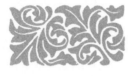

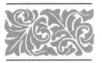

· *19* ·

America's Pianist

ON DECEMBER 20, 1963, Lyndon B. Johnson put in a telephone call to J. Edgar Hoover to ask if Van Cliburn was politically sound.

The nation was still officially in mourning for JFK, but President Johnson was preparing to receive his first head of government. The summit was to take place at LBJ's ranch, near the tiny farmhouse where he was born in the Texas Hill Country west of Austin, and its centerpiece was to be a luncheon in a converted school gymnasium in nearby Stonewall. "Cactus" Pryor, a Texas entertainer and Johnson family friend, had been tapped as master of ceremonies, and he had called Liz Carpenter, the First Lady's press secretary, to suggest an alternative to the usual country music outfit.

"Liz, wouldn't this be a good opportunity to display to the world that Johnson isn't a hick, a hillbilly, that Texans are something besides cowboys and fiddle bands?" he had asked. "Why don't we get Van Cliburn down?"

"But this is a barbeque," Carpenter had objected. "We can't present Cliburn at a *barbeque*." Still, Cactus persuaded her, Lady Bird Johnson approved, and LBJ picked up the phone. Hoover, at sixty-eight still vehemently in charge of the FBI, summarized the conversation in a memorandum that was distributed to senior staffers:

President Johnson called and asked what I know about Van Cliburn, the musician. I advised him that Van Cliburn is a homosexual.

The President then asked if there is any reason why Van Cliburn should not play for the White House, and I replied that there is no reason why he shouldn't. The President remarked that most musicians probably are homosexuals and I told him a great many are.

Johnson secretly recorded the rest of the exchange on his Dictaphone Dictabelt. Hoover added that Khrushchev had given Van a great deal of publicity while he was in Russia, but that Van's eager response was not politically motivated. "It's more, as I think, exhibitionism," he explained. "But he's a great pee-yanist, and I would see no reason why he couldn't be used for entertainment purposes." With the FBI director's political and critical blessing, the president called Carpenter. "Edgar Hoover says Van Cliburn's all right so I guess you can go ahead and invite him," he said in his husky drawl.

After supervising a candle-lighting ceremony at Lincoln Memorial that marked the end of thirty days' mourning, Johnson flew home for Christmas. On the twenty-eighth, Chancellor Ludwig Erhard of the Federal Republic of Germany landed with a large entourage. The next day, Van arrived at the Johnson ranch, also known as the Texas White House, and was handed a red-checked shirt and jeans. When he gathered that he was supposed to get into them before he played, he demurred and insisted on wearing white tie and tails.

"But Van," pleaded Carpenter, who came from the sleepy Bible Belt town of Salado, Texas, "they haven't ever seen a tuxedo in Stonewall."

"This is a concert for the chancellor of Germany," Van protested, aghast at the lapse in decorum.

"But you've never seen Stonewall!" Carpenter and Bess Abell, Lady Bird's social secretary, chorused. After a long debate a compromise emerged in the form of Van's regular business suit.

The clapboard gymnasium had been Western-themed in what Carpenter called "artistic rustic fashion," with bales of hay, red lanterns, a tack shop's worth of saddles and lariats, and yards of bunting in the German and American colors. A mariachi band welcomed the dignitaries for a chuck wagon meal of barbecued spare ribs, deer meat sausage, and hominy grits accompanied by Beethoven, Brahms, and Schumann. Afterward the president shooed the party into the pasture, where they stepped gingerly over what Vice President Hubert Humphrey called "the Republican platform," so Johnson could show off his prize herd of Texas longhorns.

"He was a man," Carpenter once said of LBJ, "like the raw land he came from, hard limestone land with twenty-seven inches of rainfall a year. He was as strong and open as the West Texas hill country." Not all the European visitors relished the drastic change from the elegant formality of JFK's reign, but the entertainment was unexpectedly well chosen: before he became an economist and then a politician, Chancellor Erhard had wanted to be a concert pianist. The "Spare Rib" summit ended with commitments to closer cooperation and renewed efforts at assuaging East-West tensions.

As he turned thirty, Van had become America's national pianist, a treasure to be wheeled out on state occasions. In 1965 he played Liszt's Piano Concerto no. 1 at the president's inaugural concert after "Landslide Lyndon" received the highest-ever share of the popular vote. He was featured at the White House Festival of the Arts, a presidential pat on the back for America's artists that turned into a public relations catastrophe when the poet Robert Lowell declined his invitation on the front page of the *New York Times* in protest at the escalating Vietnam War. That Christmas, Van attended a White House state dinner for the returning German chancellor, and then accompanied LBJ home to Texas aboard Air Force One, with Rildia Bee at his side. The two families went way back: Johnson was virtually an adopted son of the Cliburns' old friend Speaker of the House Sam Rayburn.

In 1965, Van returned to the Soviet Union for the first time since his unplanned visit three years earlier. With the world awash in

Beatlemania, he once again passed for a rock star in a country where the Fab Four were outlawed as hedonistic and corrupting and where students still danced at parties to scratched 78s. True, he was a different kind of rock star: instead of destroying hotel rooms, he liked one so much that he bought its entire contents, including the drapes—or so it was said. With his Romantic devotion, natural aristocracy, and golden boy looks, he was still every bit a *kumir*, an idol. He was mobbed in Kiev and Leningrad and Novosibirsk, the press coverage was incessant, and in Moscow the Van Club danced in constant attendance. But there was no doubt the times were grayer and cooler and less sincere. The kind of personal relationship he had had with Khrushchev was impossible under the doughty Brezhnev, and official Moscow was closed to him.

It was the first real rebuttal in seven extraordinary years. Van had always been easily discouraged and prone to paranoia, convinced that he "was not in good favor in certain places," and despite his strong Christian faith, he had looked to alternative spiritual systems for answers. Now, less sure of himself than ever, he turned to the occult for the comfort he craved. He was hardly alone—American pianist Byron Janis was an ardent believer in the paranormal—but his dabblings went far enough that they attracted the attention of the FBI. While he was in the Soviet Union, the Bureau recorded numerous conversations between Van and a female "medium or spiritualist" living in the Bronx, who was "maintaining very close control over the subject's activity." A report to J. Edgar Hoover noted that Van was "completely dependent" on her and "obeys all her orders" and gave some excerpts from their long exchanges:

MEDIUM: You seem disturbed.

VAN: I am.

MEDIUM: Do not hold a negative thought. [She says she has received a message that the spirits of all the great musicians are standing around him, holding positive thoughts and helping him.] The mind rules the body.

VAN: Could I have a shot tonight?

MEDIUM: Could you do it yourself?

VAN: Yes, I feel I need it every day.

MEDIUM: Twice daily will keep you above normal.

VAN: Should I have some beer tonight?

MEDIUM: Yes, it will relax you.

VAN: Will they like my conducting?

MEDIUM: Yes. I had a vision.

VAN: I hope you will project to my mind so I will not make any slip.

MEDIUM: The forces will be with you.

VAN: The Embassy is short of tuna fish.

MEDIUM: Send tuna fish to the Embassy. It will make a good impression.

VAN: Daddy fell. Should I call a doctor?

MEDIUM: No. It is painful but he will be all right.

*　　*　　*

HE WENT home discouraged, but from a distance the Soviet Union still figured large in his life. In the summer of 1966, Kirill Kondrashin joined him at Philadelphia's Robin Hood Dell concert venue and at the Hollywood Bowl, to resume their performances of Tchaikovsky and Rachmaninoff. In September, LBJ threw a reception at the White House for the five American prizewinners in that year's Tchaikovsky Competition, and Van was master of ceremonies. Harvey and Rildia Bee were there among a lineup of musical royalty, including Rosalie Leventritt and pianist-entertainer Victor Borge, the author of a famous crack about Van: "Tchaikovsky was born in 1840 and was a rather obscure musician until 1958 when he was discovered by a Texan." That same month, the second Cliburn Competition took place in Fort Worth. Twenty-year-old Radu Lupu, who was Romanian but had trained at the Moscow Conservatory, won first prize in a reduced field that was more than half American. To Van's dismay, the Kremlin had banned Soviet competitors from taking part, in protest at the huge American troop increases in Vietnam.

That at least was the public explanation. In truth, both super-powers were losing the automatic support of their youth that had been taken for granted in the conformist 1950s. The Shook-Up Generation of New York and the Beat Generation of San Francisco had their bored, cynical counterparts in the Soviet Union, reared on pure Marxism-Leninism but the despair of the party. "LOST GENERATION" BAFFLES SOVIET; NIHILISTIC YOUTHS SHUN IDEOLOGY, headlined the *New York Times*. The *stilyagi* were long gone, and remembered almost nostalgically; the newly disaffected youth were more materialistic and drawn to anything Western, "from a new hair-do to a belief in democratic freedoms." Girls wore nylons and spike heels or black cotton stockings and ballet pumps. Guys called each other "zhentlmen," said things such as "tip-top" and "okay," and sported Ivy League haircuts, fringe beards, tan slacks, and narrow italianate ties with horizontal stripes. Jeans, known as "kowbois" or "Texas trousers," were rare but could be counted on to infuriate party propagandists. Both sexes read *The Catcher in the Rye* and danced to Western music played by Russian jazz bands or taped from the Voice of America. "Can you show us how to do the twist?" they asked foreign visitors, between trying to discover the truth about the West. By no means were all trouble-makers: many were the educated sons and daughters of high officials, kids who spent their evenings hanging out at top hotels, including the National, where the hot bands played. "Komsomol bully squads rout them out of the restaurants and cafes and send them home," the *Times* reported. "Photographs of them are plastered on billboards under headings: 'Parasites, Get Out!' They are shipped to the virgin lands or the construction sites of Siberia." Yet nothing won them back to the cause. A few leaders quietly wondered how belief in a system that purported to be perfect could have been so easily lost to mass apathy. Most were content to revoke Khrushchev's limited freedoms, lock up dissidents in mental institutions to be cured of their infectious desire for free speech, and support Brezhnev when, in 1968, he ordered tanks into Czechoslovakia to crush the Prague Spring.

The bloody echo of 1956 further deepened the disillusion of the

Western left with Soviet-style socialism. Still, there was always Mao's China to make the Kremlin look like a model of enlightened governance.

*   *   *

IN 1961, Liu Shikun had returned from Moscow to take up a post as piano teacher at the Beijing Conservatory. That same year he had married a daughter of Ye Jianying, a prominent marshal of the People's Liberation Army. The top leadership attended the wedding, and Mao invited Liu to play at his home: "They told me Western music was not very nice," Mao said afterward, "but what you played was very nice. We cannot totally reject Western music and arts." Liu's future seemed assured when, in 1964, he was sent to live with a farmer in a Shanxi province cave dwelling with no running water and bricks piled on a stove for a bed: not as a punishment but as part of the Four Cleanups campaign, which assigned intellectuals to learn from peasants and purge themselves of reactionary thoughts.

By the time he was recalled two years later, the Cultural Revolution was already under way. Launched by Mao to "save" Communist orthodoxy from bourgeois infiltration and restore his authority after the disastrous Great Leap Forward, it soon consumed the entire nation in an orgy of denunciations and violence. Both Western music and the "feudalistic music of the old capitalistic China" were favorite targets; in their place, musicians were ordered to play "revolutionary songs which glorify Mao and are inspirational and fill one with courage." At the Beijing Conservatory, which not long before had invited Van to tour China, students formed gangs of Red Guards and pounced on its president, Ma Sicong, a venerated composer who had been a judge in the violin section of the 1958 Tchaikovsky Competition. Some threw a bucket of glue over his head and covered him with posters—one denounced him as a "Blood-sucking ghost"—while others beat him with belt buckles and boards full of nails and made him march round banging a stick on a pot. At the Shanghai Conservatory, more Red Guards denounced Gu Shengying, the other Chinese competitor in the 1958 Tchaikovsky Competition. Unable to bear the humiliation, she sent a parcel of chocolate to her father, who was still in jail, then swallowed a handful of sleeping pills and turned on the gas. She was just twenty-nine. In the same city, a whole family of classical musicians gassed themselves, while out of rage or mental derangement, a conductor tore Mao's *Little Red Book* to pieces and was shot in the head. Vast though it was, China had no room for such gentle types.

Liu returned from the countryside to find himself already the target of a campaign by a group of Red Guards calling themselves the Mao Zedong Thought Combat Team Revolutionary Committee General Service Station. At their rallies he was declared a "second-rank ghost and monster" and ordered to wear a paper hat identifying him as "Counterrevolutionary Musician Liu Shikun." Conservatory students kicked him, spat at him, and made him confess to shaking Khrushchev's hand and subscribing to Soviet revisionism. Eventually they arrested him and locked him in a storeroom with his colleagues. Each day, the prisoners were woken at six and set to read Mao's *Selected Works* or newspaper articles before being marched off to clean toilets, break stones, and chop firewood. Sometimes they had to crawl like animals, eat grass, or stand facing a wall for hours. In the evenings, they wrote confessions and sang the "Howling Song," with its chorus of forced masochism:

> *If I speak or act without permission,*
> *May you beat me and smash me,*
> *Beat me and smash me.*

The Red Guards serenaded Liu with his own ditty:

> *Liu Shikun you bastard,*
> *Now you can surrender.*
> *If you do not tell the truth,*
> *You may quickly die . . .*

One of his students repeatedly beat him with his fists and a belt, fracturing a bone in his right forearm. Ma Sicong, meanwhile, had lost thirty pounds and was too weak to pick up his violin bow. After he had tried to commit suicide several times, a doctor diagnosed him with hepatitis, and he was allowed out to seek treatment. He donned overalls, hid his violin in a bag of tools, and fled. In January he and his family escaped on a small boat to Hong Kong and defected to the United States. More than fifty of his relatives and friends were rounded up; three died, and many were jailed, including the doctor, who received eight years for his solicitude.

Liu did not try to escape, and after a year the Red Guards marched him to the public security bureau, where he was charged with spying for the Soviet Union and sent to prison. There he was kept in solitary confinement and tortured to extract proof that his father-in-law had spoken and acted against the party. By attempting to slow the pace of the Cultural Revolution, General Ye had crossed Mao's wife, Jiang Qing, whose Gang of Four happened to control the Central Special Case Committee in charge of the young pianist's case. Eventually most of the general's family and household were arrested, including Liu's wife and their little boy's nanny.

Hardly any sunlight penetrated Liu's cell, and his hair turned white. His daily rations consisted of a moldy cornmeal bun and two bowls of briny water with rotting leaves infested with nourishing worms. In cold weather, puddles turned to ice, and with only a cotton prison uniform and thin blanket for cover, he suffered from frostbite. He had no contact with the outside world and worried that if he died, no one would know what had happened to him. The only news came from the propagandistic *People's Daily*, a copy of which a guard threw in the cell each morning and collected at night. One day Liu was moved to a new cell and discovered half a copy of the paper on the floor. In his mind, he had already composed a letter to Mao, and now, one by one, he cut out the characters from the newspaper with a twig that had broken off a broom, sticking them together with morsels of the steamed buns. When the letter was finished, he waited for an opportunity to smuggle it out.

Months and then years went by, but one never came. As he bowed to Mao's portrait and confessed to his own imaginary crime, he mainly thought about staying alive. Sometimes his mind turned to the piano, and he practiced in his head or mentally composed a concerto. In those moments, he often thought about Van's playing at the competition, which had affected him so much. He puzzled over what it was that had made it sound improvised. Was it the influence of American jazz and pop music? If so, how could he absorb that himself? But that brought him back to his present surroundings and made him even more desperate to get out.

*   *   *

ON OCTOBER 14, 1967, Van landed in Washington, DC, to play an evening recital at Constitution Hall and too late realized he had left his concert apparel on the plane. So he did what any celebrity with high-placed friends would: he called the White House. LBJ told him to come over, and he was cleared to enter at 6:32 p.m. There was precious little time before the concert, and Sgt. Ken Gaddis, the president's valet, had been given time off to attend a football game. The staff flew into a panic.

Presidential aide Sgt. Paul Glynn was at home when the White House operators tracked him down. Johnson came on the phone. "Paul, I sure need some help," he said. "I gave Ken the afternoon off, and Van Cliburn has lost his black tie, he left it on the airplane. Can we do something? What size am I?" Glynn indelicately told the fifty-nine-year-old president that Van was a young man, and LBJ's dress outfit would be too big. "I'll call you back," Johnson said, and minutes later he was on the phone again. "Paul, come on in," he said, "and we'll do it." Glynn had barely had time to get ready when the phone rang a third time. "Haven't you left yet?" growled the president, who was notorious for giving reluctant congressmen the viselike "Johnson treatment."

Glynn sprinted into the White House at 6:47 p.m., found Johnson in the pool, and headed up to the family quarters. Van was practicing at the piano. Ken Gaddis ran in as well, troubled as to what was so important that he had been summoned from the game. The two men began to fit Van into LBJ's suit. At six feet, three and half inches, Johnson was the tallest president but one—Lincoln had a quarter of an inch on him—and almost a match for Van. But Johnson ate as he drank and womanized, to fill an unfillable pit, and the pants hung loose like a clown's. The aides doubled them twice in the back and pinned them. The jacket needed less pinning, but the white shirtfront billowed like a full sail and would not sit smooth. When Van was all dressed and pinned in, he changed into his regular clothes and went down to the pool, where Johnson made him get into the suit again so he could take a look. It was 7:45 p.m.

"They look fine," LBJ said, in surprise or perhaps satisfaction. Van asked if he could relate the story, and Johnson, scenting good publicity, readily agreed.

"Mr. President," Van said as he got ready to leave, "I'll return this suit, but I will not return this stud. I hope you'll hold it for a minute, and then give it back to me—and it will be something for me to treasure the rest of my life." He left at 7:50 p.m., barely in time to make the concert.

The episode was reported in virtually every news outlet.

With the help of the Texas takeover at the White House, Van had become an institution in his early thirties. Thanks to his example, American performers now rubbed shoulders with the power elite, their artistry appreciated as part of the idea of America. *Time* pronounced him a cultural hero "right up there with the Beatles and Marshall McLuhan." He was impersonated in the Marilyn Monroe vehicle *Let's Make Love*, was a regular on *What's My Line?*, and was name-dropped in *Bewitched*. In 1966 he was given an hour-long profile on NBC's *Bell Telephone Hour* and featured on a CBS tribute to Sol Hurok. He endowed scholarships at Juilliard, Cincinnati, Louisiana State, Interlochen, Texas Christian University, and the Liszt Academy in Budapest; played fund-raisers for orchestras and venues;

and accumulated honorary degrees from Baylor, Loyola, TCU, Michigan State, and Cincinnati University, where he made a pitch that his mother should get one, too: "I was moved," noted president Warren Bennis, "but declined." By late 1968, his *My Favorite Chopin* disc had been on the classical best-seller list for 138 weeks, and Van had all together sold three million albums at a time when five thousand was a good result for a classical LP; he could have sold more, but his contract, which tied him to making two records a year, did not bind him to approve any for release, and he was notoriously skittish about doing so. His audiences were loyal, his reviews often glowing, some placing him, according to one *Los Angeles Times* critic, "unmistakably in the ranks of the greatest pianists of this or any other era." He was still playing more than a hundred concerts a year, at fees starting at $7,500 for a recital. With memories of Moscow barely dimmed a decade on, to many he was a true American hero.

Yet America was changing, and one man's hero was no longer his neighbor's. The 1960s youthquake was erupting, Vietnam was burning, and the cultural outlaws were about to storm the picket fence fortresses.

*   *   *

THE VIETNAM War began because America, like the Soviet Union, had tethered its credibility to weak client states in the name of building alliances. When their clients strained in inconvenient directions, the superpowers were tugged along, absurdly but inevitably locked into unwanted conflicts that were easier to escalate than escape. At first the war attracted widespread support among Americans, but beginning with the major troop increase of February 1965, it seared itself into the national conscience. A month later the first teach-in paralyzed the University of Michigan, and the Beat Generation's barely concealed unease pushed to the surface in an upsurge of activist energy. As the war laid waste to lives and regions, for many, protest was a necessary human response that trumped Cold War geopolitics and fears of communism.

The Johnson administration had been focused on domestic re-

form: civil and voting rights, the war on poverty, and federal funding for education and health care—the "Great Society" agenda that
banned racial discrimination, lifted millions off the bread line, and
significantly extended the reach of the federal government. LBJ had
deep misgivings about the Vietnam conflict even as he broadened
it: "I don't think it's worth fightin' for and I don't think we can get
out," he told his national security adviser, McGeorge Bundy, after a
sleepless night. As a mounting chorus of criticism kept him virtually a prisoner in the White House, his large, friable ego crumbled.
He began conceiving of his opponents as traitors and slipping back
into the crude worldview of his time as a rising Texas senator, where
the "mad masters of the Kremlin" conspired to advance "the surging blood-red tide of communism." Increasingly paranoid and self-
pitying, he ordered CIA director Richard Helms to find proof that
the antiwar movement and the urban race riots that broke out each
summer were Red plots directed from Moscow or Beijing. "The communists already control the three major networks and the forty major outlets of communication," he lectured his staff, singling out the
"bunch of commies" running the *New York Times* and fuming that the
"communist way of thinking" had even infected the West Wing. By
the time Van played at a White House state dinner for the chancellor
of Austria in April 1968—the month Martin Luther King Jr. was assassinated and riots broke out in a hundred U.S. cities—Johnson had announced that he would not seek another term. After Robert Kennedy
was assassinated, the Democrats nominated Vice President Hubert
Humphrey, while Richard Nixon came back from the wilderness to
clinch the Republican nomination.

Fresh-faced, God-fearing, and wholesomely Texan, Van had suited
the 1950s as surely as chrome fenders fitted a Cadillac. Now, like
many Americans in their mid-thirties, he was out of tune with the
radical mood of young America, the angry generation that spurned
the old values of hard work, discipline, and patriotism in favor of
campus protests, pot, rock, and permissive sex. While he was never
seen without his dapper off-work uniform of dark suit, white shirt,

and dark tie, hippies were dripping beads and beards and letting it all hang out. While he adopted a gracious but stiff public persona that made him a gentlemanly throwback to an age of all of a few years ago, rebels dropped LSD and tripped out from stifling conformity. While he was utterly discreet about his personal life, Allen Ginsberg wrote openly about homosexuality and listed his partner in *Who's Who* as his spouse. While the children of the Cold War chanted, "Down with the U.S.!" and "America stinks!" Van wore his patriotism on his sleeve. Even at Carnegie Hall, audiences began to object: "Many in the full house were startled, and some annoyed, when Mr. Cliburn opened the program with the 'Star Spangled Banner,'" reported the *Times*, adding that "one woman in a stage seat pointedly refused to rise, and a few listeners were rude enough to hiss." Undeterred, he sang the national anthem at Constitution Hall with the Johnsons watching. Yet as coffins rolled in, carpet-bombing spread, and college students burned their draft cards, the country had stopped believing in the old heroes.

Van had raised the profile, status, and salaries of pianists and performers across America and had shown infinite grace under unrelenting pressure. Still, like a latter-day Paderewski, his incredible popularity had always attracted enemies, and now the chorus of complaints grew louder. Critics accused him of coasting, his rangy restlessness distracting him from sinking into the ultimate simplicities of great art. They complained that his repertoire had not expanded fast enough, though with an orchestra it stretched to Beethoven's Third, Fourth, and Fifth Piano Concertos; Rachmaninoff's Second and Third Concertos and Rhapsody on a Theme of Paganini; both Brahms concertos; both Liszt concertos; Chopin's First; MacDowell's Second; the Schumann; the Grieg; Mozart's C Major (K. 503); and Prokofiev's Third. (His recital program was longer.) A *Houston Post* writer sniffed that his once-golden tone had become "a bit ticky-tacky." Others carped that Van's interpretations were getting stale and had not matured. Privately and not so privately, some suggested that this was because he had not matured as a person, either. He was still reliving his Moscow triumph, they said, or even further back, a sanctified childhood of which he'd never let go. In interviews, he rarely mentioned Rosina Lhévinne now, only Mother, prompting a friend to dash off a furious letter accusing him of extreme ingratitude, which "shows both in your character and in your development as an artist." Perhaps it was true that with Rildia Bee eternally at his side, he stayed in the sky and never came down to earth, with its compromises and nakedness and fears learned through joy. But that was who he was.

He smarted at the criticism, but he saw nothing wrong with the way he played. As for his choice of music, it had been set in stone when he was eighteen, and during his first summer vacation, he had gone through the entire piano literature, deciding there and then which pieces were for him. Or perhaps it had been even earlier, when with his mother's guidance his keen musical instincts unfolded the plan of the great concertos to him. "Choose carefully which works to learn, and never let them go," Rildia Bee had said. "They will always be your friends." So they had been, and he saw nothing wrong with that, either.

*   *   *

ON JULY 20, 1969, America landed Neil Armstrong and Buzz Aldrin on the moon, fulfilling the pledge JFK had announced and LBJ had upheld. Yet the space race continued: within two years the Soviets launched the first crewed space station, *Salyut 1*, and three top-secret military stations followed between 1973 and 1976. Nor was the arms race in retreat. Punching through a loophole in the 1963 test ban treaty, both superpowers developed sophisticated underground testing techniques that led to an increase in U.S. detonations. By 1970 the USSR was fast closing the real missile gap, and attention moved to new destruction-enhancing innovations such as fitting many independently targetable warheads to a single missile.

From his small dacha near Moscow, Nikita Khrushchev followed events as best he could. He had spent the last few years dictating his memoirs in his usual crude, self-justifying, colorfully charismatic style. His son, Sergei, had smuggled some tapes to the West, and in

1970 they were transcribed and published under the title *Khrushchev Remembers*. In response, the Sovet authorities demoted Sergei and made Khrushchev sign a statement denying any knowledge of the work. When Moscow Radio broadcast the disavowal, it was the first time the former premier's name had been heard in six years.

On September 11, 1971, Nikita Sergeyevich suffered a heart attack and died in a suburban hospital. He was denied a state funeral or burial in the Kremlin Wall. There was no orchestra to play him on his way; instead, Chopin's "Funeral March" hissed from the speakers of the brick morgue, where he was laid out with his twenty-six military and state medals, including three stars denoting a Hero of the Soviet Union, incongruously pinned to velvet cushions at his feet. In place of a solemn funeral procession, there was a bus painted with a black border that bore the coffin and the family members sitting around it on the bumpy thirty-minute ride to the Novodevichy Cemetery, Moscow's second best.

The news had been embargoed until the day of burial, the silence a measure of the current leaders' lack of confidence in their own popularity, and there was no announcement of the place or time of interment. Even so, dissidents had been rounded up on suspicion of intent to commit an "antisocial act," and hundreds of soldiers and policemen surrounded the cemetery, the officers shouting into radios, while more waited in reserve in covered trucks. The gates were firmly shut, and stuck next to them was a scrap of paper announcing in red pencil: CEMETERY CLOSED FOR CLEANING. They opened to let in the bus and a group of mourners with passes, then closed again. The bus continued to the farthest and least prestigious corner of the cemetery, passing through a final cordon of plainclothes guards and KGB officers until it was within sight and earshot of the elevated railway that ran outside the walls.

A fine mist fell as the coffin was placed on a bier. Red-eyed women in black shawls pressed close, weeping and kissing Khrushchev's bald head. As well as family and close friends, there was a large group of Western journalists and a small crowd of artists and writers who had lately missed Khrushchev's noisy leniency. Nina Khrushchev stood with her three daughters in a black lace mantilla and dark gray coat, fighting back tears. Sergei, without coat or umbrella, strode to the mound of earth beside the grave and spoke the eulogy.

"There were those who loved him, there were those who hated him," he said in distinct, measured tones, "but few could pass him by without noticing him." The reporters held their whirring cine cameras above their heads as the rain fell harder. "We have lost someone who had every right to be called a man," Sergei added. The reproach did not need to be said. A few more speeches followed, one from an old revolutionary from Khrushchev's former hometown, Donetsk. "We remember Nikita Sergeyevich as an unbending proletarian," she testified, "one who was to us, the younger people, an example of fortitude, of heroism, of unbending will, of unbending passion in defense of the party line." A young man whose father and grandfather had been executed under Stalin thanked the deceased premier for ending the Terror.

An official hurried the mourners along as they filed past the coffin. When the final moment came, Nina caressed her husband's forehead and burst into heaving sobs. A worker in blue coveralls banged nails into the lid as a small brass band struck up a dirge. The black-suited players blared out the Soviet anthem while the coffin was lowered with ropes, and the gravediggers moved in with spades.

"You must disperse now and go on your way, comrades," the official shouted. No one moved. A few onlookers who had managed to bluff their way through the security talked in low voices.

"All the rulers of Russia have been killers," said one. "Through all our history only two have given us freedom—Alexander II and Khrushchev. And Russia took it out on them for that."

"So what do you expect?" someone else asked, "that's just our traditional way of behaving. But the important thing is that those two acted as they did."

"Nikita Sergeyevich wouldn't have wanted it to end this way," said an old man. "He'd have invited all Russia to his funeral."

Pravda announced the death of "merit pensioner Nikita Sergeye-vich" in a one-sentence, seven-line notice. The rest of the world's me-dia properly commemorated the peasant's son whose natural wit had taken him to the peak of power; the bluff, bumptious premier who tried to atone for his heinous deeds, who clung to his strong, sim-ple convictions, and who worked in his own magnificently cockeyed way for peace. "Mr. Khrushchev opened the doors and windows of a petrified structure," veteran Moscow correspondent Harry Schwartz wrote in the *New York Times*. "He let in fresh air and fresh ideas, pro-ducing changes which time already has shown are irreversible and fundamental." The headline, impossible to imagine just years before: WE KNOW NOW THAT HE WAS A GIANT AMONG MEN.

· *20* ·

Great Expectations

RICHARD NIXON had made his name as a foe of communism and had sealed his reputation in the Kitchen Debate. As president, he had begun by escalating the Vietnam War. So it was a startling turnabout when, three years into his first term, he announced plans to visit China.

The trip was a bold wager in the great game of geopolitical power. Nixon had set himself the perilous task of building a relationship with a nuclear-armed Communist country with ambitions to be a global player, in the hope of playing it off against another nuclear-armed Communist country that was already a global player. He arrived in February 1972, shook hands with Mao Zedong and premier Zhou En-lai, met with both men, and banqueted in the outsize Great Hall of the People. In the most secret session of the trip, so secret that not even the CIA knew what took place, national security adviser Henry Kissinger sat down opposite Liu Shikun's father-in-law, Ye Jianying, and briefed him on American intelligence of massive Soviet troop deployments along the Chinese border. Unbeknownst to the pianist, who was still in solitary confinement, the general had regained favor and was now defense minister in all but title; he and three other Chinese marshals had boldly advised Mao to play the "American card" against the Soviet Union, believing that the Soviets were a greater threat to China than the Americans.

Nixon's visit was in large measure designed to pressure the Soviet

Union into restarting détente. The gamble paid off, and negotiations for a presidential visit to the Soviet Union, which had been broken off twelve years before, were soon concluded. Alarmed at the Sino-American alliance, the Kremlin also noted that Vietnam, economic competition, and social unrest had shaken America's standing, and the Soviets considered that the United States would be a realistic negotiating partner in trade and arms control. Among reformers, there were even hopes that in finding themselves both outsiders in large parts of the world, the two superpowers might find themselves allies.

For this first visit of a U.S. president to the Soviet Union since Roosevelt's wartime trip to Yalta—the first ever to Russia—Sol Hurok planned a near repeat of the Eisenhower program. The impresario booked Van to appear in eight cities and Roberta Peters to perform in four operas, and then waited for a presidential blessing. For Van it was an opportunity to renew his ties and reassert his influence after seven long years. He arrived in Moscow early and found himself quartered in the monstrous Hotel Rossiya, an unloved Khrushchev legacy built to house deputies to his Palace of Congresses. Also staying in what was then the world's biggest hotel was Nixon's aide Ron Walker, a Texan code-named Roadrunner who coordinated the president's trips. "Staying" was putting it nicely: KGB agents guarded the hallways and elevator, guns in hand, keeping Walker and his party under house arrest in retaliation for Nixon's mining of Vietnam's Haiphong Harbor. The hotel set up a small top-floor dining room for the captives, and Van joined them for meals. When he complained to his fellow Texan about that perennial bugbear of Westerners in Moscow, the telephone system—he didn't like to let a day go without talking to his mother, he said, and couldn't get through to her—Walker had a word with the White House Communications Agency, and Van soon had a White House Signal phone that he could use day and night. Walker also passed on Nixon's personal request that Van perform at a Spaso House banquet for the leaders, and he happily accepted.

On May 22 the president and the First Lady arrived in Moscow and settled into a large but not overly comfortable suite in the Kremlin Palace annex. The following evening, Van opened his first Soviet tour in seven years in the Great Hall of the conservatory. To his astonishment the years had not dimmed his fans' ardor. Hundreds of women waited outside the hotel, applauding and shouting, "Vanya!" and "Vanyusha!" At the concert they swooned and threw flowers and went wild, and the line to see him backstage snaked round the building as he found the right words for each fan. Afterward the Mikoyans welcomed him back to the House on the Embankment. "What happened to you?" he said when Aschen Mikoyan opened the door. The last time he had seen her she was a teenager; now she was twenty-two, gamine, and pretty, with dark wavy hair, and she had a son. She also still had a crush on Van and, since he always called her "darling," reason to believe it was requited.

Roberta Peters was amazed all over again by the power Van held over regular Russians. He was an even more imposing presence now, with an otherworldly aura of grace that drew people in and put them at their ease. When she complained that she couldn't get hold of the best caviar, he called over the maître d' at the National (where he had managed to move) with the natural authority of a returning Romanov. "Anything for you, my dear maestro," the waiter said, and produced a giant can of beluga. Still, the atmosphere was even tenser than before. The guests at the National were ordered to keep their shades down, and when an official car was due to pass by, KGB officers knocked on doors to ensure they had complied. One morning Van was woken well before nine o'clock by a secret policeman, who insisted on watching from Van's fourth-floor window as Nixon laid a wreath at the Tomb of the Unknown Soldier, across the way. "Why did he have to do it so early?" Van said with a moan.

There were even signs that subtle differences over Van's musicianship had hardened into something stronger. "It's hard to recall any major performer whose tour received such varying reviews, such sharp conflicts of opinion, as Van Cliburn's recent concerts," noted *Sovetskaya Muzyka.* "'The pianist of the century,' 'the great conquering skill,' and, right next to it, 'boring declamation' and 'provincial sentimentality.'" Nor did Van's welcome cause the old stir back home. "Cultural exchanges have settled into a decade-old pattern," noted Max Frankel, now chief Washington correspondent for the *New York Times* but back for Nixon's trip:

> Van Cliburn is here playing the piano and Roberta Peters is singing in recital, and they are impressing the same old audiences and embracing the same old friends.
>
> Moreover, the Soviet leaders seem to have found the formula by which to protect their political system from alien ideological viruses. They are yielding on pants for women and rock music for the young, but they intend to tolerate nothing that Mr. Nixon has in mind when he speaks of a free exchange of ideas. The warmth above does not seem to reach the permafrost below. Moscow is not Peking, but it remains farther still from Washington.

And Washington remained a world away from Moscow: Western ways might have infiltrated the Soviet Union, but fourteen years after the Kitchen Debate, Nixon was still unable to comprehend the Soviets' worldview. It was as if cultural exchange had become an end in itself, rather than part of a broader meeting of minds.

This was détente without the excitement or the fun, but there was plenty of business to do. If Nixon in China had been like Marco Polo reveling in the wonder of discovery, in Moscow he was a traveling salesman working well-trodden turf, selling grain and conferences, linkups in space and arms control agreements. There were endless plenums and signing ceremonies in the Grand Kremlin Palace and meetings in Brezhnev's office or at his dacha, where in time-honored fashion he took Nixon boating. The food, service, and accommodation suffered in comparison with those in Beijing, and there were the usual bureaucratic challenges, such as telephones and telex machines that were mysteriously misplaced at inopportune moments. But by way of compensation the Soviets had *Swan Lake* to offer instead of the revolutionary Chinese ballet *Red Detachment of Women*.

After exhaustive negotiations the two parties sealed the terms of SALT 1, the first comprehensive strategic arms limitation agreement, and the Anti-Ballistic Missile Treaty, which halted work on systems to intercept incoming missiles. Peaceful coexistence, even meaningful collaboration, was once again on the leaders' lips on May 26 as they arrived at Spaso House prior to the late-night signing ceremony. After dinner, Van sat at the piano in the main hall, with its ionic columns and Montgolfier chandelier, and struck up "The Star-Spangled Banner" and the Soviet national anthem. The guests stood up, but General Secretary Brezhnev and his wife were not among them. Neither were the other top Soviet officials, Premier Alexei Kosygin and head of state Nikolai Podgorny. All four, and only those four, had gone home after dinner. Perhaps they needed to rest, but it looked suspiciously like a deliberate snub on account of Van's closeness to Khrushchev, or a refusal to accredit, as Khrushchev had, the American's expertise in their musical heritage. To Van, with his romantic attachment to Russia and deep pride in his historic role, it was the cruelest cut.

Nixon addressed the people of the United States and USSR simultaneously on TV and radio, signed a final agreement outlining the principles of future relations, visited the Baptist church that had benefited from Van's largesse, and met a group of cosmonauts. On the twenty-ninth the presidential party headed for Vnukovo Airport and, after a farewell ceremony, boarded a Soviet Ilyushin Il-62 jetliner to fly to Ukraine for the last leg of their nine-day Soviet tour. Mechanical failure kept the big plane firmly earthbound, and Premier Kosygin and President Podgorny red-facedly joined the Nixons on board while they waited for a replacement aircraft.

With relations with America improving, the Soviets and Chinese scaled down their support for North Vietnam, where it later emerged that they both had thousands of troops stationed throughout the conflict. Eight months later, American combat troops began their final pullout from the ravaged nation.

*   *   *

IN CHINA, Liu Shikun was still moldering in solitary confinement despite his father-in-law's leading role in Nixon's visit. No one came to bother him anymore, and sometimes even the *People's Daily* failed to arrive, though he could hear the doors banging as it was delivered to other prisoners. One day a copy landed on the floor, but moments later the guard rushed back. "Don't read, don't read!" he shouted as he unlocked the door and grabbed it. Yet Liu had glimpsed Ye Jianying's name on a list of leaders accompanying Mao, and realizing his father-in-law had not been ousted as his guards had claimed, Liu guessed he was still being held simply to prevent Madame Mao and her Gang of Four from losing face.

More time went by, and finally his wife, the general's daughter, came to visit. Under the table he palmed her the letter he had pains-takingly composed from specks of newspaper and sticky bun, folded very small. She slipped it in her pocket. When she got home she gave it to her father, who immediately passed it to Mao's aide Wang Dongxing, and with astonishing speed it was all over. Mao issued a "highest command"—a formulation that simply meant his word was law—and ordered the pianist's release. "You should look after Liu Shikun," he told the Central Committee. "Ask him to compose more national-style music. And he should continue his performances." The pronouncement was a deep embarrassment for Madame Mao, who was now boss of all China's cultural production, and to make the best of it, she invited Liu to her home and put on a great show of solicitude, sitting with him and two other members of the Gang of Four while they watched an American film about bullfighting that had presumably been selected for its piano score. Liu was formally ab-solved of his purported crimes and given a staggering sum of money in lieu of lost salary. Still, seven years in prison had left him with neurological problems, and he was admitted to the hospital for what would be a four-month stay. Before he went in he made a single comment to reporters asking about his treatment. "In the twentieth century," he said, with righteous clarity, slicing the air with his shaking hands, "political prisons in China during the Cultural Revolution, in terms of cruelty to inmates, are second only to Auschwitz during the Second World War."

Internal politics and smuggled letters were not the only reasons for his release. As China creaked open its borders in the wake of Nixon's visit, Premier Zhou convinced the leadership to agree to a program of cultural exchange. As one of the country's two world-class pianists—the third had defected—Liu was once again needed, and one day in October he returned to work at the Central Philharmonic. The other remaining world-class pianist was Yin Chengzong, the second-prize winner in the 1962 Tchaikovsky Competition. Yin had had a good Cultural Revolution, scoring an enormous success with the *Yellow River Concerto*, which had premiered in 1969 and was one of only two piano pieces now licensed for performance. The other was a concerto accompanied by the Peking Opera, but since there was no opera that day, Liu had no choice but to play the *Yellow River*. He had never attempted it before, but he had heard it over and over from loudspeakers hung on trees and lampposts outside his prison cell, and thanks to his father's training, he had learned it by ear. To the surprise of the musicians who had turned up to see if he could still play, it went off well, and he was given a slot with Eugene Ormandy and the Philadelphia Orchestra, early arrivals under the new cultural exchange agreement, along with basketball and swimming teams. Liu played the *Yellow River* again, and afterward the musicians, who had heard his story, silently got to their feet. Once again the international language of music was invoked to explain to confused populations why yesterday's enemy was today's honored guest.

Liu tried to put his life back together and not think about the past. Three years later Chairman Mao died, and a trio of leaders, among them General Ye and Wang Dongxing, the aide who had passed on

Liu's letter, arrested the Gang of Four. With the Cultural Revolution officially over, the *Yellow River Concerto* was banned, and Yin Cheng-zong was purged in his turn.

*   *   *

THE WORLD of politics had nearly lost Richard M. Nixon to a career in music. He was a competent amateur pianist: after one White House governors' conference, he played a duet with the great blues singer Pearl Bailey. LBJ had set great store by his fellow Texan Van, but he knew next to nothing about classical music; in Nixon, Van had a fan in the White House. The president listened to his recordings of Grieg, Tchaikovsky, and Rachmaninoff from his favorite armchair in the Lincoln Sitting Room while reading or smoking a pipe or cigar, and lobbied Van to put his favorite piece, Brahms's Rhapsody in G Minor, on vinyl. Nineteen of Nixon's White House tapes, made between February 1971 and July 1973, contain copious mentions of his favorite pianist. The president pontificated to a gruff Kissinger and others on the beauties of Van's playing. He relished his showmanship: "He's so colorful, isn't he?" he remarked admiringly. And crucially for Nixon, he counted Van as a political supporter: "He is our friend," he stressed, adding for emphasis that he was "for us."

Nixon kept Van busy. In January 1973 he played for the president's second inauguration, and the following month, he performed at the state visit of Israeli prime minister Golda Meir. Nixon upbraided his staff when Rildia Bee was omitted from the banquet and told them to get mother and son over. He also ordered them to find out if Van could perform in China. Bob Haldeman, his chief of staff, pointed out that the Chinese might have a problem with Van because he was the favorite of the Soviets. "So he could come there and screw the Russians," Nixon replied, ever triangulating, and perhaps casting his mind back to Van's snub by Brezhnev.

Van was not as dexterous as Tricky Dick, and he never accepted the mooted mission. Yet the Brezhnev snub had undoubtedly taken the shine off his value as a symbol of U.S.-Soviet friendship. Though Nixon floated the idea, Van was not called on to play for Brezhnev's

1973 visit to the United States, and not even Sol Hurok thought of sending him along on Nixon's second visit to Moscow, the following year. A brighter moment came courtesy of the fourth edition of Van's own competition, held in 1973, when Moscow Conservatory–trained Vladimir Viardo became its first Soviet winner. Van virtually adopted him, taking him shopping in Cincinnati, buying him shirts by the dozen, and smuggling jeans to him in Moscow. Yet, back home, Viardo was refused a passport and banned from traveling abroad for twelve years, seemingly for failing to bribe officials with Western gifts he was expected to buy with the fraction of his foreign earnings he was allowed to keep. The Cliburn Competition, which owed its existence to a breakthrough in the Cold War, had been diminished by it.

So, deep down, had Van. Increasingly he looked elsewhere to make grand gestures, which sometimes led him to unlikely places. At the first Nixon inauguration he had met Ferdinand and Imelda Marcos, the First Couple of the Philippines, and the three had become friends; after an assassin tried to kill Imelda with a bolo during a speech, Van visited her in the hospital. She was as energetic a patron of the arts as she was a buyer of shoes, and Van's name featured repeatedly in the guestbook of the Coconut Palace, where she put up visiting celebrities. For months prior to his concerts, radio stations and movie theaters played his records, while Filipino fashion designers produced "the Cliburn line—an array of gowns to make anyone beam with pride . . . while imbibing Cliburn's music." At a gala at the Malacañang Palace, Imelda sang Van a love song from the central Philippines, Ferdinand toasted him as "one of the most outstanding mortals of our time," and the guests belted out "Deep in the Heart of Texas" before being handed curfew passes with which they could escape arrest. Ferdinand's high standing as the islands' first elected president plunged after 1972, when he was accused of massive embezzlement and declared martial law rather than face an election, but the White House continued to back him, and Van continued to visit, playing a fund-raiser for young Filipino musicians at the huge

Araneta Coliseum in June 1973 and returning the following year to inaugurate the ten-thousand-seat Folk Arts Theater on Manila Bay. A critic wrote that his music touched minds, quickened hearts, and moved spirits, but that his dress sense offended local tastes. "Only a person of his stature can get away with such an ill-fitting coat," sniffed one columnist. "His arms are too long for his frame," echoed another. "His legs are too long to fit under the piano. His pants are a bit short above his shoes." This was not Moscow.

*   *   *

IN JANUARY 1974, Harvey Cliburn died, aged seventy-five, in the Shreveport hospital where he had been ailing for several months. His last words to Van were some of his first: "Sonny Boy, I love you," he said. "And look after your mother." He had cut a lonely figure of late; Van had occasionally convinced him to join him and Rildia Bee on tour as far away as Japan, but it was not his scene. "To tell you the truth," Harvey once told an amused Naomi Graffman in Monte Carlo, "ah'd rather be home with mah ca-ows." As they laid him to rest, Van vowed to spend even more time with Rildia Bee and began worrying that traveling was getting too much for her.

Two months later Sol Hurok, Van's other father figure, collapsed in a New York elevator and died. Months earlier Van had performed at the Met in honor of the great impresario's sixtieth year in show business, a Gilded Age–style celebration that ended with an epic party at the Pierre. With Hurok went Van's romantic dreams of backstage greasepaint in prerevolutionary St. Petersburg and fur-swaddled carriage rides through Central Park. Such dreams had already been splintered two years earlier when a bomb exploded in Hurok's Fifth Avenue office, injuring him and killing his twenty-seven-year-old secretary, Iris Kones. The Jewish Defense League, which opposed Soviet artists touring the United States, claimed responsibility for the bombing and its two Jewish victims.

Waylaid by feelings of grief and guilt as he turned forty that July, Van stopped taking new bookings. He never mentioned the word *re-*

tirement; he simply replied to requests with regrets that he had a prior engagement.

With four years' worth of commitments to work through, he was still frantically busy through the mid-1970s, pulling in record crowds to stadiums and outdoor venues; increasing his rate of album releases to include Mozart, Beethoven, Liszt, Brahms, Barber, Rachmaninoff, and Prokofiev; and picking up more awards and honorary degrees. In September 1974, a month after Nixon resigned over the Watergate scandal and Vice President Gerald Ford took over, Van was behind the piano at the newly named Lyndon B. Johnson Space Center in Houston, accompanying Soviet astronauts training for a planned U.S.-Soviet space linkup in a chorus of "Moscow Nights." For the 1975 state visit of the emperor and empress of Japan, President Ford recruited Van to play Chopin, Schumann, and Debussy and gave a speech celebrating Van's service as a catalyst of culture who had brought East and West together with his "legendary talent"; the performance was beamed live to Japan.

That year, he was also a guest at Ford's state dinner for British prime minister Harold Wilson, where he was seated at the First Lady's table, opposite the prime minister and next to gossip columnist Aileen "Suzy" Mehle. "There are so many important people at this table," Van said, turning to Mehle. "I just wish I could get all of their autographs, but I'm afraid to ask." If he was making small talk, he had not reckoned on his neighbor's brass. "What's the matter with you?" she demanded. "You're as important as they are. Give me your menu card." She signed her name and passed the card on to Cary Grant. "I want everybody's autograph, too," Grant said, and both cards did the rounds of the table.

Van was a true Romantic in his belief that playing the piano was a holy mission, but he lacked the Romantic ego that demanded, "Listen to my inner world!" He had never really believed his own press because he had never truly believed in his own legend. When fans told him he had changed their lives, he was genuinely amazed. When public figures extolled him as a hero, he all but scoffed. As he had foreseen at the time, the Tchaikovsky Competition was a burden as well as a blessing. Like Elvis, who died in 1977 after years of prescription drug abuse, Van had shot to fame in his early twenties faster and higher than any comparable musician. Ever since, he had had to restage his triumph and prove himself anew: reach the same high note of emotional connection, be a winner over and over, night after night. Nothing less would do than being the world's greatest pianist, the American Horowitz, and yet not a single interview passed without his having to rehearse the events of 1958. He did so dutifully, because he was still proud of his win and because he fully realized it was the reason he was there. Yet he knew he would always be defined by his achievement at age twenty-three and that, whatever else he did, he would never get beyond it.

He was grateful for everything, but he was ready to give it all up for the same reason he had coped remarkably well with fame: he did not care all that much for it. Fame was a vehicle for a sacred trust: to spread the glory of classical music. Yet he had done virtually nothing else for twenty years, and he was tired. He was tired of the perfectionist's edginess he had never shaken off, the excitement mixed with dread that seized him before every concert, and the self-reproach that bedeviled every curtain call. He was tired of giving his heart and being bruised by politics, first from the Americans and now from the Russians. He was tired of being hailed as a hero and being watched all the time, of hesitating to go places in case he was seen doing something he shouldn't do. He was tired of disappointments: in 1977 there were only two Soviet entrants to the Cliburn Competition after the Soviet authorities demanded higher concert fees for their winners, nearly all of which went to the state. Also, sad to say, he was tired of the piano. The eighty-eight keys were the medium he used to express himself, but they were not real. They were not even his first interest, he whispered in unguarded moments. That was the voice, but he had no voice, and he had been saddled with the piano and had spent his life trying to make it what it was not, a singing instrument.

Toward the end he was almost played out, and his habitual lateness got out of control. In 1973 he turned up for a 7:00 p.m. concert at Mississippi University for Women at 11:00. "I'm late," he said as he walked onstage before a full house. "I apologize for that. With your permission I'll get right to it." And he did, to thunderous applause. In 1977 he was supposed to take off at 2:00 p.m. for an 8:00 p.m. recital in Buffalo, New York, but at 4:00 he was still at the Salisbury Hotel. "Don't worry, honey," he told his publicist and close friend Mary Lou Falcone, "we'll get a private plane." Sometime after 7:00 they headed to LaGuardia and boarded the jet, only to run into a blizzard. He walked in at 9:30 p.m.; announced he would play only half the program, so the audience could get home; and launched into "The Star-Spangled Banner." Another time, he was desperate to see *André Chenier* at the Met the same night he was booked to play with the New York Philharmonic. He watched the first act, strode across to the concert hall, and went on without a warm-up.

Always canny with timing, Van knew his moment had passed. It was time to live for himself a little. Many of his friends were much older than he, and when Rosina Lhévinne died in 1976, he realized he would soon lose them all. That made him reflect on how much he had sacrificed by living half his life out of a suitcase. He was never quite sure when his mother had become his best friend: somewhere along the lonely road, when they prayed together before a concert, she elegant as always, perhaps in a turquoise brocade with a corsage of fresh cut sweet peas. He adored her, idolized her, but it was hardly the same thing as a romantic relationship. Oddly, it was Rildia Bee who made one possible. In the summer of 1966, when he was thirty-two and had gone to play at a small midwestern college, a nineteen-year-old student of mortuary science had been assigned to give Rildia Bee a campus tour. Tom Zaremba happened to share a family name with Tchaikovsky's composition teacher and Anton Rubinstein's successor as director of the St. Petersburg Conservatory. He was compactly built, with pallid, chiseled features, slicked-back blond hair, and the ready humor of a man at ease with himself. Rildia Bee found him so amusing that she introduced him to her son, and they took him on as an assistant. As well as helping look after Rildia Bee, the trainee mortician did Van's stage makeup, and along the way they began a relationship. Van was far too circumspect to allow it to become public knowledge; when a filmmaker played him concert footage that showed Zaremba indistinctly at the back of the frame, Van angrily refused to sanction its release. Yet in 1977, with his concert career winding down, he asked Tom to move into the Salisbury with him and Rildia Bee. Zaremba commuted back and forth to Detroit, where he taught mortuary arts at Wayne State two days a week, but he was increasingly at Van's side.

By September 1978, Van's last booking was played out and he became a private citizen for the first time in his life. "Private" was an understatement: second only to Greta Garbo, he became a legendary recluse, "the most famous dropout in American concert history."

*   *   *

VAN TOLD everyone that he had retired in order to have more time to attend the opera. His good friend Arlene Dahl had another explanation: astrology, a mutual obsession they had discovered at one of the early Hollywood parties. The years when Van stopped performing, Dahl explained, "were not terribly good years for him to be in front of the public according to astrology and his sign, which is cancer, the moon child." Sometimes Van called her at night on her private number to talk horoscopes; he told her about his investments and asked what she thought, and she read the charts and advised him as to whether to keep or sell them.

Either because of Dahl's advice or despite it, he had become a rich man. Over the years, he had taken over more rooms at the Salisbury, one at time, until he ended up with fourteen, eight on one floor and six on another. The rooms were packed with what he modestly called his "junk": a vast collection of the finest antique English furniture and European silver and jewelry, including many items from imperial Russia. Every month, he paid his hotel bill, never taking a lease.

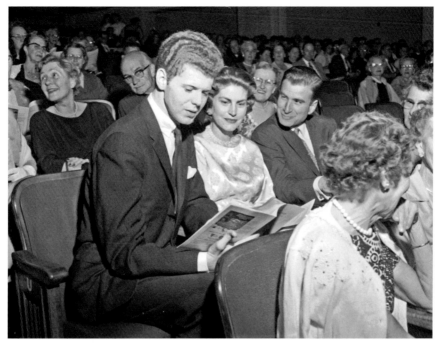

Above: Van with Rev. and Mrs. Newton White at a Tucson Symphony concert, October 1959. *(Jack Sheaffer/University of Arizona Libraries)*

Below: Soviet Deputy Premier Anastas Mikoyan and embassy officials with Van at the Soviet Embassy in Washington, DC, January 1959. Ambassador Mikhail "Smiling Mike" Menshikov is behind Mikoyan. *(AP)*

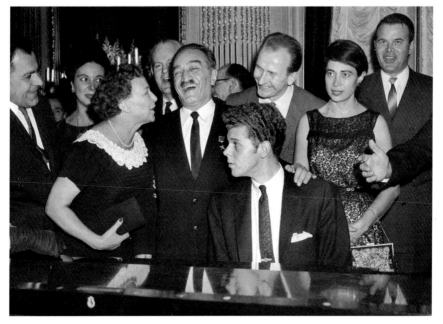

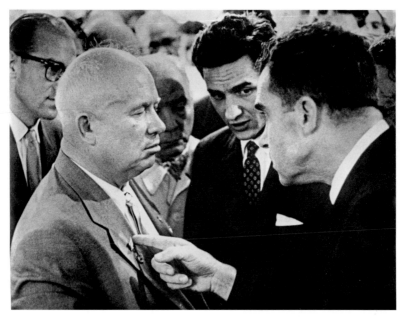

Above: Khrushchev and Vice President Richard Nixon debate outside the model kitchen at the American National Exhibition in Moscow, July 1959. This photograph was widely printed in American papers and was credited with helping Nixon to win the Republican presidential nomination the following year. *(Courtesy of National Archives)*

Below: Nikita and Nina Khrushchev welcome Van to a reception at the Soviet Embassy in Washington, DC, in September 1959 during their rambunctious tour of America. *(Ed Clark/LIFE /Getty)*

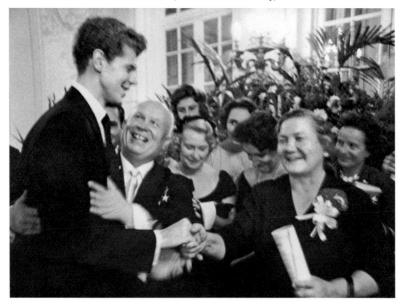

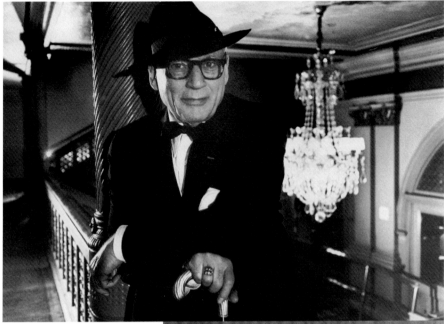

Above: The great
impresario Sol Hurok,
Van's dream manager,
photographed in
the lobby of the old
Metropolitan Opera
House. *(Walter Sanders/
LIFE/Getty)*

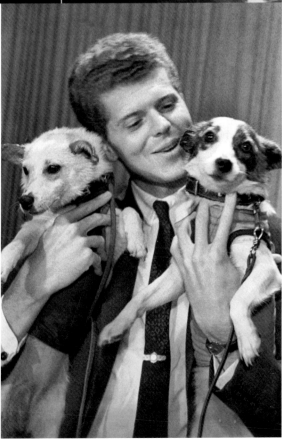

Right: Van holding the
Soviet space dogs Belka
and Strelka during
filming of the show *We
Will Meet Again* at the
Ostankino Television
Center, Moscow,
August 1960. *(Valery
Gende-Rote/TASS)*

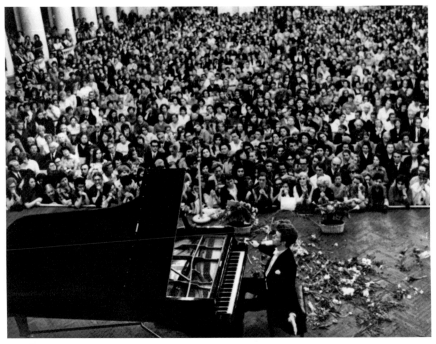

Two images of Van at concerts in the Soviet Union in 1960.

Above: Grand Philharmonic Hall, Leningrad. *(Courtesy of Cliburn Foundation)*

Below: Palace of Sports of the Central Lenin Stadium, Moscow. *(Alexander Konkov/TASS)*

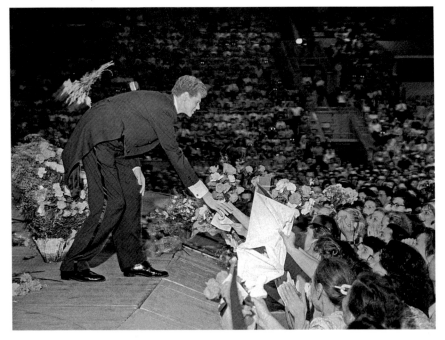

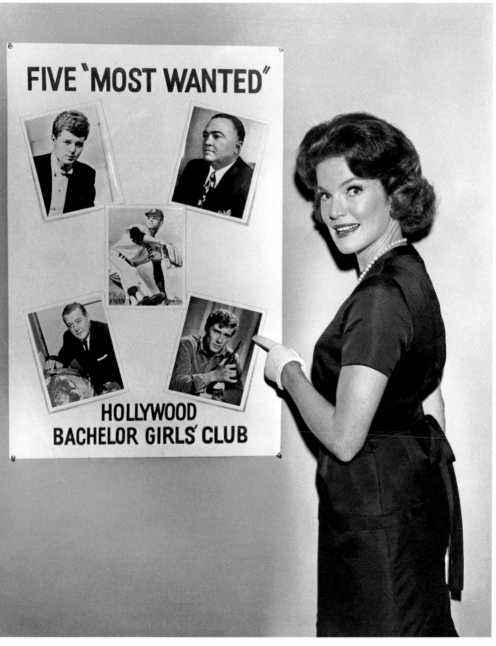

Actress Pippa Scott reveals the five most eligible bachelors of 1962, as selected by the Hollywood Bachelor Girls' Club. Besides Van the others are a TV star, baseball pitcher, U.S. senator, and FBI chief J. Edgar Hoover, whose agency took a keen interest in Van. Said Scott: "We pick the bachelors every year just to shake them out in the open as matrimonial targets. We predict that four of the five choices will be married by June 1963." *(Bettmann/CORBIS)*

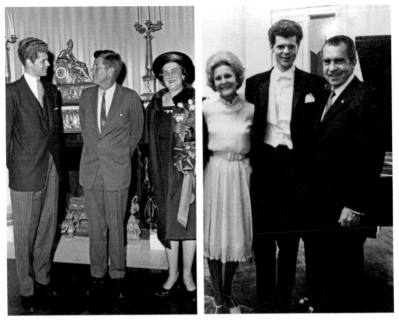

Above left: Van and Rildia Bee visit with John F. Kennedy in the White House's Blue Room, May 1963. *(Kennedy Library)*

Above right: Van with President and Mrs. Nixon after playing for an American and Soviet audience at the Moscow residence of the U.S. ambassador, May 1972. *(Nixon Library)*

Below: As President Ronald Reagan looks on, Van greets General Secretary Gorbachev and Raisa Gorbachev after playing in the East Room of the White House during the December 1987 summit. *(Reagan Library)*

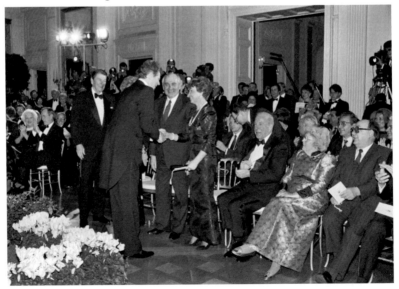

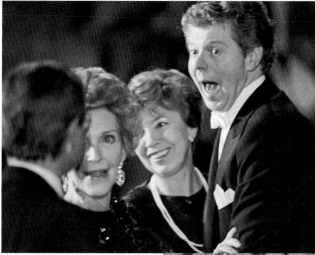

Left: Van reacts with mock horror as Raisa Gorbachev insists he play Tchaikovsky's First Piano Concerto (without orchestra) at the 1987 summit. *(AP)*

Right: President George W. Bush presents Van with the Presidential Medal of Freedom in a July 2003 ceremony at the White House. *(Cliburn Foundation)*

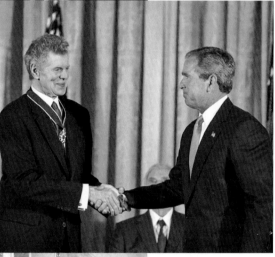

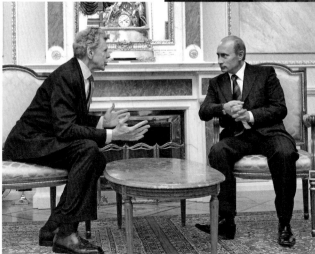

Left: Van meets with President Vladimir Putin at the Kremlin after receiving the Order of Friendship in September 2004. *(AP)*

Overleaf: Van with President Barack Obama after receiving the National Medal of Arts in March 2011. *(Getty)*

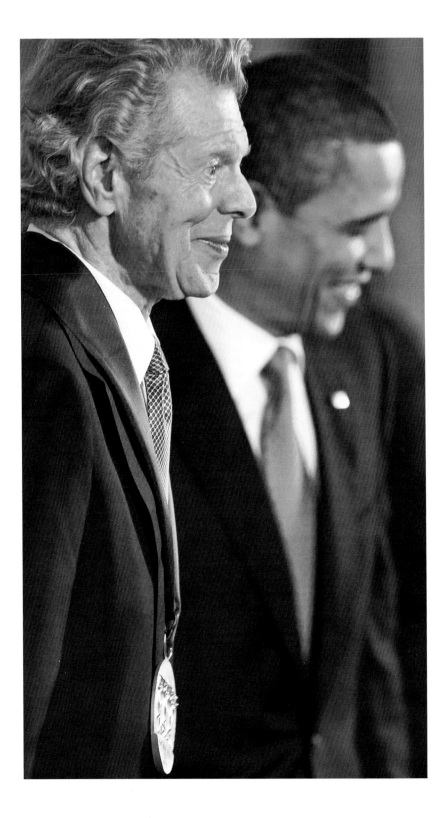

New York had always been temporary for him, and after the 1985 Cliburn Competition, he stayed on in Fort Worth to look for a home. In the fall of that year, he bought a sprawling Tudor Revival manor on an eighteen-acre estate in exclusive Westover Hills that had belonged to the grain magnate and museum benefactor Kay Kimbell, and the following spring a flotilla of moving vans headed south with the "junk." At the last minute, Van remembered a piano stored at Steinway Hall and rolled it along Fifty-Seventh Street.

Standing on a bluff, with lawns sloping down to the tree line and far-reaching views of the river valley and city, the house was as oversize and elegant and fussy and relaxed as Van was. The front door opened into a large entrance hall with smooth limestone walls and golden oak cornices and moldings. A step led down into a living room the size of an Olympic pool and lit by two Baccarat chandeliers and countless lamps, which led in turn to a sunroom. Islands of antique chairs and couches floated in a gleaming sea of silver candelabra, vases, and bowls. Nineteenth-century oils shared the walls with a full-length portrait of Rildia Bee, a gift from Ferdinand and Imelda Marcos; and a sketch of Baby Chops, a white Maltese formally known as Bootsie Costanza Cliburn. Dozens of silver-framed photographs topped the Steinway, which was out of tune and held together with Scotch tape and chewing gum. A hundred more lined a long table: Van and Nikita Khrushchev, Van and Maria Callas, Van and Sol Hurok, but mostly Van and Rildia Bee. Back in the hall another door opened into a formal dining room, which led to a family dining room, a breakfast room, and the kitchen. A third door revealed a library stuffed with memorabilia from Van's career. An elevator, necessary now for Rildia Bee, led to the multiple bedrooms. Huge sprays of flowers were everywhere, some fresh, some wilted, and some long dead, thickening the air with a perceptible bouquet of decomposing matter. "I enjoy flowers as much when they get old and dried out as when they were fresh," Van explained to a reporter. "I just look at these flowers, and in my mind, I still see the beauty they once had."

Sometimes, in the early hours, Van sat at the living room Steinway, a bust of Rachmaninoff staring gloomily from a nearby pedestal, wearing a suit and tie and playing for Rildia Bee. Occasionally he played one of the other fourteen grand pianos scattered through the house, perhaps working on the sonata he had been composing forever. More often, he left them untouched and he and his mother listened to opera, Renata Tebaldi or Leontyne Price or Cecilia Bartoli. At four or five in the morning he headed to the industrial-size kitchen, with its freezer full of leftovers from takeout and counters piled with morsels of food in tiny plastic boxes, and slurped a plate of microwaved garlic ravioli. As dawn approached he retired to his bedroom, with its balalaikas and dried flowers and photographs from Russia, and read a historical romance or watched a classic movie, perhaps *Random Harvest*, with Ronald Colman and Greer Garson, before turning in; he was also addicted to *Jeopardy!* and soap operas. He'd surface in the afternoon, stretch for a few minutes, drink a cup of hot water with lemon, go down in his torn T-shirt and dark blue bathrobe, and have poached eggs on toast for breakfast. Rildia Bee was already there, like a delicate tropical bird in her blue quilted bathrobe and bouffant pink nightcap, eating chicken as she did every day, with Tom Zaremba in his white terry cloth robe, a housekeeper or two, and a handyman.

After they got dressed Van ran errands. He loved doing everyday things such as shopping at the Piggly Wiggly and picking out fresh produce, sniffing the cantaloupes. Sometimes he went to Denny's or the Ol' South Pancake House on University Drive, always taking the same corner booth. When his favorite waitress, Dottie Satterwhite, returned after caring for her dying mother, Van met her at the door, hugged her, wept, handed her a check for five hundred dollars, and sent her flowers for two weeks. "What do you and that piano player have going?" Satterwhite's husband demanded. Late in the afternoon, he'd attend to his affairs in the sunroom, which contained more junk, including two teddy bears, a silver bowlful of Christmas baubles on a pedestal, and spun-sugar flower bouquets (from one of Rildia Bee's birthday cakes) displayed under a glass cloche. The house was Victorian in its density. Upstairs, beyond a room filled with unpacked suitcases and another housing long-wilted Christmas trees with the decorations still attached, there lurked a vast multitier replica of the cake from one of Rildia Bee's birthdays, finished in frosting but empty inside so it could be preserved forever.

Some nights, there were legendary dinner parties at the house, especially when visiting musicians were in town. They began with cocktails at 11:00 p.m., and Van came down around midnight. White-gloved valets announced the meal. Pot roast, chicken and dumplings, spoon bread, black-eyed peas, and turnip greens might be on the menu, or Rildia Bee's fabulous chicken soup, served in a lavishly ornate silver tureen that had belonged to the Grand Duchess Olga Nikolaevna, the murdered eldest daughter of the last Russian czar. Van sat next to his mother, calling her Little Precious and feeding her forkfuls of baked chicken while regaling his guests with "priceless stories populated with everyone from a European duke and a cantankerous conductor to a Hollywood starlet, a mysterious Russian plutocrat and, of course, multiple U.S. presidents." He poked fun at himself and screamed with laughter, leaping from his chair to make a point. Sometimes the company belted out Baptist hymns at the table; Van commissioned new arrangements of Rildia Bee's favorites. "Mother remembers this one," he'd say with a gasp if she joined in. "Let's sing it again." Afterward they gathered round the piano, and Rildia Bee sang comic songs from her girlhood in the early years of the twentieth century, her voice shrill and old-fashioned but her eyes bright and her delivery intact. At 4:00 a.m. Van was still sparkling, while his wilting guests desperately propped up their eyelids.

Away from the world's glare he was lighter now, an innocent-sophisticated man-child who never much cared for rules and barely noticed they existed. "In *Texas*," he said, "we like to stay *babies*." Yet the world would not stop wanting to know about him. He refused requests for interviews whenever he could, and when he couldn't escape, he kept journalists waiting until he had them on his terms.

One reporter was ushered into the library in the early hours, where Van was settled with Baby Chops on a pillow-stuffed Georgian settee, and described a scene of aristocratic leisure: "He twists a cigarette into a white holder and lights it, pressing it between his thumb and index finger, palm up, European fashion. Blue smoke curls upward in graceful rings." Van had an almost saintly aura of innocence that, to jaded reporters, seemed too good to be true, but most went away utterly charmed and none the wiser.

As time went on, he sometimes answered with mumbling or silence, as if there were places he no longer wanted to go. When Mercury was in retrograde (astrologically a bad omen for all kinds of exchange), it was impossible to get an answer out of him at all. His life story repeated for the hundredth or thousandth time became an overrehearsed routine, seasoned always with Rildia Bee's homey aphorisms. Unconsciously he overplayed himself like an aging actor, delivering his lines with overworked eyebrows. "They were so nice, very sweet, very kind," he said of everyone, emphasizing each word: "I was so thrilled." When he emerged from his seclusion to give speeches, starting with the 1978 commencement at Juilliard, he earnestly labored the same ripe lines about music being body, mind, and spirit; quoted the same wisdom from Plato, Chaucer, Rachmaninoff, and Rildia Bee; and recited an obscure Romantic poem, "Steal not away, O pierced heart," by an obscure Romantic poet named Van Cliburn.

The sentiments were deeply felt, but in reality Van was funnier and naughtier than he appeared, and he had his demons. Often he was found with friends at the bar in his favorite restaurant, La Piazza. His cousin visited to drink Scotch and smoke cigarettes, "just shy of Aunt Rildia Bee's view." There were tales of heavy drinking, including at public events. When he turned fifty in 1984, graying but still ludicrously youthful, he began worrying about his weight. His face had filled out and creased into a fleshier softness, and he had the wrinkles erased from his photographs. Sometimes he embellished his legend, perhaps carried away with the romance of it. The famous evening when Rildia Bee tended to Rachmaninoff moved back several years so it became a seminal event in Van's decision to become a pianist. The boat ride at Khrushchev's dacha extended until he and Van motored all the way into Moscow and looked up at the Kremlin Wall, an impossibility then as now.

His friends adored him, protected him, smiled at his foibles, and spoke of him with a warm glow—but few felt they really knew him. As the years went by, many told interviewers that they didn't see how he could be happy unless he returned to the stage. "Try me!" he shouted, roaring with laughter. He was scarcely alone among great pianists in shying away from performing. Liszt stopped early. Glenn Gould abandoned the stage at thirty-one. Horowitz reputedly thought his fingers were made of glass and would shatter if he touched the piano, and he took twelve years off. John Browning took off two decades. John Ogdon, who shared the 1962 Tchaikovsky Gold Medal with Ashkenazy, went mad, suffering delusions of glowing crosses, electrodes implanted in his body, and conspiracies orchestrated by Adolf Hitler. The childlike wonder and joy needed to summon up surging emotions night after night is a friable thing in a pushing world. Yet America had invested a good deal of its self-belief in Van, and the undying fascination with his disappearance suggested an anxiety about what had happened to the nation in the years since 1958. America's old insecurity about European cultural imperialism had been a powerful spur to the nation's determination to enrich itself. Yet now that that insecurity had been dispelled, above all by Van's victory in Moscow, had a vital incentive to improve and compete also been lost? Did Van's retreat from the field suggest that America was becoming complacent? Undoubtedly his premature retirement evoked a kind of melancholy, a sense even of being let down, as if by fulfilling his potential in his youth, he had tapped into an existential crisis about what the nation might be capable of in its riper years. Or perhaps the disappointment stemmed from the discovery that Van was not so much a driven, tortured genius as a thwarted homebody, that he was still a small-town Texan and not European enough after all.

*   *   *

NINE YEARS went by without Van playing a note in public, but he was still in the public eye, giving speeches and receiving honors. April 1983 brought the Albert Schweitzer Award for "a life's work dedicated to music and devoted to humanity," which was presented at Carnegie Hall with Leontyne Price singing and Greer Garson as emcee, and followed by a dinner dance for four hundred in the Plaza ballroom. But the honor came amid a month of disturbing news: of multiple nuclear tests in the USSR, the United States, and France; and a suicide bomber who killed sixty-three at the U.S. embassy in Lebanon.

Vietnam, underground testing, and the unreality of deterrence based on the potential to incinerate the earth had fostered a fatalistic nuclear apathy in the late 1970s. Yet when the Soviets invaded Afghanistan and Jimmy Carter withdrew an arms control treaty negotiated with Brezhnev, Cold War fears once again came to the fore. Bilateral exchanges fell back to a level not seen since the Stalin era, as Soviet musicians were forbidden to tour America, and the United States, along with many allies, boycotted the 1980 Moscow Olympics. Defeating Carter in that year's presidential election, Ronald Reagan abandoned détente and replaced the containment strategy that had served America since World War II with a policy of rolling back Soviet power. Reagan's rhetoric wound up in concert with a massive increase in defense spending. "The march of freedom and democracy," he affably proclaimed in a 1982 address to the British Parliament, "will leave Marxism-Leninism on the ash-heap of history." The following year, Reagan denounced the Soviet Union as "an evil empire" before a crowd of flag-waving evangelicals and proposed to weaponize space with the Strategic Defense Initiative (SDI), or Star Wars. Making Reagan's case, a Soviet interceptor shot down a scheduled Korean Air Lines flight as it crossed Soviet airspace en route from New York to Seoul, with the loss of all 267 crew and passengers, including a U.S. congressman. In 1984 the Soviet Union and every Eastern Bloc country except Romania boycotted the Los Angeles Olympics; the next year, the Soviets also boycotted the Van Cliburn Competition, as they had in 1981. Van stayed silent, but when his old friends Mstislav Rostropovich and Galina Vishnevskaya were stripped of Soviet citizenship for "activities harmful to the prestige of the state," even he was moved to comment. "I felt sad," he said, "because I know they love Russia very much. All the time I've known them I never heard anything but how deeply they adore their country."

Liu Shikun was dragged back into the Cold War, too. In 1978 his father-in-law, General Ye, had become China's head of state, and the following year, Liu was the first Chinese artist to perform in America. In contrast to his youthful pyrotechnics, his style was now broodingly romantic, the harvest of his solitary meditations on Van's playing. Yet the general's resignation in 1983 stripped Liu of his political protection, and as part of China's Anti–Spiritual Pollution Campaign against Western liberal values, the pianist was accused of smuggling and womanizing. Two years later he was visiting his eldest son in Los Angeles when a leading Republican politician heard his story and encouraged him to apply for political asylum. Everything was readied, including an FBI safe house, but despite tearful pleas, he flew back to China, convinced despite everything that the country was opening up. Still, he regretted the lost opportunity to make his name in America, never more so than the following year, when he was arrested on suspicion of drug smuggling and gold speculation after a female undercover agent working for the Beijing Municipal Public Security Bureau and the State Security Ministry befriended him to gather "evidence." When he was released he sat at home, depressed and silent and drained of any interest in music, as factions on the Left and Right continued to toy with him.

In 1983 Emil Gilels performed for what would be the final time in New York, and he and Van met for dinner. To Van's surprise, Gilels praised him for taking time off. Then he told him that he had seen in a dream that Van would play again soon, and it would have something to do with Russia. As for when it would happen, neither could say. Just as Van's triumph in Moscow had marked an uptick in super-power relations, it seemed as if his disappearance had accompanied their downturn.

Human ingenuity strives to get ahead, which, for all but an exceptional few, means negotiating the system they are given. Yet the skills needed to coax privileges from a bureaucracy are not those that promote industry and initiative, and the Soviet Union was saddled with a sacrosanct theory of history that admitted no possibility of change. After seven decades the great Marxist-Leninist experiment had become a giant charade in which the government pretended to pay, the people pretended to work, and responsibility was shunted along. In the classic Brezhnev joke, a Muscovite enraged by interminable lines for basic foodstuffs picks up a sharp knife and heads to the Kremlin to kill the general secretary. When he arrives he finds an even longer line, which he joins out of habit. He asks the man ahead of him what everyone is waiting for: "We're all queuing to kill Comrade Brezhnev," the man replies.

When Brezhnev died (of natural causes) in 1982, receiving the full state funeral he had denied Khrushchev, long-serving KGB chief Yuri Andropov replaced him at the age of sixty-eight. After fifteen months, Andropov died, still so shadowy that it was confirmed he had a wife only when one showed up at his funeral. His successor, Konstantin Chernenko, was even older—nearly as old as Reagan—and struggled through the eulogy at Andropov's funeral; he himself was dead after thirteen months. The Kremlin had become a rest home for whiskery revolutionaries, with Red Square the world's most oversize funeral parlor. Every time Radio Moscow played a slow movement of Tchaikovsky, rumors flew that another leader had expired. From top to bottom, the whole system was so sclerotic that something had to change.

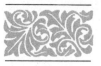

· *21* ·

The Summit

IN 1987, Nancy Reagan's office put in a call to Cliburn Foundation chair Susan Tilley. Mikhail and Raisa Gorbachev, the Soviet Union's First Couple, were coming to Washington for a summit in December and they had requested that Van play for the after-dinner soiree. Tilley took the invitation to Van, who was thrilled to be asked and panicked that he had barely practiced in years. He thought it over, tried out a few pieces on Rildia Bee; called his friend Franz Mohr, Steinway's chief concert technician, to ask him to pray hard; and the next day accepted. By now he was better known for his mysterious disappearance than for his prodigious talent, but he could scarcely have refused the chance to play for the Soviet and American leaders together at long last. He abandoned his owlish hours, began rising at 9:00 a.m., and practiced till his fingers bled.

Gorbachev had begun his career in the Khrushchev era, and like his forerunner, he launched a raft of liberalizing policies, including glasnost (openness) and perestroika (restructuring), in the hope of saving the sinking Soviet ship by encouraging initiative and weeding out corruption. Like Khrushchev, he was also eager to demilitarize foreign policy and free up precious resources. As ever, that hope depended on rapprochement with America, and in the two years since he became general secretary of the Communist Party at the sprightly age of fifty-four, he and President Reagan had met twice, in Geneva and Reykjavik, Iceland. The Soviets had plenty of bargaining chips in the form of forty-five thousand nuclear warheads, twenty thousand more than America. Yet Reagan had restarted the arms race at a time when the capitalist world was enjoying a sustained boom and the Soviet economy was teetering toward collapse. In Geneva, Khrushchev attempted to broker an agreement to reduce nuclear stockpiles, but mutual confidence was lacking. For one heady moment in Reykjavik, total nuclear disarmament was on the table, but Reagan insisted on pursuing his Star Wars initiative. Both meetings had ended without a treaty, and Washington was the make-or-break summit.

With so much at stake, tempers among the leaders' advisers were running high, and haggling over diplomatic niceties continued as six thousand journalists converged on the U.S. capital. Van flew in as well, with Rildia Bee, Tom Zaremba, Susan Tilley, and the rest of his entourage. He said nothing during the flight, staring silently out the window.

The elaborately choreographed spectacle began on the morning of December 8, 1987. Reagan and Gorbachev immediately made history by signing the Intermediate-Range Nuclear Forces Treaty, the first to abolish an entire class of nuclear missiles. Yet the treaty had been agreed to beforehand, and it eliminated only 4 percent of the superpowers' arsenal. The real business at hand was to negotiate deep cuts in the far larger stockpiles of intercontinental weapons. In public, Gorbachev was all charm and charisma, but in private, his temper was quick to flare, and as the two leaders began talks in the White House Cabinet Room, he was tough and doctrinaire. After a testy exchange over Nicaragua, Reagan cracked a joke about a professor who asked a Soviet taxi driver what he wanted to be: "They haven't told me yet" was the punch line. Gorbachev icily suggested that Reagan instruct his ambassador to spend less time collecting jokes and more time improving relations. The president took the advice badly and challenged the general secretary to prove that the Soviets had renounced their aggressively expansionist aims. Gorbachev frowned, darkened, and exploded. Every American administration in history, he snapped, gesticulating wildly, had been hell-bent on aggression and expansion. The United States and its powerful military-industrial complex were well known to be intent on world domination. Like a parent reasoning with a wayward child, Reagan quietly replied that the Soviets were even then butchering innocent men, women, and children in Afghanistan and had an iron grip on Eastern Europe. Soon he flagged as he tried to remember a Russian proverb and gave the floor to his secretary of state.

Smiles were pasted on faces at that night's candlelit White House banquet, but tempers were still high. After dinner the leaders held a short meeting while the guests took their seats in the East Room. Gorbachev was visibly tired when he entered with Raisa and the Reagans, to a smattering of applause. The president was wearing black tie; representing the proletariat, Gorbachev, like Khrushchev before him, had chosen a business suit. This irritated Nancy Reagan, who wore a black beaded gown accented with red-and-white beaded flowers paired with diamond drop earrings; Raisa, who Muscovites joked was the first spouse of a Soviet leader to weigh less than he did, sported an ankle-length brocade gown with a bodice and flared hem offset with a double strand of pearls. The two First Ladies had been conducting their own Cold War since Geneva, where Raisa had pedantically and at great length laid down the law on Soviet policy. "Who does that dame think she is?" Nancy had fumed.

In addition to the negotiating teams, the guests included 126 stars of business, science, sports, politics, and the arts. The exiled Mstislav Rostropovich and Galina Vishnevskaya were conspicuously present; also representing the world of music were jazz pianist Dave Brubeck and Zubin Mehta, the conductor of the New York Philharmonic. Billy Graham was there, with Joe DiMaggio, Claudette Colbert, and Jimmy Stewart. Vice President George Bush and Barbara Bush, Bob and Elizabeth Dole, Henry Kissinger, and Armand Hammer headed the political and business elite. Rildia Bee looked on proudly from her wheelchair.

"Ladies and Gentlemen," said the announcer: "Mr. Van Cliburn."

*   *   *

VAN WALKS onto the small stage, chest out like an icebreaker, and his nerves dissolve just as they did many years ago in Moscow. He seeks out Mikhail Gorbachev and locks eyes with him, then gives four short bows to the Reagans, the Gorbachevs, and the room. The general secretary flashes him his toothiest grin. Raisa glows: perhaps she, too, fell in love with Van in 1958.

He sits at the piano and, with a roll, plays the Soviet national anthem. In the front row the leaders exchange confused looks: this was not on the program. Foreign minister Eduard Shevardnadze is first to stand up, then the Gorbachevs, and the room follows suit. Van shakes his head and bends down, nodding as he gives emphasis to the notes, leaning his body into the music; the big, resonant sound fills the room. Then he launches into "The Star-Spangled Banner," its sunnier, simpler music requiring less movement until, near the end, the emphasis grows. The room is completely still. At the end the Gorbachevs lead the applause, and to the sound of scraping chairs and surprised murmurs, everyone sits down.

Van plays his first billed piece, Brahms's Intermezzo, op. 118, no. 6. His performance is big, slow, lyrical, and probing: the old Van, undiluted. He finishes and bows. Quickly he sits again, folding back his tails and wiping his palms on his pants. He leans forward, readies his right hand on the keys, lifts his left hand, and drops it on the first jangling, rolling chords of the Rachmaninoff "Étude-Tableau," op. 39, no. 5. He whips up a storm of sound, tossing his head at tumbling climaxes, swaying at lyrical passages, leaning back at tender moments as his right hand caresses the melodic line, shutting his eyes at the controlled passion, then corkscrewing his torso and collapsing his chest into a pivotal phrase. As the music slips away in a single note, he slides his hands off the keyboard and relaxes, slumping backward. He stands and takes three tiny bows, one hand steadying him on the piano. Gorbachev leans across and speaks briskly to Raisa, three times.

The last two pieces are the noble, soulful Schumann-Liszt "Widmung" and Debussy's L'isle joyeuse, a captivating poem of love and hope, air and grace, rendered drivingly dramatic beneath Van's hands, the tension drawn out and released at the end. Leaning into the last notes, he almost loses his balance and rights himself coming up to bow.

Bravos fill the room. Reagan approaches and shakes Van's hand, patting him on the back, then stands in front of the microphone with his prepared speech printed on cards. Before he can start, Van eagerly steps down to shake Gorbachev's hands. Then he embraces the Soviet leader, his hands splayed across his back, and kisses him on both cheeks. The general secretary's face disappears into the gabardine wool of Van's coat.

Reagan looks at his notes, grinning uncomfortably, one hand on the microphone stand. Gorbachev and Van shake hands again, and Gorbachev, smiling, sits down. Van returns to the podium and nods at Reagan.

"The American poet Longfellow once wrote that music is the universal language of mankind," the president begins, his voice husky and a little unsteady. Van gives Gorbachev a little bow, bows warmly at Raisa, raising his hand in greeting, then remembers himself and stands at attention, politely nodding his appreciation at Reagan's remarks.

"We've certainly seen that confirmed here tonight," the president continues. "There was no need to translate this magnificent performance by Van Cliburn. Van Cliburn is a musician that is known almost as well perhaps in the Soviet Union as he is here in the United States." At this, Gorbachev vigorously nods.

"For young Van Cliburn won the hearts of the Soviet people and the critics during the Tchaikovsky Competition, which he won in 1958. The tickets to his auditions in Moscow were in such demand that people lined up for three and four days in advance. And when the competition ended, Mr. Cliburn performed for Premier Khrushchev"—Van bows his head—"and then for a number of sold-out conferences"—Van shakes his head encouragingly—"in Moscow."

The president says a few words about Van's career and the Cliburn Competition, and then gets lost. He finds his place and adds that Van has not performed since 1978. "And so for this, your first public appearance, I believe, in nine years," he ends, as Van brightly smiles and the guests applaud, "you are once again speaking in that language of music. I think I can say for everyone here, we thank you from the bottom of our hearts."

Van takes Reagan's hand and gestures to himself. "May I respond?" he asks, putting his free hand on Reagan's. Taken by surprise, the president lightly chuckles and moves aside.

"Mr. President and First Lady," he begins, his arm behind Reagan's back, "I'm so grateful for the invitation to get to play. I think there comes a time in one's life when one feels one wants to have relaxation and to enjoy life. And I know the fabulous, inimitable, and incomparable Russian pianist Emil Gilels once told me, 'You are very smart to realize that because we all need enjoyment, we must enjoy life and smell the flowers.' So, unfortunately, I've thought about him so often, since he left us recently." He wreathes his hands in the air, a twitch in his neck the only sign of nerves, a sense of drama never far behind his easy eloquence.

"And when this opportunity came, I said, you know there are very few things that are as meaningful to me—first of course, I love my home country. And some people like to tease me, Mr. General Secretary, and say that sometimes they think I love Texas better than all the rest of the United States. But we want to have Texas, you know, very healthy. But in addition to that, I think you know my constancy—how very deeply I love the Russian people, and your culture and your art. And you go with me always in my life." Still looking at Gorbachev, he crosses his hands on his chest. "And it is for both my beloved president," he adds, bringing Reagan in again with his arm, "and for you that I am so happy to do this. Thank you."

Gorbachev raises his hands and applauds. Van bows to him, the room, and the president. Nancy gets to her feet, and Van comes down to kiss her, his hands on her arms. Then Raisa stands up. Reagan stands by the piano, watching as Van takes her and kisses her. The famously sharp-tongued Soviet First Lady melts. She shyly lays a hand on Van's arm and curls her fingers round his. "Play the Tchaikovsky concerto," she says in Russian, fluttering her hand across his chest. Van understands and raises his eyebrows. "Tchaikovsky!" he says, gesturing in surprise, and turns to Reagan for help. His arm round Raisa, Van laughs, wondering what to do, and vigorously scratches his forehead. "We have no orchestra," he says quietly. The Soviet interpreter comes up and translates, but Raisa says again in a merry voice, "Play the Tchaikovsky concerto."

"We have no orchestra," Van repeats, a little louder. Pulling himself up, he improvises: "If you will give me—if you will help me . . ." He looks around, nervously licking his lips, then turns back and gently pulls Raisa in. Reagan grins at him, watching a fellow entertainer at work. Van scratches his cheek and murmurs to Nancy, who looks at Gorbachev. Van looks at him, too, pointing and deferring to him. He has been warned not to go overtime; the day is scheduled down to the last minute, and the parties need to prepare for the next day's negotiations.

Van makes a decision. "I will do something," he says, "it's all right." He goes back to the piano. Raisa sits down flushed and smiling, still saying loudly, "Play the Tchaikovsky concerto." Nancy takes her seat, and the president raises his eyebrows and follows.

"This is really an aside," Van says to the audience, still standing. Gesturing to the Gorbachevs, he adds, "But I think you will also realize how very deeply this means not only to me but also to many Americans." He sits down and fiddles with the stool, inadvertently striking a high key and fluttering apologetically. Then he pulls back his sleeves and leans gently forward into the melancholy first notes of "Moscow Nights." A few bars in, he starts singing in Russian, his eyes fixed on the Gorbachevs. Raisa mouths the words, but on the fourth word, Gorbachev begins singing, first softly, then louder, then at the top of his voice. The rest of the sizable Soviet delegation joins in: Dobrynin, the ambassador; Yakovlev, the chief ideologue; even Foreign Minister Shevardnadze, who looks uncomfortable.

Between the verses, laughter breaks out: the sound of relief. The columnist George Will leans over to Adm. William Crowe, chairman of the Joint Chiefs of Staff, and whispers, "That song just cost you 200 ships."

The solemn state occasion has turned into a full-throated sing-along. Flashbulbs are popping. The Russians start applauding. Van stands up on the last note, gives a couple of hand claps to the choir, and bounds down to the guests of honor. Gorbachev jumps to his feet. Van hugs him, kisses him on the cheeks, pats him warmly on the back, speaks in his ear, and grasps his shoulder. Raisa stands up and takes Van's hand, while Nancy and Ronald Reagan wait, smiling, in the background.

"Stay around," the president quips. "I can get you a few bookings." Van laughs, unsure how to reply. He shakes Nancy's hand: "I hope that wasn't too much," he says. Gorbachev has more warm words for him, and the Reagans stand to the side. Van takes Raisa's hand and raises it to his lips, nodding deeply at Gorbachev. Then they leave: the Reagans with the general secretary, Van ushering Raisa ahead. Vice President Bush watches them leave with a look of patrician wonder. "I've never seen anything like it in this house," he says.

The next day, every network will lead with the scene of "Moscow Nights" at the White House, and Van will once again make front-page headlines around the world for drawing out the humanity of a Soviet leader. Nancy Reagan will call the performance one of the greatest moments of her husband's presidency. And Mikhail Gorbachev will be noticeably warmer as the two men begin negotiations on the most ambitious arms control treaty in history: a crowning achievement that will eliminate four out of five of the world's strategic nuclear weapons.

Coda

MIKHAIL GORBACHEV intended to reform the Soviet Union's bureaucracy and ideology, not overthrow them. Yet ever since Nikita Khrushchev renounced terror and twitched back the Iron Curtain, both had been doomed. As Western values seeped in, with music in the vanguard, the Soviet state lost credibility with its own people. Glasnost and perestroika flooded its musty recesses and found the cupboards bare. One by one, the Communist regimes of Eastern Europe agreed to multiparty elections or crumbled before popular upheavals. The Baltic States, which Stalin had annexed in 1940, declared independence after two million people linked arms from Tallinn to Vilnius. In November 1989, less than two years after the Washington summit, the Berlin Wall fell and the Cold War was over. So, after a hard-line coup against Gorbachev spectacularly backfired, was the Soviet Union, which dissolved on December 26, 1991, along with its manic fantasies and tangled byways and cockeyed masquerades.

The landing was softer than anyone had foreseen. Yet Russia's history was never likely to make it an easy neighbor or a willing accomplice of the West, whose triumphalism misjudged the centrality of national pride to Russian identity. Van Cliburn's secret was that he lovingly played back to Russia the passionate, soul-searching intensity that was its culture's great contribution to the world, while embodying the freedom that most Americans took for granted and the Soviets sorely lacked. It was a devastating combination, and so simple that it was almost certainly unrepeatable.

* * *

LIU SHIKUN, who suffered most of all the top prizewinners in the First Tchaikovsky Competition, enjoyed the greatest resurgence. In 1991 he immigrated to Hong Kong and paid his way by giving piano lessons. After a year, he had saved enough to open his own piano school. He now owns a vast network of kindergartens stretching across China, where piano is taught as the bedrock of disciplined study. Persecuted during much of his life for the vocation his father thrust on him, by making it widely available he now presides over an unprecedented explosion of Western classical music that would have dumbfounded his oppressors.

Lev Vlassenko, Liu's joint silver medalist, had a distinguished career as a teacher and concert pianist despite his fickle nerves. After thirty-nine years as a professor at the Moscow Conservatory, he took up faculty positions in Indiana and Boston before moving to Australia. He died there in 1996, aged sixty-seven, a vigorous man taken unaccountably early, loved and mourned by his large family. They still gather often at the bright green dacha, which is now well within Moscow's city limits.

Naum Shtarkman, Van's friend and the bronze medalist in 1958, was released from prison and married. For years he was permitted to teach and play only on the fringes of the Soviet music world, but after Gorbachev's reforms, he was rehabilitated and reclaimed his career as a concert pianist and a professor at the conservatory. In 1989 his son Alexander was a finalist in the Cliburn Competition. Naum died in 2006.

Van Cliburn slowly lifted himself out of retirement after his sensational comeback at the Washington summit. In the summer of 1989, the year his Tchaikovsky disc went platinum, he returned to Russia for the first time in seventeen years, at Raisa Gorbachev's invitation, taking along Rildia Bee, now ninety-two, and an entourage of friends. As the chartered jet entered Soviet airspace he sat down at his rehearsal piano and spiritedly played the Soviet anthem. The party landed in the early hours to find reporters and cameramen waiting with throngs of fans—among them the indefatigable

Irina Garmash and the rest of the Van Club—who cheered him as a returning hero. After a 3:00 a.m. press conference, he made his ritual visit to Red Square and arrived at the National Hotel sometime in the morning. Henrietta Belayeva and Ella and Aschen Mikoyan crowded into his three-room suite, along with dozens of other old friends, and stayed until the early hours. Lev Vlassenko came to visit, and Kirill Kondrashin's sons represented their father, who had died in 1981. Rildia Bee sat smiling, swaddled in a fur coat in the July heat. Outside, women thronged the sidewalk beneath Van's balcony, holding out flowers and watermelons, old programs and photographs. He greeted them by name, hugged them, and asked about their families and lives.

Mikhail and Raisa Gorbachev attended his first concert, at Tchaikovsky Hall. "We are friends," Van said in Russian from the stage: "How full my heart is." He handed over a stack of large-denomination bills as a donation to Raisa Gorbachev's Soviet Culture Fund; his earnings would also go to support Russian culture. Then, to Gorbachev's amusement, Van announced that now that private property was permitted, he was going to buy a Moscow apartment. At the end, tearful fans threw flowers and screamed and surged to the front. The Gorbachevs joined in the standing ovation, and backstage they invited Van and Rildia Bee for a long private meeting. The hosts served tea and fruit and apple pie, and Van presented them with an engraved sterling silver Tiffany plate and a Fort Worth Club jogging outfit. Gorbachev spoke of bringing peace to a world tired of war, and offered to fly the entire Moscow Philharmonic to Leningrad so Van could play in Russia's second city; the resident orchestra was on vacation, and some fans had been on the waiting list for tickets for the past seventeen years. Afterward so many well-wishers jammed the hallways that Van's party was jostled and punched and began fearing for their lives. "If you love him, don't kill him!" screamed Beth Rodzinski, wife of the Cliburn Foundation president. When Van played at the conservatory the next night for his regular fans, he came back for four encores, perspiring like a spent athlete in the hot hall but putting his whole heart into the music. On the last note he nearly fell off the piano bench but spun round toward the crowd, who threw so many flowers that he picked them up and threw them back. Afterward a police squad had to form a human shield to extract him from his dressing room.

Sweeping into a government grocery, Van commandeered all five shopping carts and filled them with cases of Sprite and Evian water, cheese, smoked salmon, a mop, a basket of fruit, perfume, wine, and carrot juice. "He loves to shop," Rildia Bee explained. Yet the bounty was for his fans and guests, not for him. Everywhere he went, he handed out red roses and goodie bags of Yankee Doodle snack cakes, pocket calculators, watches, and sodas. He ordered so many bouquets of red carnations to garland Tchaikovsky's statue that they arrived by bus. There were parties at Spaso House and the conservatory, where he was awarded a master's degree and the choir sang Rachmaninoff. At a bash for Aschen Mikoyan's fortieth birthday, he gave her 105 red roses, five more than he sent Raisa Gorbachev. Back at the suite after one concert, he stripped to his T-shirt and boxers and gabbed with his Russian friends in his bedroom, drinking vodka from a water glass and stealthily asking for refills, so Rildia Bee didn't see. One night, when he stepped onto the hotel balcony to salute the crowds, together they broke into a rendition of "Moscow Nights." After a two-week tour, the Van Club waved him away and went home to add to their treasuries of souvenirs, hoping not to have to wait so long for another visit.

Back home Van played the occasional benefit concert and threw wild birthday parties for Rildia Bee, hiring the Fort Worth Symphony or flying Roberta Peters down to sing at a Viennese evening. The Rildia Bee O'Bryan Cliburn Organ rose in their church, Broadway Baptist; with 10,615 pipes, it was the largest in Texas and the largest French-style organ in the world. In 1994 he finally made a comeback tour, with the Moscow Philharmonic, generating acres of print and front-page headlines. At Grant Park in Chicago he played to 350,000, far surpassing his earlier record and, at $125,000, his earlier fee. Yet the tour quickly stumbled. At the Hollywood Bowl on his sixtieth birthday, he suffered bouts of dizziness and dropped Rachmaninoff's Piano Concerto no. 3, instead playing some solo encores before Johnny Mathis wheeled out an enormous piano-shaped cake and asked the audience to sing "Happy Birthday"; one newspaper unkindly called the show "pathetic" and a "fiasco." Age had acted on Van's nerves like a gale on a tree, and the Rachmaninoff never returned. He recovered with a dazzling performance at the Met, but halfway through, excruciating pains in his head and right arm gave him a premonition that Rildia Bee was dying. He dedicated the concert to her, recited a poem he wrote her when he was fourteen, and rushed to her bedside in Fort Worth, where he held her hand as she passed away peacefully, aged ninety-seven.

By then Van had not been close to Tom Zaremba for some time. He sent him away, and in 1997 Zaremba sued for palimony, claiming millions in cash and property as his due for looking after Van's affairs during their partnership. For maximum embarrassment, he alleged that Van had exposed him to the AIDS virus by sleeping with men who were HIV-positive, though his lawyer acknowledged that Zaremba did not have AIDS and had no reason to believe that Van was HIV-positive. The suit failed, and failed again on appeal, and Fort Worth society closed ranks and noticed nothing. Yet, for Van, whose life had been a long exercise in discretion, it was the cruelest outing. These were difficult years, and he was a frailer figure, drinking more and occasionally getting into blazing rows with old friends. He spoke to his astrologist almost daily and fretted over horoscopes with Nancy Reagan, whose kitchen phone number was pinned to the wall next to his kitchen phone. During one concert he fainted in mid-piece and slumped to the floor.

His face was sunken now; his lips were correspondingly fleshier. His neck was sinewy, his hair a dark copper graying at the temples, his eyes moist with nostalgia and gentle kindness. In 2001 he was a guest at the summit between George W. Bush and Vladimir Putin at the Bush ranch in Crawford, Texas. He took his partner, Tommy

Smith, his loyal sustainer throughout his later years; his forced outing
and changes in the country's mores had made that possible. Tommy
and Mrs. Putin got along famously in Spanish. Three years later,
Van returned to Moscow to make a seventieth-birthday tour and
receive the Order of Friendship from Putin. The Russian president
cited Van's contribution to increasing trust and understanding. "Dear
President," Van effused in Russian, not perhaps having the full measure of his host, "I am very grateful to you, I love you and Madame,
I love the Russian language, I love Russia!" If the country had altered
beyond all recognition, his fans' ardor had not cooled one bit. When
he returned in 2009, to give his first master class at a festival in honor
of Mstislav Rostropovich, they tried to climb in through the windows, palm invitations behind the guards' backs, and break into the
hall. Two years later he was honorary chairman of the Tchaikovsky
Competition piano jury; he refused to vote, since he could never
bring himself to choose one contestant over another, as he had been
chosen. Journalists abandoned all objectivity and lined up clutching
little cameras, to have their picture taken with him. His fans, many
white-haired now, clung to him in tears and proffered embroidered
bedroom slippers and tea cozies, bunches of daises and, in one case,
a perfectly ripe pear.

As the fiftieth anniversary of his victory approached, America,
too, crowned him with laurels: the Kennedy Center Honors, the
Presidential Medal of Freedom, the Grammy Lifetime Achievement
Award, the National Medal of Arts. He had played for every president from Truman to Obama, but his real constituency was still his
regular fans. When he went on the road to plug reissued CDs, huge
lines of admirers, many young, waited for hours in malls for his autograph while he talked to each one at length, always standing up.
One spring day, he landed on the Texas Motor Speedway in a helicopter and inaugurated the newly built NASCAR track by playing "The
Star-Spangled Banner" before two hundred thousand racing fans.

Fame had set him up to be the greatest pianist of all, and he could
not quite manage that. Yet even now the old Van Cliburn sometimes

flashed out, stunning a new generation with the power and lyricism that had made him one of the greats. And he truly had been: not across all the repertoire, not all the time, but at his best. Horowitz was more dazzling, Ashkenazy more secure, but no one could beat Van's ability to communicate the sheer love and excitement of music to an audience. He called his audiences, as he called himself, to humility and quickened forgetfulness and tears of wonder.

In 2012 he was diagnosed with terminal bone cancer. Ex-presidents, movie stars, and divas called on him. Choirs sang him Baptist hymns. Among the most cherished visitors were Liu Shikun and Yuri Klimov, his driver in 1958, who had served a lifetime as a diplomat specializing in the English-speaking world. "For the first time since I was four years old and was made to be a choirboy," Van told one visitor, "I feel liberated."

He died on February 27, 2013. He had planned his funeral with the same particularity he brought to his music. The coffin was heavy with white lilacs, like Russia in the spring. The Fort Worth Orchestra played, and massed choirs sang him to his rest with his favorite hymns and "Moscow Nights." Amid the eulogies from world leaders, the most moving was from Olga Rostropovich, the daughter of his old friend Mstislav. "It is hard to describe what Van Cliburn meant to Russia, to the Russian people, and to my family," she said. "He was part of our lives. He was our heartbeat. He was our Pushkin and our Rachmaninoff. For my parents, the mere mention of his name lit up their faces."

Henrietta Belayeva, Van's loyal and loving interpreter, had predeceased him by just a few months. Irina Garmash, his most constant fan, who had written him heartfelt letters every two weeks since 1958, died two months before him, run over by a car. Yet millions of other Russians mourned him as a native son, as was fitting for a people who were his greatest love. "Van was the highlight of my life," says Aschen Mikoyan quietly, and she was far from alone.

His world was not the real world. He lived in an idealized past of nobility and goodness, elevating sadness and redeeming grace. No one was more surprised than he when his innocence and outreaching talent made a mark on the world, because, in his heart, he was simply the servant of the composers he loved. As the gears of international relations turned and, for a moment, clicked into place, he was delighted to play his part, but he knew it was not he who had eased the way. It was the music he played, the songs of humanity that, when all the leaders were gone and when he was gone, too, would be there to feed hearts for all time.

Acknowledgments

THIS BOOK, my fourth, follows three that accidentally regressed from the nineteenth century to the fifteenth and thirteenth centuries. The greatest reward of this novel up-to-dateness has been the opportunity to meet and talk with many people who were directly involved in the story. The greatest sadness was that several died during my work—in the cases of Susan Tilley, Jeaneane Dowis, and Viktor Sukhodrev, as I was arranging interviews. My biggest regret is that I never met Van Cliburn, for the simple reason that his death set me on the path to exploring his life, with amazement that I hadn't heard his full story before and determination to do what I could to enSure that it didn't fade away. Perhaps I never would have met Van: ever private in that impossibly gregarious way of his, he was famously reluctant to open up to writers and displeased with the results when he did. Some of his friends stood by his lifelong policy of discretion; some found it cathartic finally to be able to talk. In telling the story that the record presented to me with much feeling and some necessary distance, I hope I have done justice to the memory of a man who was deeply and widely loved.

At the Cliburn Foundation, Maggie Estes and Jacques Marquis started me off in the right direction and subsequently showed me many kindnesses. Richard Rodzinski, the Cliburn's former president, was an early pivot of my research. Sergei Khrushchev gave me valuable leads and discussed many points in detail. Liu Shikun spent the better part of two days telling me his life story. Aschen Mikoyan shared her family memories in Moscow's Gorky Park and corresponded with me on many matters. Ella and Irina Vlassenko and their family showed me true Georgian hospitality at their bright green dacha. Gary and Naomi Graffman were a fount of flavored vodka, food, and anecdotes in New York. Vladimir and Dody (Thorunn) Ashkenazy confided in me in the very Cold War setting of the backseat of a limo in a dark parking lot.

In the United States, vital insights came from Alann Sampson (who also introduced me to Tommy Smith), Mary Lou Falcone, Harriet Wingreen, Peter Rosen, John Giordano, Ed Wierzbowski, Shield-Collins "Buddy" Bray, Gino Francesconi, Alexander Shtarkman, Anne Walker, Kaye Buck McDermott, and, at Juilliard, Joseph Polisi, Veda Kaplinsky, Martin Canin, Howard Aibel, and Robert White.

In Russia, Sergei Dorensky, Alexander Sokolov, Elena Dolinskaya, Yury Evgrafov, Margarita Karatygina, Maria Lvova, Jeff Sexton, Maria Holkina, Elena Cheremynch, Julia Miansarov, and Natalia Klimova provided more illumination and guidance. Elsewhere in Europe, I was fortunate to talk and correspond with Norman Shetler, Tamás Vásáry, András Hernádi, and Stephen Hough. I am enormously grateful to all for their time, insights, and trust in sharing their memories with me.

For research in Russian, I was extremely lucky to have the help of Dr. Lyuba Vinogradova. Lyuba translated hundreds of pages of document, memoirs, letters, articles, and books, mostly via Skype from Mozambique, and accompanied me on a research trip to Moscow. For extra research, many thanks to Lyuba's sister, Dr. Olga Vinogradova; mother, Dr. Galina Vinogradova; and mother's friend, Zhanna Beresneva; as well as to Daria Lotareva, Alexander Netsvetaev, Angelica von Hase, Sim Smiley, and Susan Strange. I am indebted, too, to the staff of the State House–Museum of Tchaikovsky in Klin, to Elena Fetisova at the Glinka Museum, to Margarita Karatygina at the Moscow Conservatory, and to Alexander Scriabin at the Goldenweiser Museum.

For archival assistance in the United States, I am beholden to Laura Ruede at Texas Christian University's Van Cliburn Competition Archive, Jeni Dahmus at the Juilliard School Archives, David Langbart and Rob Thompson at the National Archives, Jonathan Movroydis at the Nixon Foundation, Jon Fletcher at the Nixon Library, Brigid Shields at the Minnesota Historical Society Library, Lynne Farrington and Tom Hensle at the University of Pennsylvania's Kislak Center, Bill Monroe and Jennifer Betts at Brown University, and the staffs of the New York Public Library's Music Division and the University of Arizona Library.

My thanks to Christine Peerless for interpreting at my interviews with Liu Shikun, and to Felix Gottlieb, Kirill Gilels, Yoshiko Yamamura, Allison Ouvry, Jasper Parrott, and Lily Hsu for help in various essential matters. My debts to earlier writers and scholars are acknowledged in the notes, but in particular, the two biographies of Van, by Abram Chasins (1959) and Howard Reich (1993), were rich resources for their interviews with Van and other key players, many no longer with us.

My agent and friend Henry Dunow took this project to heart and was indefatigable in perfecting the proposal and representing the book. I was thrilled to work again with Terry Karten, a true writer's editor. At HarperCollins, thanks also to Jill Verrillo, Nikki Baldauf, Mary Jo Beaman, Jenna Dolan, Cindy Achar, Fritz Metsch, Renata Marchione, and Katherine Beitner.

My wife, Viviana, instantly shared my enthusiasm for Van's story, which was just as well, since the research and writing were an intense experience for us both. But for her, this book would not exist. Our son, Orlando, who at four years of age has lived with it for more than half his life, was less thrilled by its incursions into his playtime. With confidence that he will one day understand, I dedicate it to him with the greatest joy.

Selected Bibliography

Adams, Bruce. *Tiny Revolutions in Russia: Twentieth-Century Soviet and Russian History in Anecdotes*. New York: RoutledgeCurzon, 2005.

Alliluyeva, Svetlana. *Twenty Letters to a Friend*. New York: Harper and Row, 1967.

Ashkenazy, Vladimir, and Jasper Parrott. *Beyond Frontiers*. New York: Athenaeum, 1985.

Barrett, David M. *CIA and Congress: The Untold Story from Truman to Kennedy*. Lawrence: University Press of Kansas, 2005.

Beckerman, Gal. *When They Come for Us, We'll Be Gone: The Epic Struggle to Save Soviet Jewry*. New York: Houghton Mifflin Harcourt, 2010.

Belfrage, Sally. *A Room in Moscow*. London: André Deutsch, 1958.

Berezhkov, Valentin M. *At Stalin's Side: His Interpreter's Memoirs from the October Revolution to the Fall of the Dictator's Empire*. Translated by Sergei V. Mikheyev. New York: Birch Lane, 1994.

Bertensson, Sergei, and Jay Leyda. *Sergei Rachmaninoff: A Lifetime in Music*. Bloomington: Indiana University Press, 2001.

Beschloss, Michael. *Mayday: Eisenhower, Khrushchev, and the U-2 Affair*. New York: Harper and Row, 1986.

Billington, James H. *The Icon and the Axe: An Interpretive History of Russian Culture*. London: Weidenfeld and Nicolson, 1966.

Boyer, Paul. *By the Bomb's Early Light: American Thought and Culture at the Dawn of the Atomic Age*. New York: Pantheon, 1985.

Brent, Jonathan, and Vladimir P. Naumov. *Stalin's Last Crime: The Plot Against the Jewish Doctors*. New York: HarperCollins, 2003.

Brooke, Caroline. *Moscow: A Cultural History*. New York: Oxford University Press, 2006.

Brown, Archie. *The Rise and Fall of Communism*. London: Bodley Head, 2009.

Brown, Malcolm H. *A Shostakovich Casebook*. Indianapolis: Indiana University Press, 2004.

Brzezinski, Matthew. *Red Moon Rising: Sputnik and the Rivalries That Ignited the Space Race*. London: Bloomsbury, 2007.

Carland, John M., ed. *Foreign Relations of the United States, 1969–1976*. Vol. 9, *Vietnam, October 1972–January 1973*. Washington, DC: U.S. Government Printing Office, 2010.

Carlson, Peter. *K Blows Top: A Cold War Comic Interlude, Starring Nikita Khrushchev, America's Most Unlikely Tourist*. New York: PublicAffairs, 2009.

Caute, David. *The Dancer Defects: The Struggle for Cultural Supremacy During the Cold War*. Oxford: Oxford University Press, 2003.

Chasins, Abram, and Villa Stiles. *The Van Cliburn Legend*. Garden City, NY: Doubleday, 1959.

Cherkashin, Victor, and Gregory Feifer. *Spy Handler: Memoir of a KGB Officer*. New York: Basic Books, 2005.

Chuev, Felix. *Molotov Remembers: Inside Kremlin Politics*. Chicago: Ivan R. Dee, 1993.

Cohen, Stephen F. "The Victims Return: Gulag Survivors Under Khrushchev." In Hollander, *Political Violence*, 49–68.

Conquest, Robert. *The Great Terror: Stalin's Purge of the Thirties*. Harmondsworth: Penguin, 1971.

Dallek, Robert. *Flawed Giant: Lyndon Johnson and His Times, 1961–73*. New York: Oxford University Press, 1998.

Daniels, Robert V., ed. *A Documentary History of Communism*. Vol. 2, *Communism and the World*. London: I. B. Tauris, 1985.

Davenport, Lisa E. *Jazz Diplomacy: Promoting America in the Cold War Era*. Jackson: University Press of Mississippi, 2009.

Divine, Robert A. *The Sputnik Challenge*. New York: Oxford University Press, 1993.

Dobbs, Michael. *One Minute to Midnight: Kennedy, Khrushchev, and Castro on the Brink of Nuclear War*. New York: Knopf, 2008.

Dobrynin, Anatoly. *In Confidence: Moscow's Ambassador to America's Six Cold War Presidents (1962–1986)*. New York: Times Books, 1995.

Doering, James M. *The Great Orchestrator: Arthur Judson and American Arts Management*. Urbana: University of Illinois Press, 2013.

Domracheva, T. V., et al., eds. *Apparat TsK KPSS i kultura, 1958–1964: Dokumenty* (Apparatus of the Central Committee of the Communist Party and Culture 1958–1964: Documents). Moscow: Rosspen, 2005.

Dumbrell, John. *President Lyndon Johnson and Soviet Communism*. Manchester, UK: Manchester University Press, 2004.

Dunbabin, J. P. D. *International Relations Since 1945: A History in Two Volumes*. Vol. 2, *The Cold War: The Great Powers and Their Allies*. London: Longman, 1994.

Eason, Al. *Boom Town: Kilgore, Texas*. Kilgore, TX: Kilgore Chamber of Commerce, 1979.

Eisenhower, Dwight D. *White House Years: Waging Peace, 1956–1961*. New York: Doubleday, 1965.

Fay, Laurel E. *Shostakovich: A Life*. New York: Oxford University Press, 2000.

Fehrenbach, T. R. *Lone Star: A History of Texas and the Texans*. New York: Da Capo Press, 2000.

Feklisov, Aleksandr. *Za okeanom i na ostrove: Zapiski razvedchika* (Across the Ocean and On the Island: Memoirs of an Intelligence Man). Moscow: DEM, 2001.

Frankel, Max. *High Noon in the Cold War: Kennedy, Khrushchev, and the Cuban Missile Crisis*. New York: Ballantine, 2004.

———. *The Times of My Life and My Life with the* Times. New York: Random House, 1999.

Friedheim, Arthur. *Life and Liszt: The Reflections of a Concert Pianist*. Edited by Theodore L. Bullock. Mineola, NY: Dover, 1961.

Fursenko, Aleksandr, and Timothy Naftali. *Khrushchev's Cold War*. New York: Norton, 2006.

———. *"One Hell of a Gamble": The Secret History of the Cuban Missile Crisis*. London: John Murray, 1997.

Gaddis, John Lewis. *The Cold War*. London: Allen Lane, 2005.

———. *We Now Know: Rethinking Cold War History*. Oxford: Clarendon Press, 1997.

Garrard, John, and Carol Garrard. *Inside the Soviet Writers' Union*. London: I. B. Tauris, 1990.

Gerstell, Richard. *How to Survive an Atomic Bomb*. New York: Bantam, 1950.

Gorbachev, Mikhail. *Memoirs*. New York: Doubleday, 1996.

Graffman, Gary. *I Really Should Be Practicing*. Garden City, NY: Doubleday, 1981.

Gromyko, Andrei. *Memoirs*. Translated by Harold Shukman. New York: Doubleday, 1989.

Hanhimäki, Jussi M., and Odd Arne Westad, eds. *The Cold War: A History in Documents and Eyewitness Accounts*. Oxford: Oxford University Press, 2003.

Hayter, William. *A Double Life: The Memoirs of Sir William Hayter*. London: Penguin, 1974.

Higgs, David, ed. *Queer Sites: Gay Urban Histories Since 1600*. London: Routledge, 1999.

Hixson, Walter L. *Parting the Curtain: Propaganda, Culture, and the Cold War, 1945–1961*. New York: St. Martin's Press, 1997.

Ho, Allan B., and Dmitry Feofanov. *Shostakovich Reconsidered*. London: Toccata, 1998.

Hollander, Paul, ed. *Political Violence: Belief, Behavior, and Legitimation*. New York: Palgrave Macmillan, 2008.

Hornsby, Robert. *Protest, Reform, and Repression in Khrushchev's Soviet Union*. Cambridge, UK: Cambridge University Press, 2013.

Horowitz, Joseph. *Classical Music in America: A History of Its Rise and Fall*. New York: W. W. Norton, 2005.

———. *The Ivory Trade: Music and the Business of Music at the Van Cliburn International Piano Competition*. New York: Summit, 1990.

Isacoff, Stuart. *A Natural History of the Piano*. New York: Knopf, 2012.

Ivinskaya, Olga. *A Captive of Time: My Years with Pasternak*. Translated by Max Hayward. London: Collins, 1978.

Janis, Byron. *Chopin and Beyond: My Extraordinary Life in Music and the Paranormal*. Hoboken, NJ: John Wiley, 2010.

Johnson, Priscilla. *Khrushchev and the Arts: The Politics of Soviet Culture, 1962–1964*. Cambridge, MA: MIT Press, 1965.

Kempe, Frederick. *Berlin 1961: Kennedy, Khrushchev, and the Most Dangerous Place on Earth*. New York: Putman, 2011.

Kharlamov, M. and O. Vadeyev, eds. *Face to Face with America: The Story of N. S. Khrushchev's Visit to the USA, September 15–27, 1959*. Moscow: Foreign Languages Publishing House, 1960.

Khentova, Sofia. *Van Cliburn*. Moscow: Gos. Muzykal'noe Izd-vo, 1959.

Khrushchev in America: Full Texts of the Speeches Made by N. S. Khrushchev on His Tour of the United States, September 15–27, 1959. New York: Crosscurrents, 1960.

Khrushchev in New York: A Documentary Record of Nikita S. Khrushchev's Trip to New York, September 19th to October 13th, 1960, Including All His Speeches and Proposals to the United Nations and Major Addresses and News Conferences. New York: Crosscurrents, 1960.

Khrushchev, Nikita. *Khrushchev Remembers*. Translated and edited by Strobe Talbott. Boston: Little, Brown, 1970.

———. *Khrushchev Remembers: The Last Testament*. Translated and edited by Strobe Talbott. Boston: Little, Brown, 1974.

———. *Memoirs of Nikita Khrushchev*. Vol. 1, *Commissar*; Vol. 2, *Reformer*; Vol. 3, *Statesman*. Edited by Sergei Khrushchev. University Park: Pennsylvania State University Press, 2004; 2006; 2007.

Khrushchev, Sergei. *Nikita Khrushchev and the Creation of a Superpower*. Translated by Shirley Benson. University Park: Pennsylvania State University Press, 2000.

Kissinger, Henry. *On China*. New York: Penguin Press, 2011.

Kogan, Judith. *Nothing but the Best: The Struggle for Perfection at the Juilliard School*. New York: Random House, 1987.

Korchilov, Igor. *Translating History: Thirty Years on the Front Lines of Diplomacy with a Top Russian Interpreter.* New York: Scribner, 1997.

Kramer, Mark. "Leadership Succession and Political Violence in the USSR Following Stalin's Death." In Hollander, *Political Violence*, 69–92.

Kraus, Richard Curt. *Pianos and Politics in China: Middle-Class Ambitions and the Struggle over Western Music.* New York: Oxford University Press, 1989.

Landa, Ronald D., James E. Miller, David S. Patterson, Charles S. Sampson, eds. *Foreign Relations of the United States, 1958–1960.* Vol. 10, part 1, *Eastern Europe Region, Soviet Union, Cyprus.* Washington, DC: U.S. Government Printing Office, 1993.

Landa, Ronald D., James E. Miller, William F. Sanford Jr., Sherrill Brown Wells, eds. *Foreign Relations of the United States, 1958–1960.* Volume 10, part 2, *Eastern Europe; Finland; Greece; Turkey.* Washington, DC: U.S. Government Printing Office, 1993.

Leffler, Melvyn P. *For the Soul of Mankind: The United States, the Soviet Union, and the Cold War.* New York: Hill and Wang, 2007.

Lodge, Henry Cabot. *The Storm Has Many Eyes: A Personal Narrative.* New York: W. W. Norton, 1973.

Lourie, Richard. *Russia Speaks: An Oral History from the Revolution to the Present.* New York: E. Burlingame, 1991.

MacDonald, Ian. *The New Shostakovich.* London: Pimlico, 2006.

MacDuffie, Marshall. *The Red Carpet: 10,000 Miles Through Russia on a Visa from Khrushchev.* New York: W. W. Norton, 1955.

Matlock, Jack F. *Reagan and Gorbachev: How the Cold War Ended.* New York: Random House, 2004.

May, Elaine Tyler. *Homeward Bound: American Families in the Cold War Era.* New York: Basic Books, 1999.

Mayers, David. *The Ambassadors and America's Soviet Policy.* New York: Oxford University Press, 1995.

McCormick, Lisa. *Performing Civility: International Competitions in Classical Music.* Cambridge, UK: Cambridge University Press, 2015.

Medvedev, Zhores A., and Roy A. Medvedev. *The Unknown Stalin.* Translated by Ellen Dahrendorf. London: I. B. Tauris, 2003.

———. *Khrushchev: The Years in Power.* Translated by Andrew R. Durkin. London: Oxford University Press, 1977.

Melvin, Sheila, and Jindong Cai. *Rhapsody in Red: How Western Classical Music Became Chinese.* New York: Algora, 2004.

Meyers, Jeffrey. *The Genius and the Goddess: Arthur Miller and Marilyn Monroe.* Urbana: University of Illinois Press, 2009.

Mikoyan, Sergo. *Soviet Cuban Missile Crisis: Castro, Mikoyan, Kennedy, Khrushchev and the Missiles of November.* Edited by Svetlana Savranskaya. Stanford, CA: Stanford University Press, 2012.

Mikoyan, Stepan. *An Autobiography.* Translated by Aschen Mikoyan. Shrewsbury, UK: Airlife, 1999.

Miller, Douglas T., and Marion Nowak. *The Fifties: The Way We Really Were.* New York: Doubleday, 1977.

Mitchell, Curtis. *God in the Garden: The Story of the Billy Graham New York Crusade.* Garden City, NY: Doubleday, 1957.

Mohr, Franz, with Edith Schaeffer. *My Life with the Great Pianists.* Grand Rapids, MI: Baker Book House, 1992.

Monsaingeon, Bruno. *Sviatoslav Richter: Notebooks and Conversations*. London: Faber and Faber, 2001.

Montefiore, Simon Sebag. *Stalin: The Court of the Red Tsar*. London: Weidenfeld and Nicolson, 1993.

Morrison, Simon. *Lina and Serge: The Love and Wars of Lina Prokofiev*. New York: Houghton Mifflin Harcourt, 2013.

———, ed. *Sergey Prokofiev and His World*. Princeton, NJ: Princeton University Press, 2008.

Nabokov, Nicolas. *Old Friends and New Music*. London: Hamish Hamilton, 1951.

Newton, Jim. *Eisenhower: The White House Years*. New York: Doubleday, 2001.

Olmstead, Andrea. *Juilliard: A History*. Urbana: University of Illinois Press, 1999.

Plisetskaya, Maya. *I, Maya Plisetskaya*. Translated by Antonia W. Bouis. New Haven, CT: Yale University Press, 2001.

Polisi, Joseph. *American Muse: The Life and Times of William Schuman*. Milwaukee, WI: Amadeus, 2008.

Polonsky, Rachel. *Molotov's Magic Lantern: A Journey in Russian History*. London: Faber, 2011.

Powers, Francis Gary, and Curt Gentry. *Operation Overflight: A Memoir of the U-2 Incident*. Washington, DC: Brassey's, 2004.

Radzinsky, Edward. *Stalin: The First In-Depth Biography Based on Explosive New Documents from Russia's Secret Archives*. Translated by H. T. Willetts. New York: Doubleday, 1996.

Raleigh, Donald J. *Soviet Baby Boomers: An Oral History of Russia's Cold War Generation*. Oxford, UK: Oxford University Press, 2012.

Rasmussen, Karl Aage. *Sviatoslav Richter: Pianist*. Translated by Russell Dees. Boston: Northeastern University Press, 2010.

Reich, Howard. *Van Cliburn*. Nashville, TN: Thomas Nelson, 1993.

Richmond, Yale. *Cultural Exchange and the Cold War: Raising the Iron Curtain*. University Park: Pennsylvania State University Press, 2003.

Robinson, Harlow. *The Last Impresario: The Life, Times, and Legacy of Sol Hurok*. New York: Viking, 1994.

Rosenberg, Victor. *Soviet-American Relations, 1953–1960: Diplomacy and Cultural Exchange During the Eisenhower Administration*. Jefferson, NC: McFarland, 2005.

Rothman, Hal. *LBJ's Texas White House: "Our Heart's Home."* College Station: Texas A&M University Press, 2001.

Saunders, Frances Stonor. *Who Paid the Piper? The CIA and the Cultural Cold War*. London: Granta, 1999.

Schlogel, Karl. *Moscow*. Translated by Helen Atkins. London: Reaktion, 2005.

Schonberg, Harold C. *The Great Pianists*. New York: Simon and Schuster, 1963.

Schwarz, Boris. *Music and Musical Life in Soviet Russia*. Bloomington: Indiana University Press, 1983.

Sherry, Michael S. *Gay Artists in Modern American Culture: An Imagined Conspiracy*. Chapel Hill: University of North Carolina Press, 2007.

Shultz, George P. *Turmoil and Triumph: My Years as Secretary of State*. New York: Scribner's, 1993.

Sidelnikov, Leonid, and Galina Pribegina. *25 Days in America: For the Centenary of Peter Tchaikovsky's Concert Tour*. Moscow: Muzyka, 1991.

Steinbeck, John. *A Russian Journal*. New York: Viking, 1948.

Stern, Isaac, and Chaim Potok. *My First 79 Years*. New York: Da Capo Press, 1999.

Sukhodrev, Viktor. *Yazyk moi—drug moi* (My Tongue Is My Friend). Moscow: Ast; Olimp, 2008.

Swayne, Steve. *Orpheus in Manhattan: William Schuman and the Shaping of America's Musical Life.* New York: Oxford University Press, 2011.

Tassie, Gregor. *Kirill Kondrashin: His Life in Music.* Lanham, MD: Scarecrow, 2009.

Taubman, William. *Khrushchev: The Man and His Era.* New York: Norton, 2003.

Taylor, Philip S. *Anton Rubinstein: A Life in Music.* Bloomington: Indiana University Press, 2007.

Terrill, Ross. *Mao: A Biography.* Stanford, CA: Stanford University Press, 2000.

Tomoff, Kiril. *Creative Union: The Professional Organization of Soviet Composers, 1939–1953.* Ithaca, NY: Cornell University Press, 2006.

———. *Virtuosi Abroad: Soviet Music and Imperial Competition During the Early Cold War, 1945–1958.* Ithaca, NY: Cornell University Press, 2015.

Tompson, William J. *Khrushchev: A Political Life.* Basingstoke, UK: Macmillan, 1995.

Tzouliadis, Tim. *The Forsaken.* London: Little, Brown, 2008.

Vasilieva, Larissa. *Kremlin Wives: The Secret Lives of the Women Behind the Kremlin Walls— From Lenin to Gorbachev.* Translated by Cathy Porter. London: Weidenfeld and Nicolson, 1994.

Vishnevskaya, Galina. *Galina: A Russian Story.* Translated by Guy Daniels. London: Hodder and Stoughton, 1984.

Vlassenko, Lev. *Lev Vlassenko: Articles, Reminiscences, Interviews.* Brisbane: Allstate Printing and Graphics, 2009.

———. *Lev Vlassenko: Grani lichnosti* (Facets of the Person). Moscow: Musyka, 2013.

Volkov, Solomon. *The Magical Chorus: A History of Russian Culture from Tolstoy to Solzhenitsyn.* New York: Knopf, 2008.

———. *Testimony: The Memoirs of Dmitri Shostakovich.* Translated by Antonia W. Bouis. London: Hamish Hamilton, 1979.

Wallace, Robert K. *A Century of Music-Making: The Lives of Josef and Rosina Lhévinne.* Bloomington: Indiana University Press, 1976.

Warrack, John. *Tchaikovsky.* New York: Charles Scribner's, 1973.

Wiley, Roland John, *Tchaikovsky.* New York: Oxford University Press, 2009.

Wilson, Elizabeth. *Shostakovich: A Life Remembered.* London: Faber, 1994.

Yoffe, Elkhonon. *Tchaikovsky in America: The Composer's Visit in 1891.* Translated by Lidya Yoffe. New York: Oxford University Press, 1986.

Zubok, Vladislav. *A Failed Empire: The Soviet Union in the Cold War from Stalin to Gorbachev.* Chapel Hill: University of North Carolina Press, 2007.

———. *Zhivago's Children: The Last Russian Intelligentsia.* Cambridge, MA: Belknap, 2009.

Zubok, Vladislav, and Constantine Pleshako. *Inside the Kremlin's Cold War: From Stalin to Khrushchev.* Cambridge, MA: Harvard University Press, 1996.

Abbreviations

The most frequently used primary sources are abbreviated as follows in the notes:

PRINTED MATERIAL

CCCP&C T. V. Domracheva et al, eds. *Apparat TsK KPSS i kultura, 1958–1964: dokumenty* (Apparatus of the Central Committee of the Communist Party and Culture 1958–1964: Documents). Moscow: Rosspen, 2005.

FRUS X:1 Ronald D. Landa, James E. Miller, David S. Patterson, and Charles S. Sampson, eds. *Foreign Relations of the United States, 1958–1960*. Vol. 10, part 1: *Eastern Europe Region, Soviet Union, Cyprus*. Washington, DC: U.S. Government Printing Office, 1993.

KM Nikita Khrushchev. *Memoirs of Nikita Khrushchev*. Vol. 2, *Reformer (1945–1964)*. Edited by Sergei Khrushchev. University Park: Pennsylvania State University Press, 2007.

KR Nikita Khrushchev. *Khrushchev Remembers*. Translated and edited by Strobe Talbott. New York: Little, Brown, 1970.

NKCS Sergei Khrushchev. *Nikita Khrushchev and the Creation of a Superpower*. Translated by Shirley Benson. University Park: Pennsylvania State University Press, 2000.

TOML Max Frankel. *The Times of My Life and My Life with the* Times. New York: Random House, 1999.

VC Howard Reich. *Van Cliburn*. Nashville, TN: Thomas Nelson, 1993.

VCL Abram Chasins and Villa Stiles. *The Van Cliburn Legend*. Garden City, NY: Doubleday, 1959.

YM Viktor Sukhodrev. *Yazyk moi—drug moi* (My Tongue Is My Friend). Moscow: AST; Olimp, 2008. Internet version: RuLIT.net.

RESEARCH COLLECTIONS

CWIHP Cold War International History Project. Woodrow Wilson International Center for Scholars. Washington, DC.

DDEPL Dwight D. Eisenhower Presidential Library. Abilene, KS.

FBI (FOIA) Declassified Federal Bureau of Investigation files relating to Van Cliburn. Obtained under the Freedom of Information Act.

GFPL Gerald R. Ford Presidential Library. Ann Arbor, MI.

GM Glinka Museum of Music Culture. Moscow.

JA Juilliard School Archives. Juilliard School, New York.

JABT	Board of Trustees. Minutes and reports, 1944–1981. Juilliard School Archives.
JAD	Office of the Dean. General Administrative Records, 1947–1962. Juilliard School Archives.
JAP	Office of the President. General Administrative Records, 1932–1962. Juilliard School Archives.
JH	John Hay Special Collections. Brown University. Providence, RI.
LBJL	Lyndon Baines Johnson Library. Austin, TX.
MMP	Minutes of Music Panel Meeting. International Exchange Program.
NACP	National Archives and Records Administration. College Park, MD.
PFJA	Placement file. "Cliburn, Van." Juilliard School Archive.
RLP	Rosina Lhévinne Papers. Music Division. New York Public Library.
RNPL	Richard Nixon Presidential Library and Museum. Yorba Linda, CA.
RRPL	Ronald Reagan Presidential Library. Simi Valley, CA.
SH	Serrell Hillman Dispatch. New York. May 5, 1958. Dispatches from *Time* Magazine Correspondents: Second Series, 1956–1968 (MS Am 2090.1). Houghton Library. Harvard University. Hereafter *Time* dispatches.
SHM	State House Museum of Tchaikovsky. Klin.
TM1	Tom Martin Dispatch. Dallas. May 1, 1958. *Time* dispatches.
TM2	Tom Martin Dispatch. Dallas, May 5, 1958. *Time* dispatches.
VCA	Van Cliburn International Piano Competition Archive. Mary Couts Burnett Library. Texas Christian University. Fort Worth, TX.
VCG	Van Cliburn, interview conducted for *The Cliburn: 50 Years of Gold*. Film produced by Peter Rosen Productions, Inc. for the Van Cliburn Foundation, 2012. Unedited transcript courtesy Peter Rosen.
VCJA	Van Cliburn Biographical File. Juilliard School Archive.
WSP	William Schuman Papers and Records. Music Division. New York Public Library.

NEWSPAPERS AND MAGAZINES

DMN	*Dallas Morning News*
FWS-T	*Fort Worth Star-Telegram*
KNH	*Kilgore News Herald*
NYT	*New York Times*
SK	*Sovetskaya Kultura*
SM	*Sovetsky Muzykant*
ST	*Shreveport Times*
WP	*Washington Post*

Notes

INTRODUCTION

1 **"What's goin' on":** *VCL*, 131.

1 **most famous *person* in America**: The Tchaikovsky prize, as suggested in the program note for a 1958 appearance with the Dallas Symphony, had "made Mr. Cliburn the most widely known pianist, one might almost say individual, in the United States today" (VCJA).

PRELUDE IN TWO PARTS

5 **one Viennese critic:** Eduard Hanslick, reviewing the premiere of Tchaikovsky's violin concerto in the *Neue Freie Presse* of December 5, 1981.

5 **Rubinstein asked the reticent composer:** The reconstruction is based on Tchaikovsky's letter to his patroness Nadezhda von Meck in 1887, quoted in John Warrack, *Tchaikovsky* (New York: Charles Scribner's, 1973), 78–79.

6 **bells pealing the Royal Hours . . . marriage fortunes:** The Orthodox Christmas Eve on January 6 marks the start of a traditional Slavic holiday, Svyatki, during which young women foretell their marriage prospects with wax and shadows. The Royal Hours, the services marking the times of prayer on the Eve of the Nativity, originated with the imperial services at Hagia Sophia in Constantinople.

7 **American composer:** George Whitefield Chadwick (1854–1931), "Pyotr Il'yich Tchaikovsky: Piano Concerto no. 1 in B Flat Minor, op. 23," Aspen Music Festival and School website, https://www.aspenmusicfestival.com/program_notes/view/tchaikovsky-piano-concerto-no.-1-in-b-flat-minor-op.-23/25896.

7 **hardly destined to become classical:** *The Boston Traveler*, quoted in *Concert Bulletin of the Boston Symphony Orchestra*, Seventieth Season (Boston, 1950).

7 **"It turns out":** Tchaikovsky to Vladimir Davidov, New York, April 30, 1891, in Elkhonon Yoffe, *Tchaikovsky in America: The Composer's Visit in 1891*, trans. Lidya Yoffe (New York: Oxford University Press, 1986), 62–63.

8 **quarter of a mile:** *New York Herald*, May 6, 1891.

8 **Soviet spy:** Aleksandr Feklisov, *Za okeanom i na ostrove: Zapiski razvedchika* (Across the Ocean and on the Island: Memoirs of an Intelligence Man) (Moscow: DEM, 2001), Internet version.

10 **most famous piano concerto:** On November 28, 1909, with the New York Symphony Society conducted by Walter Damrosch.

II **"six-and-a-half-foot scowl":** Igor Stravinsky and Robert Craft, *Conversations with Igor Stravinsky* (Garden City, NY: Doubleday, 1959), 41.

II **Hollywood movies:** The two described are *Mission to Moscow* (1943) and *The North Star* (1943).

II **premiere in Leningrad:** The Seventh Symphony premiered in Kuibyshev on March 5, 1942, and in Moscow on March 29. Sir Henry Wood and the London Philharmonic presented it in London on June 22, and Toscanini and the NBC Symphony Orchestra performed it in New York on July 19. The famous Leningrad premiere took place on August 9.

II **sixty-two times:** Karl Aage Rasmussen, *Sviatoslav Richter: Pianist*, trans. Russell Dees (Boston: Northeastern University Press, 2010), 124.

I: THE PRODIGY

15 **"Sug, I think":** Video recording VC-2162 (Reel 36), Rildia Bee Cliburn interviewed by Peter Rosen [1989], VCA.

15 **room 322:** TMI.

15 **"Babe . . . our family":** Rildia Bee Cliburn interview, VCA.

15 **"Harvey Lavan (Van) Cliburn":** Wayne Lee Gay, "Rildia Cliburn, Mother of Famed Pianist, Dies," *FWS-T*, August 4, 1994.

15 **met Sergei Rachmaninoff:** Van often told the tale that his parents traced his decision to be a pianist to the night when Rachmaninoff played in Shreveport at the invitation of the committee to which Rildia Bee belonged. Van was supposed to attend the concert, the story went, but had caught chicken pox and had to stay at home; instead, he listened to it on the radio, and when Rildia Bee returned, she regaled him with every detail. This appears impossible. Van generally gave the date of this concert as November 14, 1938, though some accounts say 1939; he subsequently made his Carnegie Hall debut on November 14, 1954, and often noted the coincidence. But Rachmaninoff performed in Shreveport only on January 24, 1923, and November 14, 1932 (on the fifteenth, he wrote the letter lamenting the dire attendance), before Van was born. On November 14, 1938, Rachmaninoff appeared in Ames, Iowa, and on November 14, 1939, he performed in Harrisburg, Pennsylvania; he had no engagements in Texas or Louisiana during the 1938/39 season. He did, however, play in Fort Worth on November 15, 1937 (on the fourteenth, he was in St. Louis), when Van was three. It seems that two stories—one of Rildia Bee's involvement in Rachmaninoff's 1932 visit to Shreveport, another of Van listening to his later performance on the radio—were consciously or unconsciously blended into a single parable of the passing of the torch from master to student. For a complete list of Rachmaninoff's American concert dates, see Robin Sue Gehl, *Reassessing a Legacy: Rachmaninoff in America, 1918–43* (PhD diss., University of Cincinnati, 2008), Appendix D: 252–97.

15 **railroad station agent:** TMI.

16 **"Business is lamentable":** Rachmaninoff to Eugene Somov, November 15, 1932, quoted in Sergei Bertensson and Jay Leyda, *Sergei Rachmaninoff: A Lifetime in Music* (Bloomington: Indiana University Press, 2001), 290.

17 **Shreveport paper:** Sunflower Daly, "Rachmaninoff Wins by Large Margin in Monday Night Game," *ST*, November 15, 1932.

17 **how that happened:** Van and Rildia Bee told the story many times, with minor variations. My main source is Peter Rosen's interview with Rildia Bee, VCA.

18 **regular lessons:** TM1.

18 **"Now, when we're taking a lesson":** Ibid. The lesson routine is from the same dispatch.

18 **"Well, son, we'll see about that":** Van Cliburn, quoted in *VC*, 10.

18 **medical missionary:** John Davidson, "Every Good Boy Does Fine," *Texas Monthly* 15, no. 5 (May 1987): 172. Other sources quoted Harvey as simply wanting Van to be a doctor: see TM1.

19 **"Mommy, Daddy, take me there":** VCG.

19 **born a Texan:** Rildia Bee Cliburn interview, VCA.

20 **draw off their neighbors' crude:** Stanley Walker, "Kilgore Has Oil and Van Cliburn, Too," *NYT Magazine*, September 23, 1962.

20 **ten thousand dollars:** TM2.

20 **old family friend:** Gay, "Rildia Cliburn, Mother of Famed Pianist, Dies."

20 **tiny one-story white house:** Tom Martin superciliously describes the house and its contents in TM2.

21 **"Van, you have such long hands":** TM1.

22 **"superior" fifteen times:** Ibid.

22 **"I can't play . . . and God":** Van Cliburn, "What Is Success?" *Guideposts Magazine*, February 1959.

22 **"Well, you know . . . wonderful":** Van Cliburn, interview by Paul Holdengräber, May 15, 2012, http://www.nypl.org/audiovideo/live-nypl-christies-present-van-cliburn-conversation-paul-holdengräber.

22 **"Well, all right then":** TM1.

23 **"It hurts me" . . . "help me":** Van Cliburn, interview by Paul Holdengräber.

23 **nosebleeds:** TM1. They began at age eight, when Van contracted scarlet fever.

23 **taxi driver:** Ibid. Another possibility was a preacher.

24 **insured for a million dollars:** As remembered by Coach Bradford. Gay, "Rildia Cliburn, Mother of Famed Pianist, Dies."

24 **Bob Waters . . . C. L. Newsome:** TM1.

24 **Mr. Belvedere:** TM2.

24 **Thespian Club . . . Spanish Club . . . Student Council:** TM1.

24 **Winifred Hamilton:** Ibid. Martin interviewed Michael Gehlen, the other student with a crush on her.

24 **"You already have the best teacher":** Dolores Fredrickson, "Van Cliburn Remembers His Remarkable Mother," *Clavier*, March 1996.

25 **"Sonny Boy":** Davidson, "Every Good Boy Does Fine," 172.

25 **two-hundred-dollar prize:** PFJA. A handwritten note in the same file puts the prize money at $250.

25 **with the Houston Symphony Orchestra:** On April 12, 1947. Sound recording txu-hs-0048, "Houston Symphony Concert, Apr. 12, 1947," Austin Fine Arts Library, University of Texas.

26 **"the warmonger and imperialist oppressor":** Tim Tzouliadis, *The Forsaken* (London: Little, Brown, 2008), 259.

27 **Central Committee . . . issued a resolution:** These events began in January 1948, after Stalin reacted violently to the opera *Velikaya druzhba* (The Great Friendship), by Vano Muradeli. The recriminations spread in numerous meetings, the Central Committee decree of February 10, and the First All-Union Congress of Soviet Composers, held April 19–28. See Kiril Tomoff, *Creative Union: The Professional Organiza-*

tion of Soviet Composers, 1939–1953 (Ithaca, NY: Cornell University Press, 2006), 122–51; Per Skans, "The 1948 Formalism Campaign," in Ian MacDonald, *The New Shostakovich* (London: Pimlico, 2006), 322–34; and Boris Schwarz, *Music and Musical Life in Soviet Russia, 1917–1970* (London: Barrie and Jenkins, 1972), 213–28.

27 **"grunting and scraping":** Martin Sixsmith, "The Secret Rebel," *Guardian*, July 15, 2006.

27 **"muddled, nerve-wracking":** Tomoff, *Creative Union*, 123.

27 **"enemies of Russian music":** Ibid.

28 **"Once again . . . criticism":** Letter to *Sovetskaya Muzyka*, 1948, quoted in Rasmussen, *Sviatoslav Richter*, 124.

28 **"Jump thru the window":** Terry Klefstad, "Shostakovich and the Peace Conference," *Music & Politics* 6, no. 2 (Summer 2012).

28 **"bag of ticks and grimaces":** Elizabeth Wilson, *Shostakovich: A Life Remembered* (London: Faber, 1994), 462.

28 **"hatemongers . . . outright war":** *NYT*, March 28, 1949.

29 **"suave radio baritone":** Nicolas Nabokov, *Old Friends and New Music* (London: Hamish Hamilton, 1951), 204.

29 **"not a free man":** Ibid., 205.

29 **including classical music:** At various times Elmer Bernstein, Leonard Bernstein, Aaron Copland, Lena Horne, and Dimitri Mitropoulos were under investigation.

29 **"It's by Rimsky-Korsakov":** Frances Stonor Saunders, *Who Paid the Piper? The CIA and the Cultural Cold War* (London: Granta, 1999), 196.

2: ROOM 412

31 **"Honey . . . ah've come to study with y'all":** There are several versions of this well-known line: "Ah've come to study with ya'll, honey" (Jeaneane Dowis Lipman, "Rosina: A Memoir," *The American Scholar* 65, no. 3 [Summer 1996]: 373); "Honey, I'm here to study with you" (*VCL*, 48); and "Honey, Ah'm goin' to study with you" ("The All-American Virtuoso," *Time*, May 19, 1958).

31 **Catherine the Great . . . droshky driver:** Harold Schonberg, quoted in Robert K. Wallace, *A Century of Music-Making: The Lives of Josef and Rosina Lhévinne* (Bloomington: Indiana University Press, 1976), 268.

31 **He had telephoned her:** This is one of those small but telling stories that survive in several different forms, presumably to drive biographers mad. Rosina told Abram Chasins about the phone call for his 1959 book. Van, on the other hand, told Howard Reich for his 1993 biography that this conversation took place in person, and Reich places it prior to the Juilliard entrance examinations, where he suggests Rosina heard Van play and decided to accept him. It seems unlikely that Van would have been assigned a teacher before he had auditioned for a place at the school, and Reich's version is also contradicted by the information of Jeaneane Dowis and, further on in Reich's book, of Josef Raeiff, who states that he was appointed Van's teacher when Van started at the school. Rosina told both Chasins and Robert K. Wallace the story of the impromptu meeting by the elevator, and she told both that some of her students convinced her to give Van a hearing, which seems to have been a private affair and not part of the entrance auditions. So much is confirmed by a letter Rildia Bee wrote to Rosina shortly after Thanksgiving Day 1951, in which she noted that Van "would have been terribly disappointed had you not 'squeezed' him into your class." The comment would have been redundant

had Rildia Bee already known that Van was enrolled with Rosina when she arrived with him at the start of the semester. In her notes for an interview, Rosina writes of Van, "When he was 17 years old . . . he arrived in N.Y., two of my pupils introduced him to me and he said that he wanted to study with me." It appears that Van conflated three episodes in his memory—the school audition, the telephone call, and the private audition for Rosina—possibly to make a more decorous scene out of the confusion. I have made my best stab at adjudicating between the accounts. See *VC*, 41–42; *VCL*, 47–48; Dowis, "Rosina: A Memoir," 373; Wallace, *Century of Music-Making*, 270; Rildia Bee O'Bryan Cliburn, letter to Rosina Lhévinne, n.d. [December 1951], Folder 19, Box 2, RLP; Rosina Lhévinne notes for an interview, Folder 17B, Box 29, RLP.

31 **During three summers:** Van attended the Juilliard School in the summers of 1947, 1948 (studying with Ernest Hutcheson), and 1951 (studying with Carl Friedberg).

33 **gold medals:** Josef graduated top of his piano class, ahead of his classmates Alexander Scriabin and Sergei Rachmaninoff, who won the even more prestigious Great Gold Medal for composition.

35 **five-room apartment:** The description and the following information about Van's life with the Spicers are taken from SH.

35 **"You can't love music enough":** "All-American Virtuoso."

35 **a high but unspectacular 119:** TM1 gives Van's academic credentials.

36 **Leontyne Price:** Interview by Peter Rosen, Reels 38 and 39, *Van Cliburn—Concert Pianist* elements, VCA. This vital collection includes many detailed interviews for Rosen's 1994 documentary, which was originally broadcast on the A&E Network's *Biography*.

36 **Mrs. Leo Satterwhite Allen:** *VC*, 18.

36 **"Boy, isn't it wonderful":** Mark Schubart, quoted in SH.

37 **Steinway Hall:** At 113 West Fifty-Seventh Street; when the building was sold to Manhattan Life Insurance Company, the number was changed to 111.

38 **"Well, far be it from *me* to say":** Robert White, interview with the author, February 28, 2015.

38 **a wealthy lady:** TM2.

39 **"Kremlin's ultimate intentions":** William L. Laurence, quoted in Paul Boyer, *By the Bomb's Early Light: American Thought and Culture at the Dawn of the Atomic Age* (New York: Pantheon, 1985), 340. Born in Lithuania, Laurence was the official historian of the Manhattan Project.

39 **Secret plans:** Secret report NSC-68, issued April 14, 1950, President's Secretary's File, Truman Papers, Truman Library.

39 **Third World War:** Code-named "Operation Dropshot"; first circulated in 1949.

39 **"Every effort will be made":** Boyer, *By the Bomb's Early Light*, 323.

39 **How to Survive an Atomic Bomb:** Published in New York by Bantam, 1950. The author, Richard Gerstell, was billed as a consultant with the Civil Defense Office.

40 **"leaving only the tower":** Boyer, *By the Bomb's Early Light*, 320.

40 **"fluorescence which occurs around U-235":** Ibid., 110.

40 **"a pellet of atomic energy":** Ibid., 112.

40 **"the entire world a moister, warmer climate":** Ibid., 111.

40 **"generally to tidy up":** S. Chase, *The Nation*, December 22, 1945.

40 **"If an atomic-powered taxi":** Boyer, *By the Bomb's Early Light*, 115.

40 **Science Digest . . . Scientific American:** Ibid., 115–16.

40 **Inside Room 412:** My account of Rosina at Juilliard draws on Dowis, "Rosina: A

Memoir"; *The Legacy of Rosina Lhévinne*, film dir. Salome Ramras Arkatov, 2003, DVD, Kultur, 2011; and my interviews with Van's contemporaries Martin Canin and Howard Aibel, conducted September 26 and October 16, 2014, respectively. The following quotations are from Dowis.

42 **"Very talented, quick, not *very* accurate":** Folder 10, Box 27, RLP.

42 **with great joy:** Joseph W. Polisi, "The Broad Palette of Van Cliburn's Life," *Juilliard Journal*, April 2013. "He is a great joy to work with . . . [possessing a] most unusual virtuoso talent [but] with it shows remarkable sensitivity," Rosina wrote in a teacher report.

42 **"It's too beautiful":** Wallace, *Century of Music-Making*, 271.

42 **earned him three hundred dollars:** PFJA.

42 **six-hundred-dollar Juilliard grant:** Ibid. The grant was in the name of Olga Samaroff.

42 **"Harvey Levan":** Ibid.

43 **"Excellent talent":** Folder 2, Box 27, RLP.

43 **"But Tchaikovsky":** Dowis, "Rosina: A Memoir," 375.

44 **"Well, we don't really":** Josef Raeiff, quoted in *VC*, 61.

44 **played the concerto:** On January 23, 1953.

44 **graded him "Excellent":** Folder 11, Box 27, RLP.

44 **his own showcase:** *VC*, 55.

45 **double protection:** Though the change was unusually dramatic, there were precedents: the prominent British pianist, conductor, and composer Ethel Leginska (1886–1970) was born Ethel Liggins in Hull, Yorkshire, while the British pianist Marguérite de Pachmann (1865–1952) was born Maggie Okey in Australia.

3: THE SUCCESSOR

47 **dusk on March 1, 1953:** My account of Stalin's death is based primarily on the first-hand account of the guard Pavel Lozgachev in Edward Radzinsky, *Stalin*, trans. H. T. Willetts (New York: Doubleday, 1996), 549–60. Also used were *KM*, 145–52; Simon Sebag Montefiore, *Stalin: The Court of the Red Tsar* (London: Weidenfeld and Nicolson, 1993), 564–77; Zhores A. Medvedev and Roy A. Medvedev, *The Unknown Stalin*, trans. Ellen Dahrendorf (London: I. B. Tauris, 2003), 1–33; Svetlana Alliluyeva, *Twenty Letters to a Friend* (New York: Harper and Row, 1967); Andrei Gromyko, *Memoirs*, trans. Harold Shukman (New York: Doubleday, 1989), 103; Felix Chuev, *Molotov Remembers* (Chicago: Ivan R. Dee, 1993), 236–37. The accounts often conflict: for instance Khrushchev says he arrived at Stalin's dacha early in the morning on March 2 with Malenkov, Beria, and Bulganin, whereas Lozgachev says only the first two showed up and that Khrushchev arrived four hours later.

48 **"Beat them . . . into powder":** Montefiore, *Stalin*, 558.

48 **"It has been established":** Vadim J. Birstein, *The Perversion of Knowledge: The True Story of Soviet Science* (Cambridge, MA: Westview, 2001), 64. The services named were those of America and Britain.

48 **"feverishly preparing":** *Pravda*, January 13, 1958, quoted in Jussi M. Hanhimäki and Odd Arne Westad, eds., *The Cold War: A History in Documents and Eyewitness Accounts* (New York: Oxford University Press, 2003), 427.

48 **head of the secret police:** The Soviet security service was known as the MGB, or Ministry for State Security, from 1946 to 1954, when it was replaced with the KGB, the Committee for State Security.

49 **"When Stalin says dance":** *KR*, 301.

49 **"One never knows":** Montefiore, *Stalin*, 471.

49 **warbling "Mikita":** *KM*, 146.

51 **"Come in, don't be shy":** Montefiore, *Stalin*, 572.

52 **"He sort of smiled":** *KM*, 149.

52 **Molotov saw a flash:** Gromyko, *Memoirs*, 103.

52 **"twisted by ambition":** Alliluyeva, *Twenty Letters*, 7–8.

52 **"Which specialist":** Louis Rapoport, *Stalin's War Against the Jews: The Doctors' Plot and the Soviet Solution* (New York: Free Press, 1990), 213.

53 **"Listen, please stop that":** *KM*, 151.

53 **"Khrustalev, the car":** Alliluyeva, *Twenty Letters*, 8.

53 **"He's off to take power":** Montefiore, *Stalin*, 576, quoting Anastas Mikoyan, *Tak bylo* (Moscow: AST, 2000), 587.

53 **familiar voice:** That of Yuri Levitan. See Victor Zorza, "How Moscow Broke the News of Stalin's Death," *Guardian*, March 7, 1953.

54 **"Thank you, Comrade Stalin":** Tzouliadis, *Forsaken*, 183.

54 **"I'm finished":** *KR*, 307.

54 **temporary people:** Ibid.

55 **"Our father is dead":** Vladimir Ashkenazy, quoted in Stuart Jeffries, "Back in the USSR," *Guardian*, November 8, 2002.

55 **Sviatoslav Richter:** For this episode, see Richter's recollections in Bruno Monsaingeon, *Sviatoslav Richter: Notebooks and Conversations* (London: Faber and Faber, 2001), 4–6, and in Bruno Monsaingeon's 1998 film *Richter, the Enigma*.

55 **two thousand died:** David Mayers, *The Ambassadors and America's Soviet Policy* (New York: Oxford University Press, 1995), 191.

56 **trumped-up charges:** A military panel of the Supreme Court of the USSR rehabilitated Teofil Rikhter in 1962.

57 **telephone number or apartment number:** Paul Moor, "Sviatoslav Richter: Sequestered Genius," *High Fidelity* 8, no. 10 (October 1958): 49–50.

57 **plastic lobster:** Monsaingeon, *Sviatoslav Richter*, 141.

58 **"And what a cruel—tragic—coincidence:"** Simon Morrison, *Lina and Serge: The Love and Wars of Lina Prokofiev* (Boston: Houghton Mifflin Harcourt, 2013), 271. Lina would be released in 1956, the year of Khrushchev's Secret Speech.

60 **"I did him in":** Chuev, *Molotov Remembers*, 237. Or so Molotov claimed; like the others, he had an interest in justifying Beria's execution.

60 **underage girls:** By one count, Beria had 760 mistresses, and for at least a few, his clammy embrace was the kiss of death. Larissa Vasilieva, *Kremlin Wives: The Secret Lives of the Women Behind the Kremlin Walls—From Lenin to Gorbachev*, trans. Cathy Porter (London: Weidenfeld and Nicolson, 1994), 185; Martin Sixsmith, *Russia: A 1,000-Year Chronicle of the Wild East* (London: BBC, 2011), 396.

60 **"We wiped our noses":** *KR*, 266.

60 **"Beria is getting his knives ready"** . . . **"What steps can we take":** *KM*, 189.

61 **meeting of the Presidium:** Khrushchev's account of the events (*KM*, 189–200) was for a long time the only source. Records subsequently came to light that prove it to be selective and occasionally misleading. Mark Kramer presents the evidence in "Leadership Succession and Political Violence in the USSR Following Stalin's Death," in *Political Violence: Belief, Behavior, and Legitimation*, ed. Paul Hollander (New York: Palgrave Macmillan, 2008), 69–92.

61 **"flung himself about the courtroom":** General Ivan Konev, the presiding judge at the trial, quoted in Tzouliadis, *Forsaken*, 313.

61 **got drunk and beat up the local militiaman:** Harrison E. Salisbury, "Russia Reviewed: Life of a Soviet Common Man Is a Constant Struggle," *NYT*, September 24, 1954.

62 **"not especially bright":** Mayers, *The Ambassadors*, 199.

62 **"rumbustious, impetuous . . . words of one syllable":** William Hayter, *A Double Life: The Memoirs of Sir William Hayter* (London: Penguin, 1974), 114.

62 **"For so long":** Olga Ivinskaya, *A Captive of Time: My Years with Pasternak*, trans. Max Hayward (London: Collins, 1978), 142.

4: VAN CLIBURN DAYS

63 **Rosemary Butts:** Tom Martin interviewed her; see TM1. She was then Mrs. Corwin C. Reeves, wife of a Texas Tech geology professor.

63 **fifteen hundred East Texans:** *VCL*, 54–55.

64 **check for six hundred dollars:** TM1.

64 **"East Texas Days":** On November 17 and 18, 1953. Pericles Alexander, "'East Texas Days' Named for Cliburn," *ST*, November 13, 1953; "Cliburn to Receive Honor," *KNH*, November 16, 1953.

64 **"seemed barely able":** *VCL*, 52.

64 **"After all . . . Texans are dumb":** Mark Schubart, quoted in SH.

65 **"I've never done this" . . . "hearing *about* him":** *VCL*, 58.

65 **Van was swept away:** Harlow Robinson, *The Last Impresario: The Life, Times, and Legacy of Sol Hurok* (New York: Viking, 1994), 333.

65 **overtures to Hurok:** In "American Sputnik," *Time*, April 28, 1958, Van revealed (probably not expecting it to be printed) that Hurok had passed him up. While still at Juilliard, he was confident enough to enter Hurok's name as his manager on his Placement File.

65 **"How good" . . . "even *he* knows":** *VCL*, 59.

66 **Rosalie Leventritt:** Gary Graffman provides a winning portrait of the belle of New York music in *I Really Should Be Practicing* (Garden City, NY: Doubleday, 1981), 147–49.

66 **"He's going to win":** Gary and Naomi Graffman, interview with the author, August 21, 2014. Except where indicated, my interview is the source for the following quotations from the Graffmans.

67 **Abram Chasins:** The former pianist and composer entertainingly recounts the episode in *VCL*, 24–27. The competition was held in March 1954; unaccountably, Chasins places it in the fall.

67 **"You won't forget to pray for me":** Ibid., 60.

68 **"He really loves music":** Ibid., 26.

68 **"May I explain":** Ibid.

68 **"Would y'all mahnd":** Graffman, *I Really Should Be Practicing*, 150.

68 **Van went home to the Spicers':** The following scenes are drawn from SH; *VCL*, 61–62; Wallace, *Century of Music-Making*, 271.

69 **Juilliard diploma recital:** The original program is in VCJA.

69 **"My best love to you, darling":** Van Cliburn to Rosina Lhévinne, January 13, 1954, Folder 20, Box 2, RLP.

69 **"I won't even try":** Van Cliburn to Rosina Lhévinne, June 16, 1955, Folder 20, Box 2, RLP.

70 **"Most promising student I have had"**: Folder 10, Box 27, RLP.

70 **Van was missing:** James Mathis recounts the story in *VC*, 72–73.

70 **surveyed the parterre:** The Graffmans' account is drawn from *I Really Should Be Practicing*, 151, and my interview with Gary and Naomi.

71 **"This is one . . . already been there"**: TM1. The same night Van's setting of Psalm 123, "Unto Thee I Lift Up Mine Eyes," premiered at Calvary Baptist Church.

72 **"that extraordinary guy"**: *VCL*, 66.

72 **Franz Liszt:** Ibid., quoting Donald Steinfirst's *Pittsburgh Post-Gazette* review.

72 **"Tear out this name"**: Ibid., 28. The review, in the *Denver Post*, was by Allen Young.

73 **"create on the whole globe"**: John Lewis Gaddis, *The Cold War* (London: Allen Lane, 2005), 59.

73 **strontium 90:** Boyer, *By the Bomb's Early Light*, 352–53.

73 **milk teeth:** Walter Schneir, "Strontium-90 in U.S. Children," *The Nation*, April 25, 1959.

74 **"Those who engage . . . government office"**: Elaine Tyler May, *Homeward Bound: American Families in the Cold War Era* (New York: Basic, 1999), 95.

74 **Donna Sanders:** The account of the relationship and Donna's remarks are found in her interview with *Time*'s Serrell Hillman; see SH.

74 *Arthur Godfrey Talent Scouts:* TM1.

75 **Buckingham Hotel:** Van's Juilliard Placement file gives his address as Buckingham Hotel, 101 West Fifty-Seventh Street, Apt 1104; according to Hillman's interview, Van had moved there by spring 1955.

75 **old gospel hymns:** *VCL*, 71.

75 **Jean Heafner:** SH contains her interview with Hillman.

76 **Mark Schubart, was gay:** Steve Swayne, *Orpheus in Manhattan: William Schuman and the Shaping of America's Musical Life* (New York: Oxford University Press, 2011), 62.

77 **listed the salaries:** "The Economic Situation of the Performer," quoted in Andrea Olmstead, *Juilliard: A History* (Urbana: University of Illinois Press, 1999), 164.

77 **$1,000 per performance:** *VCL*, 68.

77 **his parents' help:** VC-2159 (Reel no. 33), Van Cliburn interviewed by Peter Rosen, TCU.

78 **set about decorating:** SH; *VCL*, 68–69.

78 **pot roast sandwich:** *VCL*, 83.

78 **spent his lunch money on bouquets:** SH.

78 **"Would you call Van for me, please"**: Gary and Naomi Graffman, interview with the author; *I Really Should Be Practicing*, 312–13; James Barron, "Old Acquaintances Remember Cliburn," *NYT*, February 27, 2013.

78 **Naomi was feeling flush:** After Moscow, Van wrote her a check for one million dollars in repayment with interest for all the burgers. She did not cash it.

79 **went berserk:** Mary Russell Rogers, "A Midnight Conversation with Van Cliburn," *FWS-T*, May 18, 1997.

79 **Naomi Graffman . . . tailed him:** Interview with the author.

79 **help of a Juilliard classmate:** VCG.

80 **floating excerpts from Scripture:** By the end of 1954, the Bible Balloon Project had floated 30,000 balloons carrying 163,000 Bible texts into Russia, Poland, Hungary, East Germany, and Czechoslovakia from secret fields in West Germany.

80 **"the singing of a beautiful hymn"**: Dwight D. Eisenhower to Secretary of State,

memorandum, October 24, 1953; Eisenhower, Dwight D., Correspondence, 1953(1); Box 50, C. D. Jackson Papers, 1931–67; DDEPL.

80 **emergency presidential fund:** The President's Emergency Fund for Participation in International Affairs.

80 **made Ike's fund a permanent body:** The International Cultural Exchange and Trade Fair Participation Act of 1956. The previous year, the State Department asked for twenty-two million dollars, but the House Appropriations Committee reduced the figure by half.

80 **twelve orchestras:** Including NBC's Symphony of the Air, the Philadelphia Orchestra, the Boston Symphony, and the New York Philharmonic. Ten were approved but not used; thirty-eight were turned down.

80 **"showing the gang warfare":** MMP, February 19, 1958, Folder 5, Box 2, WSP.

81 **"We are not planning":** MMP, December 8, 1954, Folder 1, Box 2, WSP.

5: THE SECRET SPEECH

82 **"Stalin was a very distrustful man":** Robert Conquest, *The Great Terror: Stalin's Purge of the Thirties* (Harmondsworth: Penguin, 1971), 102.

84 **"horrifyingly empty eyes":** Richard Lourie, *Russia Speaks: An Oral History from the Revolution to the Present* (New York: E. Burlingame, 1991), 188.

84 **"guarding a temple":** Tzouliadis, *Forsaken*, 320.

84 **"Everyone who rejoices":** William Taubman, *Khrushchev: The Man and His Era* (New York: Norton, 2003), 96.

84 **exceeded his quota:** Ibid., 100.

86 **"the most destructive war in history":** J. P. D. Dunbabin, *International Relations Since 1945*, vol. 2, *The Cold War: The Great Powers and Their Allies* (London: Longman, 1994), 233.

86 **"the most dangerous person":** John Lewis Gaddis, *We Now Know: Rethinking Cold War History* (Oxford: Clarendon Press, 1997), 239.

86 **"The usually decorous elite":** Welles Hangen, "Boston Symphony Gets Standing Ovation at First Concert in Moscow Conservatory," *NYT*, September 9, 1956. That year the Metropolitan Opera also toured Europe with CIA money.

86 **"'Culture' is no longer a sissy word":** Saunders, *Who Paid the Piper?* 225.

86 **"reserved for criminals":** Elie Abel, "U.S. Twits Soviet on Its Own Fingerprinting Rules," *NYT*, June 2, 1956. The Moiseyev Dance Company finally made it to America while Van was competing in Moscow, thrilling audiences nationwide.

87 **"might be ready":** Dwight D. Eisenhower, *White House Years: Waging Peace, 1956–1961* (New York: Doubleday, 1965), 90.

88 **"not cucumbers":** "The New Line," *Time*, June 6, 1960.

89 **The showdown:** My reconstruction draws on *NKCS*, 228–47; Chuev, *Molotov Remembers*, 346–60; Avis Bohlen, "Khrushchev and the 'Anti-Party Group,'" working paper CAESAR XV, April 27, 1962, Office of Current Intelligence, CIA, foia.cia.gov/sites/default/files/document_conversions/14/caesar-30.pdf.

89 **"rightist deviation . . . Trotskyist and opportunist":** Bohlen, "Khrushchev and the 'Anti-Party Group,'" 18.

90 **"Only you are completely pure" . . . "Stalin's shit":** Montefiore, *Stalin*, 667–68.

90 **"You are young":** Bohlen, "Khrushchev and the 'Anti-Party Group,'" 23.

91 **World Festival of Youth and Students:** For its politics, see Pia Koivunen, "The

World Youth Festival as an Arena of the 'Cultural Olympics': Meanings of Competition in Soviet Culture in the 1940s and 1950s," in Katalin Miklóssy and Melanie Ilic, eds., *Competition in Socialist Society* (Milton Park, UK: Routledge, 2014), 125–41.

91 **CIA plants:** *TOML*, 175; John Prados, *Safe for Democracy: The Secret Wars of the CIA* (Chicago: Ivan R. Dee, 2006), 92–93. For the American contingent's experiences, see Max Frankel, "Voices of America in Moscow," *NYT*, August 11, 1957; Frankel, "Moscow Reality Cools U.S. Youth," *NYT*, July 30, 1957.

91 **Three million Muscovites:** William J. Jorden, "Gala Parade Opens Moscow Youth Fete," *NYT*, July 29, 1957.

92 **"Brodvay":** Harrison Salisbury, "'Lost Generation' Baffles Soviet; Nihilistic Youths Shun Ideology," *NYT*, February 9, 1962. In 1990 the street reverted to its original name, Ulitsa Tverskaya.

92 **"Why should anyone":** Harrison E. Salisbury, "Russia Reviewed: Life of Soviet Common Man Is a Constant Struggle," *NYT*, September 24, 1954.

92 **"like parrots":** "Soviet Youth Gets Lecture on Sloth," *NYT*, March 21, 1954.

92 **educated hooligans:** Harry Schwartz, "Hooligans Plague Schools in Soviet," *NYT*, April 16, 1954.

92 **"aristocrats and other loafers and hooligans":** Ibid. The speaker was Komsomol national secretary A. N. Shelepin; Malenkov and other top officials attended.

93 **"Today you're playing jazz":** As recalled by Lyuba Vinogradova.

93 **efforts to jam it:** By the late 1950s the Kremlin was spending more on jamming Western broadcasts than on domestic and international broadcasting combined.

93 **"told wild tales":** *TOML*, 164.

93 **one young Russian:** Alexander Osipovich, "Fifty Years Since Sax Hit the Soviet Union," *Moscow Times*, July 25, 2007.

93 **"Moscow Nights":** Vasily Solovyov-Sedoi and Mikhail Matusovsky wrote the song as "Leningradskie Vechera" (Leningrad Nights) in 1955; at the Ministry of Culture's behest, they rewrote it as "Podmoskovnye Vechera" (Evenings in Moscow Oblast).

94 **originated with the Union of Soviet Composers:** The sequence of events is unclear, but the idea seems to have been raised at the Second All-Union Congress of Soviet Composers held between March 28 and April 5, 1957; the Congress was delayed for a year to digest the upheaval of the Twentieth Party Congress and the Secret Speech, giving its doctrinaire leaders time to perform an about-face.

94 **made him feel sick:** Maya Plisetskaya, *I, Maya Plisetskaya*, trans. Antonia W. Bouis (New Haven, CT: Yale University Press, 2001), 181.

94 **arts spending:** The following figures are from Howard Taubman, "Challenge for U.S. Seen in Soviet Culture," *NYT*, July 4, 1958.

6: THE RED MOON

97 **"We are bringing you":** *The Sputnik Moment*, documentary film dir. David Hoffman, 2011, https://www.youtube.com/watch?v=GhJnt3xW2Fc.

98 **"REDS WIN SPACE RACE WITH MAN-MADE MOON":** *New York World-Telegram*, October 5, 1957.

98 **"SIGHT RED BABY MOON OVER US":** *Daily News* (New York), October 5, 1957.

98 **"ORB SPANS U.S. 7 TIMES A DAY":** Ibid., October 6, 1957.

98 **"What went wrong":** Charles Van Doren, video clip in *The Sputnik Moment*.

98 **"This is a weight":** Ibid.

98 **"slag heap":** Boyer, *By the Bomb's Early Light*, 14.

98 **"If Russia wins dominance":** Gen. Jimmy Doolittle, video clip in *The Sputnik Moment*.

98 **"In a masterpiece":** NBC radio, audio recording in *The Sputnik Moment*.

99 **"The time has clearly come":** Robert A. Divine, *The Sputnik Challenge* (New York: Oxford University Press, 1993), xvi.

100 **"Our *sputniks* are circling the world":** Nikita Khrushchev, video clip in *The Sputnik Moment*.

100 **growing crisis:** Many documents detailing the Eisenhower administration's response to *Sputnik* are accessible online via the Eisenhower Library at https://eisenhower.archives.gov/research/online_documents/sputnik.html.

100 **"OH WHAT A FLOPNIK":** *Daily Herald* (London), December 7, 1957.

100 **"KAPUTNIK," "DUDNIK," and "STAYPUTNIK":** Respectively *Daily Express*, *Christian Science Monitor*, and *News Chronicle*. The *NYT* recounted some of the international coinages in a December 8, 1957, article entitled "Enoughnik of This."

100 **"In 1957's twelve months":** *Time*, January 6, 1958. Altogether, Khrushchev would appear on the cover of *Time* nine times.

101 **Van was despondent:** Mark Schubart says so in SH; in the same dispatch, Schuyler Chapin claims that Van's career lull was deliberate policy on CAMI's part.

102 **"Wait and See":** Graffman, *I Really Should Be Practicing*, 97.

102 **"Ugh, I look so white":** VCL, 82.

103 **crossed the street:** As told to Howard Aibel by Rosina Lhévinne and recounted to the author.

103 **"Oh . . . The ocean":** SH. The same dispatch quotes Schulyer Chapin's account of Van's near drowning; Chasins gives a similar account in *VCL*, 73–74.

104 **Billy Graham's Crusade:** For the revival meetings, see Curtis Mitchell, *God in the Garden: The Story of the Billy Graham New York Crusade* (Garden City, NY: Doubleday, 1957); and Uta Andrea Balbier, "Billy Graham's Crusades in the 1950s: Neo-Evangelicalism Between Civil Religion, Media, and Consumerism," *Bulletin of the GHI* 44 (Spring 2009): 71–80.

104 **"master-minded by Satan":** Stephen J. Whitfield, *The Culture of the Cold War* (Baltimore, MD: Johns Hopkins University Press, 1991), 81.

104 **Jerome Lowenthal . . . met him:** Tim Madigan, "Van Cliburn: 'The Texan Who Conquered Russia,'" *FWS-T*, February 27, 2013.

104 **Doctors Hospital:** TM2.

105 **draft board evaluation:** Ibid.

105 **"He has won many awards":** MMP, October 17, 1956, Folder 3, Box 2, WSP.

105 **fear crept over him:** "I was at my lowest professional ebb," Van wrote in an article entitled "What Is Success?" in *Guideposts Magazine*, February 1959. "I had run up some sizeable debts, which my parents knew nothing about. The danger then was not to let fear overwhelm me."

105 **Olegna Fuschi:** The story is captured in Rosina Lhévinne's notes for an interview, Box 28, RPL. Rosina also records her instant reaction that Van was the only person she would encourage to go to Moscow, together with Van's response and her campaign to persuade him. Further details are given in *VCL*, 92, and *VC*, 92.

105 **Washington had vetoed it:** MMP, February 8, 1955, and January 17, 1956, Folders 2 and 3, Box 2, WSP.

105 **Fuschi was turned down:** MMP, May 22, 1957, Folder 2, Box 2, WSP.

106 **always reliable Emil Gilels:** Possibly Gilels was not as attuned to the Soviet regime as he appeared; see Norman Lebrecht, "The Secret Torments of Emil Gilels," December 31, 2010, http://slippedisc.com/2010/12/the_secret_torments_of_emil_gi/.

106 **"Van":** *VCL*, 92. The quotations in the following paragraph are from the same source.

107 **"You must go, Van":** VCG.

107 **"Oh Van, you must go":** Ibid.

107 **"But you can't *do* that, Rosina":** *VCL*, 95.

108 **"an agrarian country":** "American Sputnik."

108 **"The gold medal":** Rosina Lhévinne notes for an interview, Box 28, RLP.

108 **"Dear Van, I beg of you, *please* go":** *VCL*, 96.

108 **Schubart wrote to Van:** Letter of November 13, 1957, Folder 5, Box 14, JAD.

109 **He followed up with a letter:** Mark Schubart to David Wodlinger, November 15, 1957, Folder 5, Box 14, JAD.

109 **formal letter:** Mark Schubart to William Judd, December 10, 1957, Folder 5, Box 14, JAD.

109 **talented enough and willing to go:** Mark Schubart, in SH.

109 **"Take it":** *VC*, 94.

109 **Russian or Soviet composers:** For the semifinals, there was a choice of a prelude and fugue by Taneyev, Tchaikovsky-Catoire, Tchaikovsky, or Shostakovich; four pieces from a choice of sonatas by Russian or Soviet composers Alexandrov, Balakirev, Glazunov, Kabalevsky, Myaskovsky, Medtner, Prokofiev, Rachmaninoff, Scriabin, Shostakovich, or Mussorgsky's *Pictures at an Exhibition*; a movement from Tchaikovsky's Sonata in G Major or C-sharp Minor; and a work by a contemporary composer, preferably from the candidate's country.

110 **bided his time . . . until 1954:** In the *Washington Times* of August 21, 1994, Van is quoted as saying, "I began learning it in 1953, when I was 17, unbeknownst to Mrs. Lhévinne." But Van turned seventeen in July 1951. The same piece adds that he performed it for the first time "that summer with conductor Walter Hendl at the Chautauqua festival in New York." Yet Van played the Tchaikovsky B-flat Minor Concerto with the Chautauqua Orchestra on August 9, 1953, and Rachmaninoff's Third in summer 1954. Most likely he started working on the Rachmaninoff early in 1954, when he was nineteen, and performed it for the first time that summer, when he had just turned twenty.

110 **"I won't charge you now":** Martin Canin, interview with the author. Rosina's lodger and domestic helper, Fiorella Miotto, later married Canin, who was Rosina's assistant from 1959 to 1976.

110 **three, sometimes four or five hours:** Dowis, "Rosina: A Memoir," 373.

110 **"We have only three months":** *VCL*, 97.

110 **"Without hard work":** "'Vanya' Cliburn: Popular Does Not Mean Good," *Argumenty I Fakty* 39 (September, 2004). In the same interview, Van says that Rosina "forced" him to work nine to ten hours a day.

110 **"HAVE JUST MAILED MY APPLICATION":** This and the following cables and letters exchanged between Van and Shostakovich, together with Van's application materials, are preserved in Fonds 214, no. 20, GM.

111 **flare-up of colitis:** "All-American Virtuoso."

111 **convinced it was a fix:** My account of Liu Shikun's story is largely based on my interviews with him, conducted March 12 and 14, 2015. Liu claims he was the audience

favorite in Budapest from the start and that the organizing committee gave him a precious lock of Liszt's hair from the Liszt museum by way of an apology. The political currents are hard to untangle: Hungary was of course on the brink of an anti-Soviet revolution.

112 **all-union selection marathon:** The process is recounted in N. Mikhailov, "Report from the Ministry of Culture of the USSR on the Results of the Tchaikovsky International Piano and Violin Competition," April 22, 1958, *CCCP&C*, 55.

112 **Baku . . . Vilnius:** Betty Blair, "The Era of Van Cliburn," *Azerbaijan International* (Fall 1995), http://www.azer.com/aiweb/categories/magazine/33_folder/33_articles/33_vancliburn.html.

113 **Ashkenazy refused, too:** Vladimir Ashkenazy did not remember this episode when I interviewed him on September 3, 2014, but his refusal is recorded in Mikhailov's report in *CCCP&C*. After Van's sensational victory, some regretted their decision to cry off: violinist Eduard Grach entered the next competition in 1962, winning fifth prize.

113 **Lev Vlassenko:** My account is drawn from my interview with Lev's widow, Ella, conducted in Moscow on August 10, 2014, together with the collected reminiscences of Lev and others in *Lev Vlassenko: Articles, Reminiscences, Interviews* (Brisbane: Allstate Printing and Graphics, 2009), and *Lev Vlassenko: Grani lichnosti* (Moscow: Musyka, 2013).

113 **"Iron Lev":** Viktor Likht, "Shtarkman in the Memoirs of His Friends," *Zametki po Evreiskoi Istorii* 10 (October 2006), Internet publication.

113 **Hungarian students:** Tamás Vásáry, interview with the author, June 13, 2014. In the heated political atmosphere, Vásáry, quite against his nature, was the ringleader.

115 **"Oh, thank goodness . . . gelatin a day":** VCL, 98–99.

118 **State Department summoned Mark Schubart:** VC, 96–97.

118 **"Look . . . see if he can help":** *VCL*, 100.

119 **"Mrs. Leventritt . . . in my life":** SH.

119 **"I could tell":** Sid Friedlander, "He Played the Piano and the World Was His," *New York Post*, May 16, 1958.

119 **"I'm going to win":** Schuyler Chapin, quoted in SH.

120 **"The Army can do anything":** *Abilene Reporter-News*, February 12, 1958.

7: TO RUSSIA, WITH LOVE

123 **That was his first thought:** VCG; Alann Sampson, interview with the author, August 17, 2014. My account of Van's experiences in Moscow draws on dozens of interviews he gave on the subject for the rest of his life, in both the United States and the USSR/Russia. Specific references are given for quotations and unique or noteworthy details, but no attempt has been made to annotate every instance of authorial discretion in choosing among minor discrepancies and variants. Particularly useful were Peter Rosen's interview, cited as VCG; the reports of *Time* and the *NYT*; contemporary interviews in Soviet publications and press releases kept at the Tchaikovsky Museum in Klin; *VCL*; and *VC*. The documents reprinted in *CCCP&C* on pp. 41–59 are invaluable for a view from inside the Soviet government.

124 **subzero cold:** The weather conditions throughout Van's visit are taken from *Vechernyaya Moskva*, which published a daily forecast.

124 **Harriet Wingreen:** Interview with the author, May 13, 2014.

125 **boxy apartment buildings:** Dubbed *Khrushchyovka* and then *Khrushcheby* (a pun on *trushcheby*, or "slums"), the apartment buildings saw their drearily uniform design become the subject of endless Soviet jokes. In one 1975 movie, *Ironiya sudby, ili S lyogkim parom!* (The Irony of Fate, or Enjoy Your Bath!), an inebriated Muscovite wakes up at the airport, takes a taxi to his address, lets himself in with his key, and finds himself in familiar surroundings—until he realizes he took the plane to Leningrad by mistake.

126 **square of his childhood dreams:** "I feel as if I passed my childhood here, by the fantastic St. Basil's Cathedral, on the cobbles of the pavement among the pigeons," Van said in "Part of My Heart Is in Moscow," *Moskva* 11 (1962), 173.

127 **"ARRIVED SAFELY EVERYTHING WONDERFUL":** Quoted in a letter from Rildia Bee Cliburn to Rosina Lhévinne, March 26, 1958, Folder 19, Box 2, RLP.

127 **competition papers:** Fonds 96m, Nos. 79–80; 81–82; 159–60; 177–78; GM.

127 **nylon stocking:** "All-American Virtuoso."

128 **reports on him for the KGB:** This was simply taken for granted by everyone familiar with Soviet policy at the time. "In those days even the slightest detail was noted, and every word spoken by a guest was recorded," recalls Sergei Khrushchev in *NKCS*, 323. The interpreters are mostly remembered as charming people.

128 **KGB's official Moscow hotel:** Victor Cherkashin and Gregory Feifer, *Spy Handler: Memoir of a KGB Officer* (New York: Basic, 2005), 46.

128 **secret monitoring rooms:** Joy Neumeyer, "Poetry, Magic and Showgirls: The Story of Triumfalnaya Ploshchad," *Moscow News*, April 22, 2013.

128 **Hotel Ukraine:** Now the Radisson Royal. See Margarita Troitsina, "Secrets of Stalin's Seven Moscow Skyscrapers," *Pravda*, October 29, 2009.

128 **concealed microphones:** Norman Shetler, interview with the author, December 12, 2015.

128 **"Henya":** Sergei Dorensky, interview with Lyuba Vinogradova, July 17, 2014. Then a graduate student and assistant teacher who had won first prizes at competitions in Warsaw and Brazil, Dorensky was later a leading professor of piano at the conservatory.

129 **Daniel Pollack . . . the wrong pieces:** Pollack was studying at the Hochschule für Musik in Vienna; the professor responsible for the error was Bruno Seidelhofer. For his experiences in Moscow, see *VC*, 103–4; "Piano Pathways: Daniel Pollack, 50 Years Later," audio recording, *Weekend Edition*, NPR, Saturday, January 12, 2008, http://www.npr.org/templates/story/story.php?storyId=18026453; "Daniel Pollack and the First International Tchaikovsky Competition," USC Thornton press release, March 1, 2013, https://music.usc.edu/files/2013/06/Pollack_and_the_Tchaikovsky_Competition.pdf; "Interview with Daniel Pollack," bakitone.com/about/interview/daniel_pollack; "Interview with pianist Daniel Pollack," http://www.examiner.com/article/interview-with-pianist-daniel-pollack-part-i; Jeff Kaliss, "Daniel Pollack: From Russia with Love," https://www.sfcv.org/events-calendar/artist-spotlight/daniel-pollack-from-russia-with-love; Clifford J. Levy, "Piano Man, Winning Russian Hearts and Minds," *NYT*, May 29, 2009.

129 **Jerome Lowenthal:** Lowenthal, "Of Cortot, Kapell, Steuermann, and Preserving Musical Traditions," *Clavier* 41, no. 9 (November 2002); M. Uszler, "American Savoir-Faire: An Interview with Jerome Lowenthal," *Piano and Keyboard* no. 192 (May/June 1998).

129 **Norman Shetler:** Interview with the author. See also Moor, "Sviatoslav Richter:

Sequestered Genius," 49–51, 157–59. Shetler met Van in 1951 and enrolled in Juilliard to start in the fall of 1952, but he was drafted that summer and entered the army in October.

130 **"Welcome to Moscow":** *VCL*, 103; "Cliburn Finds Russian Music Lovers Sincere and Gracious" (UP), *Galveston Daily News*, April 18, 1958.

130 **competition in Lisbon:** The Vianna da Motta Competition, first organized in 1957 by Motta's protégé Sequeira Costa, who was subsequently the youngest judge for the Tchaikovsky Competition.

130 **queen of Belgium arrived:** See *The Queen Elisabeth of Belgium in the Soviet Union*, film dir. A. Rybakova, CSDF, 1958, net-film.ru/en/film-4919/; *Tchaikovsky Competition 1958*, youtube.com/watch?v=UeE4szjJQMk.

131 **Thorunn Johannsdottir:** Interview with the author, September 3, 2014. She performed under the name Thorunn Tryggvason.

132 **Soviet composer spread rumors:** Mikhailov, "Report from the Ministry of Culture," in *CCCP&C*, 51–52. Mikhailov insists the claims were pure slander.

133 **Twenty-five violinists:** The booklet of competitors' biographies, which was evidently prepared sometime before the start of the competition, lists twenty-nine violinists (twenty-four men and five women) and fifty pianists (thirty-one men and nineteen women). The final figures of twenty-five and thirty-six are given in Culture Minister Mikhailov's report in *CCCP&C*; the secretary of the jury confirms the number in S. Simonov, "On the International Piano Competition," *SM*, April 21, 1958. Abram Chasins's claim that forty-eight pianists took part suggests that the contestants themselves were unaware of the actual number.

133 **three Americans:** Evidently they were expected until the last minute; the *NYT* reported on March 25, 1958, that eight American musicians were to compete in Moscow.

133 **Six were excused:** In "On the International Piano Competition," Simonov, the jury secretary, says thirty contestants took part in the preliminary stage. Pollack had won first prize in the little-known Guild Record Festival; Lowenthal had won second prize, behind Martha Argerich and jointly with Texas pianist Ivan Davis, in the Ferruccio Busoni International Piano Competition held in Bolzano in 1957. (Jeaneane Dowis took third prize; the previous year, James Mathis had come third and Ivan Davis second; and in 1960, Mathis tried again and improved to second place.) Roger Boutry of France and Alexei Skavronsky of the Soviet Union were also excused during the first round.

133 **twelve judges from the Soviet Bloc:** Seven were from the Soviet Union: Gilels, Richter, Neuhaus, Oborin, and Kabalevsky, together with the Ukrainian composer Boris Lyatoshinsky and the pianist Pavel Serebryakov, whom Olegna Fuschi had met in Brazil. Also from the Soviet Bloc were the Bulgarian composer Pancho Vladigerov, the Romanian conductor George Georgescu, and pianists František Maxián (Czechoslovakia), Lajos Hernádi (Hungary), and Henryk Sztompka (Poland). The five remaining judges were Bliss, the Brazilian composer Camargo Guarnieri, the Belgian conductor Fernand Quinet, the French pianist Armand de Gontaut-Biron, and the Portuguese pianist José Carlos de Sequeira Costa. The last two replaced three who withdrew after the competition materials had been printed—Joseph Marx (Austria), Carlo Zecchi (Italy), and Marguerite Long (France)—making the total seventeen rather than the intended eighteen.

134 **French-kissing:** Norman Shetler, interview with the author.

134 **"LOVE AND THOUGHTS":** Van Cliburn telegram to Rosina Lhévinne, Folder 20, Box 2, RLP.

134 **voice of Russia itself:** Van recalled the episode numerous times, most evocatively in "Nobody Dares Speak Badly of Russia in Front of Me," *Trud*, September 18, 2009.

135 **Baptist, Methodist, and Presbyterian:** TMI.

136 **Smiles broke out:** For the impact of Van's appearance, see E. Gobrynina, "New Meetings with Van Cliburn," *Muzykalnaya Zhizn* 13 (1962), 16–17. Van remembered his own reactions most clearly in "Winners of the Competition Speak," *SM*, May 1958.

136 **four études:** Chopin's "Winter Wind," op. 25, no. 11; Scriabin's Op. 8 in D-sharp Minor; Rachmaninoff's "Étude-Tableau" in E-flat Minor, op. 39; and Liszt's "Mazeppa."

137 **tears glistened:** Arthur Shtilman, "In that memorable April: Fifty years ago—the triumph of Van Cliburn in Moscow," *Jewish Heritage Almanac* 2, no. 55 (March/April 2008), http://berkovich-zametki.com/2008/Starina/Nomer2/Shtilman1.htm.

138 **resented Richter's first rank:** Monsaingeon, *Sviatoslav Richter*, 31–32; Elena Cheremynch, interview with the author, August 11, 2004.

138 **denying he had ever been his student:** The issue is still controversial; the Emil Gilels Foundation claims that Neuhaus treated Gilels badly. Certainly Richter was a tricky character.

138 **missing one morning session:** Norman Shetler, interview with the author. My account of Richter's and Neuhaus's behavior on the committee draws on work by Elena Cheremynch, who examined the original records in detail. Also useful were Monsaingeon, *Sviatoslav Richter*; Rasmussen, *Sviatoslav Richter*; VC.

138 **"poor man's Prokofiev":** Monsaingeon, *Sviatoslav Richter*, 56.

138 **"deeply unpleasant . . . threadbare music":** Ibid.

138 **ganged up on the composer Nikita Bogoslovsky:** *CCCP&C*, 62.

139 **"I don't like this" . . . "speaking with God":** Sergei Dorensky, interview with Lyuba Vinogradova.

139 **full twenty-five points:** Evaluation papers for Van Cliburn for the three stages of the First International Tchaikovsky Competition, F.45, dm16No184/6, 33–64, SHM. This and subsequent marks are taken from the original slips held at the Tchaikovsky Museum; the Glinka Museum also has tabulated results from the second round.

139 **Twenty competitors:** The *New York Times* ran a brief AP piece, "U.S. Pianists Advance," on April 5, but as yet there was no notice that anything unusual was afoot.

139 **never took students:** Richter never heard Shetler play, since he was absent on the first day of the preliminary round. The two did, though, stay in touch, exchanging Christmas cards and taking walks in Central Park when Richter visited New York.

140 **admitted as much to Norman Shetler:** Interview with the author.

140 **lost her temper:** Ibid.

141 **"Hello, I'm Slava Rostropovich":** Van related the story in "Nobody Dares Speak Badly of Russia in Front of Me."

141 **"I have walked":** Undated press release, Tchaikovsky Competition Album, F.45, dm4No292/74, SHM.

142 **"No tickets left":** *VCL*, 105.

8: "VANYA, VANYUSHA!"

143 **Victory taxis:** The GAZ M-20 "Podeba" was produced in Gorky (Nizhny Novgorod) from 1946 to 1958 and was ubiquitous at state-run taxicab ranks.

144 **childhood sweetheart, Tamara:** Tamara Miansarova, "Shag dlinoyu v zhizn," *Karavan Istoriy*, January 2013.

145 **a Westerner could not win:** Norman Shetler, interview with the author.

145 **knocked him out flat:** "Van Cliburn At Home," *Ogonyok* 24 (1958), 29.

145 **hair cream:** "All-American Virtuoso."

145 **almost unrecognizable:** Shtilman, "In That Memorable April."

146 **members of the jury were applauding:** A. Zolotov, untitled article, *Moskovsky Komsomolets*, April 1958.

146 **told the press officers:** Undated press release, Tchaikovsky Competition Album, F.45, dm4No292/74, SHM.

146 **Flier, hid:** Vlassenko, *Lev Vlassenko*, 75.

146 **"nothing but golden monsters":** *VCL*, 120.

147 **"Is it true":** Ella Vlassenko, interview with the author.

147 **private capacity:** Minutes of meeting held February 7, 1958, JABT.

147 **"Is this kid" . . . "ever let him":** Madigan, "'The Texan Who Conquered Russia.'"

147 **"second or third":** *VCL*, 107.

148 **"Come on" . . . "if I'd let him":** Mark Schubart, quoted in SH.

148 **"chosen one":** *VC*, 108.

148 **"Why do you do this" . . . "music or not music":** Ibid. Reich places the scene in the first round, quoting the information of the pianist Andrei Gavrilov (born in 1955 but later a student of Richter's) that Richter was disgusted by the judges' attempt to mark down Van and mark up other contestants, especially Vlassenko, so he gave Van full marks and the rest zero. Vlassenko did not appear in the first round, in which Richter gave no candidate zero. He debuted in the second round, in which Richter gave all but seven competitors zero, and the episode must be placed here.

148 **"individualism":** Monsaingeon, *Sviatoslav Richter*, 56.

148 **other members of the jury protested:** *CCCP&C*, 52.

148 **"first international competition":** Monsaingeon, *Sviatoslav Richter*, 56.

148 **in part by Richter himself:** Richter claimed to Monsaingeon that he had given zeros to all but three others; he boasted that he acted deliberately in order "to eliminate the others and leave only Van." Ibid., 56–57.

149 **zeros were later crossed out:** Elena Cheremynch, who made a detailed study of the sheets, led me to this interesting detail. It explains the discrepancy between Culture Minister Mikhailov's report (*CCCP&C*, 52), which mentions the zeros, and the Glinka Museum's tabulation of the second-round scores, which records the threes.

149 **field of finalists:** See "2 U.S. Pianists in Final" (AP), *NYT*, April 10, 1958.

150 **slept with it under their pillows:** Maria Lvova, interview with the author, August 8, 2014.

150 **"He reminds me of my son":** Madigan, "'The Texan Who Conquered Russia.'"

151 **snapped him in the act:** Moor's photographs appeared in *Life* on April 28; his report was the basis for *Time*'s cover story on Van published on May 19. This scene is reconstructed from both.

151 **involved with the composer Aaron Copland:** Howard Pollack, *Aaron Copland: The Life and Work of an Uncommon Man* (Urbana and Chicago: University of Illinois Press, 1999), 245.

151 **Mrs. Lillian Reid:** "Writer for *Time* Plans El Paso Visit," *El Paso Herald-Post*, July 28, 1958.

151 **pupil of Arthur Friedheim:** "A Letter from the Publisher," *Time*, May 19, 1958.

151 **His right index finger was bandaged:** *VC*, 113.

152 **Harriet Wingreen:** Harriet had left with Joyce Flissler on a tour that was intended to take in Leningrad, Kiev, Riga, and Odessa, but the violinist fell ill in Leningrad, and the tour was canceled.

152 **poor French girl:** Nadia Gedda Nova, whose rehearsal Van had admired. Moor, "Sviatoslav Richter: Sequestered Genius," 51.

152 **"shy boy":** N. Mikhailov, "I'm Going to Miss Russia," *Komsomolskaya Pravda*, May 18, 1958.

153 **transported back centuries:** Van told former Cliburn Foundation president Richard Rodzinski that he visualized the Tchaikovsky concerto as an opera, with the libretto and singers' parts worked out, and staged it in his mind as he played; interview with the author, June 27, 2014. Van described the imaginary scenes in Wayne Lee Gay, "Cliburn's Tour Includes Old Russian Friends," *Washington Sunday Times*, August 21, 1994.

154 **as he had never played in his life:** Van thought so, too. "I genuinely felt at that moment that God's blessing had descended upon me," he recalled nearly a half century later. "I played like I never did again in my life." "'Vanya' Cliburn: Popular Does Not Mean Good."

154 **one-act opera:** The view is ascribed to Van in "The Reluctant Virtuoso," *Time*, July 25, 1994.

155 **"Just like Rachmaninoff":** Madigan, "'The Texan Who Conquered Russia.'"

155 **"Genius! Genius!":** "Texan in Moscow," *Time*, April 21, 1958. Max Frankel also recorded Goldenweiser's comment in "Russians Cheer U.S. Pianist, 23," *NYT*, April 12, 1958.

156 **"Oh my dear boy":** *CCCP&C*, 47.

156 **cordons collapsed:** So recalled the pianist Alexander Slobodyanik in *VC*, 118.

156 **"We were mistaken":** "'Vanya' Cliburn: Popular Does Not Mean Good."

157 **students had already written in "VAN CLIBURN":** The usual version is that Van's name had been added in large letters in a single hand, but Nina Lelchuk, who was present, recalled that many students wrote his name in. "Chudo po imeni Van Klaybern: Na smert Van Klayberna," *Sem iskusstv* 5, no. 43 (May 2013), 7iskusstv.com/2013/Nomer5/Leichuk1.php.

157 **hushed up:** *VC*, 118; and Vladimir Ashkenazy, interview with the author. Ashkenazy still rates Van's performance of Rachmaninoff's Piano Concerto no. 3 as the greatest he has heard.

157 **piano-mad schoolgirls:** Elena Klepikova, "Triumf i molchanie Vana Kliburna" (Triumph and Silence of Van Cliburn), *Russkiy Bazar*, April 17, 2008, http://russian-bazaar.com/ru/content/12287.htm.

157 **Tanya Kryukova:** F.45, dm16No185/62, SHM. On the top of the envelope (no. 63) Kryukova wrote, "Quick, quick, quick!!!"

157 **maid at a Moscow institution:** Shtilman, "In That Memorable April."

158 **"fourteen year old boy":** Heinrich Neuhaus, untitled article, *SK*, July 7, 1960.

158 **"whatever your soul tells you":** Ibid.

9: "WE ARE IN ORBIT"

159 **Max Frankel:** For his lively account of his three-year posting in Moscow, see *TOML*, 147–88.

160 **Glavlit:** The "Main-Lit" agency was the Soviet government's censorship vehicle and also monitored domestic publications.

160 **"boyish-looking":** Frankel, "Russians Cheer U.S. Pianist, 23."

161 **long dispatch marked "URGENT—SECRET":** "Report from the Deputy Minister of Culture of the USSR S.V. Kaftanov on Awarding the First Prize at the Tchaikovsky Competition to the American Pianist Van Cliburn," April 12, 1958, reprinted in *CCCP&C*, 47–48.

162 **"That's good playing":** Ella Vlassenko, interview with the author.

163 **clenched up:** Kirill Kondrashin, "An Extremely Hard Competition," *SK*, April 16, 1958.

163 **by common consensus, fared less well:** Ibid.

163 **"Apart from brilliant musical gifts":** Ibid.

164 **spoke to . . . Mikhailov, who . . . went to Khrushchev:** Sergei Dorensky, interview with Lyuba Vinogradova. Dorensky is the source for the following exchange; see also *VC*, 117.

164 **While he was in Hungary:** Van more than once remembered that Khrushchev had been in Romania, but records confirm that he was in Hungary April 2–10. Nikita Khrushchev, *Memoirs of Nikita Khrushchev*, ed. Sergei Khrushchev, vol. 3, *Statesman* (University Park: Pennsylvania State University Press, 2007), 1013.

164 **pushed back to the following afternoon:** Contestant Guide, Fonds 96m, Nos. 159–60, GM; undated press release, Tchaikovsky Competition Album, F.45, dm4No292/74, SHM.

165 **"Van, you've won . . . conservatory now":** *VCL*, 112.

165 **strode up to the piano:** The episode is described in E. Gobrynina, "Once Again in Moscow," *Muzykalnaya Zhizn* 12 (1960), 12–13. See also *VCL*, 112–13.

166 **"Van's won":** *VCL*, 113.

166 **"WE ARE IN ORBIT":** Ibid.

166 **New York Times front page:** This and the next two pieces ran on April 14. See also "Texas Pianist Wins in Moscow Over Reds" (AP), *New York Herald Tribune*, April 14, 1958; William J. Jorden, "Fruitful Exchanges: Triumph of U.S. Pianist in Moscow Provides Lessons in Building Goodwill," *NYT*, April 17, 1958.

167 **Allen Spicer stared wonderingly:** SH.

167 **Dulles ordered officers to report:** Dulles to Moscow embassy, telegram, April 15, 1958; Box 2182, RG59, NACP.

167 **KGB . . . FBI:** Khrushchev later told Van that the Soviets had been watching him: see chapter 18. The FBI's interest in Van began before his return from Moscow, and he soon became aware that agents were interviewing his friends; see chapter 15.

168 **leaked to the American press:** See for example *Gazette and Daily* (York, PA), April 15, 1958.

168 **"use his good offices":** *VC*, 119.

168 **"if I go in one day":** "All-American Virtuoso.

10: "AMERICAN SPUTNIK"

169 **gone to sleep:** Harriet Wingreen, interview with the author.

169 **devotees swarmed over:** "'Vanya' Cliburn: Popular Does Not Mean Good"; Ellen Barry, "Basking in Russia's Love Long After a Musical Triumph," *NYT*, July 1, 2011; "Kilgore Pianist Rests After Wooing Moscow" (AP), *ST*, April 13, 1958; *VCL*, 118.

170 **"So Cliburn didn't win":** Shtilman, "In That Memorable April."

170 **"Dear comrades and guests":** Undated press release, Tchaikovsky Competition Album, F.45, dm4No292/74, SHM. The ceremony can be seen in Soviet newsreel footage: http://www.britishpathe.com/video/festival-of-tchaikowsky-music/.

171 **"What is your father":** Van recalls the conversation in *VC*, 125.

171 **"Money doesn't mean anything to me":** "Word Leaks Out: Kilgore Pianist Wins Moscow Contest" (UP), *ST*, April 14, 1958.

171 **basking in the attention:** Max Frankel, "U.S. Pianist Plays for Soviet Chiefs," *NYT*, April 15, 1958.

171 **Paul Moor snapped him:** *Life*, April 28, 1958.

171 **Norman Shetler watched Moor:** Interview with the author.

172 **"Oh it's you":** *VC*, 125; Harriet Wingreen, interview with the author.

172 **"Have you heard the news":** "Word Leaks Out."

172 **"Honey, she already knows":** VCG. There are several variants on this story. In the same interview, Van says he called home after the ceremony; Chasins has him call directly upon hearing of his victory, which seems unlikely, as he was urgently required at the conservatory for the filming session and not even fame could work miracles with the international calling system.

172 **"But I'll be taking you":** VCG; "Nobody Dares Speak Badly of Russia in Front of Me."

173 **"Khrushchev is here":** VCG.

173 **"Why are you so tall":** The conversation was widely reported in the American press on April 15 and is reprinted in *VCL*, 114–15.

174 **"I was listening to you":** In an interview with *Trud*, Van quoted Khrushchev as saying, "Vanya, I listened to the second round of the competition on the radio, and I loved Chopin's F minor Fantasy in your performance." Van also recalled to Tim Madigan and Peter Rosen that Khrushchev said he had heard him playing the Chopin Fantasy on the radio, though not where, and he told *Argumenty I Fakty* that Khrushchev had heard him playing on the radio, though not what. In an interview with Paul Holdengräber, Van said that Khrushchev heard the Fantasy on the radio while in Romania. However, Abram Chasins reports Khrushchev as saying, "I have heard so much about your wonderful interpretation and wonderful playing of the Chopin F minor Fantasy . . . I love that work, and I am disappointed I didn't get to hear it in the second preliminary." And James Roos quotes Van as saying, "[Khrushchev] told me, 'I'm so sorry I didn't get to hear you in the semifinals. My daughter was there, and she told me what a beautiful performance you played of the Fantaisie in F Minor of Chopin. It's one of my favorite pieces.'" As previously noted, Khrushchev was in Hungary, not Romania, at the time, but it is impossible to establish whether he heard Van. "Nobody Dares Speak Badly of Russia in Front of Me"; Tim Madigan, "Van Cliburn: Mementos of the Musician," *FWS-T*, May 13, 2012; VCG; "'Vanya' Cliburn: Popular Does Not Mean Good"; Van Cliburn interviewed by Paul Holdengräber; *VCL*, 115; James Roos, "Stalled Van," *Times-Picayune* (New Orleans), April 24, 1983.

175 **Shostakovich opened the session:** The order of events and transcriptions of speeches are taken from "Winners of the International Tchaikovsky Competition," undated press release, Tchaikovsky Competition Album, F.45, dm4No292/74, SHM.

175 **guilty and discomposed:** VCG.

176 **drop of bad taste:** Heinrich Neuhaus, untitled article, *SK*.

176 **called him a genius:** M. Teroganyan, "Yesterday at Cliburn's Concert," *SK*, June 4, 1960.

176 **"competition has demonstrated":** "Winners of the Competition Speak."

176 **through a back door:** Mark Schubart, "Moscow Rolls Out Red Carpet," *NYT*, April 20, 1958. Another time, says Schubart, the crowds were so great that he was unable to leave at all.

177 **"Now you really have a sputnik":** Frankel, "U.S. Pianist Plays for Soviet Chiefs."

177 **"American Sputnik, developed in secret":** "American Sputnik."

177 **"Why did you let":** Ella Vlassenko, in *Lev Vlassenko*: Articles, 8.

177 **"Great man":** Liu Shikun, interview with the author.

178 **eagerly questioned Liu:** "Winners of the Competition Speak."

178 **"with grave courtesy":** "American Sputnik."

178 **"You've been a very good politician":** "Cliburn Continues as Toast of Soviet," *NYT*, April 16, 1958.

178 **"Here we are without a round table":** Ibid.

178 **"I really don't care for any":** "American Sputnik."

178 **Belgian queen left for home:** "Reception at the Chairman of the Presidium of the Supreme Soviet of the USSR K.Y. Voroshilov in Honor of the Belgian Queen Elisabeth," undated press release, Tchaikovsky Competition Album, F.45, dm4No292/74, SHM.

178 **about to be arrested:** Norman Shetler, interview with the author.

178 **telegrams and letters:** Quoted in "Let the Tchaikovsky Competition Play as a Joyful Anthem of Peace and Friendship," undated press release, Tchaikovsky Competition Album, F.45, dm4No292/74, SHM.

179 **piece for *Pravda*:** Published April 20. "Shostakovich Hails Cliburn's Success," *NYT*, April 21, 1958.

179 **workable spin:** See also M. Sokolsky, "Fame That Was Born in Moscow," *Sovetskaya Rossiya*, May 31, 1958.

179 **"*better* than Rachmaninoff's":** "All-American Virtuoso."

180 **"I dwell on these points":** Simonov, "On the International Piano Competition."

180 **leading critic:** Z. Vartanyan, quoted in "Hero's Return," *Time*, June 2, 1958. See also Howard Taubman, "Soviet Assesses Cliburn Victory," *NYT*, May 23, 1958.

180 **lengthy report:** Mikhailov, "Report from the Ministry of Culture," *CCCP&C*, 50–57.

180 **"erroneous behavior":** Ibid., 52.

180 **wanting to begin lessons:** Donald J. Raleigh, *Soviet Baby Boomers: An Oral History of Russia's Cold War Generation* (Oxford: Oxford University Press, 2012), 124. Some children forced into piano lessons by their parents were none too pleased.

181 **crowded into the small house:** Annette Morgan, quoted in Brittani Pfau, "Van Cliburn Dies at 78," *The Flare* (Kilgore College), March 1, 2013. Morgan took piano lessons with Rildia Bee from 1952 to 1962.

181 **"The best single word . . . lower middle class":** TM2.

181 **"so overwhelmed with joy":** "Word Leaks Out."

181 **regular church prayer meeting:** Annette Morgan, quoted in *VC*, 128.

181 **eighty acres around Moody:** TM2.

181 **"That's one of the things":** Ibid.

182 **"borrowed from time to time . . . left to be paid":** Ibid.

182 **compared Van to Marilyn Monroe:** SH.

182 **Mrs. Steve Roland:** Donna and Steve married in March 1956 and divorced in 1965.

Her stage career, which never progressed beyond a few musicals, in which her husband also had parts, ended at the same time. She remarried and died in 2001.

182 **nosed around Juilliard:** Mark Schubart to Patricia Berman, May 14, 1958, Folder 5, Box 14, JAD.

182 **"ALL OF US":** William Schuman to Van Cliburn, April 15, 1958, Folder 16, Box 2, JAP.

183 **"The biggest problem":** William Schuman to Mark Schubart, April 17, 1958, Folder 16, Box 3, The Joseph W. Polisi: William Schuman Research Papers, JA.

183 **a friend phoned:** *VCL*, 119.

183 **"I am afraid":** Schuman to Schubart, April 17, 1958. Chasins (*VCL*, 114) suggests that Schuman (and Rosina) got through to Van in Moscow, but this letter makes it clear that they failed to reach him.

183 ***Steve Allen Show***: Val Adams, "Cliburn Is Signed by Allen TV Show," *NYT*, April 25, 1958; Jack Gould, "TV: Van Cliburn Plays," *NYT*, May 26, 1958.

184 **"Georgie":** Gary and Naomi Graffman, interview with the author. Judd was sitting on the Graffmans' floor when he made the call. George Judd Jr. became managing director of the New York Philharmonic in 1959 but died at thirty-six of stomach cancer in 1961.

184 **"I want Kondrashin":** *VC*, 144.

184 **booked to tour Bulgaria:** Sound Recording 306-EN-G-T-5781, "Van Cliburn Washington Press Conference," May 23, 1958, RG 306, NACP.

184 **Judd called the State Department:** "Proposed United States Tour of Van Cliburn with Soviet Conductor," Memorandum of Conversation, April 17, 1958, Box 2182, RG 59, NACP.

11: THE LAST ROMANTIC

185 **flowers arrived from Khrushchev's wife:** "All-American Virtuoso."

185 **confided to an embassy official:** Richard H. Davis to Department of State, "Chaikovsky International Violin and Piano Competition: Success of American Pianist, Van Cliburn," dispatch, April 24, 1958; Box 4060, RG 59, NACP.

185 **"PLEASE DELIVER FOLLOWING TO PIANIST":** Dulles to Moscow embassy, telegram, April 15, 1958, Box 2182, RG 59, NACP.

185 **"DEAR MR. AMBASSADOR":** Dulles to Moscow embassy, telegram, April 16, 1958, Box 2182, RG 59, NACP.

186 **Tommy Thompson . . . wrote:** Thompson to secretary of state, telegram, April 17, 1958, Box 2182, RG59, NACP.

186 **Van quickly composed a reply:** Thompson cabled the State Department with the text of Van's letter:

Dear Mr. President:

I am most grateful for the message which you conveyed to me through Ambassador Thompson and it will be with great pleasure that I accept your invitation to call upon you and Mrs. Eisenhower at the White House upon my return to the United States. Signed Van Cliburn.

Thompson to secretary of state, April 18, 1958, Box 2182, RG 59, NACP.

186 **two hundred rubles a minute:** Davis to State, "Chaikovsky International Violin and Piano Competition."

186 **holy relic:** Yuri Okov, "It's a Pity to Leave Russia . . ." *SK*, May 17, 1958.

186 **made a pilgrimage:** Davis to State, "Chaikovsky International Violin and Piano

Competition." The trip took place on April 17. The often-repeated story that though Tchaikovsky's piano was played only on his birthday, the day was exceptionally moved forward several weeks for Van's benefit is spoiled by the fact that newsreel footage shows Klimov's accompanist playing it, too. See http://www.britishpathe.com/video/winners-of-tchaikovsky-competition-visit-the-comp/.

187 **"I really don't think I'm in a daze":** Moor, "Sviatoslav Richter: Sequestered Genius." The concert was on Wednesday, April 16.

187 **"a word . . . I do not use lightly about performers":** "All-American Virtuoso."

187 **Van cried again:** Ibid.

187 **"wildly pushing crowd":** "Moscow Again Hails Cliburn" (AP), *NYT*, April 19, 1958. Van's performance of the Rachmaninoff is preserved in volume 3 of *Van Cliburn in Moscow*, video recording, Video Artists International, 2008, DVD.

187 **nearly derailed:** Thompson to secretary of state, telegram, April 16, 1958; Dulles to Moscow embassy, telegram, April 16, 1958, Box 2182, RG 59, NACP. See also Davis to State, "Chaikovsky International Violin and Piano Competition."

188 **returning to Vienna:** In October, Pollack was welcomed back to the United States with a draft call; January 1959 found him a private at Fort Dix, New Jersey, serving in the six-month Army Reserve program. Ross Parmenter, "World of Music: Cash and Sherry," *NYT*, January 11, 1959.

188 **"I said to Mr. Khrushchev":** Madigan, "'The Texan Who Conquered Russia.'"

188 **"Because of his immaturity":** Thompson to secretary of state, telegram, April 16, 1958, Box 2182, RG 59, NACP.

188 **"There are no political barriers":** *Brownsville Herald*, April 18, 1958; et al.

189 **"Among Moscow teenagers":** Davis to State, "Chaikovsky International Violin and Piano Competition."

189 **schoolgirl who had watched his finals:** Klepikova, "Triumf i molchanie."

189 **others openly wept:** "All-American Virtuoso."

189 **pilgrimage to Tchaikovsky's grave:** Ibid.; "Cliburn in Salute to Rachmaninoff," *NYT*, June 1, 1958. The grave was not at Klin, as Chasins suggests (*VCL*, 121).

189 **called Rildia Bee:** Fredrickson, "Van Cliburn Remembers His Remarkable Mother."

190 **"NEW YORK AGENTS":** Herter to Moscow embassy, telegram, April 21, 1958, Box 2182, RG 59, NACP.

190 **he explained:** Thompson to secretary of state, telegram, April 22, 1958, Box 2182, RG 59, NACP.

190 **"DEPARTMENT HAS RECEIVED REPORT THAT MANAGER":** Herter to Davis, telegram, May 9, 1958, Box 2182, RG59, NACP.

191 **J. Edgar Hoover:** R. R. Roach to A. H. Belmont, memorandum, "Van Clibern [*sic*]— Internal Security," May 8, 1958, FBI (FOIA).

191 **"would play it very cautiously from now on":** A. H. Belmont to L. V. Boardman, memorandum, "Van Clibern [*sic*] Internal Security," May 9, 1958, FBI (FOIA). Hagerty's identity, redacted from the previous file, is confirmed here.

191 **his embassy day:** Van explained this sequence of events at a press conference held at Steinway Hall on his return to New York. Sound Recording 306-EN-G-T-5703, "Van Cliburn Press Conference," May 19, 1958, RG 306, NACP.

191 **lengthy telegram:** Davis to secretary of state, May 12, 1958, Box 2182, RG 59, NACP.

192 **pink floral telegrams:** *Daily Courier* (Connellsville, PA), June 24, 1958.

192 **Faculty for History and Philology:** F.45, dm16No185/76, SHM.

192 **Faculty of Soil Science:** F.45, dm16No185/39, SHM.

192 **forestry engineer . . . geographer:** F.45, dm16No185/74, 93, SHM.

192 **"Soviet telegraph operators":** F.45, dm16No185/60, SHM.

192 **"tearful verses":** F.45, dm16No185/14, 72, SHM.

192 **"Vanyusha my dear":** "'Vanya' Cliburn: Popular Does Not Mean Good."

192 **"You set our hearts on fire":** F.45, dm16No185/28, SHM.

192 **"How hard it is going to be to say good-bye":** F.45, dm16No185/88, SHM.

192 **"to all honest Americans":** F.45, dm16No185/86, SHM.

193 **"living in this nasty place":** F.45, dm16No185/37, SHM.

193 **"I would like to express":** F.45, dm16No185/41, SHM.

193 **"Look at it in your bad moments":** *VCL*, 143.

193 **"I tell you":** "All-American Virtuoso."

193 **"Oh sure," Van thought:** *VC*, 147.

193 **Central Music School:** Olesya Larchenko and Lena Varvarova to Van Cliburn, Moscow, October 1959, Folder 23, Box 9, RLP.

194 **half past five in the morning:** *VC*, 143.

194 **"We have something for you":** Ibid., 144–45.

194 **message in Russian:** Mikhailov, "I'm Going to Miss Russia."

194 **perform in America:** *VCL*, 127.

194 **"Today," he ended:** Shtilman, "In That Memorable April."

195 **next day they talked:** *VC*, 146.

195 **reporter for *Sovetskaya Kultura*:** Okov, "It's a Pity to Leave Russia . . ."

195 **fourteen extra suitcases, and one six-foot lilac shrub:** "People," *Time*, May 28, 1958. See also "Cliburn Leaves Soviet" (AP), *NYT*, May 16, 1958.

195 **4,800 rubles:** Sound Recording 306-EN-G-T-5781, "Van Cliburn Washington Press Conference," May 23, 1958, RG 306, NACP.

196 **Khrushchev allegedly ordered his death:** David Pryce-Jones, "What the Hungarians Wrought: The Meaning of October 1956," *National Review*, October 23, 2006.

196 **tit-for-tat revenge:** Harry Schwartz, "Why Soviet Is Taking Tougher Line," *NYT*, June 22, 1958.

12: "HE PLAYED THE PIANO AND THE WORLD WAS HIS"

197 **"He Played the Piano and the World Was His":** *New York Post*, May 16, 1958.

197 **missed his connection to New York:** Ibid. Van had been due to connect with SAS Flight 921 from Copenhagen, arriving New York 5:55, May 16. See Davis to secretary of state, telegram, May 13, 1958, Box 2182, RG 59, NACP.

197 **telephone interview:** TASS, "Van Cliburn in New York," *SK*, May 17, 1958.

198 **"Oh . . . you're the one:** *VC*, 148.

199 **photographers came running:** Video Recording 200-UN-31–40, "Universal Newsreel" 31, no. 40, May 19, 1958; MCA/Universal Pictures Collection, 1929–1967; NACP.

199 **shouting questions:** For the press conference, see Milton Bracker, "Jubilant Cliburn Arrives Here After Piano Triumph in Soviet," *NYT*, May 17, 1958; "Hero's Return," *Time*; Robert E. Baskin, "Interlude at Idlewild: A Happy Cliburn Returns as Concert, Parade Await," *DMN*, May 17, 1958.

200 **twenty-five hundred items:** *Daily Courier* (Connellsville, PA), June 24, 1958.

200 **"gold and white satin evening bag":** *VCL*, 123.

200 **Elizabeth Winston:** Ibid., 148.

200 ***Life* photographer:** Van's second *Life* spread ran in the June 2, 1958, issue.

201 **"He hasn't had one bite to eat":** Bracker, "Jubilant Cliburn Arrives Here."

201 **back at Idlewild:** Milton Bracker, "Cliburn Greets Soviet Conductor," *NYT*, May 18, 1958.

201 **"SOLD OUT":** "Hero's Return."

202 **"Are you Harvey Kilgore":** "Kilgore Friend of Van's Shares New York Reception," *KNH*, May 25, 1958, quoted in *VC*, 152.

202 **Abram Chasins . . . dropped by:** Chasins describes the scene in *VCL*, 140–41.

202 **notorious kleptomaniac:** John Giordano, interview with the author, August 16, 2014.

202 **Liberty Music Store:** Betty Milburn, "Fall Fabrics Drape Loosely over 'Suggested' Figures," *Tucson Daily Citizen*, July 18, 1958.

202 *Time* **sign:** *VCL*, 142.

203 **manner of dress:** Martin Bookspan described the scene in an interview with Peter Rosen: Reel 37, *Van Cliburn—Concert Pianist* elements, VCA.

203 **2,760 seats:** "Hero's Return." Before Van played, Kirill Kondrashin conducted the Symphony of the Air in Prokofiev's Symphony no. 1 in D Major.

203 **Smiling Mike:** See "Pair of Soviet Charmers on U.S. Scene," *Life*, March 31, 1958, 46–53.

203 **fastened it with a rubber band:** Gilbert Millstein, "Great Moments at Carnegie Hall," *NYT Magazine*, May 22, 1960.

203 **old Benny:** Bernard Mulryan was the artists' attendant for over thirty years, both at Carnegie Hall and Lewisohn Stadium.

204 **"She really is bursting":** Milton Bracker, "Cliburn Cheered in Packed House," *NYT*, May 20, 1958.

204 **"I'm so happy to be home again":** "Biggest in Carnegie Hall History: Cliburn Wows 'Em at Home; Given Thunderous Ovation," *KNH*, May 20, 1958.

204 **"What do you play":** *VCL*, 144.

204 **"Van Cliburn at Home":** *Ogonyok* 24 (1958), 29.

204 **"Jeepers . . . mudder-in-law":** *VCL*, 145.

204 **"We can all breathe easily now":** Louis Biancolli, *World-Telegram*, May 20, 1958. He added that Van had "exceeded all expectations." In the *NYT*, Ross Parmenter more soberly declared that Van had "lived up to expectations."

205 **"Over and over again":** Howard Taubman, "A Winner on His Merits," *NYT*, April 20, 1958.

205 **letter to** *Time:* From Henri Temianka of Los Angeles; published June 2, 1958.

206 **powerhouse of the world:** The theme is developed in Amy Chua and Jed Rubenfeld, *The Triple Package: How Three Unlikely Traits Explain the Rise and Fall of Cultural Groups in America* (New York: Penguin Press, 2014).

206 **Van Cliburn Day:** Detailed arrangements for the parade were recorded in minutes of meetings of the Department of Commerce and Public Events held on May 5 and 13, 1958, headed "Van Cliburn—Planning Meeting," Folder 16, Box 2, JAP. The parade was slated for May 14 but was moved back because of Van's Soviet commitments.

206 **with Harvey and Rildia Bee:** Rildia Bee to Bill Schuman, Hotel Pierre, June 6, 1958, Box 2, Folder 16, JAP.

207 **"He's cuter than Tony Perkins":** "Hero's Return."

207 **"You showed them Russians":** *VCL*, 131.

207 **"How does it feel":** Milton Bracker, "Van Cliburn Gets a Hero's Parade," *NYT*, May 21, 1958.

207 **his mind still a blank:** VCG.

208 **"It was a wonderful thing"**: AP, *Times Record* (Troy, NY), May 21, 1958.

208 **halibut flakes "Antoine"**: Philip Hamburger, "Tribute," *The New Yorker*, May 31, 1958.

208 **"this young, this very old diplomat"**: *VCL*, 136.

208 **Reported *The New Yorker***: Hamburger, "Tribute."

209 **"He's the Eggheads' Elvis Presley"**: *VC*, 159.

209 **"Horowitz, Liberace and Presley"**: "All-American Virtuoso."

209 **"It's a dream"**: *VCL*, 132.

210 **undignified for a musician**: Leopold Mannes of the Mannes College of Music, in "3 Bands to March in Cliburn Parade," *NYT*, May 15, 1958.

210 **"PARADE FOR PIANIST LAGS"**: *New York Herald Tribune*, May 14, 1958.

210 **"I could have gone to Moscow"**: Norman Shetler, interview with the author.

210 **"green-eyed poem"**: *VCL*, 172.

210 **"arranged" Van's victory**: Ibid., 200.

210 **report marked TOP SECRET**: "Van Cliburn," FBI summary, February 19, 1968 (FOIA). The information first appears in a report of December 21, 1963, but was presumably received shortly after the competition.

210 **"Van Cliburn is here"**: *VCL*, 149.

210 **"God bless you, son"**: Ibid.

211 **first private Soviet citizen to meet the American president**: Gregor Tassie, *Kirill Kondrashin: His Life in Music* (Lanham, MD: Scarecrow, 2009), 158. Through his State Department interpreter, Alexander Akalovsky, Kondrashin also passed on the Soviet people's compliments on the birth of a great American musician.

211 **"that kind of ordeal over there"**: Felix Belair Jr., "Eisenhower Greets Van Cliburn; Flies in Helicopter to Gettysburg," *NYT*, May 24, 1958.

211 **twelve minutes**: From 11:05 to 11:17. See Eisenhower's Presidential Appointment Book for Friday, May 23, 1958, http://www.eisenhower.archives.gov/research/on line_documents/presidential_appointment_books/1958/May_1958.pdf. The Afghan ambassador also got twelve minutes.

211 **"Yes, I think so"**: Sound Recording 306-EN-G-T-5781, "Van Cliburn Washington Press Conference," May 23, 1958, RG 306, NACP.

212 **"play it very cautiously"**: A. H. Belmont to L. V. Boardman, memorandum, "Van Clibern [*sic*] Internal Security," May 9, 1958, FBI (FOIA).

212 **"number two papa"**: Winzola McLendon, "Van Toasted in Vodka and Champagne," *WP*, May 25, 1958.

213 **"entire employment record"**: Wiley T. Buchanan Jr., "Presentation of Credentials to President Eisenhower by the Soviet Ambassador," Washington, DC, February 11, 1958, reprinted as document 37 in *FRUS X:1*, https://history.state.gov/historicaldocu ments/frus1958–60v10p1/d37.

213 **another lengthy meeting**: John Foster Dulles, "Memorandum of Conversation," Washington, DC, March 3, 1958, reprinted as document 38 in *FRUS X:1*, https://his tory.state.gov/historicaldocuments/frus1958–60v10p1/d38.

213 **"According to Coyne"**: A. H. Belmont to L. V. Boardman, memorandum, "Van Cliburn, Kirill Kondrashin—Internal Security," May 26, 1958, FBI (FOIA).

13: "HE'S BETTER THAN ELVIS BY FAR!"

214 **"You've got to let this poor boy have some sleep"**: *VCL*, 153.

214 **"What is that you're holding"**: *VC*, 161–62.

215 **three thousand dollars:** *VCL*, 146.

215 **"back to my apartment":** Abram Chasins, "Will Success Spoil Van Cliburn?" *NYT*, June 22, 1958. Chasins also recounts the following day's activities.

215 **"A great event":** "Van Cliburn's 1958 Broadcast Debut from Carnegie Hall (May 26, 1958)," audio recording, WQXR, http://www.wqxr.org/#!/story/272469-piano-legend-van-cliburn-dies-78/. Included is Abram Chasins's intermission interview with Van.

215 **"I do hope you will forgive me":** Ibid.

215 **"Y'all go along":** Chasins recounts the events of the early morning in *VCL*, 154–55.

216 *Person to Person:* The live show was broadcast on Friday, May 30, 1958.

216 **planted the sapling:** "Cliburn in Salute to Rachmaninoff," *NYT*, June 1, 1958.

217 **"MILLION-DOLLAR CONTRACT":** Rogers, "Midnight Conversation."

217 *What's My Line?:* Episode 416, May 25, 1958.

217 **Russian bear:** *VCL*, 155; "Soviet Conductor Leaves," *NYT*, June 2, 1958.

217 **"I wish you the greatest success":** "London Audience of 7,000 Hails Cliburn in Concert Conducted by Kondrashin" (AP), *NYT*, June 16, 1958.

218 **saturating the fair:** MMP, April 16, 1958, Folder 5, Box 2, WSP.

218 **with the Philadelphia Orchestra:** Walter H. Waggoner, "U.S. Hopes to Sign Cliburn for Fair," *NYT*, April 23, 1958; Howard Taubman, "Cliburn at Fair," *NYT*, July 6, 1958.

218 **"I listened to Cliburn":** Arthur Friedheim, *Life and Liszt: The Recollections of a Concert Pianist*, ed. Theodore L. Bullock (New York: Taplinger, 1961), 24. Bullock was the open-eyed listener; Rildia Bee, he concluded, had clearly been Friedheim's most receptive pupil and had become the greatest teacher of them all.

218 **Paris:** "Cliburn a 'Virtuoso' to Paris," *NYT*, June 28, 1958.

218 **arrived in the Windy City:** *VCL*, 160; *VC*, 170.

218 **eighteen thousand, for *Carmen*:** Ross Parmenter, "The World of Music," *NYT*, June 22, 1958; John Briggs, "The World of Music," *NYT*, August 31, 1958.

219 **predicted he would become a big star:** Arlene Dahl interviewed by Peter Rosen, Reel 15, *Van Cliburn—Concert Pianist* elements, VCA.

219 **audience of 22,500:** Ross Parmenter, "22,500 Hear Cliburn at Stadium," *NYT*, August 5, 1958. The concert was on August 4.

219 **nearly ended in tragedy:** SAC, New York to Director, FBI, memorandum, August 6, 1958, "Van Cliburn Information Concerning," FBI file 105–70035–6; John Edgar Hoover to E. Tomlin Bailey, director, Office of Security, Department of State, memorandum, August 15, 1958, "Van Cliburn Information Concerning," FBI (FOIA). The target of Cliburn Sr.'s ire is redacted but may be inferred from the context.

220 **"Ku Klux Klan member":** The conjecture is refuted by strong testimony that the Cliburns were free of color prejudice.

220 **Sergei Dorensky:** Interview with Lyuba Vinogradova.

220 **Van Cliburn's school:** Olmstead, *Juilliard*, 167; "2d Day in City Busy for Soviet Visitors," *NYT*, July 9, 1958.

220 **"I felt very sorry":** Sound Recording 306-EN-G-T-7952A-B, "Van Cliburn Press Conference Held at Steinway Hall," [September 25, 1958], RG 306, NACP. See also "Khrushchev Says Music Aids Amity" (AP), *NYT*, May 31, 1958. The visitor was Robert Dowling, chairman of the American National Theater and Academy, which organized the expert panels for the arts exchange program.

220 **still hoping:** "Soviet Extends Bid to Pianist Cliburn," *NYT*, August 2, 1958; "Russians Again Say Cliburn Accepted," *NYT*, August 3, 1958.

221 **"not up to them"**: "Cliburn to Join Russian Concert," *NYT*, August 10, 1958.

221 **"A young American"**: Howard Taubman, "Musical 'Summit' in Belgian Accord," *NYT*, August 18, 1958.

222 **scanning the jukebox**: Gus Schuettler, "Piano Prodigy Van Cliburn Arrives in Heidelberg," *Stars and Stripes*, August 1958.

222 **spring 1959**: "Cliburn to Tour Soviet in '59" (AP), *NYT*, November 6, 1958.

223 **one he called that September**: Sound Recording 306-EN-G-T-7952A-B, "Van Cliburn Press Conference Held at Steinway Hall," [September 25, 1958]; RG 306, NACP. Van donated the full $1,250 he had been able to take out of the USSR.

223 **Metropolitan Opera**: Ross Parmenter, "'Met' Sets a Record as Its 74th Season Opens," *NYT*, October 28, 1958.

223 **New Yorker . . . dying of cancer**: Patricia Dane Rogers, "Van Cliburn's Piano Provided a Glorious Coda to a Dying Father's Life in the 1950s," *WP*, February 28, 2013.

223 **old "friends"**: *VCL*, 173.

224 **"At Victor these days"**: "Cliburn Album Sells Like Hot Single," *Billboard*, August 18, 1958.

224 **"bottom of our hearts"**: *VCL*, 161. The concert was on September 29, 1958.

224 **"To watch Elvis"**: John W. Stevens, "Cliburn Sets Off a Teen-Age Jam," *NYT*, October 27, 1958.

224 **Boston**: "Boston to Hear Cliburn Twice" (UPI), *NYT*, September 23, 1958.

225 **November morning**: "Cliburn Hailed in Texas" (AP), *NYT*, November 24, 1958.

225 **Texas's proudest brag**: *VCL*, 151, 180.

225 **first for an honoree younger than ninety**: The earlier living honoree was John Nance Garner, who was feted on his ninetieth birthday.

225 **"PROUD HOME OF VAN CLIBURN"**: "Van Cliburn Comes Home," *The Rotarian*, June 1959, 47.

225 **"He's better than Elvis by far"**: "Noisy Ovation at Matinee: Youngsters Go Wild over Van, Forget 'Rock,'" *KNH*, December 3, 1958.

225 **play in India**: Mary Meador, "Van Cliburn Paid Honor at Shreveport," *KNH*, December 17, 1958.

226 **"rushed up"**: *VCL*, 173–74.

226 **an admirer**: Winthrop Sargent in *The New Yorker*, October 25, 1958.

226 **"flesh and blood juke box"**: *VCL*, 212, quoting Paul Henry Lang in *New York Herald Tribune*, October 18, 1958.

226 **service professional**: James M. Keller, "Van Cliburn at Bat," *Piano and Keyboard*, September/October 1993; Stuart Isacoff, "Then & Now," *Piano Today*, Summer 2001; "Deep in the Art of Texas," video recording; *Van Cliburn for the Worthington Hotel*, dir. Rick Croft and William Betaille, 1992, youtube.com/watch?v=RzezkMdy1gY.

227 **"Tucson minister friend"**: "What's with Cliburn's Teeth?" *Tucson Daily Citizen*, January 7, 1959.

227 **dining at the Cliff House**: Elaine Raines, "Happy Birthday, Van Cliburn," *Arizona Daily Star*, July 11, 2008.

227 **"arrested at Phoenix"**: "Van Cliburn," FBI summary, December 21, 1963 (FOIA).

227 **North Indian House Road**: "Acclaimed Pianist Van Cliburn Had a House in Tucson," *Arizona Daily Star*, February 27, 2013.

228 **drowned in the backyard pool**: "Mrs. Newton White," *Tucson Daily Citizen*, December 23, 1959; *Lawrence (KS) Journal-World*, February 6, 1960.

228 **rented it out:** Mary Campbell, "Not This Time," *Tucson Daily Citizen*, September 5, 1964.

228 **Newton White died:** S. C. Warman, "Rev. Newton H. White Dies; Organized 2 Churches Here," *Tucson Daily Citizen*, June 4, 1963.

228 **handsome donation:** Van donated twelve hundred dollars, to be used to defray a student's fees. Peter Mennin to Van Cliburn, October 18, 1963, Folder 10, Box 22, JAP.

14: IN THE HEAT OF THE KITCHEN

229 **"Learn from Liu Shikun":** Liu Shikun, interview with the author.

229 **Khrushchev arrived for a summit:** The events are entertainingly recounted in Mike Dash, "Khrushchev in Water Wings: On Mao, Humiliation, and the Sino-Soviet Split," May 4, 2012, http://www.smithsonianmag.com/history/khrushchev-in-water-wings -on-mao-humiliation-and-the-sino-soviet-split-80852370/?no-ist.

229 **"making him the historical pivot":** Frank Dikötter, *Mao's Great Famine* (London: Bloomsbury, 2011), 4.

230 **yet to deliver:** Khrushchev annulled the nuclear pact with China in June 1959.

230 **"transcontinental missile":** Vladislav Zubok, "The Mao-Khrushchev Conversations, 31 July–3 August 1958 and 2 October 1959," *CWIHP Bulletin* 12/13 (Fall/Winter 2001): 256; https://www.wilsoncenter.org/sites/default/files/CWIHPBulletin12–13_ p2_0.pdf.

231 **"pleasant period of thaw":** "Moscow's New Campaign," *NYT*, June 26, 1958.

231 **"blatant errors . . . gifted composers":** "On Rectifying Errors in the Evaluation of the Operas 'The Great Friendship,' 'Bogdan Khmelnitsky,' and 'From All One's Heart,'" Central Committee decree, *Pravda*, June 8, 1958. See Schwarz, *Music and Musical Life*, 263–66.

231 **printed with CIA funds:** After years of rumors, the CIA's involvement was confirmed when it declassified the relevant documents in 2014. See http://www.foia.cia .gov/collection/doctor-zhivago.

231 **called off:** B. Makarov, "Report from the All-Union 'International Book' Association to D. A. Polikarpov on the Advisability of Stopping Attempts Aimed at Preventing the Publication of B. L. Pasternak's Novel 'Doctor Zhivago' in France," February 5, 1958, *CCCP&C*, 24–25.

231 **"low-grade reactionary hackwork":** David Zaslavsky, "Reactionary Propaganda Uproar over a Literary Weed," *Pravda*, October 26, 1958.

231 **Begging Khrushchev:** Ivinskaya, *Captive of Time*, 240–41.

232 **"mangy sheep":** Solomon Volkov, *The Magical Chorus: A History of Russian Culture from Tolstoy to Solzhenitsyn* (New York: Knopf, 2008), 196.

232 **Vladimir Ashkenazy:** Interview with the author.

232 **assistant professor:** Alexander Egorov, assistant to venerable professor Konstantin Igumnov.

232 **more gay piano teachers:** Also implicated were piano professor Vladimir Belov and Ashkenazy's teacher Boris Zemylansky, who, like Naum Shtarkman, was an assistant to Lev Oborin.

233 **refused to play in Moscow:** Heinrich Neuhaus told Paul Moor the story: "Slava, the Russian," *Piano and Keyboard* 189 (November/December 1997). Moor ascribed Richter's cyclical depression, which kept him away from the piano for long stretches, to the impossibility of living a fulfilled personal life under Soviet law. See also Moor,

"Sviatoslav Becomes Svyetchik," *High Fidelity* 12, no. 10 (October 1962); Moor, "Sviatoslav Richter: A Troubled Life," *American Record Guide* 60, no. 6 (November/December 1997).

233 **"knew that Van Cliburn was a homosexual":** "Van Cliburn," FBI summary, February 19, 1968. The position of the individual concerned is redacted but may be inferred from the context. The date of the original report is unavailable.

233 **anniversary of the revolution speech:** Max Frankel, "Consumer Wooed at Moscow Fete," *NYT*, November 7, 1958.

233 **"holiday":** *Stanford Daily*, January 5, 1959.

233 **recent ultimatum:** In a speech of November 10, 1958.

233 **insisted Van be invited:** Aschen Mikoyan, interview with the author, August 9, 2014.

234 **Beaux-Arts mansion:** The embassy then occupied the current Russian ambassador's residence, the Mrs. George Pullman House at 1125 Sixteenth Street, Northwest.

234 **"Play, please play":** "Mikoyan Moved to Tears as Cliburn Plays for Him" (AP), *Milwaukee Journal*, January 20, 1959.

234 **Van's starring role:** Harrison E. Salisbury, "Cliburn a Guest at Mikoyan Fete," *NYT*, January 20, 1959.

234 **outraged housewife:** Jacqueline Stevens Hughes to Mark Schubart, January 6, 1959, Folder 10, Box 17, JAD.

235 **"ahead of the entire planet":** Plisetskaya, *I, Maya Plisetskaya*, xv.

236 **stood and cheered:** "Bolshoi Opening Hailed by Crowd," *NYT*, April 17, 1959.

236 **those of the FBI:** "Van Cliburn," FBI summary, December 21, 1963.

236 **La Scala:** "Cliburn Cheered at La Scala" (AP), *NYT*, June 17, 1959.

236 **attend the Soviet exhibition:** Farnsworth Fowle, "Van Cliburn Sees Soviet Fair Here," *NYT*, July 27, 1959; Victor Rosenberg, *Soviet-American Relations, 1953–1960: Diplomacy and Cultural Exchange During the Eisenhower Presidency* (Jefferson, NC: McFarland, 2005), 123.

236 **another fact the FBI duly recorded:** "Van Cliburn," FBI summary, December 21, 1963.

237 **"Divine indifference":** Brendan Gill and Donald Stewart, "Struggle," *The New Yorker*, August 22, 1959.

237 **"Your music and ours":** *Leonard Bernstein and the New York Philharmonic in Moscow*, CBS TV film, 1959.

237 **American National Exhibition:** My account is based on *Opening in Moscow*, documentary dir. D. A. Pennebaker, 1959; "Nixon in U.S.S.R. Opening U.S. Fair, Clashes with Mr. K," newsreel footage, Universal-International News, July 27, 1959, https://www.youtube.com/watch?v=WIGTFK2LiXs; Dan I. Slobin, "Excerpts from a 1959 Journal: U.S. Exhibition in Moscow, 2009," http://ihd.berkeley.edu/1959_Slobin_US_Exhibition_Moscow.pdf; "50th Anniversary of the American Exhibits to the U.S.S.R.," U.S. Department of State, http://www.state.gov/p/eur/ci/rs/c26472.htm; Marilyn S. Kushner, "Exhibiting Art at the American National Exhibition in Moscow, 1959: Domestic Politics and Cultural Diplomacy," *Journal of Cold War Studies* 4, no. 1 (Winter 2002): 6–26; Susan E. Reid, "Who Will Beat Whom? Soviet Reception of the American National Exhibition in Moscow, 1959," *Kritika* 9, no. 4 (Fall 2008): 855–904; Andrew Wulf, *Moscow '59: The 'Sokolniki Summit' Revisited* (Los Angeles, CA: Figueroa Press, 2010); Gregory Feifer, "Fifty Years Ago, American Exhibition Stunned Soviets in Cold War," July 23, 2009, http://www.rferl.org/content/Fifty_

Years_Ago_American_Exhibition_Stunned_Soviets_in_Cold_War/1783913.html;
NKCS, 320–26; May, *Homeward Bound*, 20–21; Taubman, *Khrushchev*, 417–18; Walter
L. Hixson, *Parting the Curtain: Propaganda, Culture, and the Cold War, 1945–1961* (New
York: St. Martin's Press, 1997), 176–81; *TOML*, 172; William Safire, "The Cold War's
Hot Kitchen," *NYT*, July 24, 2009; State Department documents 92–107 in *FRUS X:1*.

239 **"I felt like a fighter":** Richard Nixon, *Six Crises* (New York: Simon and Schuster,
2013), 258.

240 **"CATCH UP WITH AND OVERTAKE AMERICA":** *TOML*, 174. The slogan first appeared in 1957
in relation to cattle breeding, but during 1958, it came to be applied more broadly to
the Soviet economy.

15: KHRUSHCHEV IN THE CAPITALIST DEN

241 **"Only people who refuse":** *Khrushchev in America: Full Texts of the Speeches Made
by N. S. Khrushchev on His Tour of the United States, September 15–27, 1959* (New York:
Crosscurrents Press, 1960), 10.

241 **Khrushchev touched down:** My account of the visit draws on primary sources,
especially the memoirs of Khrushchev's interpreter Viktor Sukhodrev (cited as *YM*);
and also Eisenhower, *White House Years*, 432–49; *Khrushchev in America*; M. Kahr-
malov and O. Vadeyev, eds., *Face to Face with America: The Story of N. S. Khrushchev's
Visit to the USA, September 15–27, 1959* (Moscow: Foreign Languages Publishing House,
1960); and Henry Cabot Lodge, *The Storm Has Many Eyes: A Personal Narrative* (New
York: Norton, 1973), 157–82. U.S. Government records and contemporary newspapers were also consulted. Among secondary literature, Peter Carlson, *K Blows Top:
A Cold War Comic Interlude, Starring Nikita Khrushchev, America's Most Unlikely Tourist*
(New York: PublicAffairs, 2009), was essential; also valuable were Richard F. Wein-
groff, "On the Road with Ike and Niki," *Public Roads* 78, no. 6 (May/June, 2015),
https://www.fhwa.dot.gov/publications/publicroads/15mayjun/04.cfm;   Alekandr
Fursenko and Timothy Naftali, *Khrushchev's Cold War: The Inside Story of an American Adversary* (New York: Norton, 2006), 214–40; Taubman, *Khrushchev*, 396–441;
and Kevin M. Singer, "Face-to-Face with the Red Menace: Opposition to the 1959
Khrushchev Visit," Cold War Museum, http://www.coldwar.org/museum/docu
ments/face-to-facewiththeredmenaceoppositiontothe1959khrushchevvisit.htm.

242 **"old vaudeville trouper":** Warren Rogers, *New York Herald Tribune*, quoted in Carlson, *K Blows Top*, 71.

242 **"not even the end of World War II":** "Red Press Balloons Khrushchev Welcome"
(AP), *Times* (San Mateo, CA), September 16, 1959.

243 **"The next day? Even richer":** Gaddis, *Cold War*, 72.

243 **"jazzy pop combo":** Carlson, *K Blows Top*, 84.

243 *Washington Post* **noted:** Maxine Cheshire, "Van May Play on Mr. K's Red-Letter
Day," *WP*, September 20, 1959.

243 **FBI listening in:** "Van Cliburn," memorandum prepared for Secret Service, December 16, 1963, FBI (FOIA).

243 **"Third from left, Khrushchev":** Bruce Adams, *Tiny Revolutions in Russia: Twentieth-
Century Soviet and Russian History in Anecdotes* (New York: Routledge Curzon, 2005),
77.

244 **"stuck in some people's throats:"** Carlson, *K Blows Top*, 95.

244 **"What do you mean . . . to the moon":** *YM*.

244 **"murderer":** Carlson, *K Blows Top*, 85.

244 **"So what":** *YM*.

245 **"If you don't want to listen . . . great Soviet State":** Taubman, *Khrushchev*, 429.

245 **"If you've seen one skyscraper":** Nikita Khrushchev, *Khrushchev Remembers: The Last Testament*, trans. and ed. Strobe Talbott (Boston: Little, Brown, 1974), 381.

245 **"conical shape":** Tzouliadis, *Forsaken*, 324.

245 **"We the workers":** Jeffrey Meyers, *The Genius and the Goddess: Arthur Miller and Marilyn Monroe* (Urbana: University of Illinois Press, 2009), 179–80.

246 **"his eyes lit up":** "Nikita Is No Old 'Softie,' Shirley Says," *Chicago Tribune*, June 15, 1960.

246 **"Just imagine, I, a premier":** Khrushchev's famous rant is recorded in several variants by Sukhodrev, Kharlamov and Vadeyev, in *Khrushchev in America*, and in press articles. See also Carlson, *K Blows Top*, 158–59.

246 **"Screw the cops":** Meyers, *Genius and Goddess*, 179.

246 **John Wayne was there:** Cecilia Rasmussen, "Soviet Leader Met Duke but Not Mickey," *LA Times*, January 24, 1999.

246 **"Kiss him" . . . "great pleasure":** *YM*.

247 **"fat and ugly":** Meyers, *Genius and Goddess*, 180.

247 **"we do not agree":** Carlson, *K Blows Top*, 169.

247 **"We can always turn round":** *YM*.

247 **burst into tears:** Mayers, *The Ambassadors*, 202.

247 **"I can go":** Carlson, *K Blows Top*, 170.

248 **"honest girl":** *YM*.

248 **"A person's face":** Meyers, *Genius and Goddess*, 179.

248 **union bosses were traitors:** At the meeting, Victor Reuther of the United Automobile Workers addressed Khrushchev in Russian and explained that he and his brother, Walter, had spent two years in the 1930s working at the Gorky Automotive Works, "named in honor of Molotov. Is it still called that?" "Nyet," snapped Khrushchev. "We hanged the likes of Reuther in Russia in 1917," he told John F. Kennedy at their Vienna summit in 1960.

248 **reception at the Soviet embassy:** "Khrushchev Hugs Cliburn and Invites Him to Soviet" (AP), *NYT*, September 25, 1959. The reception was on the twenty-fourth. See also K. N. Nuzhin, "For Peace and Friendship!" *SM*, November 3, 1959.

248 **gave Van a tour:** "Cliburn Visits Plane" (AP), *NYT*, September 26, 1959.

249 **internal memorandum:** C. D. DeLoach to Tolson, "Van Cliburn—Pianist—Alleged Security Investigation—'Chicago Sun-Times' 9–25–59," September 25, 1959, FBI file 105–70035–7.

249 **"my kind of people":** "Van Cliburn," FBI summary, February 19, 1968.

249 **"Rildia Bee, this is Sam Rayburn":** Madigan, "Mementos of the Musician."

250 **"Berlin is the testicles of the West":** Gaddis, *Cold War*, 65.

250 **at a wake:** *KR*, 413. State Department memorandums confirm that Nixon was present at lunch on September 26, not September 27, as is sometimes said.

250 **Eisenhower was astonished:** Eisenhower, *Waging Peace*, 447.

251 **memorandum of the conversation:** Llewellyn Thompson, Memorandum of Conversation, Camp David, September 27, 1959, 1–1:45 p.m., "Quality of American Chocolates; Van Cliburn," reprinted as document 134 in *FRUS X:1*, https://history.state .gov/historicaldocuments/frus1958–60v10p1/d134. Other records relating to Khrushchev's visit form documents 108–39.

252 **"wise statesmanship":** Robert V. Daniels, ed., *A Documentary History of Communism*, vol. 2, *Communism and the World* (London: I. B. Tauris, 1985), 280.

252 **"Main Street Americans":** Vladislav Zubok, *A Failed Empire: The Soviet Union in the Cold War from Stalin to Gorbachev* (Chapel Hill: University of North Carolina Press, 2007), 131.

253 **"Don't you dare spit on us":** For a transcript of the bad-tempered conversation, see "Memorandum of Conversation of N. S. Khrushchev with Mao Zedong, Beijing, 2 October 1959," *CWIHP Bulletin* 12/13 (Fall/Winter 2001): 262–69.

253 **"Duke, Merry Christmas. Nikita" . . . "Nikita. Thanks. Duke":** Rasmussen, "Soviet Leader Met Duke but Not Mickey."

16: BACK IN THE USSR

254 **group of twelve:** Marianna N. Tishchenko, "Crossing the Iron Curtain," *Harvard Crimson*, June 1, 2009. The eight men and four women also included an actress, an engineer, and an accordion player.

254 **"It is clear to me":** A. Krivolapov, "Shadows and Light in New York," *Komsomolskaya Pravda*, December 13, 1959. The episode is reconstructed from this article.

254 **breakfast with Rosina:** Ella Vlassenko, interview with the author.

254 **readers of *Sovetsky Muzykant*:** Lev Vlassenko, "My Impression from a Visit to the United States," *SM*, n.d. [1959].

255 **"Wonderful sounds":** Krivolapov, "Shadows and Light."

255 **audience of 16,100:** John Briggs, "Russian Adieu," *NYT*, February 15, 1960.

256 **swept the young pianist into his offices:** *VC*, 207.

256 **"Get rid of the bum":** Robinson, *The Last Impresario*, 384.

256 **heard complaining:** Howard Aibel, interview with the author.

256 **"What's the matter":** Donna Perlmutter, "The Long Road Home," *LA Village View*, July 1, 1994.

256 **Roberta Peters:** Van and Peters had had something of a mutual appreciation society ever since she eyed him when he was a young man in the coffee shop of the Buckingham Hotel. Later they shared an elevator ride: she spoke first, and he admired her floor-length mink. Roberta Peters, interview by Peter Rosen, Reel no. 40, *Van Cliburn—Concert Pianist* elements, VCA.

256 **Ike himself had personally requested:** Ibid.

257 **spindly black plane:** The Eisenhower Library has put many documents pertaining to the U-2 crisis online at http://www.eisenhower.archives.gov/research/online_documents/sputnik.html. See also Francis Gary Powers and Curt Gentry, *Operation Overflight: A Memoir of the U-2 Incident* (Washington, DC: Brassey's, 2004); "May Day Over Moscow: The Francis Gary Powers Story" (2015), News and Information, Central Intelligence Agency, https://www.cia.gov/news-information/featured-story-archive/2015-featured-story-archive/francis-gary-powers.html.

257 **six R-7s:** Two were based at Plesetsk in northwest Russia, two at Baikonur. In 1962 the sites reached their maximum capacity of ten active ICBMs.

257 **"The way to teach these smart-alecks":** Taubman, *Khrushchev*, 442.

258 **Sverdlovsk:** Now (as previously) Yekaterinburg.

258 **seat was rigged to explode:** Stepan Mikoyan, *An Autobiography*, trans. Aschen Mikoyan (Shrewsbury, UK: Airlife, 1999), 260.

259 **"Comrades, I must tell you a secret":** "Excerpts from Premier Khrushchev's Remarks on U.S. Jet Downed in Soviet," *NYT*, May 8, 1960.

259 **veins bulging:** *TOML*, 185.

259 **"could not help but suspect":** Thompson to Department of State, telegram, Moscow, May 9, 1960; reprinted as document 50 in *FRUS X:1*, https://history.state.gov/historicaldocuments/frus1958–60v10p1/d150.

260 **"I would like to resign":** DDE [ACW] Diary May 1960, Box 11, Eisenhower, Dwight D.: Papers as President of the United States, 1953–1961 (Ann Whitman File), DDEPL.

260 **still going to the Paris peace conference:** For the unraveling of the summit, see Sherman Kent, "The Summit Conference of 1960: An Intelligence Officer's View," *Studies in Intelligence* 16, special edition (1972), Library, Central Intelligence Agency, https://www.cia.gov/library/center-for-the-study-of-intelligence/csi-publications/books-and-monographs/sherman-kent-and-the-board-of-national-estimates-collected-essays/8summit.html; *NKCS*, 380–83; Michael Beschloss, *Mayday: Eisenhower, Khrushchev, and the U-2 Affair* (New York: Harper and Row, 1986), 234, 242–52, 274; David M. Barrett, *CIA and Congress: The Untold Story from Truman to Kennedy* (Lawrence: University Press of Kansas, 2005), 386–400.

260 **"My feeling . . . grim prospect":** Mayers, *The Ambassadors*, 206.

261 **"stupid U-2 business":** George Kistiakowsky, *A Scientist at the White House* (Cambridge, MA: Harvard University Press, 1976), 375.

261 **anti-American propaganda:** *NKCS*, 391.

262 **B-47:** "Memorandum of Telephone Conversation Between President Eisenhower and Secretary of State Herter," July 11, 1960, reprinted as document 158 in *FRUS X:1*, https://history.state.gov/historicaldocuments/frus1958–60v10p1/d158.

262 **"Well, I'm not going" . . . "wants you to continue":** Madigan, "Mementos of the Musician."

262 **courtesy calls:** The *DMN* of May 25 ran a photo of Van with Lacy taken the previous day.

262 **another American pianist:** Byron Janis, *Chopin and Beyond: My Extraordinary Life in Music and the Paranormal* (Hoboken, NJ: John Wiley, 2010), 106.

262 **yelling teenagers:** In "Moscow Acclaims Cliburn on Return" (UPI), *NYT*, May 27, 1960, the figure is given as two hundred; Sol Hurok claimed that five thousand turned out.

262 **journalist from *Teatr* magazine:** Viktor Gorokhov, "Van Cliburn: The Boy Is Me, Kind Neighbors That's You, Parents That's America," *Teatr* 9 (1960): 144–46.

264 **green wooden dacha:** Now dacha no. 30; according to *Teatr*, it was then no. 15. As well as the *Teatr* article, the episode is reconstructed from newsreel footage, photographs, and my own visit to Ruza. Van remembered his time there in "Nobody Dares Speak Badly of Russia in Front of Me."

265 **Richter kept vigil:** A well-known story: see Norman Lebrecht, "A Fusion of Piano and Cerebellum," *Standpoint*, March 2013. That Richter played is confirmed in Ivinskaya, *Captive of Time*, 327.

265 **eloped with Neuhaus's wife:** Neuhaus's wife, Zinaida, became Pasternak's second wife in 1934.

265 **"We excommunicated Tolstoy":** Ivinskaya, *Captive of Time*, 331–32.

265 **quietly freed:** Olga Ivinskaya was officially rehabilitated in 1988, the year *Doctor Zhivago* was finally published in Russia. Her role remains controversial: see Alessandra Stanley, "Model for Dr. Zhivago's Lara Betrayed Pasternak to K.G.B.," *NYT*, November 27, 1997.

265 **spoils included:** *TOML*, 185.

266 **party of young Soviets:** Roberta Peters, interview by Peter Rosen.

266 **"Does America really want war":** Ibid.

266 **his ex-wife, Tamara:** Miansarova, "Shag dlinoyu v zhizn."

266 **Thorunn Johannsdottir:** Interview with the author.

266 **Liu Shikun:** Interview with the author.

266 **he saw a mob:** Walter Cronkite, interview by Peter Rosen, Reel no. 30, *Van Cliburn—Concert Pianist* elements, VCA.

267 **clutching at his clothes:** Freers to State Department, July 18, 1960.

267 **"Aw, look at that":** CBS archival footage, Reels no. 116 and 117, *Van Cliburn—Concert Pianist* elements, VCA.

267 **huge bouquets of flowers:** Roberta Peters, interview by Peter Rosen.

267 **Outside the conservatory:** Seymour Topping, "Van Cliburn Wins Moscow Ovation," *NYT*, June 4, 1960.

267 **"Madame" Furtseva:** Teroganyan, "Yesterday at Cliburn's Concert."

268 **"Soviet cultural officials":** Thompson to State Department, telegram, June 4, 1960, quoted in Rosenberg, *Soviet-American Relations*, 123.

268 **"TO NIKITA S. KHRUSHCHEV FROM DWIGHT D. EISENHOWER":** "U.S. to Return Nikita's Boat to Its Maker," *Chicago Tribune*, June 15, 1960.

268 **"could do his own country . . . Russian leader":** F. B. Fritzell, letter to *Chicago Tribune*, June 15, 1960.

269 **"In the summer heat":** "Packed House Hails Cliburn in Moscow," *NYT*, June 6, 1960.

270 **Aschen Mikoyan:** Interview with the author.

270 **Van spoke glowingly of Rildia Bee:** Roberta Peters, interview by Peter Rosen.

270 **"bounced out of his arms . . . Russian-American friendship":** "Van Cliburn is hailed" (AP), *NYT*, June 17, 1960.

270 **Tbilisi:** A. Machavariani, "Van Cliburn Is Playing," *Zarya vostoka* (Tbilisi), June 19, 1960.

270 **political statement:** Van Cliburn, [interview], *Literaturnaya gazeta*, July 30, 1960.

270 **sang lustily along:** "Halfway Coexistence," *Time*, July 18, 1960.

271 **"More than 1,000":** "Cliburn Is Cheered by 20,000 in Moscow" (UPI), *NYT*, July 20, 1960; see also "People," *Time*, September 5, 1960.

272 **Anastas Mikoyan warned Van:** Van Cliburn, interview by Ed Wierzbowski, Moscow, 1989.

272 **Young Aschen:** Aschen Mikoyan, interview with the author.

272 **speaker after speaker:** Rosenberg, *Soviet-American Relations*, 133.

272 **page two of *Pravda*:** On August 25, 1960.

272 **FBI was less impressed:** "Van Cliburn," FBI summary, February 19, 1968.

273 **eighty thousand rubles:** About eight thousand dollars at the time, at the official exchange rate, or some sixty-four thousand dollars today.

273 **"of the heroes of the cosmos: Belka and Strelka":** The text of the TASS article is partially recorded in SA Leonard A. Butt to SAC, New York, June 19, 1961, FBI file 62–12802–2. Butt was conducting surveillance on the journalist who interviewed Van in the United States on behalf of TASS.

273 **On board was Barbara Powers:** "People," *Time*, September 5, 1960.

17: SOLE DIPLOMACY

274 **Khrushchev set out for New York:** My reconstruction draws substantially on the eyewitness account given by Viktor Sukhodrev (*YM*), together with Khrushchev's

own recollections in his *Memoirs*, vol. 3, 264–91. Also used were *NKCS*, 410–16; Taubman, *Khrushchev*, 474–77; *Khrushchev in New York* (New York: Crosscurrents, 1960); and contemporary newspaper reports.

275 **Federal-style town house:** The former Percy Rivington Pyne House at 680 Park Avenue, now the headquarters of the Americas Society.

275 **"Okay, let's go get some fresh air":** *YM.*

276 **"Dammit, I've even broken my watch":** *YM.* This was the explanation, related by Sukhodrev, that Khrushchev gave that day to socialist leaders who were riding with him in his car to the Soviet mission. There are several versions of the story, some of which Khrushchev spun to account for his actions. In his memoirs, Khrushchev claimed he had promised a member of the Spanish international workers' movement that he would expose Franco's men as criminals and that he deliberately banged his shoe to emphasize his point. Sergei Khrushchev says that a journalist stepped on his shoe on the way into the hall, and rather than struggle to bend down in front of the cameras, he had a staffer bring it to his desk wrapped in a napkin.

277 **"So you, chairman"** . . ."**closing the session":** *YM.*

277 **"God bless him":** *Ibid.*

277 **advanced spacecraft:** Robert Reeves, *The Superpower Space Race: An Explosive Rivalry Through the Solar System* (New York: Plenum, 1994), 315–16.

278 **Richter arrived in Chicago:** Rasmussen, *Sviatoslav Richter*, 156, 159.

278 **"the shopkeeper":** *NKCS*, 391.

279 **"military-industrial-congressional complex":** Eisenhower used the term in his farewell address on January 17, 1961.

279 **"How old are you, Mr. President . . . even older":** *YM.*

279 **"He beat the hell out of me . . . He savaged me":** Frederick Kempe, *Berlin 1961: Kennedy, Khrushchev, and the Most Dangerous Place on Earth* (New York: Putman, 2011), 255–56.

280 **"Yeah, well":** *YM.*

280 **no mercy in politics:** Kempe, *Berlin 1961*, 253.

280 **"a meeting of a giant and a pygmy":** *YM.*

280 **televised address:** On July 25, 1961.

280 *Life* **ran a feature:** May, *Homeward Bound*, 1.

280 **Sunday sermons:** *TOML*, 238.

281 **Khrushchev's aides joked:** Vladislav Zubok, "Khrushchev and the Berlin Crisis (1958–1962)," CWIHP Working Paper no. 6 (May 1993), 24.

281 **new spy satellites:** The Corona project, launched August 1960, was a by-product of *Sputnik*, which set a precedent for the free exploration of space.

281 **"second strike capability":** Roswell Gilpatric, October 21, 1961, reprinted in *Documents on Disarmament, 1961* (Washington, DC: U.S. Arms Control and Disarmament Agency, 1962), 545.

282 **"at least three busts of Van Cliburn":** "Moscow Glitters for Party Rally with Special Effort in Culture," *NYT*, October 29, 1961.

282 **"monstrous crimes . . . historical justice":** Stephen F. Cohen, "The Victims Return: Gulag Survivors Under Khrushchev," in Hollander, *Political Violence*, 63.

283 **"not just as part of our arsenal":** Hope for America: Performers, Politics, and Pop Culture, Library of Congress, http://www.loc.gov/exhibits/hope-for-america/government-support-for-the-arts.html.

283 **Van played for him twice:** At the fund-raiser for the National Cultural Center, re-

named the Kennedy Center after JFK's assassination, which Van closed on November 29, 1962; and at a Congressional Club breakfast on May 2, 1963, following which he and Rildia Bee visited with the president in the Blue Room of the White House.

283 **relying on Jackie:** "President Obama Opens White House Evening of Classical Music," November 6, 2010, https://www.whitehouse.gov/photos-and-video/video/president-obama-opens-white-house-evening-classical-music.

283 "VAN CLIBURN PLAYS FOR FREE BERLIN": *DMN* (UPI), August 31, 1961.

283 *Ed Sullivan Show:* The episode aired on CBS on October 8, 1961.

283 **"I recognize the divine spark":** Bruno Walter to Van Cliburn, draft of letter, Series I, Folder 99, Bruno Walter Papers, Music Division, New York Public Library. Van played for Walter's last live concert appearance, on December 4, 1960, with the Los Angeles Philharmonic; Walter died in 1962.

284 **invited Van to conduct:** Van made his conducting debut on March 5, 1961, in a memorial concert for Dimitri Mitropoulos, who had died after falling off the podium at La Scala, Milan. Leopold Stokowski was supposed to conduct but had broken his hip.

284 **all the great orchestras:** Van also had a close relationship with Eugene Ormandy and the Philadelphia Orchestra; see their correspondence in Eugene Ormandy Papers, Kislak Center for Special Collections, Rare Books and Manuscripts, University of Pennsylvania.

284 **"first time that a long-hair artist":** *VCL*, 162.

284 **"Thank you for sending us Van Cliburn":** Lyde and Charles Devall, "Cliburn Acclaimed on Anniversary of N.Y. Debut: Music World, Friends Join to Honor Van," *KNH*, November 22, 1964.

284 **she wrote complaining:** See their correspondence in Folders 21 and 22, Box 2, RLP. By contrast, the collection contains four folders of letters from John Browning.

284 **Van's old friend:** Dowis, "Rosina: A Memoir," 374.

285 **Winifred Hamilton:** TM1.

285 **office and living room:** G. Kuznetsov, "Van Cliburn: Music Is Not a Collection of Sounds," *SK*, April 25, 1963.

285 **rented out his apartment:** Campbell, "Not This Time." "I'm in transient status in New York," Van explained. "I couldn't afford to keep a flat in a hotel."

285 **back to Shreveport:** In 1960 the Cliburns moved to 455 Wilder Place, a smart two-story redbrick Colonial revival.

285 **"Oh, Daddy" . . . "buy something else":** Van Cliburn, interview by Paul Holdengräber.

285 **"crappiest hotel in history":** Howard Camner, *Turbulence at 67 Inches: The Autobiography* (Xlibris, 2009), 261–63.

286 **"Well he's a nice boy":** *VC*, 218.

18: ENDGAME

287 **thirty-nine international competitions:** Over the five years to 1961. Culture Minister Furtseva reported the figures in a speech to the Twenty-Second Party Congress. Rasmussen, *Sviatoslav Richter*, 153.

287 **Vladimir Ashkenazy:** Interview with the author.

288 **American intermediaries:** Special Agent Leonard A. Butt of the FBI recorded four such requests—including one from *Pravda* and one from TASS—between June 1961

and March 1962 in the course of surveillance of one stringer for the Moscow press; see FBI files 62–12802–2/3/4/5.

288 **Van's salutation:** SAC, New York, to SAC, Albany, memorandum, April 9, 1963; FBI file 62–12802–8.

288 **"addressed to his friends":** SA [. . .] to SAC, New York, memorandum, November 5, 1963, FBI file 62–12802–11.

288 **FBI logged the conversations:** Van's declassified FBI files include fourteen reports of calls originating in Moscow between December 31, 1962, and January 3, 1968, on both business and personal matters; in several, Van thanks the caller for gifts.

288 **told the Bureau:** "Olga Baquero, Also Known as Mrs. Alfonso Baquero, Internal Security—Russia," July 13, 1964, FBI File SI 105–1612.

288 **"Some politicians maintain . . . friendship":** SA Leonard A. Butt to SAC New York, June 19, 1961, FBI file 62–12802–2.

288 **park on the Black Sea:** *NKCS*, 483.

289 **tracked Van down in Helsinki:** N. Agayants, "Art Brings the Nations Closer," *Komsomolskaya Pravda*, June 19, 1962.

289 **festival of modern music:** The first Modern Music festival was held in Gorky (Nizhny Novgorod) June 9–13, 1962.

289 **Rildia Bee . . . urged him to accept:** Drannikov (APN Novosti), interview with Van Cliburn, *Pravda Ukrainy*, June 16, 1962.

289 **"I saw the faces . . . I wanted to play for them":** "Part of My Heart Is in Moscow," *Moskva* 11 (1962): 173.

289 **set off for Moscow:** For evocative footage of Van and Rildia Bee in Moscow, including Rildia Bee at the piano, see "Van Cliburn Is Playing," film dir. Z. Tulubeva, CSCF (RCSDF), 1962, http://www.net-film.ru/en/film-5656/.

289 **lost himself on the cobbles:** "Part of My Heart Is in Moscow."

290 **Lenin Hills:** Now Sparrow Hills, near Moscow State University in southwest Moscow.

290 **Sukhodrev received an urgent call:** Sukhodrev recounts the episode in *YM*.

290 **Janis was already booked:** Janis, *Chopin and Beyond*, 113–14.

291 **"Kleeburn! Kleeburn!":** Ibid., 106.

291 **welcomed Van as its own:** "He was received here as a son that had come home," wrote A. Zolotov in a piece headed "See You Again Soon" in a July 1962 edition of *Izvestiya*.

291 **"not to my humble person":** "Part of My Heart Is in Moscow."

291 **falling-out with Kondrashin:** Tassie, *Kirill Kondrashin*, 155, 162.

292 **dacha outside Moscow:** Van's day at the dacha is captured in video recording RR185 [June 17, 1962], Sergei Khrushchev home movies, JH. See also *NKCS*, 504–5; *YM*; "First Photo of USSR's No. 1 Family," *Life*, September 21, 1959, 38–41; "Red's Dacha Is Luxurious" (AP), *Milwaukee Journal*, July 27, 1959.

292 **"We've been watching you . . . you love classical music":** Madigan, "Mementos of the Musician." In the same interview, Van is quoted as saying that Khrushchev took him "on his boat from his dacha and we motored into the middle of Moscow so we could look up at the palace of the Kremlin." As Sergei Khrushchev pointed out to me, it was and still is impossible to ride by boat from the Gorki-9 dacha to Moscow through the Rublevskaya Dam, which has no locks.

293 **"Because you are too skinny, Vanya":** "'Vanya' Cliburn: Popular Does Not Mean Good."

293 **"Wouldn't you like" . . . "Kvass, never":** *NKCS*, 504–5. Apparently Van quickly developed a taste for *okroshka*, or at least he claimed to love it when Viktor Sukhodrev's mother cooked it for him and Rildia Bee (apparently on this same visit), even asking for seconds.

294 **useful political cover:** Khrushchev's show of charm to Van appears to have been part of a pattern. On May 30, Khrushchev and his family had also attended a Benny Goodman concert in Moscow, part of the first officially sanctioned jazz tour of the USSR, despite his well-known dislike of jazz. As the first ships carrying weapons for Cuba were setting sail, Jane and Tommy Thompson were dining with Khrushchev at Dacha no. 9 for the last time before leaving Moscow at the end of their diplomatic posting.

294 **"insolent American imperialism":** *NKCS*, 493.

294 **royal audience:** Agayants, "Art Brings the Nations Closer."

295 **"Da da, ochen khorosho . . . Ya lyublyu Moskvu":** "Yes yes, very good. I love Moscow."

295 **"I think the cultural exchange . . . enough for that":** Drannikov, interview with Van Cliburn.

295 **"Whenever he appeared . . . boyish naiveté":** Albert Goldberg, "Israelis Acclaim Pianist Van Cliburn," *LA Times*, September 6, 1962.

296 **Operation Mongoose:** Many documents are reprinted in *FRUS 1961–1963*, vol. 10, *Cuba*.

296 **photographs and gifts:** Lelchuk, "Chudo po imeni Van Klaybern."

297 **filled up a large file:** FBI files 105–1451–1 to 105–1451–31.

297 **"Willy, Waylon or Garth . . . achy breaky hearts":** Mike Cochran, "Van Cliburn Competition Turns Cowtown into Classical Mecca," *Scranton Times* (PA), May 16, 1993.

297 **disassociating himself from it:** Mark Schubart to Van Cliburn, December 14, 1961, Folder 3, Box 28, JAD. Schubart recalls Van several times expressing "serious misgivings about the Competition and the manner in which it was launched and was to be conducted. You remember, I am sure, how concerned you were; and if I am not mistaken, at one point you were seriously considering the possibility of withdrawing from it altogether."

297 **Juilliard fund-raiser:** See the lengthy correspondence on the matter in Folder 10, Box 22, JAP.

298 **"For three hours":** Irving Spiegel, "West Meets East as Bolshoi Opens," *NYT*, September 7, 1962.

298 **New York City Ballet:** For the tour, see Naima Prevots, *Dance for Export: Cultural Diplomacy and the Cold War* (Middletown, CT: Wesleyan University Press, 1998), 81–87; Clare Croft, *Dancers as Diplomats: American Choreography in Cultural Exchange* (Oxford: Oxford University Press, 2015), 35–65; Rachel Marcy, "Dancers and Diplomats: New York City Ballet in Moscow, October 1962," *The Appendix* 2, no. 3 (July 2014), http://theappendix.net/issues/2014/7/dancers-and-diplomats-new-york-city-ballet-in-moscow-october-1962.

298 **Khrushchev leading the applause:** Marjorie Hunter, "President Cheers the Bolshoi Ballet; He Goes Backstage," *NYT*, November 14, 1962.

299 **"It shall be the policy of this nation":** "Text of Kennedy's Address on Moves to Meet the Soviet Build-Up in Cuba," *NYT*, October 23, 1962.

300 **played Rachmaninoff:** Paul Hume, "Symphony Does Ives Second, Van Cliburn Rachmaninoff," *WP*, October 25, 1962.

300 **Alexander Feklisov:** The spy went under the alias Alexander Fomin.

300 **"If there is no intention . . . ready for this":** The full text is available at John F. Kennedy Presidential Library and Museum website, at http://microsites.jfklibrary .org/cmc/oct26/doc4.html.

301 **attacked the sub:** The episode was not revealed until 2002; see William Burr and Thomas S. Blanton, eds., "The Submarines of October," *National Security Archive Electronic Briefing Book* no. 75 (October 31, 2002), http://nsarchive.gwu.edu/NSAEBB/ NSAEBB75/.

301 **U-2 pilot accidentally trespassed:** Michael Dobbs, *One Minute to Midnight: Kennedy, Khrushchev, and Castro on the Brink of Nuclear War* (New York: Knopf, 2008), 254–64.

302 **"stinking double cross":** Ibid., 189.

302 **ready to die:** The so-called Armageddon Letter, written on October 26, whose contents were first disclosed in the portion of Khrushchev's memoirs first published in 1990. See *NKCS*, 628–30; "Fidel Castro, Nuclear War, and the Missile Crisis: Three Missing Soviet Cables," *CWIHP Bulletin* 17/18 (Fall 2012): 325–30.

302 **"Can you imagine . . . global catastrophe":** Mikoyan, *Autobiography*, 277.

302 **dispatched their ever-reliable father:** "The Soviet Cuban Missile Crisis: Documents on Anastas Mikoyan's November 1962 Trip to Cuba," trans. Svetlana Savranskaya, *CWIHP Bulletin* 17/18, 331–48.

303 **"applauded louder and longer":** Hunter, "President Cheers the Bolshoi Ballet; He Goes Backstage."

303 **commenced an affair:** Pia Catton, "A Life in the Lively Arts," *New York Sun*, August 8, 2005. The conduit was Maxim Gershunoff, in Sol Hurok's office; see Gershunoff and Leon Van Dyke, *It's Not All Song and Dance: A Life Behind the Scenes in the Performing Arts* (Pompton Plains, NJ: Limelight Editions, 2005).

304 **"dog shit . . . asshole art":** Vadislav Zubok, *Zhivago's Children: The Last Russian Intelligentsia* (Cambridge, MA: Belknap, 2009), 193.

304 **strangled:** The advice came from party ideologue Mikhail Suslov.

304 **"The thaw is over . . . smash the Hungarians":** Robert Hornsby, *Protest, Reform, and Repression in Khrushchev's Soviet Union* (Cambridge, UK: Cambridge University Press, 2013), 275.

304 **"Society has a right . . . tool for their ideology":** Schwarz, *Music and Musical Life*, 418–19.

306 **"cunning yet insecure . . . rule a superpower":** *TOML*, 277. The two men had met in September 1959, when Johnson was Senate majority leader: Khrushchev said he hated LBJ's speeches, and Johnson told Khrushchev he would make an outstanding senator.

306 **"dogs peeing against curbstones":** Gaddis, *Cold War*, 114. Khrushchev was referring to Central Committee members, a third of whom he ordered to resign at each election. He also split regional party committees into parallel bodies for industry and agriculture; both acts cost him much of the support that saved him in 1957.

306 **insulting Khrushchev:** Starting in September 1963, Mao published nine polemical letters that tore into every aspect of Khrushchev's leadership. One was titled "On Khrushchev's Phony Communism and Historical Lessons for the World" and accused the Soviet leader of revisionism and risking the return of capitalism.

307 **"I'm old and tired . . . I won't put up a fight":** Taubman, *Khrushchev*, 13.

307 **"You smeared me all over with shit":** Gaddis, *Cold War*, 113.

307 **"In order to be victorious":** Rasmussen, *Sviatoslav Richter*, 168.

19: AMERICA'S PIANIST

311 **"Liz . . . at a *barbeque*"**: Hal Rothman, *LBJ's Texas White House: "Our Heart's Home"* (College Station: Texas A&M University Press, 2001), 175.

312 **"President Johnson . . . a great many are"**: John Edgar Hoover to Tolson, Belmont, De Loach, Sullivan, December 20, 1963; FBI file 105–70035–10. Despite Hoover's equanimity, in 1963 it was still dangerous to be gay in America. That year, the FBI had to correct a rumor that Van had "picked up a young man in the mens [*sic*] room" at a hotel; in fact, a memo explained, it was a different pianist who picked up "an informant of the Washington Field Office, who is an active, aggressive homosexual" and told him to come to his room, where they "engaged in a homosexual act." The report added that the informant identified a photograph of the pianist in question, whom he cattily said he "considered as a more talented pianist than Van Cliburn." A. Rosen to Belmont, "Van Cliburn Information Concerning," December 21, 1963, FBI file 105–70035–9.

312 **"It's more . . . entertainment purposes"**: Recording of Telephone Conversation Between Lyndon B. Johnson and J. Edgar Hoover, December 20, 1963, 3:35 p.m., Tape K6312.11, PNO 2, Recordings and Transcripts of Conversations and Meetings, LBJL. Johnson signaled to his secretary to press a switch and activate the recorder, and the first part of the conversation summarized in Hoover's memo is missing.

312 **"Edgar Hoover says . . . invite him"**: Recording of Telephone Conversation Between Lyndon B. Johnson and J. Edgar Hoover, December 20, 1963, 3:36 p.m., Tape K6312.11, PNO 3, Recordings and Transcripts of Conversations and Meetings, LBJL.

312 **Ludwig Erhard . . . landed:** The White House Motion Film Unit filmed the visit, including Van's performance. Video Recording MP801, December 28/29 1963, Materials Relating to "Visit of Chancellor Ludwig Erhard of West Germany" Project, 12/28/1963–12/29/1963, White House Naval Photographic Center Films, LBJL.

312 **"But Van" . . . "artistic rustic fashion"**: Rothman, *LBJ's Texas White House*, 175.

313 **"the Republican platform"**: Dorothy Austin, "Liz Carpenter Recalls the Johnson Years," *Milwaukee Sentinel*, July 5, 1978.

313 **"He was a man . . . West Texas hill country"**: Transcript, Elizabeth (Liz) Carpenter Oral History Interview V, 2/2/1971, by Joe B. Frantz, Internet Copy, LBJL.

313 **public relations catastrophe:** Dwight Macdonald, "A Day at the White House," *New York Review of Books*, July 15, 1965; Henry Raymont, "Professor Says President Infuriated by Viet Critics at 1965 Arts Festival," *Eugene Register-Guard*, December 25, 1968.

313 **accompanied LBJ home to Texas:** President's Daily Diary, December 20 and 21, 1963, LBJL, http://www.lbjlibrary.net/collections/daily-diary.html.

314 **bought its entire contents:** Paul R. Rundle, "In the Key of Life: Van Cliburn and the Piano Double," April 4, 2013, http://www.huffingtonpost.com/paul-r-rundle/van-cliburn-_b_2807508.html.

314 **press coverage was incessant:** See Viktor Merzhanov, "Van Cliburn," *SK*, June 15, 1965; Sofia Khentova, "Van Cliburn, Pianist and Conductor," *Leningradskaya Pravda*, June 25, 1965; Soloveichik, "The Charm of Talent," *Komsomolskaya Pravda*, June 25, 1965; Jakob Milshtein, "At Van Cliburn's Concerts," *Muzykalnaya Zhizn* 17 (1965): 9–10.

314 **"was not in good favor"**: SA Leonard A. Butt to SAC, New York, memorandum, July 23, 1962, FBI file 62–12802–6. The subject of the surveillance adds that Van was "very discouraged."

314 **"medium or spiritualist"**: SAC, New York to Director, FBI, memorandum, "Har-

vey Lavan Van Cliburn Miscellaneous Information Concerning," July 7, 1965, FBI file 62–12802–16.

315 **reception at the White House:** President's Daily Diary, September 7, 1966, LBJL.

315 **crack about Van:** *VCL*, 171.

316 **"'LOST GENERATION' BAFFLES SOVIET":** Harrison Salisbury, *NYT*, February 6, 1962.

317 **Liu Shikun:** Again, my account is based primarily on my interviews with Mr. Liu, with further sources detailed hereafter.

317 **"They told me . . . music and arts":** Liu Shikun, interview with the author.

317 **"feudalistic . . . fill one with courage":** "Defector Ma Ssu-tsung [Ma Sicong] Tells of Cultural Persecution on Mainland," *Taiwan Journal*, April 23, 1967. Sicong was known in China as King of the Violinists; as well as president of the Central Music Academy, he was also vice president of the Union of Chinese Musicians and a deputy to the National People's Congress.

317 **invited Van to tour China:** In 1960 and 1962. Rogers to Paris embassy, March 23, 1973, State Department cable 1973STATE053785, RG59, NACP; https://aad.archives. gov/aad/createpdf?rid=77902&dt=2472&dl=1345.

317 **"Blood-sucking ghost":** Sheila Melvin and Jindong Cai, *Rhapsody in Red: How Western Classical Music Became Chinese* (New York: Algora, 2004), 241.

317 **denounced Gu Shengying:** Ding Zilin, "Three People Deeply Imprinted on My Memory," April 8, 2001, HRIC, http://www.hrichina.org/en/content/4665.

318 **shot in the head:** Melvin and Cai, *Rhapsody in Red*, 240.

318 **"second-rank ghost" . . . "Counterrevolutionary Musician":** Richard Curt Kraus, *Pianos and Politics in China: Middle-Class Ambitions and the Struggle over Western Music* (New York: Oxford University Press, 1989), 167.

318 **"If I speak . . . smash me":** Melvin and Cai, *Rhapsody in Red*, 242.

318 **"Liu Shikun you bastard":** Kraus, *Pianos and Politics in China*, 165.

320 **called the White House:** This episode is largely reconstructed from a note by Paul Glynn; see "Remembering Van Cliburn," February 27, 2013, LBJL, http://www .lbjlibrary.org/press/lbj-in-the-news/remembering-van-cliburn. Unless otherwise indicated, quoted speech is from this source. Also see President's Daily Diary, October 14, 1967, LBJL.

321 **"They look fine":** "People," *Time*, October 27, 1967.

321 **"Beatles and Marshall McLuhan":** "The Artist as Culture Hero," *Time*, November 22, 1968.

321 **regular on *What's My Line?*:** Van appeared in episodes 426 (August 3, 1958), 461 (April 19, 1959), 604 (March 11, 1962), and 791 (April 5, 1964).

321 **name-dropped in *Bewitched*:** In episode 3 of season 5, "Samantha on the Keyboard," broadcast October 10, 1968, ABC.

321 *Bell Telephone Hour:* *Van Cliburn: A Portrait*, Video Artists International, 2004, DVD.

322 **"I was moved . . . but declined":** Warren Bennis, *Still Surprised: A Memoir of a Life in Leadership* (San Francisco, CA: Jossey-Bass, 2010), 145.

322 **"unmistakably in the ranks":** Albert Goldberg, "Van Cliburn Proves His Greatness," *LA Times*, October 3, 1963.

323 **"I don't think it's worth fightin' for":** Recording of Telephone Conversation Between Lyndon B. Johnson and McGeorge Bundy, May 27, 1964, 11:24 a.m., Tape 64.28, PNO III, Recordings and Transcripts of Conversations and Meetings, LBJL; reprinted as Document 53 in *FRUS 1964–68*, vol. 27, *Mainland Southeast Asia: Regional Affairs*.

323 **"mad masters . . . tide of communism":** John Dumbrell, *President Lyndon Johnson and Soviet Communism* (Manchester, UK: Manchester University Press, 2004), 9.

323 **"The communists already control":** Kelley Shannon, "Tapes Reveal LBJ's Vietnam Conversations," *WP*, November 18, 2006.

323 **"communist way of thinking":** Robert Dallek, *Flawed Giant: Lyndon Johnson and His Times, 1961–73* (New York: Oxford University Press, 1998), 279.

324 **"Down with the U.S.!" and "America stinks!":** Saunders, *Who Paid the Piper?* 361.

324 **"Many in the full house":** Robert Sherman, "Cliburn Startles Recital Audience," *NYT*, May 5, 1972. At the White House, Nixon read part of the article to his chief of staff, H. R. "Bob" Haldeman, adding that he wanted to back Van. OVAL 726–1, May 19, 1972, White House Tapes, RNPL.

324 **sang the national anthem:** "President Hears Van Cliburn Sing National Anthem" (UPI), *Chicago Tribune*, October 13, 1966. Van had promised the rendition as self-punishment for missing the start of yet another concert.

324 **Critics accused him:** Joan Barthel, "Eight Years Later: Has Success Spoiled Van Cliburn?" *NYT*, October 9, 1966.

324 **"a bit ticky-tacky":** Davidson, "Every Good Boy Does Fine."

325 **"shows both in your character and in your development as an artist":** Helen G. Coates to Rosina Lhévinne, New York, October 17, 1966, enclosing a letter to Van dated October 16, Folder 20, Box 2, RLP. "All his talk about his Church and what it means to him is idle talk when it comes to showing it in deeds," Coates fumed. "I'm afraid he is a very self-centered, and ungrateful young man."

326 **Nikita Sergeyevich . . . died:** My account of Khrushchev's funeral draws on Rudolph Chelminski, "The Quiet Passing of Nikita Khrushchev," *Life* 71, no. 13 (September 24, 1971): 40; Edward Gwertzman, "Son Lauds Khrushchev at Rites," *NYT*, September 14, 1971; "Friends, Admirers Attend Funeral of Khrushchev" (UPI), *Ludlington Daily News*, September 13, 1971; Georgy Fyodorov, "Khrushchev the Liberator," trans. Brian Murphy, Great Britain-Russia Society, http://www.gbrussia.org/reviews.php?id=167.

326 **"antisocial act":** Gwertzman, "Son Lauds Khrushchev."

326 **"CEMETERY CLOSED FOR CLEANING":** Fyodorov, "Khrushchev the Liberator." Fyodorov, an archaeologist and writer, talked his way through several rings of security to get to the graveside.

327 **"There were those . . . called a man":** Gwertzman, "Son Lauds Khrushchev."

327 **"We remember . . . defense of the party line":** Ibid.

327 **"You must disperse now":** Fyodorov, "Khrushchev the Liberator."

327 **"All the rulers" . . . "acted as they did":** Ibid.

327 **"Nikita Sergeyevich . . . Russia to his funeral":** Chelminski, "Quiet Passing of Nikita Khrushchev."

328 **"merit pensioner":** "Friends, Admirers Attend Funeral of Khrushchev."

328 **"Mr. Khrushchev opened the doors":** Harry Schwartz, "Khrushchev: We Know Now That He Was a Giant Among Men," *NYT*, September 12, 1971.

20: GREAT EXPECTATIONS

329 **Henry Kissinger sat down opposite . . . Ye Jianying:** Memorandum of Conversation, February 23, 1972, 9:35 a.m., Box 92, HAK Office Files, National Security Council Files, Nixon Presidential Materials Project, NACP.

330 **Sol Hurok planned:** Roberta Peters, interview with Peter Rosen. Hurok, quoted in "U.S. Stars Due in Soviet at Same Time as Nixon," *NYT*, May 15, 1972, maintained that the two events had nothing to do with each other. To believe that Van's first

visit to Moscow in seven years just happened to coincide with Nixon's is to underestimate Hurok's talent for public relations.

330 **Nixon's aide Ron Walker:** Anne Collins Walker recalled the events in "Remembering Van Cliburn," on *GramAnne*, March 6, 2013, http://gramanne.blogspot .co.uk/2013/03/remembering-van-cliburn.html, and in e-mails with the author.

330 **Nixon's personal request:** Nixon first discussed the invitation with Bob Haldeman. He gave three reasons: he would get the visit off to a "great start" by doing a "huge favor to the Russians"; since Van was already there, it would save money; and he wanted to back Van after the audience at Carnegie Hall hissed at his rendition of "The Star-Spangled Banner." OVAL 726–1, May 19, 1972, White House Tapes, RNPL.

331 **"What happened to you":** Aschen Mikoyan, interview with the author.

331 **Roberta Peters was amazed:** Roberta Peters, interview by Peter Rosen.

331 **"Why did he have to do it so early":** "Soviet Agent Wakes Cliburn" (AP), *Des Moines Register*, May 25, 1972.

331 **"It's hard to recall . . . 'provincial sentimentality'":** E. Romadinova, "Define Standards," *Sovetskaya Muzyka* 10 (1972): 77–87. The same pages, though, featured an extremely long and largely glowing appreciation by M. Sokolsky entitled "Van Cliburn and Russian Music."

332 **"Cultural exchanges . . . from Washington":** Max Frankel, "A Reporter's Notebook: Comparing the Journeys," *NYT*, May 25, 1972.

333 **All four . . . had gone home:** Appendix C, President's Daily Diary, May 26, 1972, RNPL, http://www.nixonlibrary.gov/virtuallibrary/documents/dailydiary.php. When Brezhnev visited the United States, Nixon made a point of inviting Van and Rildia Bee to the White House dinner and introducing the two men: see "Appendix B" to President's Daily Diary, June 18, 1973.

334 **Liu Shikun:** Interview with the author.

334 **staggering sum of money:** Liu received eight thousand renminbi in compensation for lost salary; the average monthly salary was ten or twenty renminbi. The blame for his imprisonment was pinned on senior leader Lin Bao, who had conveniently died in a plane crash.

335 **shaking hands:** They still shake today, though it has not affected his piano playing.

335 **Philadelphia Orchestra:** Francis B. Tenny, "The Philadelphia Orchestra's 1973 China Tour: A Case Study of Cultural Diplomacy During the Cultural Revolution," *American Diplomacy* (September 2012), http://www.unc.edu/depts/diplomat/ item/2012/0712/fsl/tenny_orchestra.html.

336 **played a duet:** On March 7, 1974. "You don't play as well as I sing," joked Bailey, "but I don't sing as well as you govern." When he started on "Home on the Range," she interrupted: "Mr. President, I wanted to sing a song, not ride a horse."

336 **listened to his recordings:** Jerrold Schecter, "The Private World of Richard Nixon," *Time*, January 3, 1972.

336 **his favorite piece:** Frank Gannon interview with Richard Nixon, February 9, 1983, part 1; Walter J. Brown Media Archives and Peabody Awards Collection, University of Georgia Libraries, http://www.libs.uga.edu/media/collections/nixon/ohms/index.html.

336 **"He's so colorful":** Conversation with Julie Nixon Eisenhower, WH Telephone 43–142, February 21, 1973, White House Tapes, RNPL.

336 **"He is our friend . . . for us":** OVAL 867–16, March 2, 1973, White House Tapes, RNPL.

336 **upbraided his staff:** OVAL 867–8, March 2, 1973, White House Tapes, RNPL.

337 **Van virtually adopted him:** John Giordano, interview with the author.

337 **visited her in the hospital:** Pablo A. Tariman, "Van Cliburn of Imelda's Splendorous Days," September 14, 2012, http://verafiles.org/van-cliburn-of-imeldas-splendorous-days/. Van was also friendly with the Marcos entourage: when he played at the White House for the Golda Meir visit on March 1, 1973, he invited as his guest Romeo Amansec, a Marcos bodyguard. President's Daily Diary, March 1, 1973, Appendix C, RNPL.

337 **"the Cliburn line . . . mortals of our time":** "Minicult Blooming Over Van Cliburn" (AP), *The Capital* (Annapolis, MD), June 15, 1973.

337 **"Deep in the Heart of Texas":** Davidson, "Every Good Boy Does Fine."

338 **"Only a person" . . . "above his shoes":** "Clothes Don't Make the Pianist" (AP), *Kansas City Times*, June 23, 1973.

338 **"Sonny Boy, I love you":** Greta Beigel, "Finally, a Return Engagement," *LA Times*, July 3, 1994.

338 **lonely figure:** Davidson, "Every Good Boy Does Fine."

338 **"To tell you the truth":** Gary and Naomi Graffman, interview with the author.

338 **Iris Kones:** Gal Beckerman, *When They Come for Us, We'll Be Gone: The Epic Struggle to Save Soviet Jewry* (New York: Houghton Mifflin Harcourt, 2010), 238–39. The bomb exploded on January 26, 1972; another did so at the CAMI offices, but no one was hurt.

339 **accompanying Soviet astronauts:** Caption to photo stand-alone, *Guardian*, September 21, 1974.

339 **"legendary talent":** "10/2/75—Introduction of Van Cliburn, State Dinner," Box 17, President's Speeches and Statements: Reading Copies, GFPL.

339 **"There are so many" . . . "everyone's autograph, too":** Bob Colacello, "The White House's Dinner Theater," *Vanity Fair*, June 2010.

340 **two Soviet entrants:** One, Georgian pianist Alexander Toradze, came second.

340 **whispered in unguarded moments:** VCG.

341 **"I'm late":** Reader's comment appended to Tim Page, "Van Cliburn, Celebrated Classical Pianist, Dies at 78," WP, February 27, 2013.

341 **"Don't worry, honey":** Mary Lou Falcone, interview with the author, August 22, 2014.

341 *André Chenier:* Untitled clipping, VCJA.

341 **Tom Zaremba:** Davidson, "Every Good Boy Does Fine"; "Palimony suit filed against Van Cliburn" (AP), *Bangor Daily News*, May 1, 1996.

342 **Van's stage makeup:** Page, "Van Cliburn Dies at 78."

342 **refused to sanction:** Peter Rosen, interview with the author, August 23, 2014.

342 **"most famous dropout":** Donal Henahan, "What Makes a Gifted Artist Drop Out in Mid-Career?" *NYT*, August 17, 1986.

342 **"not terribly good years":** Arlene Dahl, interview by Peter Rosen.

342 **"junk":** Rogers, "Midnight Conversation." Many of Van's choicest objects were auctioned at Christie's on May 17, 2012, and March 4–5, 2014. See James Barron, "For Sale: The Practice Piano That Made Van Cliburn Perfect," *NYT*, May 16, 2012; Marilyn Bailey, "Items from Van Cliburn's Estate to Be Auctioned at Christie's," *FWS-T*, February 20, 2014; Madigan, "Mementos of the Musician"; "The Van Cliburn Collection," video recording, http://www.christies.com/features/the-van-cliburn-collection-2283-3.aspx.

342 **never taking a lease:** Davidson, "Every Good Boy Does Fine."

343 **Scotch tape:** Richard Rodzinksi, interview with the author; Michael Kimmelman, "Playing When He Wants, and Remembering," *NYT*, July 30, 2000.

343 **"I enjoy flowers as much":** Davidson, "Every Good Boy Does Fine"; and see Joyce Saenz

Harris, "Van Cliburn: Myth and Reality on a Legendary Scale," *DMN*, May 23, 1993.

344 **tiny plastic boxes:** Perlmutter, "Long Road Home."

344 *Random Harvest:* Rogers, "Midnight Conversation."

344 **sniffing the cantaloupes:** Susan Tilley, interview by Peter Rosen, Reel no. 60, *Van Cliburn—Concert Pianist* elements, VCA.

344 **"What do you and that piano player have going":** Tim Madigan, "Diner Waitress Remembers Years Serving Van Cliburn," *FWS-T*, July 21, 2013.

345 **White-gloved valets:** Bob Merrill, interview by Peter Rosen, Reel no. 59, *Van Cliburn—Concert Pianist* elements, VCA.

345 **Pot roast:** Bernard Holland, "Van Cliburn: Man Behind the Contest," *NYT*, March 27, 1989.

345 **Olga Nikolaevna:** "The Van Cliburn Collection."

345 **"priceless stories":** Andrew Marton, "Remembering Van Cliburn," http://www.dfw.com/2012/09/25/686901/van-cliburn-tribute-fort-worth.html.

345 **"Mother remembers":** Shields-Collins Bray, interview with the author, August 17, 2014.

345 **"In Texas . . . we like to stay babies":** Joseph Horowitz, *The Ivory Trade: Music and the Business of Music at the Van Cliburn International Piano Competition* (New York: Summit, 1990), 35–36.

346 **"He twists a cigarette":** Rogers, "Midnight Conversation."

346 **commencement at Juilliard:** A copy of the address, given on June 2, 1978, is in the "Commencement 1978" file, JA.

346 **"just shy of Aunt Rildia Bee's view":** Micke Brown, *Salisbury Post* obituary comment, February 27, 2013, http://www.legacy.com/guestbooks/salisburypost/van-cliburn-condolences/163346926?&page=27.

346 **wrinkles erased:** Horowitz, *Ivory Trade*, 36.

347 **"Try me":** Ibid., 32.

348 **Albert Schweitzer Award:** Bill Zakariasen, "An Award for Cliburn, but Not a Note from Him," *Daily News* (New York), April 20, 1983; "Suzy," *Daily News*, April 19, 1983.

348 **"The march of freedom":** "Text of Reagan's Address to Parliament on Promoting Democracy" (AP), *NYT*, June 9, 1982.

348 **"an evil empire":** "Excerpts from President's Speech to National Association of Evangelicals" (AP), *NYT*, March 9, 1983.

349 **"I felt sad":** "Cliburn Helped Open Door to Cultural Exchange," *Odessa American* (Odessa, TX), April 15, 1978.

349 **first Chinese artist:** Gail Jennes, "Pianist Liu Shih-Kun Wins Bravos in Boston After Years of Forced Silence in a Peking Prison," *People*, April 16, 1979. The orchestra players nicknamed him "the man who never smiles."

349 **smuggling and womanizing:** Kraus, *Pianos and Politics in China*, 187–90. Yet again the accusations appear to have been part of a campaign to discredit Ye Jianying.

349 **something to do with Russia:** Perlmutter, "Long Road Home."

350 **classic Brezhnev joke:** Caroline Brooke, *Moscow: A Cultural History* (New York: Oxford University Press, 2006), 101–2.

21: THE SUMMIT

351 **Susan Tilley:** Susan Tilley, interview by Peter Rosen; *VC*, 310–11.

351 **called his friend Franz Mohr:** Franz Mohr with Edith Schaeffer, *My Life with the Great Pianists* (Grand Rapids, MI: Baker Book House, 1992), 68.

351 **mysterious disappearance:** Speculation about the reasons and the likelihood of a return were rife during Van's self-styled "intermission." See, for example, "Pianist Van Cliburn Plans to Perform Again After Self-Imposed 'Intermission' of 4 Years" (AP), *Newark Star-Ledger*, December 11, 1984.

352 **The elaborately choreographed spectacle:** An essential resource for the Soviet view of the summit is Igor Korchilov, *Translating History: Thirty Years on the Front Lines of Diplomacy with a Top Russian Interpreter* (New York: Scribner, 1997). Korchilov covers the summit in detail on pages 41–140, and Van's concert on pages 100–101. Also consulted were the relevant Executive Secretariat, NSC files and President's Daily Diary, both at RRPL.

352 **talks in the White House Cabinet Room:** Korchilov, *Translating History*, 79; Memorandum of Conversation Between President Reagan and General Secretary Gorbachev, December 8, 1987, 2:30–3:15 p.m., National Security Archive, http://nsarchive.gwu.edu/NSAEBB/NSAEBB238/.

353 **their own Cold War:** Howard Chua-Eoan, "Gorbachev: My Wife Is a Very Independent Lady," *Time*, June 6, 1988.

353 **126 stars:** Barbara Gamarekian, "The Summit: A State Dinner for the Gorbachevs: Front-Row Seat on World History," *NYT*, December 9, 1987.

353 **Rildia Bee looked on proudly from her wheelchair:** YM.

354 **Van walks onto the small stage:** My account is from video footage of the event: "Van Cliburn Performance at the White House, December 8, 1987," Reel no. 112, *Van Cliburn—Concert Pianist* elements, VCA.

358 **"200 ships":** Hugh Sidey, "Not Since Jefferson Dined Alone," *Time*, December 21, 1987.

358 **"I can get you a few bookings":** True to his word, Reagan faxed Van to ask him to appear at the opening ceremony for the Bob Hope Cultural Center in Palm Springs, whose producers had been pursuing him, to no effect; he gave in and played for the invited audience, which included the Reagans.

358 **"I've never seen anything like it":** Korchilov, *Translating History*, 101. As president, Bush invited Van back to play on state occasions and famously nodded off during one concert: see Melinda Bergreen, "Lullaby: If Van Cliburn Puts Bush to Sleep, Who Is Safe?" *Seattle Times*, March 15, 1992.

358 **noticeably warmer:** Susan Tilley, interview by Peter Rosen.

CODA

360 **played the Soviet anthem:** *VC*, 329.

361 **swaddled in a fur coat:** Aschen Mikoyan, interview with the author.

361 **flowers and watermelons:** Alann Sampson, interview with the author.

361 **"We are friends . . . full my heart is":** Aschen Mikoyan's private recording.

361 **invited Van and Rildia Bee:** "Cliburn Plays in Moscow" (AP), *NYT*, July 3, 1989.

361 **jogging outfit:** Susan Tilley diary, quoted in *VC*, 333.

361 **"If you love him, don't kill him":** Richard Rodzinski, interview with the author.

361 **played at the conservatory:** Ed Wierzbowski, e-mail message to author, April 1, 2016. The concert was on July 3.

362 **"He loves to shop":** "Nice Guy," *Orlando Sentinel*, July 13, 1989.

362 **arrived by bus:** John Giordano, interview with the author.

362 **Back at the suite:** Ed Wierzbowski, e-mail message to author, July 3, 2016.

362 **rendition of "Moscow Nights":** Aschen Mikoyan, interview with the author.

362 **occasional benefit concert:** Each was accompanied by a flurry of press coverage. See, for example, Donal Henahan, "A Celebrity Returns, Undimmed," *NYT*, July 2, 1989; and Otto Friedrich, "The Return of Van Cliburn," *Time*, July 3, 1989.

362 **flying Roberta Peters down:** For Rildia Bee's ninety-fourth birthday. David Daniel, "Rildia Bee," *The New Yorker*, December 17, 1990. Van's celebrations at home of Rildia Bee's ninety-fifth birthday are touchingly captured in *My Precious Mother*, video recording, dir. Rick Croft and William Betaille, 1992, youtube.com/watch?v=NXBv8dVSfII.

362 **Rildia Bee O'Bryan Cliburn Organ:** The organ was dedicated before Rildia Bee's death; construction began in 1994 and finished in 1996.

362 **played to 350,000:** John von Rhein, "Cliburn's Back on Top," *Chicago Tribune*, June 20, 1994. For further useful coverage of the comeback tour, see Lynette Rice, "The Ultimate Piano Man," *LA Daily News*, July 11, 1994; Michael Walsh, "The Reluctant Virtuoso," *Time*, July 25, 1994. See also Mark Stryker, "Cliburn's Retreat Enhances His Mystique," *Deseret News* (Salt Lake City), May 19, 1996; Rick Rogers, "Van Cliburn: As Career Intermission Draws to a Close, Legendary Concert Pianist Returns to Spotlight," *NewsOK*, July 21, 1996, http://newsok.com/article/2544761.

362 **$125,000:** Donna Perlmutter, "At Home with Van Cliburn: A Little Night Music," *NYT*, March 3, 1994.

363 **"pathetic" and a "fiasco":** *Baltimore Sun*, quoted in Stephen Wigler, "Pianist's Comeback Fails to Strike Right Chord," *Guardian*, August 23, 1994.

363 **Rildia Bee was dying:** Terry Teachout, "Cliburn Gives the Met a Show of Virtuoso Reality," *Daily News* (New York); "Van Cliburn's Mother Dies," *ST*; Lawson Taitte, "Rildia Bee Cliburn Dead at 97," *DMN*; all August 4, 1994.

363 **sued for palimony:** Kevin O'Hanlon, "Van Cliburn Sued for Palimony" (AP), *Daily Gazette*, May 1, 1996, and widely reprinted; "Former Partner Sues Van Cliburn in AIDS Allegations" (Reuters), *Daily News* (New York), May 1, 1996. For a thorough investigation of sexuality, classical music, and Van, see Joey DiGuglielmo, "Classical Closet?," *Washington Blade*, March 7, 2013.

363 **failed, and failed again on appeal:** *Thomas E. Zaremba v. Harvey Lavan Cliburn, Jr.*, Docket 17–236771–96, Seventeenth District Court, Tarrant County, Texas; COA Docket 02–96–00238-CV, Second Court of Appeals, Fort Worth, Texas.

363 **blazing rows with old friends:** Van blew up at Susan Tilley after she advertised herself as his manager; he never spoke to her again.

363 **astrologist . . . horoscopes:** Ed Wierzbowski and Richard Rodzinski, e-mail messages to the author, March 26 and 29, 2016.

363 **fainted in mid-piece:** Wayne Lee Gay, "Pianist Van Cliburn Collapses Onstage," *FWS-T*, May 14, 1998. For Van at the turn of the millennium, see Michael Kimmelman, "Playing When He Wants, and Remembering," *NYT*, July 30, 2000.

364 **Tommy and Mrs. Putin:** Alann Sampson, interview with the author.

364 **"Dear President . . . I love Russia":** "Pianist Is Honored for Charity in Russia" (AP), *Houston Chronicle*, September 21, 2004. During his visit, Van gave a concert dedicated to the victims of the Beslan school siege; see "Van Cliburn Will Give a Concert in Memoriam," *Rossiiskaya Gazeta*, September 8, 2004; and "Praise the Pianist!" *Rossiiskaya Gazeta*, September 24, 2004.

364 **climb in through the windows:** Olga Rostropovich, interviewed in *Kultura*, February 21, 2014; "Van Cliburn: One Should Not Worry About Classical Music. It Is Never Going to Die," *Rossiiskaya Gazeta*, March 1, 2013. For another interview during this trip, see "Classical Music Is Forever," *Samarskie Izvestiya*, July 18, 2009.

364 **clutching little cameras:** Richard Rodzinski, interview with the author. See also

Van Cliburn Conference in Moscow 2011, video recording, youtube.com/watch?v=BZ
vBaQI34-Y.

364 **His fans . . . clung to him in tears:** Barry, "Basking in Russia's Love." See also "Moscow Gave Me the Name," *Rossiiskaya Gazeta*, June 29, 2011.

364 **fiftieth anniversary:** Media coverage was widespread and included a number of
valuable interviews with Van. See Anthony Tommasini, "Cold War, Hot Pianist.
Now Add 50 Years," *NYT*, March 9, 2008; Richard S. Ginsell, "The Buzz Is Just
a Little Less Forte Now," *LA Times*, April 27, 2008; Angela K. Brown, "Cliburn
Still an Icon, 50 Years After Winning Moscow Piano Contest" (AP), VCJA; "Van
Cliburn: Treasuring Moscow After 50 Years," audio recording, NPR *Weekend
Edition*, March 1, 2008, http://www.npr.org/templates/story/story.php?story
Id=87771963; "'Russians Conquered My Heart': Pianist Van Cliburn Reflects
on 50 Years of Music Making," audio recording, *PBS NewsHour*, April 11, 2008,
https://www.youtube.com/watch?v=d4Z1e6HWV3Y; "Van Cliburn: The Man
and His Music," audio recording, 2008, http://keranews.org/post/van-cliburn
-man-and-his-music.

364 **Kennedy Center Honors:** Van was honored on December 2, 2001, alongside Julie
Andrews, Quincy Jones, Jack Nicholson, and Luciano Pavarotti.

364 **Grammy Lifetime Achievement Award:** At the Forty-Sixth Annual Grammy
Awards in Los Angeles, 2004.

364 **Texas Motor Speedway:** Raad Cawthon, "Track Is a Texas-Size Step Forward," *Philadelphia Inquirer*, April 6, 1997.

365 **"I feel liberated":** Yoheved Kaplinsky, interview with the author, October 8, 2014.

365 **He died on February 27, 2013:** Obituaries and appreciations of Van were valuable
starting points for my research. In addition to those already noted, among the most
useful were those by Scott Cantrell, *DMN*; Anthony Tommasini, *NYT*; Olin Chism,
FWS-T; Peter Dobrin, *Philadelphia Inquirer*; Ben Finane, *Listen*; Jeremy Eichler, *Boston Globe*; Terry Ponick, *Washington Times*; Jeremy Siepmann, *Guardian*; Stepan
Ivanov, *Russia Beyond the Headlines*; in *The Economist*, March 9, 2013; and in *Clavier
Companion*, September/October 2013. Equally revealing and often deeply touching
was the outpouring of readers' comments and personal reminiscences, including
Mary Daily, "Van Cliburn and My Two Enchanted Evenings," August 3, 2013, http://
www.huffingtonpost.com/mary-daily/van-cliburn_b_2824510.html; Miriam Elder,
"Van Cliburn's Star Never Faded in Russia Even as He Left the World Stage Behind," *Guardian*, February 27, 2013; Evans Mirageas, "Remembering Van Cliburn,"
blog post, http://www.evansmirageas.com/blog; Noel Morris, "Remembering Van
Cliburn," http://blogs.wfmt.com/offmic/2013/02/27/van-cliburn/. Prudence Mack-
intosh's elegiac "In Search of Van Cliburn," *Texas Monthly*, February 2013, poignantly
coincided with Van's death.

365 **"It is hard . . . their faces":** Alan Peppard, "Cliburn Eulogized by Presidents, Pals,
at Fort Worth Funeral," *DMN*, March 3, 2013. The statement belies the notorious
charge, leveled in the course of an attack on "sissies" in American concert music,
that Mstislav Rostropovich told an American colleague, "We knew Cliburn was no
great talent, but we thought it would be politically opportune to show that we can
be friends." Anna Frankenheimer, "A Much-Needed Upbraiding of Long-Hair Music," *Fact* (November–December 1964): 11–17.

365 **"highlight of my life":** Aschen Mikoyan, interview with the author.

Index

About the Author

Nigel Cliff is a historian, biographer, critic, and translator. His first book, *The Shakespeare Riots,* was a finalist for the National Award for Arts Writing and was chosen as one of the *Washington Post's* best books of the year. His second book, *The Last Crusade: The Epic Voyages of Vasco da Gama,* was a *New York Times* Notable Book. His most recent book is a new translation of *The Travels* by Marco Polo. A former film and theater critic for the London *Times* and contributor to the *Economist,* he writes for a range of publications, including the *New York Times Book Review.* He lives in London.